MISS CHASE
SANTA BARBARA'S TRAILBLAZER

SIMON KERRY

Published in 2023 by
Unicorn, an imprint of Unicorn Publishing Group
Charleston Studio
Meadow Business Centre
Lewes BN8 5RW
www.unicornpublishing.org

ISBN 978 1 911397 73 1
10 9 8 7 6 5 4 3 2 1

Design by newtonworks.uk
Printed in Malta by Gutenberg Press

Frontispiece: Image of Pearl

CONTENTS

Great Spirit Prayer

Oh, Great Spirit,
Whose voice I hear in the winds
and whose breath gives life to all the world.
Hear me! I need your strength and wisdom.
Let me walk in beauty, and make my eyes
ever hold the red and purple sunset.
Make my hands respect the things you have made
and my ears sharp to hear your voice.
Make me wise so that I may understand
the things you have taught my people.
Let me learn the lessons you have hidden
in every leaf and rock.

Help me remain calm and strong in the
face of all that comes towards me.
Help me find compassion without
empathy overwhelming me.
I seek strength, not to be greater than my brother,
but to fight my greatest enemy: myself.
Make me always ready to come to you
with clean hands and straight eyes.
So when life fades, as the fading sunset,
my spirit may come to you without shame.

Chief Yellow Lark, Lakota, 1887

CHASE FAMILY TREE

(Pearl was the last of her family to share the name Chase)

Aquila Chase (1580–1641) = Martha Stewart Jelliman (1588–1643)

Aquila Benjamin Chase (1618–1670) = Anne Wheeler (died 1687)

Moses Chase (1663–1743) = Anne Follansbee (1668–1708)

Samuel Chase (1690–1743) = Hannah Emery (died 1776)

Samuel Chase (1728–1769) = Saraha Stewart (1732–1813)

Amos Chase (1770–1852) = Judith Little (1776–1860)

Hezekiah Smith Chase (1805–1893) = (1) Elizabeth Schuyler (1816–18

Elizabeth S Chase (1553–1870

Hezekiah Griggs Cha

Pearl Chase (1888–197

Caroline Mercer-Naime

Charles Mercer-Naime = Frances
9th Marquis of Lansdowne

Arabella Rachel Simon Wil

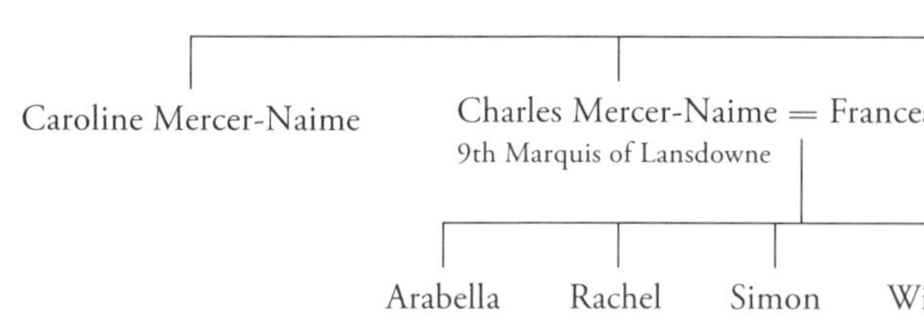

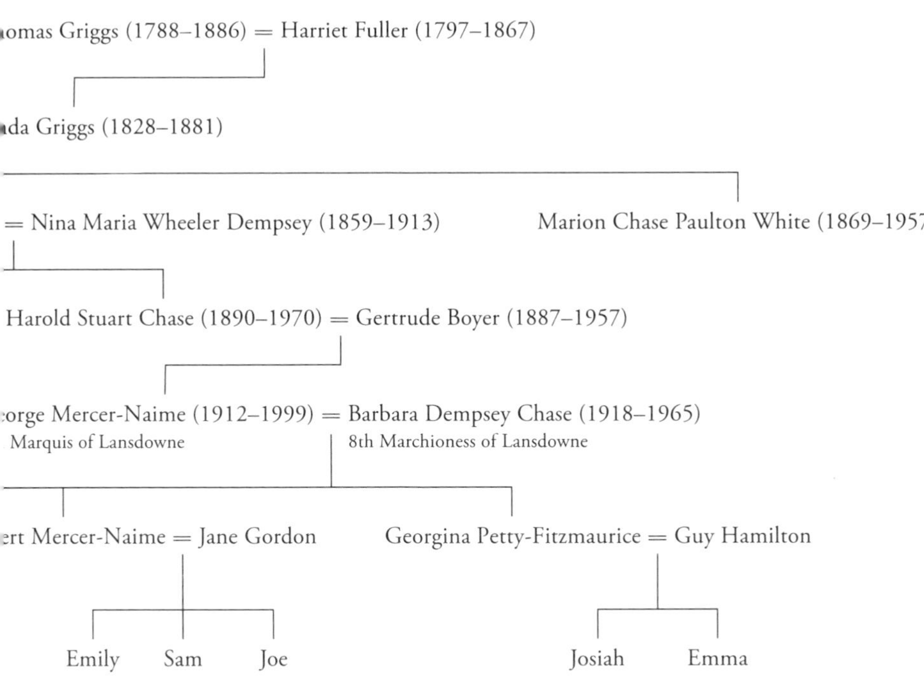
omas Griggs (1788–1886) = Harriet Fuller (1797–1867)
da Griggs (1828–1881)
= Nina Maria Wheeler Dempsey (1859–1913)
Marion Chase Paulton White (1869–1957)
Harold Stuart Chase (1890–1970) = Gertrude Boyer (1887–1957)
orge Mercer-Naime (1912–1999) = Barbara Dempsey Chase (1918–1965)
Marquis of Lansdowne
8th Marchioness of Lansdowne
ert Mercer-Naime = Jane Gordon
Georgina Petty-Fitzmaurice = Guy Hamilton
Emily
Sam
Joe
Josiah
Emma

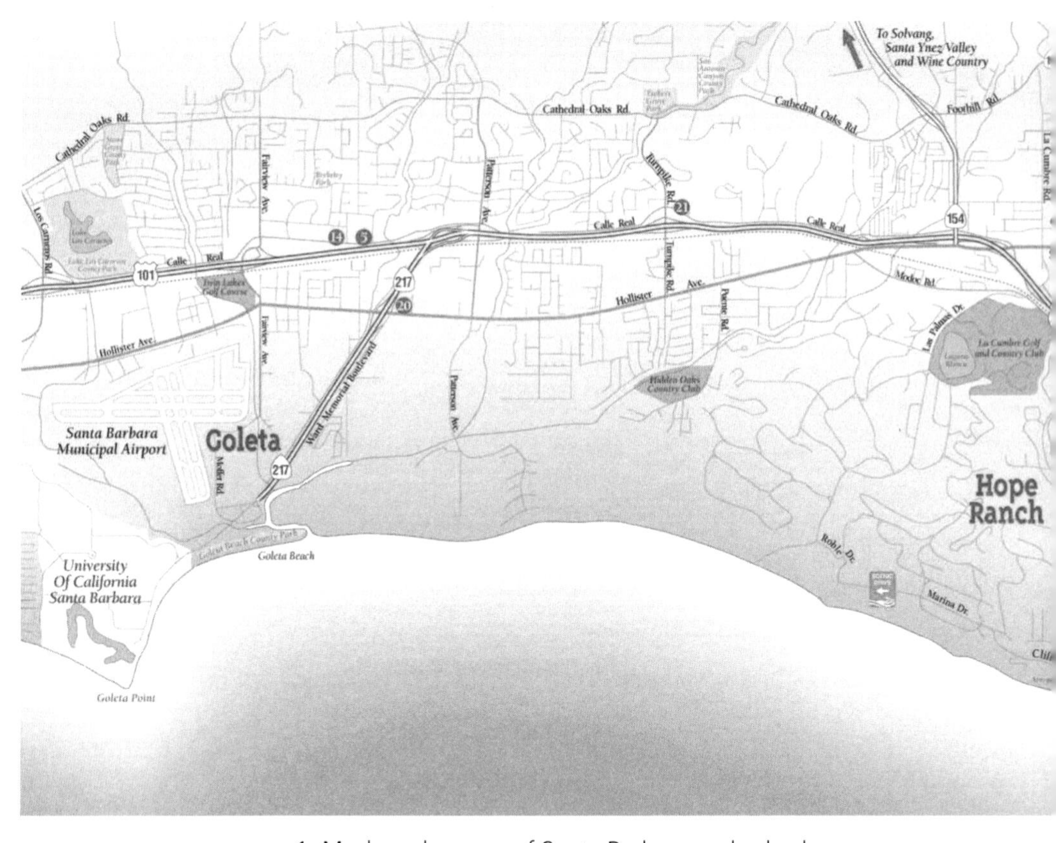

1. Modern day map of Santa Barbara and suburbs

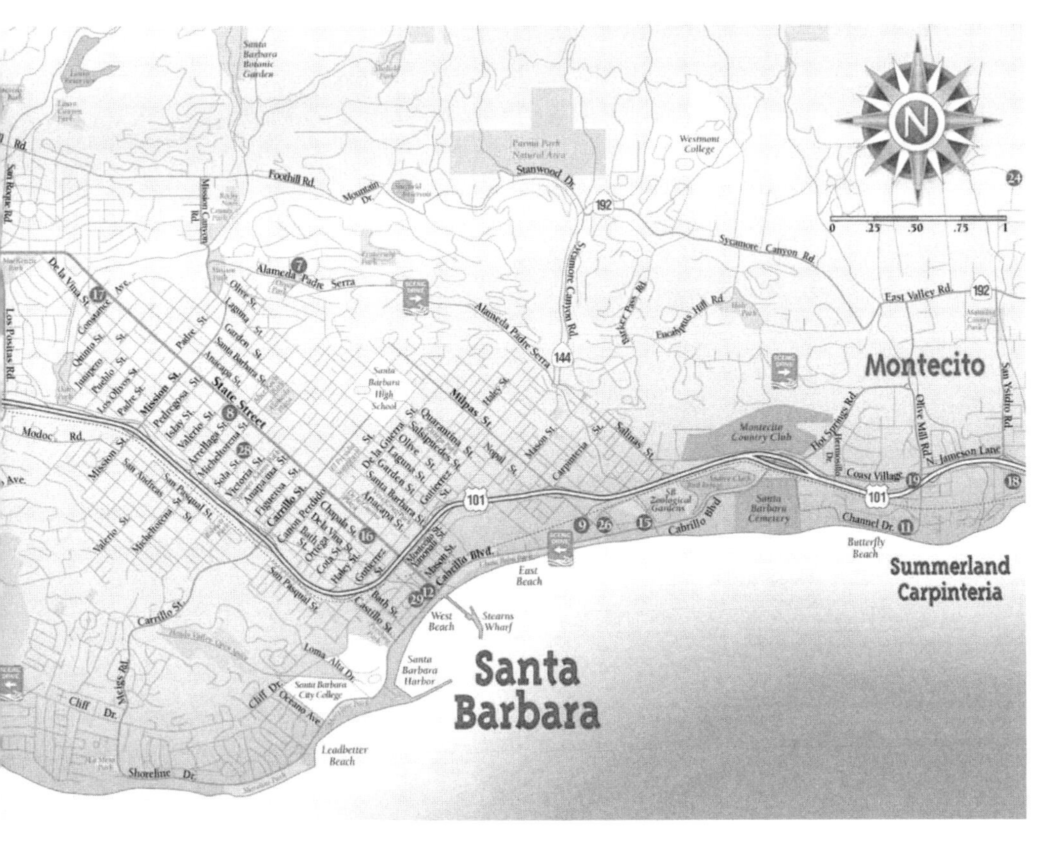
Santa Barbara Botanic Garden
Westmont College
Foothill Rd.
Mountain Dr.
Stanwood Dr.
192
Sycamore Canyon Rd.
Alameda Padre Serra
Mission Canyon Rd.
San Roque Rd.
Los Positas Rd.
De la Vina St.
Constance Ave.
Olive St.
Laguna St.
Garden St.
Santa Barbara St.
Anacapa St.
State Street
Mission St.
Padre St.
Pedregosa St.
Islay St.
Valerio St.
Arrellaga St.
Micheltorena St.
Sola St.
Victoria St.
Anapamu St.
Figueroa St.
Carrillo St.
Canon Perdido
Chapala St.
Bath St.
Castillo St.
Haley St.
Cota St.
Ortega St.
Gutierrez St.
Milpas St.
Quarantina St.
Salsipuedes St.
Nopal St.
Mason St.
Carpinteria St.
Salinas St.
Santa Barbara High School
Modoc Rd.
San Andres
San Pasqual St.
101
144
Barker Pass Rd.
Eucalyptus Hill Rd.
East Valley Rd.
Montecito
San Ysidro Rd.
Olive Mill Rd.
N. Jameson Lane
Hot Springs Rd.
Coast Village
Montecito Country Club
Channel Dr.
Butterfly Beach
Santa Barbara Cemetery
SB Zoological Gardens
Cabrillo Blvd.
East Beach
West Beach
Stearns Wharf
Santa Barbara Harbor
Summerland
Carpinteria
Santa Barbara
Carrillo St.
Loma Alta Dr.
Meigs Rd.
Cliff Dr.
Santa Barbara City College
Oceano Ave.
Leadbetter Beach
Shoreline Dr.
0 .25 .50 .75 1

2. Modern day map of California

Introduction

For as long as I can remember I have been fascinated by my American ancestors. When I started to learn about my great-grandaunt I was treated to numerous anecdotes about powerful individuals, invariably men, who confessed to a feeling of dread when they were told that Miss Chase had called. It habitually meant that a cherished plan they were hatching was about to be exposed to public scrutiny. I wrote this book to satisfy my curiosity. How, I wondered, could a single woman, who did not appear to have had the benefit of any great institution behind her, evoke such feelings? What motivated her, enabled her to overcome the odds and be successful? The answer I discovered was her vision. A vision of beauty and possibility.

One of the great joys of being a biographer is that you get to delve into the life of another person. However, the concern a biographer has is that there will not be enough material to make this possible. In their own way, all lives are fascinating, but most lives leave behind little trace. I was fortunate in that this was not so with Pearl Chase. At the time of her death in 1979 she was widely acknowledged as having been Santa Barbara's woman of the twentieth century.

Over a seventy-year period, she served on hundreds of committees and on the boards of organizations and received over eighty national, state, and local awards, including two honorary doctorates. Modest to a fault, she liked to joke that the only reason she got so many accolades was because she lived such a long life. Speaking up for Indigenous peoples, conservation, historic preservation, public health, social services, education, civic planning—she was involved in it all, devoted to improving the lives of those around her.

She was an intrepid, forward-thinking, practical-minded person who worked to advance public understanding. No one individual did more to transform the style and character of Santa Barbara. The Hispanic motifs of the buildings, the architectural standards of excellence, the renowned waterfront and acres of lush parks free from commercial development were due to her perseverance and courage.

She was charming, talented, and highly persuasive, but she was no saint. As a woman having to operate in a man's world, she applied righteous indignation laid on thick. While she preached a doctrine of quiet cooperation between private citizens and public agencies, she was a strong activist. Merging the public and private spheres of her life with her work Pearl was married to her workplace. Santa Barbara was her long-term love and she had a unique ability to see before anyone else what Santa Barbara could become—and, thanks to her, did become.

Apart from the purely personal, the life of an individual serves as a window into the world in which they lived. In the case of Pearl Chase America's story as it unfolded into the twentieth century is told through the development of one community in the state of California. Against the background of two world wars, the Great Depression, the emancipation of women, the explosion of consumerism and what was often violent political discord, Pearl was an unflagging social entrepreneur long before the expression had been invented.

To be happy, individuals needed to live in wholesome, beautiful communities which they felt able to treat as their own. That was her belief. It was as simple as that. To that end they had to be involved, be on their guard against decisions being taken over their heads, be prepared to solicit the best advice available and, if necessary, go well beyond signing fine-sounding petitions, while always recognizing that improvement was a continuous process.

3. Pearl

Even though this book is about the life of Pearl Chase it is also a rich source of information on women's lives, on the history of Santa Barbara and California, and on American history. Taken together, they make up a valuable resource relating to the betterment of the human condition and, until now, the untold personal story of the growth and development of an American community.

Many of the people that knew and worked alongside Pearl have already left the scene, but of those still living I have attempted to try and tell her story with as many "live" voices as possible and I am deeply indebted to the numerous individuals I spoke with for sharing so much with me. From over forty people I amassed many hours of conversation. Much of this material is interspersed in the book. It's my hope that including these voices makes it even more inclusive—Pearl, whose ears I suspect are burning, would like the collaboration.

In my research I have been struck by how few stories have been told about the accomplishments of foresighted American women. I aim to applaud one such American woman and commemorate both her legacy and the places where she made history. Despite Pearl's remarkable life of service, no one had written an authoritative account of her life and career. Where she had received attention from local historians, the studies had a specific focus on single aspects of her career. Here, I aim to help fill the gaps in these accounts.

Even if Pearl received less than the attention she deserved until now, she herself understood the importance of her contribution to both Santa Barbara and the state of California; she saved all her papers, both public and private. Known as the Community Development and Conservation Collection, Pearl's papers are housed at University of California, Santa Barbara. They comprise a voluminous special collection of around 735 linear feet, or 1,500 boxes, enough to fill the trailers of two trucks. Contained within the collection are family papers, photographs, diaries, newspaper clippings, books, and business records dating from the 1830s, when the Chases were operating three shoe factories in New England, to the early 1900s when they were running a Santa Barbara real estate office, through to the late 1970s, when Pearl was the last surviving family member. Much of this material has never been researched before, and this work makes the most extensive investigation of the papers to date.

Throughout America I consulted archives in many states—Massachusetts, Maine, Connecticut, New Jersey, New York, Illinois, Indiana, Minnesota, Washington, Colorado, Oregon, and California—and sourced thousands of other records. Pearl was a national figure.

It was important to Pearl that everything she worked for be educational. She taught people the importance of being responsible citizens and caring about communities. There was a remarkable depth in her commitment to developing, among all people, a realization that America's cultural and environmental resources must be protected. Deepening a connection with this woman, what she left behind, and how she is still inspiring people, is another reason why I wrote the book.

Pearl's story intersected with many of the most important trends of twentieth century America: universal suffrage, women's rights, governmental reform, public health reform, professionalization of social work, educational expansion, city planning, historic preservation, and the environmental movement. These issues that she advocated are as important now as they were then and not just in the US. What happens in the US has an impact on the UK, where I live, and beyond. If this account of her life can help others at least to understand the urgency to act, I hope, I will have done her justice.

CHAPTER 1

Early Years

On November 2, 1979, a warm and sunny Friday afternoon, a ceremony was held at Mission Historical Park in Santa Barbara, California: "A Joyous Celebration for a Great Lady," a community-led memorial service in honor of Pearl Chase.[1] The congregation included British aristocracy, Native Americans, Franciscan Friars, Santa Barbara citizens, and local, state, and national officials working in conservation, planning, historic preservation, and community development. The tone was set by a Chumash tribesman, reciting, in his native language, Pearl's favourite piece of Native American writing, "Great Spirit Prayer." Superior Court Judge John Rickard, acting as Master of Ceremonies, remarked at the start of the service, "No one likes to imagine what Santa Barbara would have been without her." The *Santa Barbara News-Press* described the scene later that week: "Bells rang out at the Old Mission Towers and the invocation was given by Father Virgil Cordano, Pastor of the Mission."[2] After songs and "we remember" talks, Rickard concluded, "Chase was a born leader. A skilful and intelligent one. She earnestly pursued her objective by enlisting the aid of the right people, at the right time, all the time."[3]

How did such a life well lived begin?

Pearl, the first child of Hezekiah and Nina Chase, was born in Boston, Massachusetts on November 16, 1888. Her parents deliberately neglected to give her a second name, assuming she would take "Chase" after marriage. Her family was of ancient lineage in both America and England and could trace their roots to Mayflower passengers John Alden and Priscilla Mullins.

4. Hezekiah Smith Chase and Pearl, 1890

Hezekiah was the son of Hezekiah Smith Chase. Hezekiah Smith's first wife died at thirty-nine in 1855, leaving behind a daughter, Elizabeth. Remarrying a Brookline, Massachusetts resident, Amanda Griggs, he fathered two more children: Hezekiah Griggs, Pearl's father, in 1861, and Marion, born eight years later. Hezekiah Smith was a half-owner of Chase, Merritt & Co., a manufacturer of boots and shoes headquartered in Boston with factories, in Massachusetts and Maine. Prone to speculating, he invested heavily in transportation, communication, and mining. At his death in 1893, he had enough stock to paper a room.[4] A practicing Baptist, serving as Deacon of the Clarendon Street Baptist church, he was motivated by the Puritan belief that work is pleasing to God. He was opposed to slavery, supported Abraham Lincoln, and being too old to fight in the Civil War, advanced money to outfit an entire regiment from Kansas.[5]

After being awarded a Franklin Medal in Boston's public schools, Pearl's father went on to study at the Massachusetts Institute of

Technology.[6] His university education was cut short when in 1880 his father lost his sight and Hezekiah was compelled to take on the family business. The following year, upon his mother's death, he also became head of the household.

Reputed to have slept on a haircloth sofa at the end of his father's bed with the gas burning to keep warm, Hezekiah found little time for a personal life or recreation.[7] It was fortunate that in 1885, through his local church, he met and fell in love with Nina Maria Dempsey. In some ways their meeting may seem unsurprising, given that he went to church twice on Sundays, taught Sunday school, and attended a Wednesday prayer group meeting.

Nina, too, came from a well-connected and devout family. She was a Wheeler, also of English origin, a family that settled in Concord, Massachusetts. In 1799, a branch of the family emigrated north to Norridgewock in Maine. Although the Wheelers were quite clannish and kept in close touch with each other, by the 1870s, different family members were living in a number of states such as California, New York, South Dakota, and Massachusetts.

Nina's mother, Maria Wheeler, remained in Maine. In 1849 she married Hugh Dempsey, an immigrant from Northern Ireland.

5. Maria Wheeler

With a common interest in theology, they lived firstly in Newton Centre, a village within the Boston suburb Newton, where Hugh completed his studies at Newton Theological Seminary, and then later in Fairfield, Maine, where he was a popular Baptist minister. A lover of fast horses, Hugh was killed at forty-three in a runaway accident involving his buggy and a skittish horse. Maria was six months pregnant with Nina at the time. She later remarried, but when her second husband died shortly after, she moved back to Boston with her three children. They were privately educated, and Nina then went on to attend the New England Conservatory.[8]

Aside from her interest in art and music, Nina was a strong Baptist, faithfully attending the Clarendon Street Church where she met Hezekiah. After a brief courtship, spent mainly on streetcars between their respective houses, they were married on December 30, 1886. Nina was a calm, patient woman with a tender sympathy and an iron resolve. She was perfectly matched to Hezekiah, an ambitious, generous, and athletic man. Both believed that they had, in each other, a precious gift from God.

Pearl was born two years after the Chases wed, and another two years later they welcomed a son, Harold Stuart. Among Pearl's family papers I discovered a photo of Nina breastfeeding the newborn with Hezekiah standing proudly by her side. It's clear that the Chases were a remarkably close family from the start.

After his father's death in 1893, Hezekiah paid off his siblings with the valuable part of the estate and took, as his share, the debts of an unscrupulous business partner—debts he knew he would not collect. While America celebrated the Chicago World's Fair, the nation was also facing one of the worst economic recessions in decades. The Chase family firm was affected by the downturn and labor disputes; Hezekiah struggled to keep the business going and, in his efforts, suffered a nervous breakdown. In a letter to Nina, he told her how God was giving them a chance to make a turning point in their lives.[9]

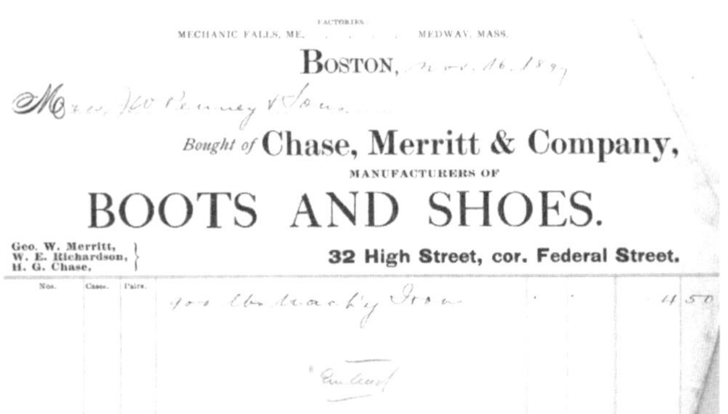

FACTORIES:
MECHANIC FALLS, ME. MEDWAY, MASS.

BOSTON, Nov. 16, 1897

M

Bought of **Chase, Merritt & Company,**

MANUFACTURERS OF

BOOTS AND SHOES.

Geo. W. Merritt,
W. E. Richardson,
H. G. Chase,

32 High Street, cor. Federal Street.

Nos.	Cases.	Pairs.		
				4 50

6. Chase, Merritt & Company

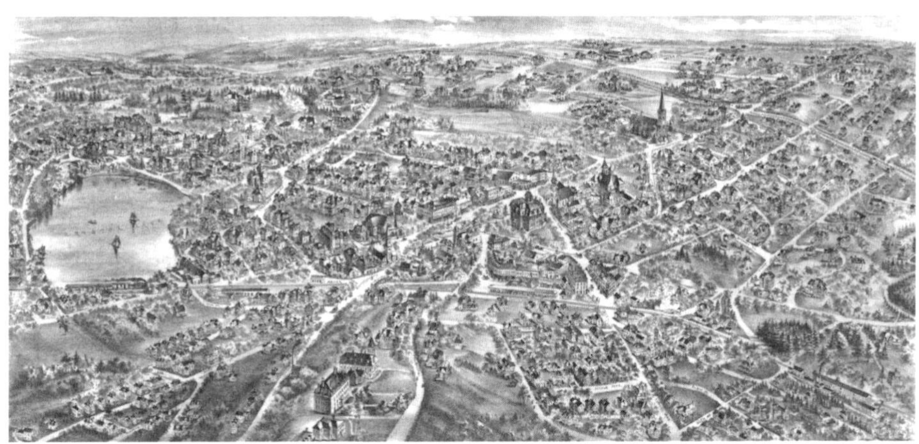

7. Newton in the 1880s

8. The Chase house at 19 Parker Street

The following year he sold their house in Chester Square in Boston's South End and moved the family into a substantial mansard roof property on Parker Street in Newton Centre. Newton, then a growing suburb seven miles west of Boston, was within walking distance of Nina's mother. Living in a large house with a barn, on grounds planted with many fine trees, Pearl enjoyed her new home and a carefree childhood. Surrounded by people who loved her and a variety of domestic animals including a Saint Bernard and a horse, she was never without attention. In later life she fondly recalled many companions, including the housekeeper who read to her, the family coachman who danced with her, and a young neighbour who wrote plays Pearl would act out. She attended the local kindergarten and went to Sunday school where she developed an abiding interest in mythology and the Bible.[10]

Despite moving to "the country," Hezekiah's condition did not improve and following his doctor's advice he and Nina took a long vacation in Europe. Upon returning to Boston he sold the family business and in March 1900, freed of this responsibility and motivated by both new economic prospects and adventure, the Chases travelled to Perris, California, where Nina had a cousin.

9. Nina, Pearl and Harold, 1893

10. Arlington Hotel, 1880s

After a stay of three months, when it became "too darned hot" for them, the Chases travelled by train, stage and coach, 165 miles northwest to Santa Barbara where it was only seventy-two degrees Fahrenheit. Nina had visited Santa Barbara in 1885 during a tour of California, a year before her marriage, and had stayed with her uncle who was the then manager of the Arlington Hotel. Regarded as one the most genial hostelry men on the coast and a person of deep public spirit, Charles Wheeler ensured Nina had a wonderful stay she never forgot.

Nina, like thousands of other tourists, became enraptured with the city and state.[11] Santa Barbara, with its Mediterranean climate, sun-drenched beaches, rolling hills, oak trees, morning mists, and the moral and intellectual atmosphere of a New England community, acquired a reputation as one of the world's most ideal health and tourist resorts. Acting as the social center for young and elderly, rich and near-rich alike, the Arlington Hotel was justly famous. Its ninety guest rooms featured marble-mantled fireplaces, running water, gas light, and a speaking tube to call the front desk. Of course, Santa Barbara was much more than a luxury break.

11. Aerial view of Santa Barbara, 1880s

12. Downtown Santa Barbara, 1890s

Returning to settle with her family in Santa Barbara fifteen years later in 1900, Nina's accommodation was not quite so comfortable as the Arlington Hotel, and the town had changed out of recognition. A real estate boom had increased the population from just over 3,500 to 6,600. The city's evolution was evident: the principal streets were lit with electric arc lamps, the first telephones had been established, trolley wires had replaced mule-drawn cars, and the Santa Barbara Sloyd School (renamed the Anna Blake Manual Training School), modelled after the Sloyd schools of Sweden and

13. Downtown Santa Barbara, c.1905

Boston, had been founded. What was once an essentially inward-looking culture, brought about largely by its isolation, was transformed into the spotlight by the arrival of the first Southern Pacific train from Saugus in 1887. Travel by steamship or stagecoach over bad roads was no longer the only means of getting in and out of the city. However, because of a long and tedious layover at Saugus, the rail journey from Los Angeles to Santa Barbara could sometimes take up to ten hours, making the city less than appealing to empire builders. Pacing up and down the Saugus railway platform did not appeal to men like Harrison Gray Otis, future publisher of the *Los Angeles Times*. Establishing himself in the late 1870s as the owner of the *Santa Barbara Press*, he left for Los Angeles not long after, commenting that the local gentry were too unambitious by his standards.[12]

Despite this perceived lack of ambition in the community there were still no decent houses to rent, and the Chases spent their first year in Santa Barbara living in a barn house with no proper kitchen save for an oil burner on which they cooked eggs and coffee. Although their situation was quite different from their life in New

England, they made friends quickly, and Pearl and Harold were admitted to the city school.

Nina felt happy and wanted to settle permanently, but Hezekiah was still uncertain. Twelve months after his breakdown his health had recovered, but his economic prospects had not. As he considered his next step, he fancied himself as a mining superintendent.

Among his father's wide-ranging speculations, from buying real estate in Chicago to outfitting the Kansas regiment, in 1877 Hezekiah Smith had invested in a silver mine in Idaho Springs, which his son inherited. Mining at that time was highly profitable as prospecting changed from an individual to an industrial endeavour, and ore production from the Murray Mine was estimated to have been worth $160,000 ($4.1m in 2023). Confident it would continue to provide a comfortable income for his family, Hezekiah persuaded his sister and stepsister to go into partnership with him. They paid $10,000 each to buy the title to the mine.

Moving to Colorado in 1901, the Chases rented a house in Denver at 1105 East Alameda Avenue, and Pearl and Harold were admitted to Denver West High School that September. The school motto was "Age Quod Agis," which translated literally means "do what you are doing." But practically, it acts as encouragement to

14. Denver West High School

15. Hezekiah and Nina Chase at Lawson

keep going and concentrate on the task at hand, making it an applicable motto for their father, as well. The Murray Mine was situated at the foot of the Columbia Mountain at an elevation of 8,250 feet, a quarter of a mile from the railway station at Lawson, seven miles from Idaho Springs, and forty-four miles from the smelting works in Denver. Despite the occasional wash-out, the wagon roads were in good condition, and no one depended on pack train transportation.

Taking lodgings in the bracing air of Idaho Springs, Hezekiah hired an experienced four-man crew and bought equipment to work the mine. He underestimated the complications of mining between two unworked claims, and in the first few months he and his team worked night and day in eight-hour shifts, pumping water from all three mines. Initially, the sight of his men shovelling dirt and rock from their 170-foot platform inspired him to write a love poem to Nina.[13] His excitement was short-lived, as it soon became apparent there was not even enough ore to meet the cost of blasting and timbering. In January 1902 he decided to cut his considerable losses and sell the mine.[14] With no desire to return to Massachusetts and at Nina's encouragement, he travelled to Corona, California, and stayed on a lemon ranch with a family with Boston connections. Taking Pearl and Harold, Nina headed east, back to Newton

Centre with instructions to sell the house. The sale was completed in the summer, and Nina shipped the unsold furniture west to Santa Barbara, where the family had decided to permanently relocate.

In her nine months at Denver West, Pearl had grown in both confidence and intellect. She made friends easily and excelled in rhetoric and Latin. Living one mile high, riding the Georgetown Loop, and traveling into the bowels of the earth in a mining bucket had also given her a sense of adventure.[15]

16. Pearl, aged 7

CHAPTER 2

School Years

If one believes that timing is everything, 1901 motioned two of the most important events in Santa Barbara's modern history: the completion of the Southern Pacific Railroad coastal route between Los Angeles and San Francisco, and Milo Potter's purchase of the thirty-six-acre site for his hotel. Built within two years, the Potter Hotel put Santa Barbara on the map as a year-round place to vacation.[1] With first-rate transport connections and accommodations, Hezekiah, whose health had recovered in the mild Mediterranean climate, decided to permanently settle in the city, mindful that it would grow steadily, bringing many business opportunities.[2] Pearl was excited to start a new life in a city, one with ample outdoor activities and many children her age to play with, including Milo Potter's daughter.

17. Santa Barbara, c.1901, with the railroad and train

Potter was one of America's leading hotel builders. It was said that "wherever he put his foot red geraniums sprang up. They were his favourite flower and he had them potted by the thousands for his guests."[3] His energy was abundant and his interests many, from training employees to training racehorses.[4] Although he was not particularly superstitious, the nineteenth day of the month was his lucky day, and he never started anything unless it was touched by the number nineteen.

Costing $1.5 million (nearly $49 million in 2023), the Potter Hotel covered six city blocks. Directly behind the Potter, the Southern Pacific built their new station with a pathway leading straight to the hotel. Unsurprisingly, the hotel opened on January 19, 1903. Among the cream of American society to visit the fashionable hotel in the early years, those to sign the guest register included Carnegie, Rockefeller, Vanderbilt, Astor, Studebaker, Harriman, Cudahy and Spreckels.[5]

Many of these guests found Santa Barbara to their liking and decided to build their own residences. Whether for part or full-time use, many of these wealthy families built great estates in the upmarket area known as Montecito and lavished their philanthropy on

18. The beach with the Potter Hotel behind

the city. One commentor cynically remarked that "a resort for the wealthy and unhealthy is all Santa Barbara aspires to now."[6]

The Chases began their new life renting a house at 1530 Garden Street before moving, two years later in 1905, to 2012 Anacapa Street. Covering 2,900 square feet, their rented two-story clapboard and shingle house was regarded as in "the country." Located several blocks from the downtown commercial core and linked to lower State Street by a streetcar line, the city's upper-middle and wealthy classes were attracted to this neighborhood.

Set back from the ungraded street by a front garden, the Chases' house faced west. In the morning the family cooked their breakfast with the sun streaming into their kitchen over the heavily planted rear garden. Sash windows on all floors filled the house with sunlight. An entrance hall led into a parlor and a drawing room; a second drawing room and the kitchen completed the ground floor. The four bedrooms and two bathrooms were accessed by two wooden staircases, one used by their servant and the other, more decorative, by the family and their guests. With the exception of a gas-fired stove in the kitchen, the interior of the house would be familiar to us today. Running water and sewage were on the mains,

19. 2012 Anacapa Street nowadays

electricity and a gravity heat system provided light and warmth; a fireplace in the parlor was largely aesthetic and for enjoyment. A telephone connected the family to the outside world via the service of the Home Telephone Company.[7] The home had wood flooring throughout except the tiled bathrooms and the kitchen, where Nina chose linoleum—easier to clean. Rugs covered many floors. Wallpaper and artwork were used in the principal rooms, and the servant's room was painted. In awe of indigenous plants as well as those from abroad, the family filled the garden with walnut, lemon, orange, palm, and bougainvillea trees. They stabled their horse and carriage on Lower Anacapa, calling for someone to bring it to them when needed.

Hezekiah's new life brought out an outgoing and confident side of his personality that had lain dormant in New England. He established himself as a realtor, selling and renting property, with an office in the heart of downtown only a six-minute walk from the house. With his integrity and skill of salesmanship he excelled, fast becoming the city's leading agent. Such was his success that he was later labelled "a master builder" and reputed to have sold over half the county at one time or another.[8]

20. Hezekiah Chase, c.1910

A perk of working in real estate, viewing ranches was what he enjoyed most. Driving on trails through the Santa Ynez Mountains, he and his clients would often camp overnight or stay in taverns. When not showing customers, he often drove out with his family and spent weekends in the back country, camping under oak and pine trees at Zaca Lake.[9]

Further demonstrating his newly regained extroversion, living in a growing city allowed for Hezekiah to get to know the local movers and shakers, and he spent time socializing with them. Soon they were all connected in different ways, making things happen and growing their community together. Pearl developed her understanding of community building by watching and listening to her parents.

With a tradition of wealthy family involvement in city affairs and improvements, Santa Barbara was and still is notably civic-minded. Even though the position of mayor was typically filled by a member of one of the leading families, Santa Barbarans were inherently distrustful of city government and government in general; they felt they should have a say in any decisions affecting their city, as understandably, they knew what was and was not good for it. Pearl felt this strongly, later remarking, "Government officials are really temporary. They come and go. And this constant turnover means that many citizen organizations have far greater continuity and relative importance in community affairs."[10] Indeed civic-minded, Santa Barbara was known as a city of meetings, where nothing got done until a meeting was called to discuss it.[11] Leading these discussions were the Chambers of Commerce, Social Service Clubs, and Women's Clubs. While each organization had different agendas and membership, all were motivated toward making their city bigger, better, and more beautiful than any other in their state.

At a time when the position of American women was beginning to shift in the direction of greater individual autonomy, Nina also took on a philanthropic role in the community. New ideas of what

21. Nina Chase, c.1910

it meant to be a woman and about their role in society were met with a variety of interpretations. Without the political power of the vote, benevolent women found that social welfare activities provided them with a voice in public affairs and a means to influence community politics; many of these women found in benevolence work a means of breaking down gender divisions.

The newness of Santa Barbara and its strong civic spirit offered a space in which to pursue this. By raising the issue of women, children, and families and thereby promoting a healthier, cleaner, and morally upright city, their efforts laid the groundwork for the later development of feminism. Pearl believed that her job was to "get the message across and make politicians feel they must pay attention to the people."[12] It helped that Santa Barbara men approved wholeheartedly and encouraged women's community work financially (although one suspects that nothing would have stopped these women in their important work).

Medical charitable work, in particular, appealed to Nina and offered her welcome exposure to a wider world outside her home. Joining the all-female board of directors of the Cottage Hospital, she soon found herself chairman of the Building Committee and vice-chairman of the board. Her husband's contacts in the real estate and contracting trades were no doubt invaluable in helping to strengthen her influence. As in other American cities with charitable boards, the directors were part of an elite group. Unsurprisingly, this not only helped them to raise funds but also smoothed out legal difficulties. Among the elites or otherwise, Nina was motivated by both the cause and the act of getting involved, and she found her greatest concern was in working for the expansion of the hospital facilities. Constantly imagining what she could do for others, her work took her out of herself. Pearl was impressed by her mother's volunteerism, once telling her, "It has always been that you think of other people's welfare and not your own."[13]

While Nina and Hezekiah continued to be guided by their Baptist faith, neither parent forced nor encouraged Pearl or Harold to follow the strict religious upbringing they themselves experienced. Subsequently, Pearl developed a broad interest in world religions like Buddhism, as well as various denominations and movements of Christianity such as Congregationalism, Episcopalian, Christian Scientist, and Catholicism. She rarely went to church except for weddings and funerals.

Pearl was a curious and inquisitive child. She found learning enjoyable. She was at an impressionable age when she started at Santa

22. Santa Barbara High School, as it was when Pearl attended

23. Pearl, aged 14

Barbara High School at fourteen. Founded in 1875, the school was, by 1903, highly regarded, attracting three times the national average intake of students.[14] While the primary focus of study was college preparation, there was also a broader focus on vocational courses. Pearl pleased her parents with her report cards for literature, math, science, history, and geography, and in turn they encouraged her in learning Latin, French, Spanish, and German, languages for which she had natural aptitude.[15]

Socially, she made friends easily and demonstrated leadership skills quite mature for someone her age. Standing five feet eight inches tall with long black hair often tied in a bun, she was admired by girls and loved by boys for her warm, seductive smile, peaches-and-cream complexion, and visible zest for life.

With plenty of outdoor pursuits in Santa Barbara, she excelled at team activities and athletics. Whether swimming in the ocean, horseback riding in the mountains, cycling, captaining the girls' basketball team, or playing hockey or tennis, she was handicapped by convention and costume. Swathed in long, heavy, voluminous skirts, one wonders how she was able to move at all; in fact, as she related many years later, she was once fortunate to escape sudden death when jumping from a high pier, her head and arms getting tangled in her flannel bathing skirt.[16]

In June 1904, Pearl and thirteen other boys and girls graduated from Santa Barbara High. While she was fully prepared at fifteen to start her studies at the University of California (UC) at Berkeley, she was refused admission because of her age, and she returned for a fifth year of high school coursework. Since she was born in Boston, it was expected by her wider family that Pearl would attend college in Massachusetts. However, she knew that in her college years she would make friends for life, and by staying and studying in California she would see her friends more frequently.[17]

Her parents supported her decision—Berkeley was well known to them. Under Benjamin Ide Wheeler (no relation), the university was emerging as a major institution. Abandoning all but a few vestiges of the traditional American college so familiar to her father—mainly of New England origin, based on religious piety, rote learning of the classics, and an overall commitment to building character—Berkeley was becoming a democratic stronghold of polite, traditional culture and a center of specialized research.[18]

24. Berkeley Campus, c.1901

Named after the Anglo-Irish philosopher George Berkeley it was situated on the eastern shore of San Francisco Bay lying ahead of the Berkeley Hills. This public institution was born out of a vision of a university in the state constitution that would "contribute even more than California's gold to the glory and happiness of advancing generations."[19]

Interestingly, there does not appear to be any record that Pearl or her parents visited the campus before she enrolled, but I suspect that Nina, whose cousin was a Regent, would have taken her daughter to see it. Charles Stetson Wheeler was one of San Francisco's most famous attorneys. Active in Republican politics, he made his fortune handling the estates of the gold rush millionaires and their wives. Among his clients and personal friends was Phoebe Apperson Hearst, widow of the "outrageously rich silver and land baron and United States senator George Hearst" and "mother of William Randolph Hearst, crusading publisher of the *San Francisco Examiner*."[20] Encouraged by the example of what Mrs. Jane Stanford was achieving with her fledgling university in Palo Alto, and advised by Stetson Wheeler, Phoebe's architectural plan for the Berkeley campus included the Hearst Memorial Mining Building, Hearst Greek Theatre, Hearst Hall, Hearst Museum, and other major financial benefactions.[21] She was especially interested in helping women to attend the university and strengthen their place once there.[22]

25. Berkeley Campus, c.1901

During Pearl's visit to California in 1900, she met Phoebe while staying with Wheeler at "The Bend," his ranch in Siskiyou Country. While there is no archival evidence, it can be assumed that Pearl first heard talk about Berkeley during this visit.

Between October 1870, when UC Berkeley enrolled its first women students "on equal terms with men," and when Pearl arrived in September 1905, the debate about women in higher education was constantly raging.[23] At a national level, the issue related to more general controversies about "changing constructions of sex and appropriate roles for educated women" and society, while at a local, campus level, it concerned a fear that women were outnumbering men and effeminizing the university.[24]

While researching Pearl's happy years at Berkeley and visiting the campus myself, I was reminded of Mike Nichols's 1967 movie *The Graduate*, shot at the university. While the movie was created by and for its time, I could not help wondering whether many of the settings—including an all-male rooming house, a fraternity, and conventional classrooms—and middle-class white people everywhere might not have been all that different sixty years earlier. Of course, the university in 1905 was not a hotbed of social activism, but it *was* a hotbed of social awakening.

Even though conditions for women students had improved since the nineteenth century when they lived in isolation from one another and the university community, Pearl arrived at a school harbouring an uneasy and turbulent power struggle between sexes. That this tension existed on a campus where women made up nearly half the student population is extraordinary by today's standards.

Knowledge was controlled by chauvinistic male professors, keen to preserve their own power, and women students were repeatedly told they were inferior to male students both in public and in print. They were "excluded from most class officers, from intercollegiate competition and sometimes from scholastic honors."[25] Moreover, President Wheeler held very traditional views regarding women, deeming their education preparation for marriage and motherhood only, making them "serviceable as wives and mothers."[26] Encouraging separatism in this way devalued the meaning of coeducation.

Despite these conditions, by 1905 there were some signs of change emerging. Under Wheeler's predecessor, Martin Kellogg, male students "had built their campus life around the structure of class traditions and interclass rivalry." Students were "initiated, sometimes violently, into college rites as freshmen."[27] While violence and pranks did not disappear during Wheeler's presidency, male students redirected their aggression away from their own campus toward their archrival, Stanford. A few months before Pearl arrived, freshmen and sophomores formed a human chain and buried the 'rushes'(contests), which pitted the two classes against each other by building a large "C" (symbolizing Californian spirit) in the Berkeley Hills.[28]

Even if male student inter-class rivalries had lessened, their attitudes toward women were still hostile. Most of these men had probably gone to coeducational primary and secondary schools and become accustomed to the presence of women there; why did they have difficulty dealing with their female classmates both as intellectual equals and objects of romance? The traditional conventions of Victorian culture prescribed separation of the sexes and gave men the reins of power, but as women steadily assumed more of their own power, men felt threatened. In many ways this fear still exists today, often taking the form of abusive conduct and bullying.

Ironically, it was this separatism that spurred the development of a culture in which women could be free to create their own forms of personal, social, and political relations. Pearl was quick to grasp redefining womanhood by the extension, rather than by the rejection, of the female sphere of influence.

During a period of changing cultural norms and confusion about the meaning of those changes, women banded together and found deeper strength. Furthermore, with the support of women administrators, benefactors like Phoebe Hearst, and teachers like Jessica Peixotto, a brilliant scholar and instructor of political economy, UC Berkeley women learned how to unite as a community in ways their peers at other American universities could not.[29] Accepting that their community was different from the men's, Berkeley women were committed to equality and fostering a greater influence on campus. The reform-minded spirit of the so-called "new woman" took root, and its implications were troubling to men.[30]

CHAPTER 3

University Years

Arriving at Berkeley with a definite purpose to prepare herself to earn a livelihood, it did not take long for Pearl to understand the dynamics of her situation. She was the epitome of the Gibson Girl, the then ideal of femininity and attractiveness named after the illustrator Charles Gibson, and popularized in magazines such as *Ladies' Home Journal*. The Gibson Girl was a young, single, "all-American girl" dressed in a bell-shaped skirt with a large bosom and narrow, corseted waist. Portrayed outdoors, in some athletic pursuit, or at dances and dinner parties, she was presented as an "object of men's desires whose aim was to find a suitable partner and get married." She embodied a "confident and assertive type of femininity that

26. Pearl, aged 18

carried a potential challenge to existing sexual hierarchies, this challenge framed as playful romanticism in relationships with men, not as a demand for political rights."

UC Berkeley was a small city of about ten thousand people, with more than three thousand students from all over the state. With no dormitories or approved housing for women students, they were unable to participate fully in campus life and remained divided as a community. This was especially so for students who commuted from their own homes, often at some distance. Pearl spent her first semester living at Snell Seminary, a private school for girls a ten-minute walk from campus.

27. Pearl's sketch on card of her address at Snell Seminary

Within just a few days of unpacking her suitcase, Pearl was feeling unhappy at Snell and longed to be closer to the center of university life. In order to live close to campus in those days, her only option was to join a sorority. There were seven sororities at Berkeley in 1905 with 145 girls. Having discussed the matter with her Wheeler cousins, she decided to join the Omega chapter of Kappa Alpha Theta (KAT), the oldest and most prestigious sorority at the university, chartered in 1890.

On September 11, Pearl sent a message via Pacific Telegraph and Cable Company to Hezekiah: "Pledged Theta. Having a good time.

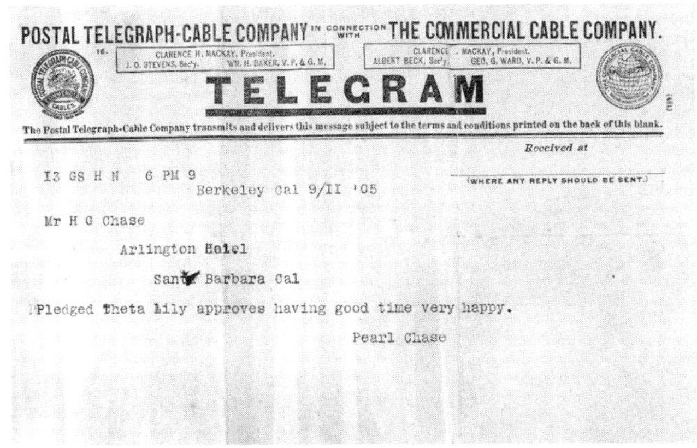
POSTAL TELEGRAPH-CABLE COMPANY IN CONNECTION WITH THE COMMERCIAL CABLE COMPANY.

CLARENCE H. MACKAY, President. J. O. STEVENS, Sec'y. WM. H. BAKER, V. P. & G. M.

CLARENCE H. MACKAY, President. ALBERT BECK, Sec'y. GEO. G. WARD, V. P. & G. M.

TELEGRAM

The Postal Telegraph-Cable Company transmits and delivers this message subject to the terms and conditions printed on the back of this blank.

Received at

(WHERE ANY REPLY SHOULD BE SENT.)

I3 GS H N 6 PM 9
Berkeley Cal 9/II '05

Mr H G Chase

Arlington Hotel

Santa Barbara Cal

Pledged Theta Lily approves having good time very happy.

Pearl Chase

28. Telegram 'Pledged Theta'

Very happy." Kappa Alpha Theta was the most important institution to shape Pearl's undergraduate years; it was literally a life-changing experience. From her first day as a Theta, the KAT force started to run through her veins, and she could think of nothing else.

Living with her KAT sisters, Pearl found the closest thing to a home beyond the domestic sphere. It was also a good instrument "through which to experiment with self-government, particularly as the sorority was managed and governed without university supervision." It also provided her with career opportunities she had not previously considered. The friendships she made through this network were enduring, and she remained an active member all her life. Among them she found like-minded women supportive of one another's intellectual and social aspirations. More importantly, she discovered that sisterhood was a responsibility and a time commitment, and allegiance to the sorority identity was fundamental. With this awareness, she was able to have a lot of fun.

One of the most significant developments for the Thetas during Pearl's college years was the construction of a new chapter house in 1908. It was entirely fitting that they should commission one of their own to do the work, and Julia Morgan was in a unique position to help. Graduating from Berkeley in civil engineering in

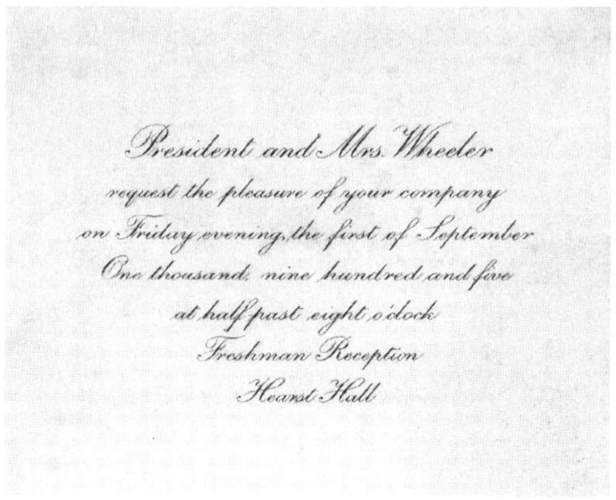
President and Mrs. Wheeler
request the pleasure of your company
on Friday evening, the first of September
One thousand nine hundred and five
at half past eight o'clock
Freshman Reception
Hearst Hall

29. Invitation to Freshman Reception, 1905

1894, she was the first woman to be admitted to the École des Beaux Arts in Paris and the first woman architect licensed in America. In her career, "it seems that she often tried to conceal her sex in order to advance professionally," and much of her work was in designing female spaces, many of her commissions coming from former Theta housemates. Her design at 2723 Durant Avenue made quite an impression on the Theta sisters, including Pearl, who loved the house. While the design was quintessentially Californian, it drew on both rustic Arts and Crafts styles and Classical modes for inspiration. The house was neither pretentious nor expensive to run, and on Pearl's moderate income it met all her requirements. She and her Theta sisters had many house rules, one of which was to keep an elegant home.

As a pioneer woman architect involved with Berkeley, Morgan's work caught the eye of Phoebe Hearst and her son, William Randolph Hearst, who commissioned her to design Hearst Castle. Many architectural historians regard her as the greatest woman architect in America of the twentieth century, designing over eight hundred buildings during her forty-five-year career.

Outside the US, fraternities and sororities are "somewhat mysterious entities, often portrayed with drink-laden parties, hazing

30. Julia Morgan's design for 2723 Durant Avenue

or initiation controversies, and raunch comedy movies like *Animal House* and *Neighbors*." In reality these societies and the houses associated with them "are institutions at the centre of university social life." So it was for the Theta sisters at 2723 Durant Avenue in 1908. When Pearl became president of the chapter in her final year, she was determined to ensure the sisters bonded with one another and the house was well kept.

Among the most important records of her university life is a ninety-page scrapbook, which includes, among many other mementoes, photographs of her Theta sisters and their house. Pearl was passionate about visual storytelling as both a photographer and collector of postcards. Her love for collecting in this way started in high school, where she produced a twenty-four-page pamphlet on women of all nations using magazine cuttings.

Although the Berkeley Thetas were not politically outspoken on suffrage and the national politics of the day, they were among the most determined students for equal rights for women on campus. Pearl's two best friends, Connie Stratton (1906–07) and Maude Cleveland

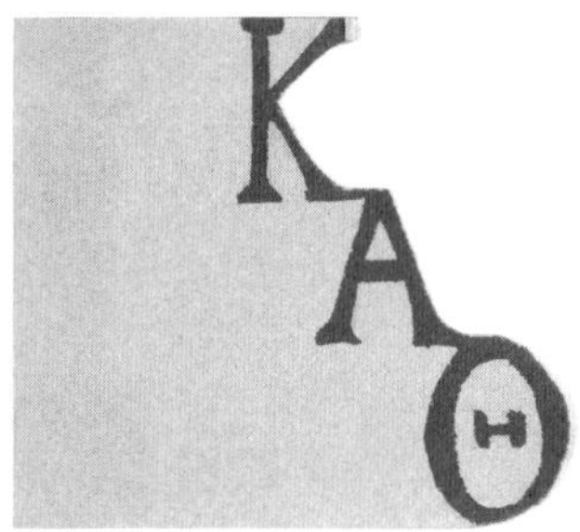

31. Pearl's KAT notebook

(1908–09), were both presidents of the Association of Women Students. The AWS was founded in 1894 by Berkeley women seeking to bring their community closer together and deal with questions of conduct, housing, finance, and social affairs. This proved challenging, not least because the "AWS was dominated by sorority women, and it followed that those women who were excluded from the sororities might also find the AWS an unwelcoming group."

It was also seriously undermined by the Associated Students of the University of California (ASUC). For every AWS yearly due of one dollar, a fee of twenty-five cents was paid to the ASUC to participate in their organization; despite this, women had no representation on the ASUC. It was a subject of resentment, but "no one suggested merging the groups, partly because men would have not tolerated equality within one organization and partly because neither sex considered it appropriate for men to supervise women's social lives."

Pearl participated in committees involved in a wide range of AWS events, from arranging the Annual Reception, to helping to organize the inaugural Women's Day celebration, to spearheading the fundraising campaign to build a new women's dormitory, to acting and ushering at theatrical events. She was committed to helping her women colleagues; she took the work all in stride while feeling that she could "accomplish a good deal more by not letting other things and people distract" her. Her accomplishments in co-ed activities were recognized publicly after she graduated when the Torch and Shield, the senior women's honor society, elected her a member.

In expanding career prospects for women, Pearl believed that her own education was the key to her future. She remarked:

> I am publicly educated. I have always gone to public schools since kindergarten and everyone who has done the same owes something for that free education. [...] The difference between intelligence and wisdom is important. You can be knowledgeable about something but unwise in how and when to use it.

Her ambition was to learn a little about a great many things. She enrolled in more classes than were usually permitted and soon after found the choice unwise. Most women students tended to take literature, foreign language, and history courses rather than life sciences. Of the forty-nine courses Pearl completed, thirty-four were in the former disciplines, with sixteen in history alone. Among the courses she wanted to study but did not, geology was uppermost. She also neglected to take the prerequisite courses for upper division political science and economics, and was unable to enrol in the department headed by Jessica Peixotto, the forerunner of the university's school of social work.

While Pearl had appreciated history since childhood, it was the inspiration of Professor Henry Morse Stephens's teaching that brought it to life for her at university. Morse, as he was better known, was born in Scotland in 1857 and educated at Balliol in Oxford. He immigrated to the US in 1894 and took up a position at Cornell where he taught European history. Arriving at Berkeley in 1902 as Sather Professor of History and Director of the University Extension, he quickly became one of the most popular of all lecturers—in fact, students from other disciplines often went to listen to him.

Living in the west wing of the Faculty Club to be close to his students, he attracted a circle of friends. Undergraduates like Pearl

32. Henry Morse Stephens

who were "admitted to that circle found themselves just as welcome as professors and quite as much at their ease." With an emphasis on the scientific approach to history and the importance of going to the original source material, Morse was dedicated to rigorousness, exhaustive analysis, and the amassing of factual evidence. He was a prolific writer, most well-known for his three-volume history of the French Revolution.

As a member of the Bohemian Club, an elite, invitation-only, all men's social club based in San Francisco, Morse was also known socially to Charles Stetson Wheeler, a fellow member. Although Morse recognized Pearl's talent and strong intellect, it seems likely that his friendship with Wheeler influenced his decision to take her on as his student. Pearl recalled later that she was the only senior in her year he allowed to read from original Spanish documents held in the Bancroft Library.

CHAPTER 4

University and the San Francisco Earthquake

On April 18, 1906, Pearl's university experience was profoundly shocked. On that day she witnessed a 7.9-magnitude earthquake and the three-day fire that followed, killing an estimated 3,000 people, leaving 250,000 homeless, and destroying 28,000 buildings on 490 city blocks. Three quarters of San Francisco had become ash and ruins.[1]

33. Photo possibly taken by Pearl of the San Francisco earthquake

Inspired by the event, and the fact that it was history-making, she wrote a letter to her parents in the form of a three-meter-long scroll, sharing her extraordinary experience during the first few days after the earthquake. Referring to herself as "your special reporter in the field," she began:

> I can hardly realize that it was only last Wednesday that I woke to find the house rocking and shuddering as if some giant had grasped it by the shoulders. The girls were screaming, and I saw a vision of three white-clad figures pushing in their doorways, shaking their hands and screaming, "Why doesn't it stop? Isn't it dreadful? Oh my, oh my, everything is smashed! I know it is and we're all going to be killed!" Then it did stop. We gathered in the "jolly room," had a consultation, and much to their disgust after finding that our chimney wasn't down, and that besides some spilled bookshelves, little damage had been done, I left the girls and went to bed again and [slept] undisturbed til nearly ten. By that time we had learned that the college had closed, and for the rest of the day we could do nothing but listen and add to the rumours which came to us from every side. A train took a large part of the cadets to the ferry late in the afternoon. By that night the fire had gained headway and we could see the flames as they rose and fell in the city across the bay. It was a line of fire, not scattered, as might be expected. During the days that followed a huge cloud of grey smoke hung over the city, which changed every evening into a charging, seething mass of orange flames shading into the black sky. Some say that the reflection and the glare in the night sky might be seen over 200 miles out at sea. To us who watched, it was a gloriously terrible sight, made more impressive as now and then some dull report reached us, showing that the dynamiters were at their work. And they did work day and night as long as their supplies lasted. Early Thursday morning some of those who anxiously waited for the first refugees started to gather supplies and prepare for their reception, for Oakland and Berkeley [are]

but thirty minutes from San Francisco, expected to shelter great numbers.

At noon the first train came in and we must have wept had there not been almost as many ridiculous and pitiful sights. Few were weeping or lamenting tho many had lost everything in the world except that which they carried with them. One old lady, I remember, burdened by an enormous quilt-load + carpetbag also carried a ferocious red and green parrot in an enormous cage who kept up the most terrific stream of language that I ever want to hear. All along the line we found pets, and most of them much more tenderly cared for than the little tots, who for the most part, aside from the discomforts of grime and hunger (which were soon to be removed) were cheerfully important under the attention showered them and were voluble in the tales told of nights spent walking the streets or in crowded sheds where they lay on the straw among all sorts and kinds of people.

In Berkeley relief committees were quickly formed and their system and management improved every day. As the people left the trains they were met by college girls or boys, who fed them at once and then found lodgings for them, through a card system of those who were willing to take the refugees into their homes. A great many of the better class went to friends or to respectable boarding houses so that really what we had to handle were those of the slums or class just above. All were grimy, with eyes swollen from the smoke more or less peculiarly clad and laden with the most outlandish possessions.

All those not too proud to ask for aid were given clothes, food, and shelter. There were many, however, who needed medical and surgical attention, and I saw a good deal of this part of the work for I spent the greater part of my time helping in the makeshift hospital. One morning from eight o'clock til eleven we washed and dressed twenty-five babies, from a few days old to two years of age. The poor little things were those to suffer most from the privation. One little baby was brought to us on Friday morning, its mother had been lost since Wednesday noon (we learned through an interpreter) and all that it had during that time was some coffee sucked through its father's old bandana handkerchief; of course the baby was extremely weak and after we had made it as comfortable as possible there was nothing to do but carry it.

It died that afternoon in my arms, very quietly, it had whimpered a little and the poor little hands had grasped convulsively before the tiny body went to sleep, that was all. There were some cases even sadder than this that we saw.

What helped everyone, however, during the hard time was the common sympathy. Those who gave time and money to help the homeless people found everywhere a calm acceptance of loss and the spirit that made the best of whatever came. Undoubtedly some of the wanderers had never been so comfortable and well cared for before and there were but few thankless and unresponsive to mar our impression of them. I suppose that many were too dazed to realize their position and that realization is but now forcing itself on those who will have to begin at the bottom and work up all over again. Some

34. One of the many relief queues established after the earthquake

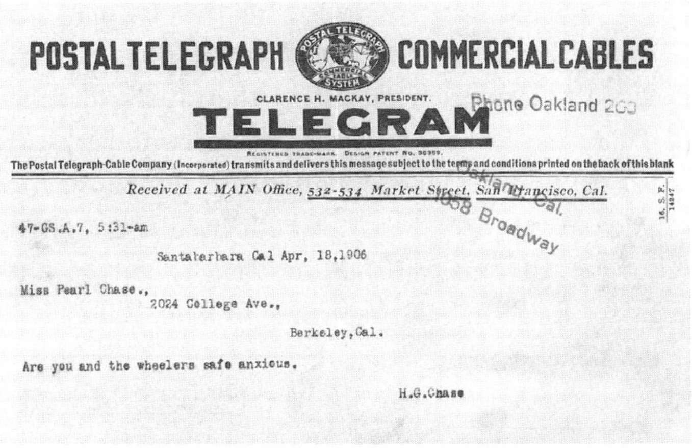
POSTAL TELEGRAPH COMMERCIAL CABLES

CLARENCE H. MACKAY, PRESIDENT.

TELEGRAM

Phone Oakland 263

The Postal Telegraph-Cable Company (Incorporated) transmits and delivers this message subject to the terms and conditions printed on the back of this blank

Received at MAIN Office, 532-534 Market Street, San Francisco, Cal.

Oakland, Cal. 1058 Broadway

47-GS.A.7, 5:31-am

Santabarbara Cal Apr, 18,1906

Miss Pearl Chase.,
2024 College Ave.,
Berkeley, Cal.

Are you and the wheelers safe anxious.

H.G.Chase

35. Telegram from Hezekiah Chase to Pearl, April 1906

> fortunes will be made out of the fire—we seldom speak of the earthquake now but more will be spent in building up what people say is going to be a greater and better San Francisco and all the resources of the state will be taxed to support those left on its hands by the great fire for the number is not small.[2]

Nina and Hezekiah were understandably shocked by the events, but greatly relieved that Pearl was safe. They sent her money with the advice "not to let your heart run away with your pocket."[3]

Two years after the earthquake, Pearl was asked by Professor Stephens, who had been appointed a member of the Earthquake History Committee, to help him unpack and sort through Hubert Howe Bancroft's library, which the university had purchased in 1905 and which had survived the earthquake. Comprising 50,000 volumes of materials on the history of California and the North American West, it was the largest collection of its kind in the world. Housed in the attic of California Hall, Pearl worked alongside Stephens's history PhD and master's students. She considered it an honor, and she was the only woman.

The campus at Berkeley suffered almost no damage from the earthquake but for a few chimneys. Financially, however, the university suffered losses of over $100,000 from its commercial assets in San Francisco. The state met these losses with a grant.[4] Even with the disruption caused by the massive destruction and fire of 1906, San Francisco was still the eleventh largest city in the United States and the most important city in the American West. In a show of resilience, the city rebuilt itself at rapid speed. Over the following years, everyone visiting the city and Pearl, too, could sense the spirit of San Francisco rising from its ashes.

In the wake of the disaster, the academic council of faculty at Berkeley suspended coursework for the rest of the academic year except for the cadets who continued to supervise the refugees. Examinations were left in the hands of the instructors to decide on the final mark. Commencement continued without the senior ball or extravaganza.

In true American spirit, university life returned to normal the following September, and freshmen entering fraternities and sororities were pledged and hazed. Returning sophomores, juniors, and seniors shared their summer vacation stories. Pearl liked nothing better than to get together with her sorority girlfriends and gossip about such matters. Her letters are full of news about who was seeing

36. Clippings of 'the Big Game' from Pearl's Berkeley scrapbook

who and who was doing what.[5] It was not that she simply took an interest in their lives, but that she cared deeply about her friends.

As a Theta, she also cared about maintaining the reputation of the sorority as being the best at Berkeley. Attracting the most talented new girls was important to her. Advised to "impress with the fact that you are clever entertainers, more clever than any others, and that nothing is too much trouble,"[6] Pearl made a huge effort. Her parties and dinners, often incorporating Asian themes, were legendary. She was a competitive, fun-loving extrovert.

In her final year at Berkeley, Harold enrolled. Up to this point their education had proceeded in tandem as part of a conscious effort by their parents to foster a closer relationship between them. The sibling solidarity took on a new form at college where, for the first time, both siblings were living away from home. Pearl adopted a role somewhere between mother and helpmeet, speaking to Harold every day and seeing him every other. On her recommendation he joined the Beta Theta Pi fraternity, where he was a popular student, eventually becoming president of the Mandolin Club, managing the

37. Harold and Pearl, c.1910

Blue and Gold and winning his captain's C on the track team.[7] At six feet two inches tall with the same brown hair and eyes as Pearl, he was handsome and athletic. Pearl delighted in his accomplishments, often attending his sporting events. She loved to describe the way many women students would gather near the track when he was competing because he had such handsome legs.[8]

The reciprocity was clear and exhibited in customary ways. Popularly known as "Pearl's younger brother," Harold assumed the role of traveling companion, partnered with Pearl at social events, and introduced her to many of his friends. Brotherly concern took the form of making sure she did not go without, a concern that continued all their lives.

Among his male friends were Earl Warren, who went on to become governor of California and chief justice of the United States Supreme Court; Horace Albright, a conservationist who became director of the National Park System; and Newton Drury, a conservationist who also served as a director of the National Park System and executive director of Save the Redwoods League. Quite possibly because of the age difference, Pearl had no romantic interest in Harold's friends, but they remained close friends of hers, often collaborating on conservation projects well beyond their college years.

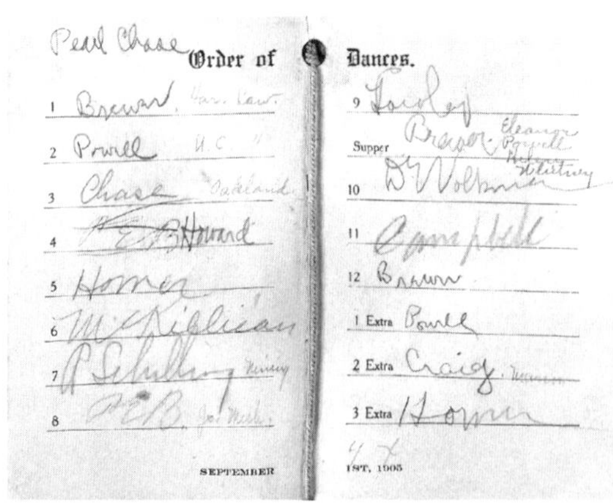

38. Freshman reception dance card, 1905

As she later remarked, "I've always been very proud of that class of 1912 and its leaders."[9] And, "They were men who came to college to learn, who were interested in people, and they were proud of their university, glad to be of service."[10]

Given her energy, beauty, and popularity on campus, Pearl attracted and enjoyed a great deal of romantic attention from the opposite sex. At a time when the standard of morality was very high and only occasionally were hasty marriages arranged after too-ardent lovemaking, there was, however, nothing to stop students from having affairs. Commenting on her student life years later, she said, "I probably danced more miles than anybody in college. It was said that I went to more dances and more parties than anyone else."[11] While many women students at the time treated their education as preparation for marriage, Pearl thought otherwise. She was in no hurry to rush in, but she enjoyed the company of men and getting to know them without the need for any physicality beyond

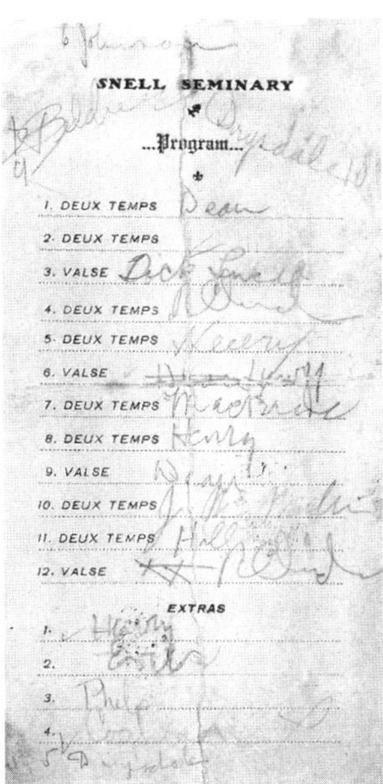

SNELL SEMINARY

...Program...

1. DEUX TEMPS
2. DEUX TEMPS
3. VALSE
4. DEUX TEMPS
5. DEUX TEMPS
6. VALSE
7. DEUX TEMPS
8. DEUX TEMPS
9. VALSE
10. DEUX TEMPS
11. DEUX TEMPS
12. VALSE

EXTRAS

1.
2.
3.
4.

39. Snell Seminary dance card

kissing. She won a wager for having been given the most fraternity pins.

Among her suitors, Robert Van Sant and Dean Witter were the two main contenders for her affections. From her correspondence it appears that she dated both simultaneously, somewhat to the confusion of her sorority sisters. Witter was good-looking, honest, and ambitious. He joined the Zeta Psi fraternity and rowed for the university. Years later he cofounded Dean Witter & Company, which became the largest investment house on the west coast.

He was one of Pearl's earliest dance partners when she was living at the Snell Seminary. Their shared interest in dance continued throughout their years at Berkeley. There is very little surviving correspondence between Pearl and Witter, but among their friends it

40. Dean Witter

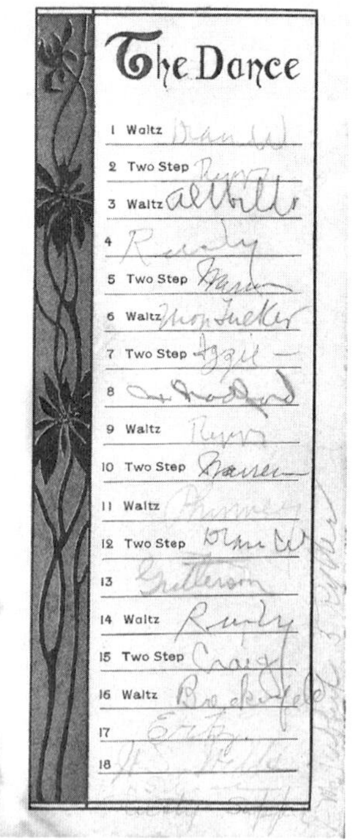

41. Dance Card, Dean Witter gets the first dance

was rumoured that they had become engaged a year after they graduated. Many stories have been told about this incident but the one that gets repeated most often, even among family circles, is that she decided to break off the engagement and returned the ring. Other stories have Pearl losing the ring and Witter calling the wedding off.

If dancing was what attracted Pearl to Witter, it was an intellectual connection with Robert Hayes Van Sant, Jr. He was an honor student three years older than Pearl. Through his father's construction company, his family had played an important part in the development of Oakland. During his years at Berkeley, he was a senior member of the ASUC and organizations editor for the college's first-ever senior yearbook, the *Senior Record, Volume 1*, for the class of 1907. Pearl and "R," as she lovingly referred to him, began seeing one another in 1908 and continued for another three years after she graduated. The nature of the relationship was a mystery to Pearl's friends, and even Harold. Her parents also had no awareness of it, as she kept it a secret from them.

In their correspondence both expressed a heartfelt love for each other and a wish to get married, but they were beset by doubts. Robert worried about his finances, his ability to support Pearl, and whether their social worlds were compatible. She questioned his controlling tendencies and his personal aspirations, which she saw as separate from his career goals. A further obstacle that dampened the affair was the physical distance between San Francisco and Santa Barbara and neither party's willingness to relocate.

Given Robert's uncertainty, it is surprising that Pearl held out for a proposal and did not look for another partner. She disliked reticence. One reason for her patience might be peer pressure; any proclamations her sorority friends had made of remaining eternal bachelorettes during their Berkeley years were soon forgotten shortly after graduation. Her correspondence is filled with gossip of their engagements and marriages.[12] These girls and their contemporaries found that the social context of their lives beyond campus

42. Sketch of Pearl with bougainvillea in her hair, from her Berkeley scrapbook

contained little to sustain their idealism, and that it was easier to settle for marriage and family life. Another reason might simply be that the strain of hiding their relationship created toxicity.

I suspect, given Pearl's strong-mindedness and intellectual ambitions, that she found neither man was equal to her. Pearl's eventual decision to break with "R" brought her independence. She was glad to be out of the relationship and free to focus on her career.

In addition to having a full social life and many responsibilities on campus, Pearl worked assiduously throughout her years at Berkeley and impressed her teachers. In her final year, despite suffering from sudden blurred vision brought on by a fall at Nojoqui Falls in Santa Barbara County, and having been forbidden to read for some months, Pearl completed her studies. Such was her output that she earned all her credits for graduation by December 1908. Despite this, Pearl continued to push herself academically during her final months. On May 12, 1909, commencement was held in the Greek Theatre, and Pearl graduated summa cum laude with a Bachelor of Letters (BL) in history. She was surprised by her success; her friends, less so.

Over a century later as I walked around campus, I could not help noticing that a lot of what surrounded me was imagined and influenced by women. Pearl's contribution in making Berkeley a better place for women was part of a collective effort which continues today.

43. Commencement Day, May 12, 1909. Pearl is standing in the middle

CHAPTER 5

Home Economics

With her Berkeley experience and belief in both the conservation and volunteerism spirit of the progressive movement, Pearl had a very definite vision for her future. It had taken root in 1907 when she returned to Santa Barbara from Berkeley for a holiday. "I remember alighting from the train at the old Victoria Street station coming home for the holidays, and how ashamed I was of Santa Barbara's shabby buildings, dusty streets, and lack of landscaping. Then and there I resolved to dedicate myself to making Santa Barbara a more beautiful place to live in."[1]

Education was, to Pearl, the most natural career path toward achieving her vision. Despite its low pay, teaching offered one of the highest-status careers at the time. Nonetheless it was a commitment, not least because she needed to graduate from an approved program for her teaching certification. Undoubtedly, her decision was made easier by the 1909 opening of the Santa Barbara State Normal School of Manual Arts and Home Economics under the leadership of Ednah Rich.[2] It was the first school of its kind in the US, and Ms. Rich, as director, was then the only woman in the US to serve as president of a state normal school.[3]

With a faculty of four, including Rich, the school opened on August 30th. Pearl was one of fifteen students in the home economics department. Located in a huge Victorian building in the downtown district, it took Pearl twenty minutes to walk from her house at 2012 Anacapa Street. Her courses included domestic science and domestic art. While there were many who thought it was absurd to

44. Ednah Rich standing in front of the trolley to the Normal School campus

teach cooking and sewing, and that it was just common sense, others thought the improvement of the home was one of the greatest moral and social reforms imaginable. Maternal instinct was no longer considered the only prerequisite for ensuring a child's health and well-being. Pioneers such as Rich believed that by applying scientific principles and efficiency to domestic topics such as good nutrition, pure foods, proper clothing, and sanitation, women would have more time for pursuits other than cooking and cleaning.

At this time there were no prescribed standards for teaching these subjects, as such standards had not been recognized by authority. Given that there were not a great many books on the topic, Pearl and her associates found themselves breaking new ground. Finding her new life more disciplined than her sorority life, she remarked, "It's an awful struggle to keep aprons and dresses neat and clean. I'm not of the proper disposition."[4] However critical Pearl was of herself, the normal school fostered a sense of professionalism. Reminiscing years later she explained how the instruction she got in home economics was to become the fundamental formal education experience of her life.[5]

In 1911 a state directive forbade Rich from holding the job of president of the state normal school and superintendent of home economics for the city of Santa Barbara. Rich asked Pearl to take the latter post and continue to train student teachers. Pearl took the required courses, obtaining her secondary teaching diploma in July, 1912, and taught her first class at Santa Barbara High School the following September. Pearl was the first university graduate to secure a certificate in home economics from the normal school. For the next three years she combined teaching at the high school and supervising practice teachers from the normal school.

Pearl adopted modern teaching methods that put the student in the center. She was familiar with John Dewey's progressive theory that teachers should not be in the classroom to act simply as instructors, but she also believed in the traditional view that a teacher's role was to pass information to students that would help prepare them for life beyond school. She took a scientific approach to her work; it was essential to not only get the facts correct but know the subject in detail.[6]

Teaching at the high school, Pearl established a reputation for herself among the faculty as "a dear mind set to lofty purposes."[7] Among her many students, Martha Graham went on to become a famous dancer and choreographer. Pearl enjoyed the sociability of her colleagues but teaching left her feeling, "tired, cramped and limited in her pleasures."[8]

These pleasures she found while volunteering in social work at civic-oriented clubs and associations including the Neighborhood House Association. Such was her enthusiasm that in 1910 she was elected to the board of directors. Wasting no time toward improving the city, one of her first actions was to appoint Margaret Baylor, a

45. Martha Graham

trained professional, to serve as superintendent "to curb a rising tide of juvenile delinquency caused by Santa Barbara children having nothing to occupy their leisure time."[9] Born in Boston in 1880 to a wealthy family, Baylor had by 1910 become prominent in Cincinnati social work. "Arriving in Santa Barbara she sized up the existing problem very quickly. While wealthy tourists had golf courses and polo fields, Santa Barbara youth was virtually ignored. She also saw an extreme need for clean, decent, low-cost housing facilities for unmarried working women."[10] Pearl thought Baylor was "remarkable and interesting."[11] She admired her ideals, respected her training and knowledge in community service, and felt "she put us in line."[12] With her appointment, Santa Barbara had a true expert in social welfare. In collaboration they organized the construction of a recreation center modelled on the settlement house movement and Hull House in Chicago, where Baylor had trained as a college graduate.

The recreation center included a large auditorium with a dance floor undergirded with coiled springs to give it a bounce. This facility, Baylor predicted, would both attract Santa Barbaran youth and reduce juvenile misbehaviour and racial friction in schools. It worked, with over two and a half thousand people visiting the building during its first year.

It was no surprise given Baylor's experience in social work that the center was geared more toward helping women than men. Soon after it opened Baylor recognized that additional lodging was needed for single women and girls. It took a further eleven years before this became a reality, and Baylor never lived to see the final result, passing in 1924. It was Pearl who saw the project through and helped form a committee to raise money for the building. Julia Morgan was hired to design the plans. Total construction costs reached $245,000 and the hotel, which opened in March 1927, was named the Margaret Baylor Inn. It replicated what had been proved so successful by the Young Women's Christian Association organizations across the US.

As Pearl's vision for Santa Barbara evolved, she discovered in herself a talent for "recognizing and encouraging leadership qualities in others."[13] Through her membership and participation of the Santa Barbara Woman's Club, she found a group of women eager to get involved in the public sphere. Most of the members were the wives and daughters of wealthy men in prominent positions, and with the ability to access funds and generate support for their projects, the Woman's Club was in many ways a "counterpart to the male power structure."[14]

One of the issues that brought all clubwomen together in the years leading up to the First World War was suffrage. In 1914, the General Federation of Women's Clubs endorsed the movement taking the view that women could best achieve their reform goals through the vote. Santa Barbara had a long association with suffrage; at the forefront of the drive to enfranchise women in California were club women and teachers. The former were motivated largely by a desire to nurture civic activism in women, and the latter to provide equal pay for equal work.

It would seem that Pearl must have engaged in lengthy discussions on the subject. Unfortunately, there is scant information on the process by which Pearl's close associates formed their political beliefs and the ideological conflicts among them and their male counterparts. Suffice to say, Rich was a suffragist, as were some of Pearl's fellow teachers at the high school.

Pearl was happy to attend suffrage talks in Santa Barbara, but she never discussed her feelings publicly. Nonetheless, she cared deeply about advancing women's work, later supporting the 1960s feminist movement and the 1972 Equal Rights Amendment.[15] Whatever her views were, she understood that the suffrage movement was more than simply about the legal ability to vote; it expanded women's social and political power and their ability to participate more fully in the public affairs of society through political engagement and civic action.

In 1911, California became the sixth state to give women the franchise joining Wyoming, Colorado, Utah, Idaho, and Washington. In a very real sense, the victory paved the way for the adoption of the Nineteenth Amendment in 1920. Pearl was delighted that the franchise was passed but she did not view suffrage as the wellspring of women's rights or the ultimate goal. The ballot was a tool that women could use to accomplish their civic duties.

Alongside these changes in society, the automobile became both a symbol of freedom for American women and a tool in the fight for suffrage. The appearance of the car ushered a key force for change in twentieth-century America. The first local to own an automobile in Santa Barbara was in 1900. Two years later there were eight cars in the city; passers-by viewed them with mixed feelings, not least because horses became so frightened by their "sight and noise that they did everything but fly."[16] In the early days, horses had the right of way within the Santa Barbara city limits. The speed limit was eight miles an hour.

By 1910, with a population of over eleven thousand, the number of automobiles had grown to over three hundred. However, Santa Barbara City Council remained loyal to the horse until 1912 when it authorized the first purchase of a Ford Model T for $685 for council use.[17] The mail continued to be delivered with horse-drawn carts until 1922 when the carrier was given a car to cover Montecito.[18] It is interesting to note that across the US there were only 250 miles of concrete road at this time.[19]

Hezekiah bought his first car, a Buick, in 1911, as it was no longer suitable to conduct real estate viewings by horse; his clients expected to be driven, a much quicker option. In 1912, Pearl was one of the first women to drive in Santa Barbara and one of thirty-three original members of the Automobile Club of Southern California.[20] In these years, there were few directional signs, roads were in poor condition, and motorists often got lost while taking a drive. The auto club members took on the responsibility of signposting thousands of miles of streets and highways.

The transition from the horse age to the motorized was not only liberating but also very dangerous. There were no stop signs, warning signs, traffic lights, street lighting, brake lights, or posted speed limits. Accidents were frequent, even in Santa Barbara where many of the cars were chauffeur-driven. On Saturday July 12, 1913, tragedy struck the Chases when Nina was killed in a car Hezekiah was driving. Returning from the theatre, Hezekiah accidently crashed his car through the wall of the wooden garage at their home. The brakes failed and the car shot through the rear wall and a crossbeam caught Nina across the chest. She died instantly. Hezekiah survived fatal injury due to the steering wheel catching the force of the impact. The entire community was shocked, and the news spread swiftly around the city. Grief was widely shared and expressed, as Nina had an unusually large circle of friends.[21]

46. Nina Chase, c.1912

To compound the tragedy, neither Pearl nor Harold were in the city at the time and they could not be contacted. Harold was visiting the Channel Islands thirty miles from the mainland and, with no radio, was not informed until the following morning when a local ship's captain reached him. Pearl was on a trip to Alaska and did not hear the news until the following week when she received a wireless communication from family friends in Tacoma. By the time she reached Santa Barbara, the funeral service had already been held. Four days after the accident, Hezekiah and Harold took Nina's body to Los Angeles for cremation, a decision that was likely to have been her own; Santa Barbara had no facilities for cremation.

Pearl had been very close to her mother, and her death meant the loss of the unconditional love experienced only as a daughter. It is hard to imagine what she must have felt to have missed her mother's funeral. She never mentioned publicly what she felt, but she kept the memory of her mother alive, reminding her father and brother at anniversaries of Nina's birthday of the importance of the date.

To Pearl, the shock of her mother's death was swiftly replaced by the worry of seeing her father so broken-hearted and racked with guilt. Aged fifty-two, a part of him shut down and he became extremely depressed. Without his wife, he became very lonely. Faced with having to cope on his own, he begged Pearl never to leave him, and she agreed. She later explained, "I promised him that I would stay with him as long as he lived, so I couldn't ever leave Santa Barbara."[22] She also decided that she could not marry and leave her father. Among Pearl's records and by her own account, there are references to many men who wanted to make her their wife. She thought they wanted "to be taken care of, awfully rich ones, some of them."[23]

At only twenty-four, her mother's death changed Pearl's life. In many respects she took the place of Nina, both in a social sense and as a confidante with her father. Although they had always been close, she became emotionally closer to him and started to make decisions on his behalf. She was already mature for her age, but Nina's death brought about more maturity.

Nina's death further bonded what was already a close family. Neither Harold nor Pearl expressed their grief in public; it was not that they were unfeeling but that they did not express such emotions openly. In a letter Pearl wrote her brother many years later, she remarked, "I knew my life would be subject to change as his [Hezekiah's] condition and your life patterns changed, and I have always been ready though through all the years there have been fewer variations in your life and mine than is usual."[24]

CHAPTER 6

Car Crash

Pearl narrowly escaped death when on January 29, 1916, she was in a car accident as she, Harold, and some friends were driving to a party at Hope Ranch after recent rains had made the narrow road particularly treacherous. Swerving to avoid another car stuck in mud, and an oncoming car, Harold drove into the road bank. In her account of the story, Pearl said:

> The other car hit the car I was in and drove the mudguard right through, so I had a horizontal and vertical thrust on my back at the same time. Two men came and said, "How are you?" One of the other passengers said, "I think we are alright but for one of the girls here." Of course, my brother was terrified because of my mother's death less than three years before. Harold's car couldn't move and they wanted to get me out, so someone had to get in the car and lift me by the shoulders so I could come out feet-first. I had something which has always amused me. I had this magnificent embroidered Chinese pink brocade skirt given to my mother by Harry Fonda, a famous actor. As my feet went out of the car door, I had the very feminine thought, "I'm glad to have pink silk stockings on." In an accident I was all dressed up for it and then I fainted for a moment only. It was about the only time I ever did. Harold took me right to the osteopath's office on Victoria Street. Doctor Myra Sperry had been treating me since I got back from college. My life would have been ruined if it hadn't been for Dr. Sperry. She laid me face down on the table and began working. It was so soon after the accident the hard stiffening had not begun, and

> the muscular contractions had not taken hold. My brother screamed when he saw my back because it came down there and you could put your whole fist right in beside where my back was bent. She worked for an hour loosening and then pressed, and I screamed, and it went straight. Because of my mother I was allowed to have her come to the cottage hospital. Normally they do not allow osteopaths in the hospital. But this treatment has kept me going.[1]

Pearl's injuries gave her family and friends a fright. A few days later as she lay in bed recovering, Hezekiah and Harold asked her what she wanted to do, and she told them that she was never going to teach again.[2] She had been considering a change of career for several months, and it came as no surprise to anyone when she resigned her teaching positions the following July.

Despite her accident and confinement in the hospital, Pearl continued to work. She was in the middle of organizing Santa Barbara's child welfare week, in collaboration with the Association of Collegiate Alumnae. She ordered a telephone to be installed by her bed and from there she sent messages to all her various social work committees. Knowing that publicity was critical to the success of her social welfare causes, she made sure that the local newspaper heard about her determined resolve. Such fortitude won her many plaudits and plenty of positive local media attention.

Pearl's association with Santa Barbara's normal school, neighbourhood house association, recreation center and woman's club had ignited a passion for social work. In 1913 she participated in the Santa Barbara County Social Service Conference (SBSCC). Meeting with government social agencies; civic organizations, including relief committees of lodges and labor unions; and private citizens, she felt that the "varied activities connected with the development of public health, was probably what I could serve the best."[3]

Her first proper foray into this work started in 1914. Following instructions from the county Board of Health, she took charge

47. Pearl in her garden at Anacapa Street, aged 24

of a subcommittee of the SBSCC to inspect several food-related businesses, including a foul-smelling slaughterhouse in a residential neighborhood. Getting rid of the unsanitary eyesore, she and her committee "raised such a hullabaloo" that the health officers condemned the building.[4] A few months later, a raging typhoid epidemic in Santa Barbara revealed the need for the pasteurization of milk. Working along educational lines she launched a campaign of dairy sanitation, pure milk, and a movement for the prevention of tuberculosis, which was a major cause of infant mortality.

Such was her success that Santa Barbara's unclean dairies became "model creameries."[5] In like manner, under the Children's Bureau at Washington DC and through the local parent-teacher association, a "Better Babies Week" was held in 1915. Never before had the community's responsibility for its babies been so well presented and publicized. Among the many findings of her campaigns was the poor standards and inefficiency of the county hospital. Naturally, she made it her duty to reorganize it.

Pearl also noticed that although there were intelligent college-educated women, among the SSC community there were too few experts trained as social scientists who could address public health concerns. In 1915, she helped resolve this with the formation of the Santa Barbara branch of the Association of Collegiate Alumnae. Pearl noted that this was the first time "intelligent women, trained women, college women, who were peculiarly able in furthering social things" had gathered together and "saw the opportunity of making studies and surveys."[6] With their support, she embarked on tackling the civic jobs "that everybody said somebody ought to do but which nobody did."[7]

At a time when newspaper headlines blazed with the violence of the First World War, then sweeping across Europe; when women in Washington, DC chained themselves to fences to protest their lack of franchise; when half of all American families lived in rural areas or towns with populations below 2,500 and more than half the country's population was under 25; when very few people owned a refrigerator; and when clothes washers, dryers, air conditioning, and television sets were a distant dream, social welfare was a minor consideration across large parts of the nation. However, from New York to San Francisco, well-educated citizens were leading spirited campaigns to improve living standards in their communities. In the great American cities of Boston and Chicago, social health workers were pioneering new techniques, and it was from their example that Pearl looked for inspiration and knowledge.

Realizing her vision of a better Santa Barbara, she introduced modern techniques of social planning and efficiency. What Pearl initiated was a new way of working, highly organized, motivated, far-sighted, and not afraid to use all means of media communication. To understand how Pearl transformed Santa Barbara and herself along with it, it is worth exploring how she operated in these early years.

Among her papers I was struck by the thousands of newspaper clippings she kept on matters of public health. By staying informed, she became an expert on her subject. Her education and training gave her a foundation to work upon, but she was determined to build on it with the spirit of a pioneer. Seeing what other communities were doing in the US and Europe, she cherry-picked the best cases for Santa Barbara. She realized that the future of the city depended on looking outward and that for too long it had been both a physically and mentally insular place.

Pearl was an activist. She felt that people needed to be nudged now and again so they could see the bigger picture. While she made it her business to know her stuff and be as prepared as a generalist could be, she accepted that there were experts who knew more than her and that only by building relations with them would everyone benefit. Pearl believed that she would be of most use to her community by taking matters to the highest authorities, many whom she knew socially, armed with the very best information and a clear explanation how to approach matters differently.

She was not afraid to use any means possible. In 1918, a mysterious stomach disorder struck the town. When twenty-five citizens died in one week, Pearl brought a committee to see the city health officer. As Jim Little describes in *Mother Pearl*:

> They demanded that he send for an epidemiologist from the state Department of Health to diagnose the malady but he refused.[8] […] When forty more Santa Barbarans died, however, Pearl and her committee decided to play hardball. Knowing the doctor had a morphine habit, they sat in his office all afternoon deliberately keeping him from his fix. Not surprisingly he sent the telegram and the epidemiologist discovered salmonella in city water wells. The epidemic ended and Pearl learned a valuable lesson in political persuasion. A lesson she never forgot.[9]

To win support from both the public and officials, she realized she had to walk a tightrope between many different communities.

She learnt much from her father and brother about the business world. Like other businessmen at the time, they understood that Santa Barbara was in competition with other cities as a market for business, people, and institutions. In the face of risks and costs, the city needed investment to enable itself to adjust to changing circumstances. They taught Pearl that "playing up atmosphere paid dividends to the business community".[10] Fortunately, both men also wanted to build a beautiful Santa Barbara from which the entire community would benefit. Unlike many developers and realtors, they were not simply in it for themselves—it was equally important to their business that Santa Barbara remained an attractive place to live. Given that both men were socially prominent and members of prestigious organizations, they were able to open many doors for Pearl. They did not, however, influence her decisions, which were sometimes at odds with their interests. They knew that her work was important, and they respected that fact. She realized this and knew she "had a peculiar and very valuable independence. They never once asked her to quiet down or not discuss any particular subject that might affect their business."[11]

Despite plenty of evidence that she placed equal emphasis on economics as on aesthetics to persuade her supporters and donors, this was the language they themselves understood—nor did Pearl discriminate as to who she collaborated with in getting the job done. There was nothing remotely venal about her motives; it was enlightened self-interest in the best sense.

Tackling the enduring inequities that separated the experience of women and men, she generally chose to understand, accommodate, and adapt to cultures that were instituted by men for men. By attempting to navigate these male-dominated cultures, she paid a significant emotional price.

Alongside her influential women friends, Pearl developed close relations with some of the most powerful men in the city and state. She learned that she could accomplish more behind the scenes, and that the nominal leader of any successful campaign needed to be a man. Appointing "a man as a figurehead," aligning herself with that person and keeping an eye on his goals, she rode the coattails of men into public life.[12]

Conducting herself in meetings she was persistent, business-like, and entirely focused on her objectives. She was able to see ahead and zero in on the key issues—she was not one for small talk. She wanted to change the perception held by men that women in public health work were sentimental rather than scientific. However, while she preferred to speak about social justice in scientific and civic terms, she used maternalism when she felt it supported her work. In choosing her words, Pearl relied on her expertise to promote reform in education, public health, and women's status. She was also careful in the way she promoted women's professional work within public health. It was not enough for her to know about the factors that would influence citizens' health in the future, but she attempted to be a healthy role model herself.

48. Pearl's book plate

The atmosphere around her was calm. She would always have a notebook with her and make sure that she wrote down everybody's names. Nothing was ever lost to her, and every moment mattered. She was a complete professional and always well-mannered, always able to encourage and bring out leadership qualities in her volunteers that they themselves had never been aware of. She worked long hours, every day, and even on weekends and holidays.[13] By remaining in her father's home she had the benefit of a housekeeper, a cook, and a gardener, and could devote all her time to her work. Her dedication to and love for Santa Barbara satisfied her more than any lover could. By living to serve she created a sense of belonging which met her professional needs, and naturally such unselfish service matched with her brilliant capabilities was rare and encouraged by the community.

In June 1916, having fully recovered from her car accident, Pearl enrolled at Berkeley on a one-year post-graduate course in public health and psychology with a special focus on community programs. However, she returned to Santa Barbara after two months to take care of her father.[14] At the same time, Harold met and fell in love with an heiress and divorced mother of two who was three years his senior. Gertrude was the youngest daughter of Joseph Boyer, president and majority shareholder of the Burroughs adding machine company.[15]

After a whirlwind romance Harold and Gertrude were married on July 28, 1917, much to the surprise of Hezekiah and his relatives living in Boston and Sioux Falls. They worried that Pearl must be "a little sad at the parting of the ways."[16] It was also a parting of ways in other respects, as many of the men in the city, including Harold himself, rushed to enlist for war duty. Despite the feeling that Europe was far away from California, Santa Barbarans had followed the events of the First World War closely since 1914. When the US entered the conflict in spring 1917, the community rallied to "do its bit." Many men did not return until 1919.

While America advanced during the progressive era inspired by social justice and economic equality, during the First World War the

49. Pearl with Trudie and Fred Stearns, at the marriage of Harold to Gertrude Boyer Stearns, 1917

nation was also stirred by international democracy. America's entry into the war had the support of the National American Woman Suffrage Association and women's clubs. Hundreds of thousands of US women worked with voluntary agencies on the home front, and over six thousand women volunteered for service abroad. Santa Barbaran women rallied for the promotion of war bonds and the Belgian relief work.

In 1917, Pearl was elected chairman of the committee for the Santa Barbara County joint campaign of the Young Men's Christian Association (YMCA) and the Young Women's Christian Association (YWCA) to secure financial aid and raise awareness of the women employed in war industries. She was also asked to reorganize the local chapter of the Red Cross. Having at first declined an offer from the organization, Pearl accepted the position of executive secretary on the condition that she was given a free hand, and that she took it for two months only. As she remarked, "By then [The Red Cross chapter will] be organized but you will be very glad to get rid of me."[17] Once the war began, "she took 60 days to write the bylaws, establish two offices in the state, recruit 13,000 members, and raise $33,000."[18] Her work was quite a sensation.

So great was her success that she was selected to represent the organization at the 1917 California Conference on Social Work (CCSW) in San Francisco. Despite the meeting being mismanaged, Pearl triumphed. The mismanagement stemmed from the fact that almost every relief agency across the state had sent a delegate who was given three minutes in which to make a summary report of their work. This proved beyond the capability of most of the men, who talked over time. Pressed for time, the presiding officer announced that the remaining speakers, including Pearl, had two minutes each. Pearl gave the shortest speech of her life, taking less than a minute, and so impressed were the state organizers that they asked her to accept the presidency of the CCSW. Reminiscing years later of that meeting, she said:

> There was a big struggle within this organization of professional workers and directors of social agencies. The former law partner of the graft prosecutor in San Francisco wanted to be president, and was the active representative of the Catholics. The representative of an insurance company was president of a big Los Angeles insurance firm. And what do you suppose were the problems in 1917 that they were fighting about? Birth control and social insurance. The insurance companies didn't want the social workers to endorse social security. The Catholics didn't want birth control. So there were these two forces represented by these two very important men. So they took me into a smelly service room on the second floor of the Oakland Hotel and said, "Do you want to be president? Because they'll stop fighting if a girl gets into the picture." I wasn't thirty yet. So the men dropped out.[19]

Pearl thought the method of her election was "funny," but she was quick to grasp the enormity of it.[20] The two-year term of office was her first opportunity to prove herself in social work at the state level and she knew that all eyes would be on Santa Barbara the following year for the tenth annual meeting. On April 16, many of the most prominent state officials, writers, lecturers, church leaders, clubwomen, and educators, private or public in California, gathered in Santa Barbara for the four-day conference. The aim was to promote understanding and cooperation between existing social agencies and war relief activities. All the more important, state commissions and boards participated through their representatives as well as the numerous war organizations.[21]

It was reported that never had "any California city entertained so many division bureau heads at one time."[22] The conference met its objectives and Pearl received glowing press coverage and letters of encouragement. One, from Aurelia Reinhardt, President of Mills College in Oakland, said:

> Do let me congratulate you again on the truly remarkable week which you planned for the delegate. I think you are too much a part of the work itself to realize in how orderly and effective a way the program was presented and how full of constructive ideas it was from first to last. Thanks for certain delectable drives up mountain roads.[23]

Pearl and Reinhardt went on to become lifelong friends.

On November 11, 1917, an armistice with Germany was signed and opposing armies on the Western Front began to withdraw from their positions. America had much to celebrate: they had saved Britain and France and destroyed the German Army. However, during the transition to peace that followed, the US faced hard economic times and problems related to labor, race, and reintegration of veterans into American society.

50. Aurelia Reinhardt, c.1919

In the hope of salvaging the fine spirit of cooperation and centralization of effort that had developed, Pearl proposed the creation of a Santa Barbara community chest. The idea was not widely practiced at the time but had been adopted by some large American cities, which she studied as part of her social service conference work.[24] Based on her findings, she decided to put pressure on the city leaders to unite the city's community fundraising organizations, which had been traditionally in competition with one another, to form a financial federation to collect greater funds with less effort. Pearl was determined the chest should be designed to meet the neglected needs for joint work in public education.[25] With her input, it achieved this, but it also became a public relations arm of private and professional social work, convincing ordinary people to support community service as a fundamental civic obligation.

Although Pearl's public self was in its ascendancy in the years immediately following the end of the war, her private self was confused and vulnerable both emotionally and intellectually. She shared some of her anxiety in correspondence with Ralph Hiett, a US Airman sent to France, whom she met in 1917 and who was infatuated with her. Arranging to meet up for the first time after his return from France in 1919, she wrote, "I am not sure what kind of person I am, for just now I'm full of doubts and big, big questions about my future. Nothing seems settled in my mind, even how I am to respond to anyone of half a dozen approaches on your part."[26]

As her circumstances changed further, she drafted a will. Among her few distributions, all her technical books were for the normal school, all her clothes to her cousins, something to each of her aunts, and all her papers but for those with an association name were designated to be destroyed.

In a few short years Pearl had passed through a baptism of fire. With her taking a lead, Santa Barbara could claim to have one of the most organized groups of female social workers in the state. By the end of 1919, the troops were home and the world pandemic (erroneously dubbed the "Spanish Flu") had departed. A feeling of optimism was in the air and a cultural renaissance was taking shape. Reading between the lines it is easy to see Pearl had been steadily drawn in by circumstances unfolding around her, and was finding ways to put her own stamp on them.

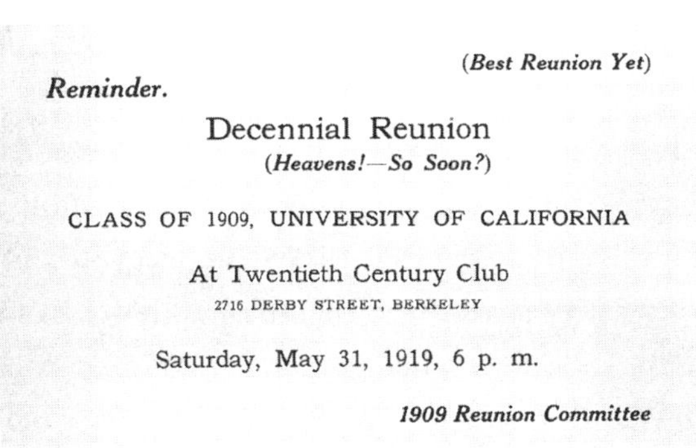

(Best Reunion Yet)

Reminder.

Decennial Reunion

(Heavens!—So Soon?)

CLASS OF 1909, UNIVERSITY OF CALIFORNIA

At Twentieth Century Club

2716 DERBY STREET, BERKELEY

Saturday, May 31, 1919, 6 p. m.

1909 Reunion Committee

51. Pearl's invitation to the Class of 1909, Decennial Reunion at Berkeley

CHAPTER 7

Renaissance

Shortly after the war, a new group of magnanimous philanthropists and cultural leaders discovered Santa Barbara, and determined to leave their own mark on the community. Pearl liked to think that "these people, who were patriots and to whom others looked for leadership, were pretty much bound to their communities and to their obligations in the East but with the end of the war some of them just spread their wings. They wanted to do things and know things and get away."[1] Escaping the disillusion that overshadowed many of America's great cities and the declining values in society, these altruistic leaders wanted to rebuild their world. Pearl saw an opportunity to help them, and her vision for a better Santa Barbara with it.

Entranced by a place that seemed foreign and exotic, these "hill barons" as they were known, were able to create a whole new life for themselves and live in a way that they never dreamed of. It gave an extraordinary sense of adventure. Blending athleticism and gentility, a Santa Barbara style developed not that dissimilar to its counterpart on Long Island. But being so new, it was at once privileged and "touched by a frontier that was only a horseback ride away in the backcountry."[2] Naturally, their standard of taste became most vigorously expressed through architecture as well as "yachting, riding, and polo."[3] They turned increasingly to the Mediterranean Revival and Spanish Colonial style.

Fortunately for Santa Barbara, not unlike the prosperous bankers of Renaissance Florence, these men and women recognized philanthropy as an appropriate enhancement of their community and, in the process, themselves.[4] Their civic and personal celebration extended into every important segment of life and their names assumed a geographic permanence in the cultural landscape. Frequently taking charge and demonstrating leadership when the local government either would not dare or could not financially afford to, the city developed a strong sense of civic self-reliance. Undoubtedly these individuals contributed toward and established the culture of giving that permeates Santa Barbara today.

Wishing to spend six months of the year in Santa Barbara and the rest of the year in their homes in the East, some of these newcomers relied on locals to guide their civic projects in their absence. This is where Pearl saw an opportunity to champion city culture and planning.

What made this post-war influx of wealthy newcomers so important and different from any previous was that they wanted to change the existing inward-looking culture, and introduce new forms of sophisticated and worldly entertainment. As Pearl noted, "They wanted drama, they liked entertainment, and they liked the people who could further that type of living."[5] Collectively, these men and women demanded a level of culture and education far beyond what might have been expected.

Of course, none of their philanthropy would have been possible had there not been the talented artists, architects, and designers to create their dreams. During my research I was fortunate to meet Marc Appleton, who is one of today's leading architects in southern California and a direct descendant of one of the philanthropic families that developed the city. A board member of numerous Santa Barbara institutions, he is also a prolific writer on architectural subjects with a particular interest on George Washington Smith. Eating burritos and tacos in his office in downtown Santa Barbara, Marc described memories of his grandparents, Peter and Angelica Schuyler "Girly" Cooper Bryce, and Florestal, the family's former

52. George Washington Smith

home in Hope Ranch designed by Smith and regarded as his finest residential work.

> I like to think my grandparents were not that unusual, the more I research these southern California architects. You had these very well to do entrepreneurial people coming from Chicago or New England to California. You have this wonderful pioneer spirit at work and you have competent architects who followed them. You cannot talk about architecture unless you talk about it in the context of the people involved and their lives, of society, of economics of the cultural environment at the time and politics. It is all intertwined.[6]

It was no coincidence that across the United States a new flowering of the arts happened at the end of the war in reaction to the mass slaughter in the trenches. With philanthropists, talented artists, and community organizers like Pearl, Santa Barbara was able to pioneer a real contribution to American cultural and civic life.

Santa Barbara had a head start on many other communities. Toward the end of the nineteenth century, the city had developed into an important art colony. Drawn to the natural beauty of the region, artists including Alexander Harmer, Frederic Remington,

Ed Borein, Carl Oscar Borg, John Marshall Gamble, Albert Herter, and Fernand Lungren set up studios in the area. These artists did much to awaken a cultural and artistic movement that would influence the city's Hispanic architectural and cultural evolution.

Eager to build on this reputation and start a college of art, Lungren, in 1920, established the Santa Barbara School of the Arts. Alongside the rich artistic tradition in 1919 a group of music lovers decided to bring out-of-town musical events to Santa Barbara. Calling themselves the Civic Music Committee (CMC), now known as the Community Arts Music Association, they enlisted the support of David Gray, whose family were major shareholders in Ford.[7]

At the same time the CMC was taking shape, a small group of residents, including Pearl, met to discuss creating a small theatre group. Calling themselves the Community Arts Players (CAP), they had their first performance at the Potter Theatre in August 1920. Enthusiasm ran high. A direct result of this work was the chrysalis of a group known as the Community Arts Association (CAA), which was tentatively formed the following month.[8] Much to Pearl's delight, of the thirteen original members, eight were women.

In late 1920, Pearl and her colleagues began to discuss merging the three branches of drama, art, and music into their CAA. From a financial and logistical standpoint, it was effective to consolidate, as duplication and insufficient funds were weakening the impact of the different branches. Negotiations were also smoothed by the fact that the various officers in the branches knew each other socially and had similar aspirations for the association. The music branch merged with the CAA in the spring of 1921 and the School of the Arts in the fall of 1921. A fourth branch, Plans and Planting, was established, and joined in the spring of 1922.

The CAA began innocently enough with Pearl herself writing the constitution and bylaws. The CAA was formally organized on February 18, 1921, with a slightly reduced number of officers acting as executives and directors and women outnumbering men. The purpose was to coordinate and correlate the work of the different branches. Initially Pearl served as secretary and manager of the music branch under the chairmanship of Adele McGinnis Herter, who had offered the branch a small orchestra directed by the talented young musician Roger Clerbois.[9] Pearl thought Adele and Albert Herter "beautiful people personally and at the heart of the cultural renaissance in the city."[10] She particularly loved and admired Adele, "as one of the women who had a very considerable influence on my life in connection with the development of Santa Barbara."[11]

Her relations with Adele took off during the winter of 1920 when they worked together on a community Christmas celebration as an offshoot of the CAA. At a time when no one in the city hosted any sort of pageant they started a festival committee to bring something of the holiday to those who might not otherwise have had one. Anyone could drop into the recreation center to sit around a blazing fire, eat and drink, and take part in a program of games and carols.

As with many of her previous projects, this was a real community affair. However, it also had a spiritual quality she wanted to share. The true significance of Christmas, she hoped, could be blazed out in the tree of light. In 1920, a pine tree on the grounds of the

53. Adele Herter

54. Albert Herter

courthouse was illuminated; a few years later, a ninety-five-foot Norfolk pine was used downtown.[12] The sight was a true spectacle, and the white lights could be seen from the Santa Ynez Mountains on one side and from far out in the channel on the other.

In 1919, another couple hailing from the East Coast, Bernhard and Irene Hoffmann, arrived in Santa Barbara with hopes that their daughter Margaret, who was diabetic, could be treated.[13] Under the care of Dr. W.D. Sansum, one of the primary developers of insulin, she responded readily to treatment and the Hoffmanns decided to remain in the city until she had convalesced.

From that moment forward, Hoffmann started making a profound impact in civic volunteerism. Although his interests were many, they were strongest in beautification and preservation activity.[14] It was logical, then, that he would join the CAA. In September 1921, he was appointed an officer of the association. Shortly afterward, the Hoffmanns bought the Casa De La Guerra, a century-old, tile-roofed adobe in the heart of downtown which, like many such buildings, was falling into decay. As they set about restoring the building, they commissioned James Osborne Craig, a Scottish

55. Bernhard Hoffmann

architect who they had also used to design their Santa Barbara home, to design a complex of shops, offices, and restaurants adjacent to the adobe.

El Paseo, the first shopping complex west of the Mississippi, was the result of James's efforts, and the Spanish flavour of the red-tiled roofs, central fountains, stairways, and ironwork, which set off the whitewashed stucco to great advantage, "created a sensation" and gave Santa Barbara a unified architectural look.[15] Caught up in the whirlwind of architectural planning in the spring of 1922, Hoffmann then proposed establishing a fourth branch of the CAA called the Plans and Planting Committee (P&P).

When the CAA was incorporated as a nonprofit in the summer of 1923, it established as one of its purposes "to afford individuals an opportunity for self-expression, training, and education in music, drama, and the allied arts, and to aid in the cultural improvement of the people and the beautification of the City of Santa Barbara."[16] As the CAA grew in influence so the number of paying members rocketed from 166 in 1921 to over 1,500 in 1923. Its membership read like the who's who of the city and included Lolita Armour, Cornelius K.G. Billings, Clarence Black, Miss Amy du Pont, Major Max Fleischmann, Louise Knapp, Francis Forrest Peabody, and his wife, Kathleen Burke.

Functioning through the four branches, the CAA oversaw 33 committees with 140 individuals. A male president presided over eight directors including four women. Pearl acted as secretary.[17] Given free rein, she was frequently assertive and demanding, and people quickly saw that she was a shining example of how much one person could accomplish. Her colleagues found it rewarding to work with her; she recognized strengths in people that they did not think they had, and she was generous to give praise where it was merited.

In Bernhard Hoffmann, Pearl found someone who shared her vision for a better Santa Barbara. She readily accepted when offered the role of his secretary with the P&P, giving up her position with the music branch. She later remarked, "In college, typing was required, and everybody wanted me to be a secretary of their committees. I said I was never going to be that. I would do something on my own, so I have had to raise enough money to pay secretaries to do the typing."[18] Unsurprisingly, settling into the role with P&P, she refused to do any typing. However, through organizing the committee and its projects, she soon became Hoffmann's right-hand woman. Over the next five years, working together, they became the most influential individuals in the development of the city in the Hispanic tradition.

As journalist Jim Little once commented: "Contemporary Santa Barbara developers, who think they have a rough time trying to get their projects past county and city planning commissions, should be grateful they weren't around when Hoffmann and Chase worked as a team. Those two had such clout they were able to persuade banks and lenders not to make loans on any project that didn't meet their aesthetic standards."[19]

While the P&P was establishing itself, Pearl, as secretary of the CAA, wrote to Henry Smith Pritchett to solicit funds. Pritchett was a former President of MIT and the then head of the Carnegie Foundation, and had recently made his home in Santa Barbara. She

56. Henry Smith Pritchett

thoroughly enjoyed making the application and presenting her case, and it is hard not to imagine nepotism did not play a part in the final decision to grant funding to the CAA.[20]

Carnegie and his close associate Charles Taylor had been frequent visitors to Santa Barbara early in the century. Moreover, Pritchett, as a member of the Santa Barbara Club, socialized with the city's leading citizens, including Hoffmann and both Hezekiah and Harold Chase. Pearl described Pritchett as a constant source of inspiration.[21] In the fall of 1922, the CAA received a five-year annual grant of $25,000 to use in any way it saw fit.[22] Without this, it's unlikely the CAA would have succeeded as it did. Hoffmann described the funds as of tremendous importance; with its finances secure, the Association embarked on an experimental project of civic improvements designed to serve as a model for other US cities. Of all the branches, the P&P was the least expensive to maintain. This was because neither Hoffmann nor Pearl took a salary for their work. In fact, Hoffmann spent a great deal of his own—or rather, his wife's—money on making his vision a reality.[23]

Hoffmann and Pearl were acutely aware that their vision relied on successful city planning, and they devoted a great deal of attention to related problems. At a time when Charleston, South Carolina, was creating a historic district, the P&P urged the city toward formulating a plan to redesign the entire city in the Hispanic tradition. In September 1923, Santa Barbara's first Planning Commission, one of the first to be established in the US, had its initial meeting. Planning consultants Charles H. Cheney and the Olmsted Brothers firm were hired by the city. During the consultation process, these men were required by law to report to P&P on equal terms as the elected officials who had instructed them: "A non-elective, non-appointive citizens' committee now had the same power as the city's duly elected officials."[24] Pearl "saw no problem with the less than democratic nature of the relationship between city government and the citizens group."[25]

Pearl, who had no formal training in architecture or planning, learnt much from these men. Her view of city planning was that: "A city that develops finely should delight the eye, feed the intellect, and lead the people out of the bondage of the commonplace."[26] The Santa Barbara Planning Commission, once established, met some resistance from the public, not so much because it advocated a push toward a unified Mediterranean style but more so because of "a concern of too much government control over property owners' rights in the form of a zoning ordinance."[27]

The intensity of effort Pearl and Hoffmann demonstrated in the first years of the P&P was beginning to show results, and while progress was not as rapid as they would have liked, by the end of 1924, the spirit of Santa Barbara had begun to change in their desired direction. Developing Santa Barbara and its community had become a calling.

CHAPTER 8

The Santa Barbara Earthquake

Santa Barbara's paradise turned into hell at 6:43 a.m. on Monday, June 29, 1925, when an earthquake measuring 6.3 on the Richter scale ripped through the city, claiming thirteen lives.[1] The sound was described as like "a million dogs crunching bones."[2] In residential neighborhoods, windows shook, chimneys fell, and people were thrown out of their beds; in the downtown area, 85 percent of buildings were destroyed, leaving behind shambles of masonry and fallen brick; and in the hills above the city, the twin towers of the Mission collapsed and the earthen dam of the Sheffield reservoir gave way, sending 45 million gallons of water flooding through Sycamore Canyon to the sea. A gas company engineer became a hero when he shut off the city's gas supply, avoiding fires like those

57. Santa Barbara earthquake damage

that destroyed San Francisco in 1906.[3] At 2012 Anacapa Street, Pearl and Hezekiah were unscathed save for some broken china and ornaments.

Pearl was due to meet Julia Morgan to discuss plans for the Margaret Baylor Inn later that day. Unlike in 1906, she did not keep a personal record of the events, but she did write articles about the earthquake and its effect on both the community and development of the city. Harold and Gertrude, then living in Hope Ranch, also felt the quake but suffered no damage. The Chase office at 1012 State Street was badly damaged, but Harold, seeing an opportunity, struck a deal with the owner from whom they rented and bought the property for $32,000.[4]

Santa Barbara, Pearl noted:

> Pulled herself together, literally, in a moment. Less than forty-five minutes after the quake the Red Cross had set up its headquarters in a tent in the City Hall Plaza. A few hours later a relief unit from the Los Angeles chapter of the Red Cross arrived in a special train lent by the Southern Pacific. The doctors and nurses quickly discovered that there was a greater need for tents, blankets and lanterns than for medical services.[5]

There was a general sense of relief that the quake struck early in the morning. If it had occurred, instead, just a few hours later when the streets and sidewalks were busiest, hundreds may have been killed or injured by falling debris.

A "temporary police force was organized of Los Angeles police officers and deputy sheriffs to prevent looting."[6] It was not deemed necessary to impose martial law. "President Coolidge dispatched the USS Arkansas, a dreadnought, to steam up from San Diego and administer relief."[7] The following morning the city council established a Board of Public Safety and Reconstruction, made up of eleven citizens, including city council members and Pearl's brother, Harold. This board was given full power to meet necessary emergencies and plan for reconstruction. The estimated damage was $10 million, and the total cost of reconstructions and new buildings was $15 million. On July 11, city council, charged with raising and distributing money to revitalize the city and restore the damaged Mission, set up a relief fund. Among its eight members were Hoffmann, Harold Chase, Frederick Forrest Peabody, and Pritchett, who, through the Carnegie Institution, provided $1 million.[8]

The earthquake was more than a disaster: it marked a major turning point in the history of the community. As one observer remarked, "the measure of Santa Barbara's greatness was not in the fact that the city was restored, but the way the restoration was conducted."[9] As in 1906, the Board of Public Safety and Reconstruction was looking for an instant positive spin to counteract the rumours of death and destruction, and in this Hoffmann and Pearl saw an opportunity to promote their vision for the city. Confronted with a massive rebuilding effort, city leaders needed the assistance of the P&P. Owing to P&P's ongoing educational campaign, Santa Barbarans understood the value of sensible building practices and architectural harmony—the city had already established a City Planning Commission, drafted a comprehensive building zone ordinance, and hosted meetings and conferences on city beautification and zoning legislation.

Further strengthening the P&P's credibility, not least in economic terms, was that all the structures built in the Spanish Colonial style had withstood the earthquake. "The fact that El Paseo, the Lobero Theatre, City Hall, and the *Daily News* building sustained no appreciable damage was credited to hollow tile and concrete girdle construction; however, from the very beginning, 'better building' was conflated with the Spanish idiom itself."[10] Given the situation they found themselves in, it is hard not to imagine that Hoffmann and Pearl thought it a blessing. What might have taken years to achieve through human endeavour nature had forced in nineteen seconds. The earthquake had made possible their vision of building in a unified Spanish Colonial Revival Style, or, as Pearl liked to call it, "California style."[11]

Few, if any, of the city's 24,000 inhabitants disagreed with this idea. State Street was fast becoming a blot on the cityscape, a "succession of little wooden shop fronts."[12] Moreover, the city council was only too happy to be relieved of some of the stress and work that followed the earthquake. Hoffmann and Pearl's lobbying was met with success, and on July 1, the front page of the *Daily Press* announced: "Spanish Architecture to Rise from Ruins."[13]

In the following weeks, Pearl and Hoffmann secured further publicity in newspaper articles and public speeches as they appealed to the public to support their endeavour. In August, *Survey Graphic*, a progressive social welfare periodical distributed nationally, published a five-page article by Pearl entitled "Santa Barbara Resurgent." Proud of the universal courage shown by the city, she stated the people of Santa Barbara were "mustering their forces in a concerted effort to show what an American community can do in mastering and in shaping its own life and environment."[14]

The idea of a disaster makeover caught on, and letters of encouragement soon came in from all over the US—from concerned individuals, to the California Federation of Women's Clubs, to the AIA. Setting an example to other communities across the nation, Santa Barbara and the campaign to rebuild State Street was front-page news.

A few days after the earthquake, Harold and the other members of the public safety and reconstruction board established an Architectural Advisory Committee (AAC), not unlike the one Hoffmann had started in 1922. This time, however, its purpose focused on the preparation of a building code which would ensure safer construction of earthquake- and fire-resistant buildings. Santa Barbara became the first city in the US to do this. Hoffmann was appointed chairman with two other directors, and an advisory board was formed of forty-two prominent citizens with diverse interests and experience levels in community organization, law, business, and property management.

A few days later, on July 16, the city council formed an Architectural Board of Review (ABR) as a subcommittee of the city Building Department. This board, the first unelected, decision-making entity of its kind anywhere in the US, had six members and was chaired by a City Planning Commission member, with Hoffmann acting as secretary. The other four members were architects George Washington Smith, William Edwards, Carleton Winslow and John Frederick Murphy.[15] The ABR had the power to review and hold up every building permit issued by the city for twenty days, and to discuss with property owners the style of architecture and quality of design. If an owner failed to agree with the board's recommendation, by the end of twenty days, a public hearing on the disagreement had to be held before the city council before a permit could be issued.

The ABR was similar to the Palos Verdes Art Jury "in the sense that both members were appointed from lists of nominees submitted by professional organizations, and both had powers of veto."[16] It differed significantly from the AAC in the scope of its powers, and in the Community Drafting Room (CDR). The CDR was a most original inspiration of Hoffmann's and did a huge amount of work of unusual character. Realizing that offices of local architects would be inundated with plans, he created the CDR so that outside architects might offer practical assistance.[17] This body operated under the AAC, with personal funding from the Hoffmann and Gray families.

No records of its accomplishments were published. Among those to work in the fully-equipped architectural office were Reginald Johnson and William Templeton Johnson. The office drafted the desirable changes in plans referred to it by the ABR; almost all their services were free. Within a month the ABR "had approved 102 reconstructed permits, virtually every one in the Spanish style."[18] Comprised of only men, Pearl was not invited to sit on any of the reconstruction and architectural boards created after the earthquake.

She did, however, follow their proceedings closely and kept copies of their minutes. Because of his increased responsibilities, Hoffmann offered to resign as president of the CAA and asked Pearl to take his place as chairman of P&P. He was quite confident that Chase was capable of fulfilling the role.

As one commenter has mentioned, "For the first time in California and perhaps American history, preservationists, planners, and aestheticizers [*sic*] had gained control of a city and were refashioning it to their purposes."[19]

While Pearl thought the idea of a uniform style of architecture took like wildfire,[20] she and Hoffmann faced an uphill struggle convincing the State Street property owners to rebuild in the Spanish style. While they had plenty of support—including the editor and owner of the *Morning Press*, Reginal Fernald, a Stanford- and Harvard-educated Republican progressive—there was a minority of discontent.

Leading the opposition to the ARB were Thomas M. Storke, who, through his newspaper the *Daily News*, possessed a powerful hold on public opinion, and Howard Sweeney, a local contractor and former school supervisor. "Both men believed that each property owner was the master of his or her own property. The dispute was a disagreement over the degree to which private interest should give way to community interest."[21] The merchants wanted to develop their business center to its maximum. Planning and zoning, they maintained, were subservient to property rights and business expansion. They believed that the board was a "dictator" over all building in the city, and because outside interests had elected the members, it represented the elite of the city.[22] They argued this elite included the city council and the Planning Commission. The argument against the board was not about the use of the Spanish style, but for exercising "aesthetic censorship."

While the two newspapers battled on the subject, readers might not have wondered if the age-old family feud for control of Santa

Barbara between the Fernalds and the Storkes was not behind the print. The Fernalds had been in Santa Barbara since 1852, and the Storkes since 1872. As the second generation continued the battle, exchanges grew uglier and uglier. Fernald, a bachelor *bon vivant* rarely seen in the office before lunch and always at a Montecito party, was no match for Storke, whose Democratic party connections and appointment as Santa Barbara Postmaster General in 1914 made him the most powerful person in Santa Barbara.

In support of their scheme, Hoffmann and Pearl used a combination of economic and aesthetic arguments. They often referred to New Orleans as a comparison, remarking that the "average person, when thinking about New Orleans, visualized the charm of the old French and Spanish quarters, and would be more inclined to make a pilgrimage with such an objective than to see more modern developments of high buildings, fine parkways, and the like, which presumably they can find in their own regions."[23]

The issue came to a head on December 1st during the municipal election. A political upheaval stirred up by the *Daily News* supplanted the "city manager" form of government by the old "mayor and council" scheme. Pearl thought it was "the end of the Renaissance period, as far as government went."[24] Several of the newly elected councilmen had pledged to their constituents to vote for the repeal of the ordinance granting the ABR power to review and hold up every building permit issued by the city. The fate of the ABR was sealed. On January 7, the new mayor introduced an ordinance to repeal the powers of the ABR, and two months later it was disbanded. In the following months, "as work was completed and scaffolding was removed along State Street, the result of the ABR's iron-fisted control was more apparent than ever."[25]

In its brief nine-month existence the board "processed some 2,000 design proposals" for the city Planning Commission.[26] Pearl later remarked that Hoffmann was "deeply grieved and shocked, because he realized that it ended the cooperation of the city government officially, and to an extent, spiritually, in the architectural development of Santa Barbara."[27] When writing his memoirs in 1958, Storke dodged mentioning his objections that had brought down the ABR, and praised Hoffmann as "a vigorous leader with whom my newspaper could cooperate in arousing our citizens to a new consciousness of civic beauty."[28]

In May, 1926, Hoffmann was invited by the CAA to be their president once again, and he remained in that role until health problems forced him to step down the following year. Pearl resigned from her role as secretary while maintaining her chairmanship of the P&P. With the five-year Carnegie award due to expire in 1927, the directors were concerned about their funding. It cost them $80,000 a year, of which $30,000 came from membership and events. Reapplying to the Carnegie Institute, they were granted a final extension of five more years, receiving a total of $100,000 plus a $25,000 bonus for earthquake relief.[29]

Ironically, the demise of the ABR helped to boost the role of the P&P. The committee's educational campaign continued its efforts to promote architectural harmony, and it became the guardian of the city planning. Writing to the owner of a department store on State Street and now the newly appointed mayor, Charles Milton Andera, Pearl urged him to provide a means by which the rapid growth of

"A DREAM CITY COME TRUE"

"The silver lining to Santa Barbara's recent cloud, discloses the old buildings of the mutilated business district, damaged by the first earthquake in over a century, now being replaced by the finest examples of modern and substantial construction. The lovely lines of Spanish architecture are making a new dream city. It reveals residence districts with minor damage quickly repaired. It shows already an influx of new visitors who know that nowhere else in America may such a marvelous climate, such scenery and such delightful living conditions be found, through every season of the year."

H. G. CHASE & ASSOCIATES
(ESTABLISHED 1903)
REAL ESTATE AND RENTALS
1012 Estado Santa Barbara, California Phone 125

58. H. G. Chase real estate advertising

Santa Barbara may be as effectively directed along the lines which had already so greatly added to the reputation and beauty of our city.[30]

As her confidence grew, she would pick up the phone or visit in-person to get the measure of a new incumbent entering a powerful position. It was usually a man, and he would usually be stunned. Pearl would mention some of her pet projects and describe how she would be able to help him. When advising the mayor on what would be good actions for him to take, she was sometimes successful and sometimes not, depending on the person's ego. She knew how important it was for nonprofit organizations and ordinary, concerned citizens to become familiar with these different people, and for these officials, too, to realize who was who for getting things done.

One notable example of her early success was convincing the Southern Pacific Railroad company to redesign its roundhouse on East Cabrillo Boulevard, which had been damaged in the 1925 earthquake, in the Spanish style. She went up to the company's headquarters in San Francisco with pictures of the bullring of Seville, Spain and demanded they adopt that design instead of a stock roundhouse. They acceded, and until the building was demolished

59. The Locomotive Roundhouse, designed to resemble the bullring in Seville

in December, 1982 to make way for a resort hotel, it was proof that even a railroad roundhouse could be made a thing of beauty.[31]

On June 29, 1926, exactly a year after the earthquake, Santa Barbara recorded the last and most devasting aftershock, which killed a small boy. A few days later, *Architect and Engineer* published an article by Irving Morrow, the architect best known for designing the Golden Gate Bridge, entitled "New Santa Barbara." Praising the cautious but determined leadership of the P&P, he concluded, "I look to Santa Barbara as a sort of laboratory experiment in California architecture. Once she has assimilated her present available architectural material and adjusted herself to a viewpoint in harmony with the real necessities of the modern situation, she should provide the inspiration and the leadership for a movement genuinely modern and genuinely Californian."[32]

The architectural ideal underlying Santa Barbara's rebirth was best expressed by the design for the county courthouse.[33] Completed in 1929, it was designed as a metaphor for a Spanish castle, replete with towers, arches, turrets, and Moorish paintings. "The sunken gardens resembled, in castle terms, an inner bailey."[34] The city's worst disaster proved to be its finest hour.

60. Santa Barbara County Courthouse

CHAPTER 9

Better Homes in America[1]

"Santa Barbara Divides Prize with Atlanta," reported the headline in the *Los Angeles Times* on July 16, 1925. "Santa Barbara tied for first prize with Atlanta, Georgia, in the national Better Homes contest according to notice received here today by Miss Pearl Chase, Chairman of the committee."[2] The award, presented by the nationwide campaign for homeownership, Better Homes in America (BHA), was official recognition that Santa Barbara was one of the most beautiful residential environments in the nation.

Over the following months, more than fifty national magazines and hundreds of newspapers devoted space to Santa Barbara's campaign. Herbert Hoover, the future president of the United States and the then president of BHA, congratulated Pearl personally, remarking, "You have not only furnished an example to the building industry, but have gone far to awaken a keen desire and appreciation in the people of your community which will create a demand for a craftsman-like product."[3] Pearl's vision for a better Santa Barbara was reaching a wider audience than ever before, and with such prominence and distinction came new demands on both her and the community.

Hoffmann and Pearl's success was due in part to the fact that they did not see eye to eye and had different emphases for their beautification projects. Hoffmann preferred to work with business owners, while Pearl preferred the residential sector, especially the less well-off families and particularly the Mexican poor. Drawing on her social work experience, she believed that "architectural harmony and beautification of lower-income residential neighborhoods proceeded hand in hand."[4]

The success of her 1919 survey had earned her a reputation as a "pacesetter" for doing worthwhile work in housing.[5] In September 1922, the P&P held a design contest to "stimulate an interest in the community in more harmonious and artistic, and fitting buildings and dwellings in Santa Barbara."[6] The aim was to promote Spanish Colonial architecture across all sections of the community. The following year, they offered support to those building small houses by arranging exhibits, publishing leaflets, and sponsoring an architectural competition for homes costing about $5,000. In 1924, the directors of the CAA published *The Book of Small House Designs*, which Pearl produced in collaboration with local architects. Suited to the type of building going on in Florida and California, the featured designs were adapted to those climatic conditions. So significant was its popularity that inquiries came from as far as Costa Rica and Cuba.

While furthering her work in housing, Pearl had closely followed the Better Homes in America movement. In 1921, Herbert Hoover became Secretary of Commerce in Warren Harding's Republican administration. One of his primary goals was to fix the acute housing shortage in America. He believed that homeownership was a prerequisite for good citizenship and that Americans needed a property stake in society. Looking to "the private sector for a solution," he found "a willing and able partner in the social enterprise: Better Homes in America."[7]

This movement was started by Marie Mattingly Meloney, a journalist and socialite, who edited *The Delineator*. Using the magazine as their instrument, with its circulation to over one million women readers, in 1922 Meloney formed a partnership with the US government.[8] The campaign encouraged home ownership as a financial, social, and patriotic undertaking with homemaking and consumerism at its core. The first BHA "demonstration week" in October 1922 was held in over five hundred communities across

61. Marie Mattingly Moloney

the country. The following year, that figure was doubled. The movement appealed to the public because "it was one of action as well as discussion, and concrete improvements could be seen as well as intangible assets which came with friendly cooperation in service to the community."[9]

Toward the end of 1923, *The Delineator* relinquished all connection with the movement and BHA was incorporated as a nonprofit, educational organization. Hoover agreed to serve as president and Calvin Coolidge, then Vice President of the US, became chairman of the advisory council.

Shortly before this, Pearl, who referred to Meloney as "the Godmother of the movement" and admired her influence, ability, and interest in the American home, sent her details of Santa Barbara's small house design contest.[10] Given that the BHA was an educational campaign endorsed by national, state, and local governments; had access to funding and resources from Washington; was supported by the General Federation of Women's Clubs, the National Federation of Business, and Professional Women's Clubs and the American Civic Association, it was natural for Pearl to consider affiliating the P&P program with it.

BHA promoted its educational messages through activities that concentrated on home improvement, community improvement, urban-rural relationships, and dissemination of information on housing and homemaking subjects.[11] While each local committee across the nation followed the BHA guidebook on how to organize their own campaign, they were encouraged to add their individual interpretations of the needs of the average American family. Efforts in these areas were made through the annual national Better Homes Week (usually held in mid-May); collaboration with national, state and local organizations; and press coverage and publications.

In the BHA guidelines, a condition for participation was that chairmanship had to be held by a woman. Not one to turn down a learning opportunity while appreciating the campaign was a year-round commitment, Pearl put herself forward. She saw it as an extension of the work P&P was already doing in advancing the cause of a harmonious architectural image of Santa Barbara. With her training in home economics and her studies in architectural design, interior decorating, and landscaping, she was perfectly suited for the role. She later said of her work that it kept her in touch every year with all the local organizations and business firms involved in the home, and those contacts were useful and the experience had been helpful ever since.[12]

In November 1924 aged thirty-six, Pearl entered the city for the 1925 BHA. It cost nothing but the price of the guidebooks. Using the P&P office as her headquarters, she started by organizing an executive committee with seven women and five men, including Hoffmann. These men and women included representatives of the city government, community chest, recreation center, county federation of women's clubs, the ministerial union, the Federation of parent-teacher associations, the social service conference, the central labor union, the building trades council, and the CAA. In addition to this committee, an advisory committee was formed, including the presidents of the cooperating organizations, service clubs, women's clubs, social agencies, civic and commercial organizations, and religious and academic groups.

Fourteen subcommittees were established to carry on the work of the campaign and report to the executive committee. These ranged from a house-furnishing committee, to a home economics committee, to a publicity committee. By starting the program after the summer holidays had ended, all the agencies, particularly the women's clubs, were available. Proclaiming that "the improvement of the American home was the greatest challenge to the women of America today," these clubs played an important role in recruiting local volunteers.[13]

Pearl supplemented funds from the CAA with her own fund-raising effort, remarking: "much of a beggar during the year, I have always felt loath to ask for money for projects I was running."[14] However, she had a nose for money and targeted selectively. She was also supported by her brother Harold, who provided secretarial help and real estate assistance through his office.[15] Never before had Pearl worked with so many different parties—she felt cooperation was the keynote of the whole project.

Both the *Morning Press* and *Daily News* gave the demonstrations publicity and lent their pages to educational material supplied by Pearl. Over 2,500 people attended lectures and discussion meetings held in the recreation center, and 3,000 viewed special exhibits and supplementary demonstrations presented in locations across the city. Churches, clubs, and schools participated actively in the campaign. Such was the enthusiasm for the campaign that it was impossible to tell whether the CAA, the library, the schools, the women's clubs, the businessmen, or the newspapers did more to contribute to its success.[16] The highlight of the 1925 campaign was the Better Homes Week which ran from April 25 to May 1. Among the attractions were the five demonstration houses, planned and, in three cases, furnished for families of modest means, to illustrate the sort of houses that could be built. Over nine and a half thousand people visited Santa Barbara's principal house, called "the house that budget built," which had six rooms arranged on one floor.[17]

62. The cost of this winning demonstration house was $1544.90 to build and $394.67 to furnish

Submitting their campaign report in mid-May, Santa Barbara had a four-week wait before hearing Santa Barbara had won equal first prize with Atlanta, Georgia. It added a dramatic climax to their months of strenuous work. The 1925 campaign was the largest to date, with 2,000 communities across the US participating.[18] The BHA published its national guidebook the following October for the 1926 campaign, and out of nineteen illustrations, nine were of Santa Barbara houses.[19]

Delighted by the positive response to the campaign, Pearl appointed herself secretary for the 1926 campaign and, in characteristic style, handed the role of chairman to another female colleague from the business division of the Chamber of Commerce. Needless to say, Pearl ended up doing most of the work, as the chairman turned everything over to her.[20] While this took all her time, strength, and energy she harboured no ill will, reasoning in her very logical way that "[the chairman] worked hard but her experience had not been such as to make her realize the necessity of staying on the job and keeping at it."[21] When Santa Barbara won the first prize of $500 by unanimous vote in July, Pearl was requested by her other committee members to inform the Washington office that her name be included as Associate Chairman.

Pearl introduced two novel features through the Santa Barbara campaign: garden tours, and house and garden competitions. The latter was such a valuable contribution to the BHA national campaign that James Ford, the executive director, informed all participating chairpersons, and soon afterwards similar competitions were organized in scores of other communities in the 1926 campaign.

The following year, the BHA started featuring competitions of this sort as part of their program. *House Beautiful* magazine followed suit in 1928 with their famous Small House Competition. Santa Barbara was not just winning the BHA, but also making a real contribution to the movement. The educational value of the Santa Barbara campaign was exercising a deep influence upon the housing and home lives of families throughout America.[22] Pearl believed that "in many communities the small homeowners are inarticulate and lack leadership, and the city governments and the subdividers lack vision;"[23] further, Pearl also believed that "beauty pays the best dividends in the world."[24]

With this beauty in mind, garden tours were arranged with the hope that the opportunity of seeing the most beautiful and interesting places in Santa Barbara and Montecito would delight visitors and inspire them to study the diversified collections and arrangements of trees, shrubs, and flowers, many of which were adapted to a small garden environment.[25] The idea of garden visits had been suggested long before 1926; the fact that nothing came of the idea was due to owners being somewhat shocked by the prospect of meeting strangers on their garden paths, and reluctant to open their gates.[26] While there were many examples of garden tours across the US from which to gather inspiration, it was difficult for Pearl to find gardeners and owners ready to speak on the telephone, and organizing the event required hundreds of calls. To oversee the effort running smoothly, she formed, through the P&P, a special tours committee representing all local organizations interested in gardening.

63. Las Tejas, Montecito. One of many gardens Pearl visited on her garden tours

Pearl considered both landscaping and gardening arts, believing they contributed immensely to the character of a community,[27] improved quality of life, and generated overall happiness for citizens. She was a member of the Garden Club of Santa Barbara and Montecito as well as the Garden Club of America. Through the P&P and through the organization of the garden tours, Pearl made a major contribution in educating citizens of Santa Barbara's unique natural properties. Collaborating with the city's park and recreation authorities, Pearl also promoted improvement of public space landscaping, advising on street tree planting and park development. She also subsidized and established the *Santa Barbara Gardener* magazine with Elizabeth and Lockwood de Forest, the renowned landscape architects, as editors.[28]

Horticulturally speaking, Santa Barbara had been in good hands since the 1870s. Nurserymen from Europe, particularly England, Italy and Holland, settled in Santa Barbara, drawn to its Mediterranean-like weather pattern creating a long growing season and allowing many kinds of plants from around the world to flourish.[29] Twenty years later, the Santa Barbara horticultural society was formed and held a city flower festival that attracted hundreds of visitors, including President Benjamin Harrison and his wife.

In 1926, forty-one garden tours ran from April to October on Tuesdays and Fridays at a cost of fifty cents each. Along with the tours, the P&P-formed committee hosted lectures, exhibits on gardening and landscape design, flower shows, wildflower planting events on vacant lots, and competitions for floral arrangement and small garden design. The committee also published pamphlets to help gardeners best use their plant material. Using local guides, thousands of visitors from all over the world were able to see ninety gardens, large and small. Referred to as the "most friendly and delightful example of hospitality for which Santa Barbara from Old Spanish Days has been distinguished,"[30] the owners enjoyed the appreciation, and the visitors returned to their own communities with new ideas about how to make their own gardens more beautiful.

Pearl considered the publicity generated by the tours, which included regular articles in national publications, "an enhancement of Santa Barbara's reputation."[31] Such was the success of the tours that they became an annual event, enabling Pearl to bring in tourists, school clubs, and convention groups. Although the garden tours were initially associated with the BHA movement, they outlived it by thirty years and became a staple visitor attraction.

After winning first prize in the 1927 BHA competition, Santa Barbara's Chamber of Commerce appointed a publicist to promote the city on a full-time basis,[32] and Pearl was asked to consider the newly created role of BHA State Chairman. In his offer to her regarding the role, James Ford said, "You would have all the latitude you need in making your selection of the State Committee, and could have both a working board of directors and an advisory council made up of the presidents of the various state organizations which cooperate in the movement, [and] university presidents and other outstanding personalities of the state whose names or whose help might be of value."[33] Pearl politely refused: "I have too many part-time jobs already to take on a new one, which sounds like one and a half."[34]

The discontinuation of the Architectural Board of Review in 1926 and Hoffmann's decision to step down from the chairmanship of the P&P at the end of 1927 caused Pearl "regret and astonishment,"[35] but provided her an opening to assume civic leadership of the architectural and landscape development of Santa Barbara as chairman of the P&P.[36] Planning was central to her vision for the city. Hoffmann had started the work, pressing for the formation of a city Planning Commission in 1923, and Pearl expanded and developed his efforts after he retired. As to why she took on the role, she once jokingly remarked it was "because no one else wanted the job."[37]

Much of Pearl's success in obtaining local support for her planning efforts was a result of her association with the BHA and the confidence it inspired. In 1928, her ambition grew beyond city lines. County planning was a relatively new field at this time, and exact procedural rules and tested laws to guide planners were few. Working with Leon Deming Tilton, Santa Barbara Planning Commissioner, Pearl argued, "The same need for planning existed in the county as it did in the city, differing only in degree, according to the number of people and values affected."[38] Facilitating discussions on zoning regulation, subdivision ordinances, parkland acquisition, shoreline protection, traffic projection, and comprehensive planning all came at a time when such efforts were unheard of; when heard only with suspicion, Pearl went far to transform Santa Barbara's image.[39]

Many of her ideas were incorporated in Santa Barbara's 1928 annual BHA campaign. Dividing the county into three districts, each with their own female chairman and with representatives from every organization in the locality assisting on subcommittees, it was said that not since the First World War had so many citizens worked together: "Never before had there been such unified effort for the improvement of the community."[40] Pearl developed an education program which covered the field of housing and home life very thoroughly.[41] Every public, private, and parochial school in the county participated; in nearly every area of schoolwork done during Better Homes Week, the subject matter was related to the home. Every town in the county with sufficient population to contain a civic or professional organization such as farm bureau, woman's club, or parent-teacher association, participated. Ford thought the effort was "little short of phenomenal," and that the 1928 "Better Homes Demonstration [was] the best that has ever been held in the history of the movement."[42]

Winning first prize for the fourth time brought with it astonishingly favorable publicity throughout the country. Pearl soon found herself advising other communities outside of Santa Barbara on planning and community betterment. This success also triggered a little envy from competing cities. Writing from Greenville, South Carolina, the local BHA chairman, whose community had been runner-up to Santa Barbara, remarked that if she wanted first place, the only way she knew how to get it was "to move to Santa Barbara and then lick Greenville."[43]

The BHA movement continued under the directorship of Ford until 1935, by which time the number of communities participating had reached 10,000. Due to lack of funding, the corporation had to be liquidated in 1935, and its research and publications were transferred to the Housing Research Foundation at Purdue University.[44] The momentum generated by the BHA campaigns continued up until 1942 despite no organized backing for the work.

Between 1925 and 1942, with Pearl as president, Santa Barbara entered the competition sixteen times, winning either first place or highest merit in thirteen of those years. As the BHA's model community, it was an exemplar to the country of how American families could make their homes more convenient and attractive. The city so impressed Herbert Hoover that he made a campaign stop at Santa Barbara on August 12, 1928, on his way to a landslide presidential victory.

CHAPTER 10

Washington, DC Conferences on Social Problems

On October 29, 1929, known as "Black Tuesday," a historic stock market crash brought a dramatic end to a booming era of consumer confidence and unprecedentedly lopsided prosperity in the United States. During the good times, many ordinary working-class citizens had made stock investments, and many had purchased on margin (on borrowed money). In the days following the crash, panic grew and worsened as people found themselves unable to withdraw their money from banks, because bank officials had invested it in the

64. Stock Market Crash, NYSE
1929

market. Bank failures exacerbated an already dire situation: thousands of banks and companies went bankrupt, and many more investors and ordinary people alike lost everything.

"The nation was woefully unprepared for the crash" and President Hoover's administration was slow to respond.[1] Initially, Hoover did not believe solving the crisis was the job of the federal government, instead asking state governments to undertake public works projects, for companies to keep workers' pay steady, and for labor unions to stop demanding pay increases. Throughout the nation, "the shantytowns that were popping up as people lost their homes were nicknamed 'Hoovervilles' as an insult to the president's hands-off policy."[2] A consequence of a massive change in the world's financial system, the Great Depression that followed, then brought untold misery.

The crash was soon felt in Santa Barbara, and the wealthy in Montecito were among the hardest hit. It was a time of concern for Pearl, who not only relied on residents of Montecito's contributions but was also friends with many of them. Having to make tough financial decisions, some homeowners sold their estates, but the majority retrenched, leaving hundreds of gardeners, butlers, chauffeurs, and both skilled and unskilled workmen unemployed. Life after Black Tuesday was never the same, and in the years that followed, the "hillside baron" estates were broken up. According to a local historian, "the appalling stagnation of growth in Santa Barbara during the 1930s was documented by the US Census Bureau, which listed the city's population of 33,623 going into the decade and only 34,438 in 1940, an average annual increase of only 80 persons."[3]

Hoover's opposition to direct relief federal government programs was not one of indifference toward those suffering; in fact, his humanity for those in need was vast. "A voluntary deed," he believed, "is infinitely more precious to our national ideal and spirit than a thousand-fold poured from the Treasury."[4] In July 1929, three months before the stock market crash, he issued a call for a

65. During the unemployment crisis in 1930–32, unemployed men carried out road repairs under the supervision of a committee chaired by Pearl's brother Harold

conference "to study the present status of the health and well-being of children in the United States and to report what is being done, to report what ought to be done and how to do it."[5]

A planning committee of notable physicians, social workers, educators, and laymen was formed to raise awareness on issues affecting children and to prepare reports of their research. To chair the conference, Hoover appointed his lifelong friend Ray Lyman Wilbur, an Iowa-born medical doctor who served as Hoover's Secretary of the Interior, previously holding the positions of president of Stanford University and president of the BHA campaign. The committee's findings were ready in November 1930, at which point Hoover invited 2,000 delegates to Washington for the White House Conference on Child Health and Protection to hear the reports, discuss them, and agree on a final course of action.[6] Pearl was among those invited to the conference, owing to her growing network of friends and her reputation in BHA and social circles. Out of these discussions came recommendations covering prenatal care, parenting skills, education, health, and development of social skills for all children. Thirty-one volumes of information prepared by the White House Conference were incorporated into a nineteen-point

66. Ray Lyman Wilbur

statement and designated the national Children's Charter. This formal designation "carried [with it] a promise from all delegates that they would try to make it a reality."[7]

The success of the conference ensured a second in a series of social studies undertaken by Hoover's administration. Pearl was once again invited to Washington to participate in Hoover's Conference on Home Building and Home Ownership. Distances, she remarked "mean very little to me except as they represent dollars and cents and hours spent on the train."[8] On August 30, 1930, when Hoover announced the conference, the crisis in American housing was reaching an acute stage; construction of new homes had almost come to a halt, repairs were going unfinished, and slums had expanded. The announcement was well received, as many believed that an upturn in construction was key to stimulating economic recovery. Applying the scientific method popular at the time, the primary goals of the conference were to bring together facts concerning housing throughout the US; to determine the factors that influenced housing, favourably or unfavourably, and how they were interrelated in cities, in smaller communities and in rural areas; and to bring attention to the problems of home ownership and to suggest means of meeting them.[9] The conference was chaired by Robert Lamont, Secretary of Commerce: a tall, spare man with kindly blue eyes, and not one given to verbose utterances of unwarranted enthusiasms.[10]

The number of women assigned major roles on the committees was widely reported. Pearl, who was appointed chairman of the committee on Home Information Services and Centers, found herself sharing the platform with the likes of Mrs. Henry Ford, president of the Women's National Farm & Garden Association; Mrs. Hugh Bradford, president of the National Parent-Teacher Association; Mrs. John Sipple, president of the General Federation of Women's Clubs; and many others. Despite the substantial advances made by women, the message taken up by journalists reporting on the conference was the traditional belief that women belonged in the home and not at work. During the Depression, "society viewed working women as un-American money grubbers, stealing jobs from men who needed them to support their families."[11] Progressive ideals of equality, fine for contemplation during economic boom times, failed to proliferate during a period of economic turmoil.

"From frying pan into fire," Pearl quipped as she left Santa Barbara by train in early May 1931, traveling to Washington to meet and spend ten days with her Home Information Services and Centers committee colleagues to discuss the project.[12] Her vice chairman was Helen Atwater, an author and first full-time editor of the *Journal of Home Economics*, twelve years Pearl's senior. Marion Hall, her secretary, was twenty-six and came from the Department of Commerce. Pearl thought she was a "charming girl, very quiet and unobtrusive."[13] Completing the administrative team was Merle Frampton, a field assistant and vice president of the University of the Ozarks in Arkansas. The twenty-five-member committee comprised thirteen women and twelve men with expertise in many diverse fields, such as small homes, museums, adult education, libraries, and architecture. Some of these individuals became lifelong associates of Pearl, including Blanche Halbert, the research director of the BHA movement, and H. Roy Kelley, a much-revered architect and secretary of the southern California chapter of the American Institute of Architects in Los Angeles.

With little previous work done on Home Information Services and Centers, Pearl's study was highly original. Devoting themselves fully to the project, she and her team collected their materials and opinions from all over the country within five months. On September 20, she returned to Washington with a trunk full of papers and spent the following week meeting members of the conference planning committee. Among them was Dr. John M. Gries, who had organized and, for several years, supervised the Division of Building and Housing in the Department of Commerce, and was appointed executive secretary of the conference. Writing to Hezekiah and Harold, Pearl explained,

> I met Dr. Gries and had a very charming visit. He is a big, grey-haired man who is working terrifically hard. He has a whole-hearted smile and a great interest in people and a great grasp of subjects with which the conference is concerned. You can imagine the variety of questions and the multiplicity of interviews which come his way. Since the newspaper release of the 15th [President Hoover's statement announcing Conference], there has been a constant stream of persons with axes to grind who are hard to dispose of.[14]

67. John Gries

Pearl's family were proud of her Washington work. As realtors, they had been advertising homeownership since 1904. One of their slogans was, "Homeowners are rent-savers. Own your own home! It is one of the greatest daily joys of life to own a home of your own."[15] In what little spare time she had, Pearl continuously wrote detailed accounts of her experience to Harold:

> I had my first meeting with a few members of my committee on Tuesday. On Thursday we met from nine til six, all together, adjourning only for an hour and a half for lunch at an attractive tea-room two blocks away which has been made out of an old stable and stable yard. After dinner, with the men's committee we talked until twelve. Meetings began again on Friday and lasted from nine until six and after dinner from ten o'clock with a small group of the women. On Saturday we had a meeting of half the committee from 11:30 until one and then they scattered. I must admit that the ladies on my committee did ten times as good a job as the men with whose total accomplishments I am not at all satisfied. Don't think that I haven't thought of you lots every day. I have wondered what you were doing but I just haven't had time to write anything more than thoughts that I had to get ready for presentation to the committee. It is no joke running a committee of thirty people from all parts of the country, experts in all sorts of lines, and keeping them interested in each other's reports for forty or fifty hours. None of them were worn out and all stuck to the finish except for the very rich Mrs. Storrow from Boston [President, American Homemakers], and she came for a day and a half, which is more than she has done for anything else in years.[16]

Working at the Commerce Department Building within the Federal Triangle as well as from her bedroom at the American Association of University Women on Eye Street, Pearl found herself faced with papers and more papers:

> A lot of those I have brought have been put on the fire but more and more have come to take their place. It is going to be a great old job of editing—"rehashing" is the word. I haven't quite decided which kind of expert assistance I need the most. People who can think, people who can write, people who can type, I need them all and for the first time in my life I wish that I were an author within an assured style and an unlimited vocabulary.[17]

Although Pearl had hoped she could return to Santa Barbara and deal with some pressing local issues before the conference in December, her committee's report kept her in Washington. She trusted that her P&P secretarial support back in California could manage without her. And although the work was challenging, it's evident from her correspondence that Pearl enjoyed both it and being in another city. "The end of the month has stolen upon me unawares. It is disgusting how many people there are who are doing interesting things that I would like to see and talk to and how few of them I have a chance to even hail."[18]

Among the people she did see was Miss Harlean James, a BHA director whom Pearl had met through the movement. Eleven years older than Pearl, James was a Stanford alumnus who, after moving east in 1911, "transformed the Baltimore women's civic league into a

68. Harlean James

progressive city beautiful group. When the US entered World War I, she rose through the wartime housing bureaucracy, eventually taking charge of the boarding houses built around the Capitol. Her management caught the attention of Frederic Delano, a railroad man and Federal Reserve vice chair with a lifelong interest in grand plans. After the war, Delano hired James to work as executive secretary in the American Civic Association (ACA)."[19] Pearl shared much in common with James: both were powerful, single women who appreciated beauty and whose values appealed to other women. Their friendship developed in Washington and lasted until James's death in 1969. Pearl thought James was "outstanding, one of my teachers."[20]

Among the findings in Pearl's report on Home Information Services and Centers, the problem of education was the most apparent. Despite the many excellent existing agencies, public and private, homeowners, builders, and homemakers had nowhere to turn for authoritative advice on many of the problems arising in the home. Presenting a plan to address this deficiency, Pearl's report focused on the different needs of urban, farm, and village communities. As she explained to her brother, it was heavily edited:

> I have learned a lot about myself and other people, and I certainly pity Wickersham[21] and all the other commissions that have produced volumes and volumes and seen it largely pass into oblivion. Sometimes we have a hundred pages of material mentioned in a sentence. The results of 200 letters summarized in another, and so it goes.[22]

Despite heavy-handed editing, the report's conclusion was characteristically Pearl:

> Any community regardless of its size can start some type of home information service. The beginning of such a service might be no more than a committee of representative citizens but the development of the service into a perfected organization providing unbiased information on a wide range of subjects

should be the concern of every person interested in home and community improvement.[23]

Put the work in and you can achieve anything. Pearl was, of course, a living embodiment of this.

Between December 2 and 5, 3,000 presidential invitees with experience in housing matters from every state, as well as Hawai'i and Puerto Rico, gathered in Washington to consider the reports and recommendations of the committees. As described by Natasha Porfirenko and James Ryan in their finding aid of the 1931 President's Conference on Home Building and Home Ownership, "The pooling of so much experience to discuss and evaluate fact and opinion was without precedent in the history of housing. It revealed for the first time the immense scope of the subject as well as its organic unity."[24] The findings were important but did little to "halt the slide of the housing industry or the worsening predicament of homeowners."[25]

The efforts put forth by volunteers across the country in the BHA movement "could and did make considerable effort to stimulate the utilization of the findings of the conference including publishing the reports."[26] In 1932, the committee reports were published in eleven volumes. Owing to the cost of publishing, the editor was forced to cut out some of Pearl's original work. She didn't complain, aware of the difficulties her former colleagues were facing: "I can barely imagine how difficult the winter has been in Washington, with the uncertainty as to jobs and salary, the Bonus Army, and a hectic political condition generally. I certainly am sorry for a lot of the people in the mess."[27,28]

Having worked on one committee report continuously for six months, travelled over 16,000 miles by train and car, and accumulated expenses of $5,000, Pearl left for California on December 8, 1932. She expected to stay at home for some time. Compared to the mess in Washington, she found that life in Santa Barbara was "very quiet."[29]

CHAPTER 11

Roadside Reform[1]

Despite life in Santa Barbara being quieter than her time in Washington, Pearl's work toward beautification was never busier. If there was one aspect of the city's, county's, and state's growth that Pearl found particularly engaging, it was roadsides.

One of her pet peeves was poor signage. She was not alone: during the early 1920s, many women's groups, including General Federation of Women's Clubs (GFWC), and the Garden Club of America made concerted efforts to control roadside billboards that sprang up along national road systems connected with the rising use of the automobile. In 1923, Elizabeth Lawton, a GFWC member from New York, along with her engineer husband, created the National Roadside Council (NRC)[2] to speak out against the

69. Highways or Buy-ways? Anti Billboard cartoon, 1929

impending blight on the landscape caused by outdoor advertising. In Santa Barbara, illegal signs were rarely removed, and indiscriminate placing of billboards along with signs being tacked on trees, fences, and barns threatened to drive away rather than attract the tourist. Lawton's antagonists were the "billboard barons" and their industry machine: the Outdoor Advertising Association of America.[3] Labelling Lawton and her civic-minded women followers as the "scenic sisters," deriding them as idle bourgeois "do-gooders" whose fragile sensibilities could not be allowed to trump free market forces, the association was prepared for a lengthy fight.[4] So was Lawton.[5]

Pearl believed there was a place for advertising, but that it should be regulated within zones and with civic welfare at heart. In 1924, the P&P became the first civic group to cooperate with Lawton's campaign. Pearl considered it a privilege to work with Lawton; she knew of no one else who waged a more intelligent and persistent battle against powerfully entrenched opponents.[6]

The main voice of opposition to outdoor advertising in the state was the California Roadside Council (CRC), an organization dedicated to fostering public appreciation of roadside scenery.[7] Composed primarily of women, the CRC was established in 1929 with Cora Felton, a San Franciscan lover of natural beauty and wife of US Senator Charles Felton, as chair. The group's leading spirit was Helen Baker Reynolds.[8] In 1929, while working as an artist in San Francisco, she began to take an interest in roadside beautification. After meeting Cora Felton in 1930, Reynolds joined the CRC as its secretary. Feeling passionate that California was really growing hideous with so many billboards, Reynolds became an activist and took on the most powerful lobbyists in the state. Described by Reynolds as "obese, cynical and crude," Frew Morton, lobbyist for Foster and Kleiser, and Artie Samish, the liquor lobbyist, called the shots on legislation far beyond their own fields. Artie Samish's famous statement was "Don't make no difference who is governor of California, I'm Governor of the Legislature." Describing Morton and Samish, Pearl recounted, "They were the Goliaths of whom we little innocents went forth to do battle."[9]

Pearl had nothing but respect for Helen Reynolds, saying she thought her "remarkable." At the same time that Reynolds began to consider a career in roadside activism, Pearl decided to affiliate P&P with the CRC. She was eager to help them get organized by promoting their cause and disseminating their literature.[10] The timing could not have been more appropriate.

In May 1929, the California legislature authorized the appointment of a joint committee to "investigate the possibility of regulating and controlling the location of gasoline stations, hot dog stands, advertising signs, and other structures of a commercial nature along scenic roads and highways."[11] The report of the committee was ridiculed by the NRC, who found evidence that one-third of the text was taken from a 1928 Foster and Kleiser publication.[12]

While the joint legislative committee was reporting, Pearl started a county-wide organization to correlate the records and efforts of the local organizations and departments interested in preserving the beauty of the rural scenery. Collaborating with groups from all over the county, she developed a series of educational campaigns and printed pamphlets and reprints, thousands of which were distributed in Santa Barbara County, and in California. By 1930, the county's "Master Highway" plan for the relief of billboard blight was attracting national attention. In the annual report of the Billboard and Roadside Committee of the Garden Club of America, Pearl's work was referred to as an inspiration to other communities by its chairman, Hope Goddard Iselin, (a sailor, horsewoman, gardener, famous beauty, and wife of Charles Iselin, a banker who three times defended the America's Cup). The following year, the NRC and the American Nature Association published a California roadside study made in collaboration with the CRC. It concluded that, while the state revealed a progressive attitude toward roadside planting and improvement on the part of the state departments, as well as an aroused sentiment on the part of many civic groups, it likewise showed a condition of domination, both political and otherwise, on the part of the outdoor advertising industry.[13]

As the reform movement increasingly made state and county zoning its priority, the issue of aesthetics became displaced by arguments about speed and safety. To counter the accusation that billboards along the highway were a source of danger, the billboard industry provided research reports and testimonials from insurance companies to prove there was no relationship between signs and accidents. Nevertheless, Pearl and her colleagues used the issue to support their increasing legislative efforts. Since aesthetics would not be a category of public welfare (on which zoning was based) until the mid-1950s, highway safety was the next best thing.[14] In 1936, Pearl was invited to sit on the California Traffic Safety Advisory Committee.

Pearl's success in reforming the state's roads came from a mixture of her persistence and confidence, having not been afraid to visit the federal and state departments in Sacramento in person. These offices were not too used to lone women visiting. This practice of meeting Washington and Sacramento colleagues not just in legislature but also in administrative departments was highly effective. As she later remarked, "I spend more time and money becoming informed of the latest practices than anybody else I know in this field because I don't have to wait to be asked and have my expenses paid."[15]

70. Santa Barbara road sign

Such was her reputation that *Los Angeles Times* reporters nicknamed her the "Carrie Nation of the Billboards."[16] Occasionally, she got caught out by her own competence. In 1939, a subcommittee of county schoolchildren working for her against banners, posters and signs disposed of all the temporary markers put up by another of her committees promoting a pilgrimage tour to the old mission and ranches in the Santa Ynez Valley. "I had a taste of my own medicine," she remarked.[17]

Interestingly, she gathered so much relatable sentiment against billboards in certain areas where companies had previously placed them that those same companies then pointed, with pride, to the fact that they no longer did so, in the hope of gaining public approval.

Keeping up Santa Barbara's community individuality, character, and charm in the face of rapid roadside development, Pearl not only fought against billboards but also devoted her attention to assuring good street tree planting, getting county highways landscaped, dealing with litter, promoting fire prevention, and improving the appearance of roadside stands and service stations.

In March 1931 Pearl took local roadside matters into her own hands and established the Santa Barbara County Roadside Committee to take charge of a competition for the improvement of

71. Casa Loma station. One of many architectural gems dotted about the county which received Pearl's attention

Santa Barbara County service stations. Pearl had been inspired by watching other individuals take up the cause, including Mrs. John D. Rockefeller, Jr. In 1927, while motoring through New England, Mrs. Rockefeller was so shocked by the hideousness of roadside refreshment stands that she established a competition to improve the appearance and usefulness of those buildings in every state.[18] However, the Santa Barbara competition was the first of its kind in the US, in which the emphasis was not simply on the design of the building, but also on signs, color, and plantings.

In fact, many service stations in the county had already incorporated the Mediterranean and Spanish Colonial style in their building design, encouraged by local architectural firms and the opportunity for good public relations. These endeavours did not go unnoticed by Pearl, who, during the late 1920s, presented a number of stations with P&P awards for civic and commercial architecture. While gratifying, "Pearl was not one to be complacent," and architectural design was only one aspect of the overall aesthetic.[19]

Cooperating with the Garden Club of Santa Barbara and Montecito and the Montecito Roadside Committee, the Santa Barbara Chamber of Commerce, and other agencies, Pearl brought together some of the most prominent county leaders in her struggle to defend Santa Barbara's beauty. She worked hard to get full cooperation from the service station operators and district managers of the oil companies that owned them. By telephoning and writing letters with enclosed photographs of substandard stations to the national headquarters of Texaco, Union, Associated, and Shell, she gradually won their support. As one of her colleagues noted, Pearl never abandoned a program prematurely, and "when she got her mind made up, she would see it through."[20] Pearl herself found it "such fun to work with the spirit of cooperation and education in eliminating signs and improving color and planting."[21]

With sufficient funds and interest from the owners, she directed her committee and groups of women volunteers to visit, inspect, and photograph each service station in the county. Her advice was that if they saw an eyesore, they should take a photograph of it, because pictures never lie;[22] more importantly, that they should work in teams so that misunderstandings were kept to a minimum and the women had a witness in each other.[23] What started slowly in March 1932 rallied during the summer, and altogether ninety-five out of a possible two hundred service stations within the county submitted application forms for the competition. These ninety-five included the most conspicuous.[24]

Twenty-nine awards were made including five in the first category. One first-prize winner was Patrick Maher, wartime Mayor of Santa Barbara, who owned two Richfield stations in the city.[25] He thought "it was a very good program." Accommodating of Pearl's persistent prodding, he remarked, "My only trouble with Miss Chase was trying to keep up with her." The key to her success, he added, was "she was so well organized."[26]

The competitions continued annually until 1938, by which time the county could boast of having service stations that were truly architectural gems. Texaco and Shell went further and extended their Hispanic-Mediterranean design nationwide. Pearl often argued that "good style is good business." The oil companies listened and agreed.

Today, standing alone among towering eucalyptus trees bordering a golf course on the former Ellwood Oil Field, is the Barnsdall-Rio Grande station, built in 1929. Featured in the 1980 sultry movie remake *The Postman Always Rings Twice*, this former service station reminds us of something Pearl knew only too well: first, everything has a history, even a gas station, and secondly, something as mundane as a gas station can be designed to contribute interesting beauty to the environment.[27]

In 1934, Pearl went one step further and established the Santa Barbara Roadside Council (SBRC) with members from her Roadside Committee.[28] Its aim was to provide the citizens of Santa

72. Barnsdall-Rio Grande station today

Barbara County with more effective means for expressing their interest in highway safety, park and highway improvement, community beautification, and related problems of community development, and to promote cooperation between official civic and commercial agencies for the betterment of the region. It worked in cooperation with the CRC. She felt comfortable knowing the active leadership in the state's roadside campaign remained. Continuing as the Santa Barbara representative of that organization until 1976 and a member of the SBRC until 1966, Pearl was able to protect Santa Barbara's reputation of being quite "restrictive and stiff" about billboards and outdoor advertising.[29]

Today, the stretch of Highway 101 between El Rincon and the Gaviota Pass is widely regarded as one of the most stunning in California. Twenty-one miles of the road between Goleta and Gaviota was recently designated a California Scenic Highway. The absence of billboards and the attractive landscaping is part of Pearl's lasting legacy.

CHAPTER 12

Another Car Crash and a Fork in the Road

Despite the great hardship created by the Great Depression, it is testament to Pearl and the Santa Barbara community that so much beautification was achieved during these years. It was, however, not without cost, and by 1931 the P&P's finances were strained.[1] Given her resourceful nature, Pearl was able to sustain her work by soliciting funds from friends.

Pearl cultivated friendships with some of the wealthiest patrons in America. Mary Harkness, wife of the philanthropist Edward "Ned" Harkness and daughter of wealthy New York attorney Thomas Stillman, met Pearl while visiting Santa Barbara with her husband during the 1920s. They both became members of the CAA, and Mary also joined the P&P after Adele Herter put in a good word for Pearl.[2] Ned, whose fortune he inherited from his father, a silent partner in John D. Rockefeller's Standard Oil company, is reputed to have made bequests of over $129 million (equivalent to over $2 billion in 2023), including many millions to Yale University, his alma mater. Pearl was reported to give a throaty chuckle and smile when recalling that the gothic dormitories with small windows which bore his name were nicknamed "the darkness dormitories."[3]

Over several years and through regular correspondence and personal visits when in New York, Pearl became close to Mary Harkness. Describing Mary's involvement in the work of the P&P, "[Mary] said it was the first time she had ever had her finger on the pulse of the community."[4] Given Pearl's close ties, it was not unusual for people to ask her to make an introduction on their behalf. One such case was Aurelia Reinhardt, who wished to interest the Harknesses in Mills College, telling Pearl in 1937, "I would forfeit anything to help in strengthening this western college to which I have given many years of work."[5]

Aside from her wealthy patrons, her brother Harold, and what she could raise from events such as Garden Tours, Pearl was also able to rely on financial assistance from her fellow committee members, all of whom volunteered their time at no expense.

The largest overhead was Pearl's office and secretarial support. During the busiest months of the year, she could have up to four women working for her. On June 15, 1932, she moved the P&P from the office at 929 Paseo Carrillo to a garden-level studio at 912 Santa Barbara Street on a plot which was owned by the CAA, taking 40,000 articles with her. She had to build on a storeroom to house the reserve supplies. The large area provided space for office conferences and meetings in a convenient, central location. Pearl enjoyed the new premises immensely and found it particularly useful in that she could ask people to "come and see us here rather than calling on men in their offices where they are constantly interrupted."[6]

Pearl did not type her own letters and publications; she had something of a reputation for using fountain pens and for filling the entire page in her letters.[7] She abhorred the waste of government officials who sent letters with two lines of text and a signature on the second page. All her typed letters were mimeographed and filed away. By her own admission she did not write easily, and she struggled to produce publicity material.[8] She always kept postcards and photographs which she believed "tell better than one can in words the variety of scenes and people I have encountered."[9] Her office's output was phenomenal, with thousands of letters typed and hundreds of thousands of pamphlets sent to local, state, and national organizations each year.

73. Pearl

Interestingly, although Pearl assisted numerous authors with books on subjects ranging from planning to housing to education, she only wrote one herself. It was published in 1930 during a time when Santa Barbara was home to an unusually large number of small gardens, and a gardening fad for growing cactus plants. *Cacti and Other Succulents*, written with her desire to further increase an interest in the public in gardening, included an annotated list of 943 species cultivated in the Santa Barbara region. It was compiled with help from Bernhard Hoffmann's brother Ralph, who was establishing the species at the Museum of Natural History, and Edward Owen Orpet, an English-born horticulturalist, former Santa Barbara city park superintendent, and husband of one of Pearl's secretaries.

The work took over a year to complete and Pearl became something of an expert on the subject, giving lectures and advising other gardeners and authors including retired teacher Victoria Padilla, one of the region's best-known horticulturalists, who wrote a definitive book on southern California gardens in 1961.

Pearl's office became something of an informal clearing house. It was called upon day in and day out for advice and information by individuals and public officials on all sorts of subjects, but particularly on zoning, tree cutting, parks, planning, parking, historical matters, billboards, signs, and employment. Questions about planting were very frequent. This is partly due to the fact that the committee had maintained membership and cordial relations with state and national organizations and departments for many years, and was receiving up to date communications and publications from them. A great deal of correspondence was warranted, as was the time involved in collecting and filing the material and information for the citizens with inquiries.[10]

Her central office location and her influential relations with local leaders played integral roles in establishing and maintaining Pearl's authority with her volunteers, clients, and interested parties. From 1:30 to 5:30 each weekday afternoon, the office was open to anybody from the private or public sector interested or curious about community development, conservation and preservation. In operating her own office, she established a progressive work culture that emphasized camaraderie over competition and hierarchy, generosity over greed, and merit and skill over knowing it all. Work was at the core of what she did, but being realistic and making a positive difference in people's lives were equally important to Pearl. As one male admirer told her, "You are in the midst of your work, happy in making other people happy. My dear, you are the blessing for so many less fortunate people. Service is indeed the highest aim in life!"[11]

Managing her office during the Great Depression, at a challenging time for Santa Barbara's philanthropic tradition, was not lost on Pearl:

> …this is a time when we must carefully analyze the value of and the service rendered by our activities and adapt our programs to present needs. When the good old times return, we can perhaps continue growing along some of the lines which now must be put aside but not forgotten. I have seen the pitiful sight of good men and women fighting [blindly] to preserve the status quo of social agencies when the same energy could, if better directed, [make] their public work of increasing community value.[12]

While Pearl adapted her affairs to the challenges facing American society, her own world was nearly brought to an abrupt end when she was involved in a car accident on April 19, 1932. After attending some garden club meetings in northern California, she was traveling south of Eureka on the Redwood Highway with Mrs. Harriet P. Miller, a friend from San Francisco who was a member of the Garden Club of America. They were riding in Mrs. Miller's chauffeur-driven Packard. The chauffeur, who had been awake the night before with a toothache and taking aspirin for the pain, fell asleep at the wheel. Near the town of Weott, where the road ran close to a sheer cliff above the South Fork Eel River, the car left the pavement and collided with a huge redwood stump about three feet from the side of the road. As Pearl's secretary Mildred Orpet later remarked, "It was fortunate that the stump was there, as it probably saved them from going over the precipice."[13]

Pearl suffered numerous injuries: a skull fracture, a broken nose, back strain, bent ribs, a broken ankle, torn ligaments, and four cuts on her face requiring ten stitches. Mrs. Miller was equally injured. They were hospitalized for one week in Scotia in Humboldt County, treated by two fine local surgeons. It took one of the surgeons an hour and a half to extract all the pieces of broken glass and black straw hat from Pearl's face and head. Alice Bentz drove up from San Francisco to care for Pearl. Mrs Miller received support from her family who took her back to San Francisco once the stitches were removed. The chauffeur survived with minor injuries.

After returning to Santa Barbara, Pearl spent a further two months housebound, getting around with crutches and a brace. Despite her condition, she played down the pain and discomfort she was in and, as her secretary reported, "She would have us think that there's nothing wrong, and she acts the part well enough to get away with it."[14] Indeed, as Pearl later remarked, "I have had a fine rest out of it all and my friends seem to approve of that part of the performance."[15] In fact, her friends were concerned she had been overdoing it. Prior to the accident she regularly had a resting heart rate of 120, was unable to sleep well, and had an acute pain in her chest for three days.

Among those to wish Pearl a speedy recovery was Newton Drury. As a very close friend of Harold and Pearl from UC Berkeley, he heard about the accident and wrote, "As [my wife] Elizabeth told you over the telephone, we feel sort of responsible for whatever happens on the Redwood Highway, but I am very glad that large stump was where it was, as from all indications it was responsible for keeping your machine from going over the bank."[16]

Having to keep fairly still so as to let her body recover, meant Pearl had "a much longed for chance to communicate with my far-away friends and be at home to my nearby ones."[17] Describing her daily routine: "I'm still following the same regime," she remarked, "and have found daily use for a rather colorful satin pyjama suit. Imagine me lying down with pale blue-green trousers and a Peach colored jacket, with an embroidered Spanish shawl over my nether extremities. I never felt so different from my usual self."[18]

By August, Pearl was getting along nicely and had dispensed with her cane. Her nose healed in good shape and her scars were mended, though her ankle remained bandaged a couple of months further. Accident insurance provided a small indemnity, which helped pay for one month of medical bills. Due to her injuries, Pearl missed the track and field events of the Summer Olympics, which were taking place in Los Angeles between July 30 and August 14. She did, however, spend two days at the games during the final week. Thirty-seven nations competed before an estimated one million spectators. Pearl thought the event was "wonderfully managed," noting that "The sales of tickets and concessions amounted to $2,000,000, one-half of which will go to pay off the state bond issue underwriting the affair."[19]

Reflecting on her situation, she drew a parallel between the car accident she survived in 1916 and the one she had just survived, detailing her thoughts in writing to family friend Carl Dennett:

Just as that accident put a period to my short teaching career this is I believe marking the end of the "career," if one can call it that, of varied civic service which I have indulged in for the last sixteen years. I've taken the opportunity to resign from all the organizations whose multiplicity of demands for thought and service have helped to make life a little too hectic at times. Of course, I have a few left which really need me and which have "unfinished business" which would be seriously embarrassed if deserted now. I had hoped to study this summer, but can't get up and away for the postgraduate work in psychology always tempted me since I had to give up work in it when war and father's illness stopped me in 1917. Father has been well ever since I came back from the East. He really needs me less, except for company, than at any time since mother died, so it's a bit ironical that now when I'm free to have a job and be a bit self-supporting that all the jobs are needed by others probably more than I.

You remember I confessed I never had wanted to be paid for what I did or for what I gave of myself, and I don't now, but on the contrary, I'm beginning to think that I might not like to be dependent on my brother for years and years. Not but that he's dear and generous, but that I've heard so much from the "supporters" lately that I've imagined how sensitive such a situation might become even between people as fond of each other as we are. Possibly the accident has made me imagine what it would be like to be unable to do for oneself or for others, and to be dependent too.

All this unusual report of my own ponderings you called down upon yourself when you hoped I could stop, and said, "Now I think you have earned your 'well done' and I wish I might see you expanding in a sunny soul atmosphere." It sounds thrilling, and so perhaps my stopping now was to give a chance to the expanding process, but I wonder what you would call a sunny soul atmosphere for me.

Anyway I'm at the fork in the road and I'm not going to worry, to hurry or even to think about the future very much.

> There are a lot of people who need me now and I'm stirred as they come and sit beside my sofa in the sunny bay window and talk over their problems, of course I can only encourage them to go on striving and cheerfully working for their own, and perhaps guide them directly to the source of practical help which is most appropriate to their needs. To many of us one of the tragedies of poverty and family disasters is that the individuals have often to be passed through so many hands before their helper turns up.[20]

Pearl cut back on her social welfare commitments, resigning as director of the recreation center and delegated more of the Better Homes work to the county chairpersons. In June, she tendered her resignation as director and member of the CAA, to John Gamble, then president, noting the difficulty of her decision: "The connection of eleven years is not broken without long considerations."[21] Pearl was not the only director to resign during this time,[22] and it was difficult for Pearl to see the thing that she had worked so hard for "just ruined."[23]

Gamble was a distinguished artist, but as president of the school of the arts and the CAA, he was, in Pearl's view, "hardly 5 percent effective. Poor man, he hardly knows what it is all about."[24] By 1932, he was also suffering from a serious heart ailment.

As meetings lapsed, some of the CAA directors began to question the direction the association was taking. Among the four branches, P&P was the most active. As Pearl remarked, "we worked frightfully hard to keep the name of the Association before the public in a favorable and interesting way, particularly during the summer when the other branches were largely inactive."[25,26]

In October, Pearl decided to also resign as chairman of the P&P. She wrote, "I had been feeling so miserable for so long that there is just no use in continuing to keep up the pace that tires me out."[27] In fact, her heart had been in a condition which demanded a long rest if she was not to cause permanent or chronic damage,[28] and so this resignation was wise. Since 1930 she had hoped that Bernhard Hoffmann would return and take on the role again; however, in August, 1932, he suffered a severe heart attack. Pearl then swapped roles with John Frederick Murphy, who was, in her view, "a splendid co-operator and fine architect."[29,30] With this, she knew that she would still have a "good many irons in the fire but will not have to be so continually pushing other people on that will be a change and improvement."[31] The feelings of many were summed up by Bernhard Hoffmann in a letter to Pearl:

> Never have I known anyone who so consistently and courageously and so generously gave of his or her time and effort for so many worthwhile activities. It's difficult, nay impossible, to express my admiration and respect for your accomplishments.
>
> What you have given to your friends, your community, and your country would be notable even in any one of the several lines that you seem to have been able to pursue simultaneously; so if you find it wise or desirable or necessary to step aside from the active conduct of one or more of your many specialities, you will still be able to feel you have more credit than most for your civic and neighborhood activities. I hope that you will find it possible and easy to spare some time for Pearl Chase. But this wasn't meant to be a note of suggestion; merely a most sincere expression [of] admiration and deep appreciation and affection. This note may make you think the climate or my convalescence has gone to my head; but its [*sic*] really only my lame use of the chance this gives me to say what we are always thinking and we don't want you to think we take it all as a matter of course.[32]

Within days of stepping back, Pearl remarked, "There are numberless other [jobs] popping up and trying to take their place, but I am saying 'no' very often."[33] She did not abandon the role for long. In January 1935, with her health fully recovered, she returned to the position of chairman of the P&P.

CHAPTER 13

The State Park Movement and Conservation

> Popular wisdom has it that in times of scarcity or economic contraction, the relative luxury of land or resource conservation loses its viability and appeal. Yet, during the Great Depression, the conservation movement, which had reached an apogee during the Progressive era, continued within a core of organizations and especially within the federal government.[1]

Caught up in the evolving movement, Pearl found herself shaping and being shaped by conservation ideas. In August 1932, seven months before Franklin Delano Roosevelt was inaugurated as thirty-second president of the United States, as Pearl was deciding to reduce her committee work, she was also thinking about starting a new, statewide project for conservation. "It is the psychological moment to start projects which depend upon volunteer activities," she told a friend. "There is the same spirit abroad that moved people to work and give as during the war."[2] Like many of her projects, California Conservation Week (CCW) started out as an experiment and rapidly grew into a highly organized annual event. Realizing that the Garden Clubs were not equipped to handle such an event, Pearl established a nonprofit citizen's group which she called the California Conservation Council (CalCC). If any of her colleagues suspected that she'd grown tired of serving her community, she quickly proved them wrong.

Having worked in social welfare, highway beautification, and civic planning, it was logical that Pearl would want to bring attention to the conservation of natural resources. As a child she was fascinated by the debate raging over America's goal of conquering nature and grasping its ultimate meaning. In the rush to settle and develop the West, congress gave away to speculators and business interests, western lands, minerals, and grazing rights, without developing any coherent policy. By the late nineteenth century, American citizens organized to challenge unregulated development and investigate how to best conserve the natural environment. Because of its vast scope, these efforts proved to be challenging. Among one of the most problematic aspects of conservation was how best to define it. What did terms such as "nature," "wilderness," "garden," "conservation," and "environment" really mean when used interchangeably? Such terms meant different things to different people from one generation to the next, and they continue to cause confusion today.[3]

Soon after arriving in Santa Barbara, Pearl became friendly with Stewart Edward White, a local landowner, spiritualist, preservationist, and author with a vested interest in natural history and outdoor living. He convinced Pearl of the remarkable value of the strange, varied, and ragged backcountry of Santa Barbara and how it should be carefully protected.[4]

A few years later, as an admirer of John Muir, she followed the debate over the damming of Yosemite's Hetch Hetchy Valley and the eventual passage of the Raker Act in 1913, which permitted

74. Stewart Edward White

flooding of the valley. The debate brought the fledgling conservation movement and its two factions: the preservationists and the practical conservationists to a crossroads.

Muir, a Scottish American naturalist, author, romantic philosopher, and cofounder of the Sierra Club, favored wilderness preservation and believed the valley should be preserved for its inherent aesthetic beauty and for recreation. Opposing Muir was Gifford Pinchot, a wealthy American politician who served as the first head of the US Forest Service and was a close friend of President Theodore Roosevelt. He believed in a utilitarian ideal of using natural resources for the "greatest good of the greatest number for the longest time."[5]

After becoming president in 1901 Theodore Roosevelt used his authority to help establish 230 million acres of public lands, 150 million acres of which was set aside as national forests. In 1905, he created the US Forest Service, as an organization within the Department of Agriculture. An adamant proponent of utilizing the country's resources, "Roosevelt wanted to ensure the sustainability of those resources."[6] Forests, rangelands, and water should be managed for productivity, sustained yield, and year-round conservation, with private developers prevented from wholesale destruction. "Put simply conservation sought the proper use of nature, while preservation sought protection of nature from use."[7]

The Hetch Hetchy controversy pitted the needs of San Francisco, a rapidly growing city trying to find a large and reliable source of water, against the proponents of a newly formed Yosemite National Park. Between 1905 and 1913 a bitter battle was fought. An influential "opposition led by John Muir and the Sierra Club worked to protect the Hetch Hetchy Valley in Yosemite National Park from a dam, believing that its beauty should be enjoyed by the American people. On the other side, James Phelan, the Mayor of San Francisco believed it was his civic responsibility to provide his 750,000 constituents with an abundant source of water. Congress finally decided the issue by passage of the Raker Act, granting the valley to San Francisco's use."[8]

For the first time, Americans had to decide what the designation of a national park actually meant. The Santa Barbara Woman's Club, which Pearl was a member of, and the wider General Federation of Women's Clubs (GFWC), which had formerly supported utilitarian forestry and Pinchot, both offered their support to Muir over Hetch Hetchy. In the following years many women's clubs along with hiking and outdoor clubs promoted the wilderness ideal and the preservation of parks.[9]

With their vast network, the women's clubs made a significant impact on conservation during these years. Their success lay not simply because they had the time and financial resources but also because the conservation movement with its scientific, rational, efficient impulses, was a critical part of progressive reform. In the struggle to beautify the nation's communities and preserve its wildlands, many women believed that "man the money maker had left it to woman the money saver to preserve resources."[10]

Clubwomen capitalized upon concern for the environment to advance broader public agendas including both municipal housekeeping and progressive political reform. The Women's Club movement identified conservation with such cherished white middle-class values as motherhood, family, community, religion, and patriotism. Club women never tired of extolling God's natural resources and American abundance, which they hoped to save for America's children; they "lifted conservation above a political agenda to an American ideology."[11]

By articulating a gendered view of conservation, "women's club leaders encouraged women's interest in nature, helped organize followers for collective action, and eased male anxiety over women's movement into political and economic areas formerly the exclusive domain of men."[12] In effect, women's clubs used conservation to expand the public and political influence of their own gender.[13]

The controversy of Hetch Hetchy led the GFWC and other agencies including the American Civic Association (ACA) to press for a national parks bill. They believed such a measure would separate wilderness areas from the US Forest Service and other federal agencies and thereby protect their integrity. Setting aside their differences, both practical conservationists and preservationists came together in 1916 with the creation of the National Park Service (NPS). According to Pearl's close friend from UC Berkeley, Horace Albright, who assisted first NPS director Stephen Mather, and later succeeded him as the second director in 1929:

> The general philosophy at that time was "use." Resources were to be used. There'd always be more. Men like Theodore Roosevelt and Gifford Pinchot were for "preservation with use." Hence the National Forest idea. Our group and followers were conservationists and preservationists. No use of resources, no change in the general state of national park areas. But roads to enjoy the outstanding, easy-to-visit features of a park while leaving most areas in wilderness, accommodations for the people of all incomes in a wide price range, conveniences for health and safety. Dollars would be doled out according to the number of visitors.[14]

Key to fostering public appreciation for the parks, saving them from private exploitation and proving to Congress the usefulness of the national park idea was travel and tourism.

"In viewing recreational tourism effectively as the highest and best use of the national parks' scenic landscapes, and developing the parks for that purpose, Mather and Albright took a 'wise use' approach to the parks, an approach reflected in the NPS's capitalist-oriented growth and development rhetoric. Through the promotion of tourism in the national parks, scenery itself became a kind of commodity."[15]

Pearl supported this type of park use, which delivered a massive boost to the conservation movement. Outdoor recreation in the parks fit neatly with her desire to improve social welfare by providing better public health among children and instilling youth with love of country through nature education. State parks became part of "the grand experiments in social engineering associated with the progressive era."[16]

For the visitors themselves, it was proven that visiting parks not only improved their education and understanding of wilderness but indirectly through sharing their stories and photographs, they "recruited potential supporters to the conservation ethic."[17] Pearl encouraged such behaviour, often reminding her associates when they traveled outside of Santa Barbara, "You will be gathering ideas and comparing what you see with what we have done or might do in your home community."[18] Emphasizing the importance of spending a few weeks or months each year traveling, she found American state and national parks especially rewarding to visit. On alternate years from the late 1920s onward, she made trips to the southern, eastern, and central states while in the years between she visited the Pacific states.[19,20]

Ironically, the increased use of the national parks and forests provided by improved roads and automobiles brought its own new set of problems, which have been the subject of debate ever since. Pearl felt roadside improvement was the most discussed and most cussed subject in connection with conservation.[21] Seeing the rolling tide of humans rushing through park after park concerned her, and she resolved to campaign that humans could both use the parks and protect their beauty and special charm.[22]

Five years after establishing the NPS, Mather, a millionaire industrialist turned conservationist, was faced with two choices: either adding parks to the national system that were worthy of being established but were not of national significance, or promoting state park systems to establish the locally significant parks. This idea created a perception of state parks as the second tier of the nationwide park system, "A second filter to catch those park 'rejects' and thereby relieve the pressure on the national park system to compromise its

75. Stephen Mather

quality standards. Who better to take on this important responsibility than the state governments, where interest in state parks was already spreading?"[23] Sometime in 1920, Mather came up with the idea of calling a nationwide conference on parks. If he could get the key movers and shakers together in one place, it would be infinitely easier to set his plan in motion.

In 1921, the National Conference on State Parks (NCSP) was convened in Des Moines, Iowa. The successful meeting laid the groundwork for its perpetuation with an executive committee. With her interest in social welfare, planning, roadside beautification, and conservation, Pearl was determined to get involved with the California state park movement. Nepotism helped. Pearl was slightly in awe of Stephen Mather, who she knew over a long period before his death in 1930. A native Californian and alumnus of UC Berkeley, graduating in 1887, Mather moved to New York and became a wealthy businessman after founding a borax mining company. With financial independence, he was able to pursue personal projects, most notably working to preserve US parkland. After lobbying for a bureau to operate the national parks, he was appointed the first director of the NPS in April 1917.

During his career he moulded the NPS into one of the most respected and prestigious arms of the federal government. Like Pearl's father, Mather came from a solid New England family and suffered from periodic bouts of depression. When he retired for health reasons from the NPS in 1928, Pearl wrote, "I hope you realize that you have held a unique position among the many in government service and that your contribution to the development of the national parks in their preservation and to the health and pleasure of our people has been a real contribution to American life." She concluded by remarking, "I am delighted that Mr. Albright is able and that his long experience with you has been recognized."[24]

The following year, Horace Albright succeeded Mather as the second director of the National Park Service. Pearl had known Albright and his wife, Grace Noble, from UC Berkeley. They were in the class of 1912 with Harold Chase, where they were universally popular and very much alike. In fact, it was often hard to talk about Horace without mentioning Grace. Over a fifty-year correspondence, many of Pearl's letters are addressed to both. Where Mather had a talent as a promoter, Albright was a gifted organizer. He could not boast the charisma or sheer physical energy of Mather, but he "possessed extraordinary personal charm as well as a rare political sensitivity. He could coax and persuade and manoeuvre with the most accomplished politicians in the nation's capital. Most of all, he attempted to carry out the preservationist policies that he and Mather had pioneered."[25] Pearl once remarked:

76. Horace Albright

> Horace, I think, is the friendliest man I know. He writes more people with more kindly goodwill and spirit than anybody I know. He's written thousands of letters to thousands of people through the years both in his official and in his industrial career. And in his later years, as he has represented or been asked to represent corporations and foundations and so forth, his good judgment, his reasonableness, his concern for others has been outstanding.[26]

Spotting her enthusiasm for the park movement and her talent for California roadside beautification, in 1928, Pearl was invited by Mather and Albright to serve informally as an advisor on NPS matters in the development and growth of the state park system. By 1925, the number of California state parks had grown to nearly five; however, these parks were managed by independent boards and commissions with no fundamental policy to govern their administration or creation. A unifying system was needed to oversee park acquisition and management. Save the Redwoods League (STRL), established with the goal of protecting and restoring redwood forests by purchasing groves and creating parks in 1918 by John C. Merriam, Madison Grant, and Henry Fairfield Osborn, established a California State Parks Committee to advocate for legislation for a comprehensive state park system in 1927. The legislative campaign was directed by Newton Drury.

Drury, like Albright, was a native Californian from the Berkeley class of 1912 and on close personal terms with Pearl and Harold. A highly motivated, bright entrepreneur and future fourth National Park Service director, Drury was known for his "impeccable character, his consistency, humility, and reasonableness."[27] With a background in advertising and public relations, in 1919 he was appointed executive secretary of the Save the Redwoods League.

In 1927, the formation of a single State Park Commission to administer a unified park system was signed into law. At the same time, plans were made for submission to the voters of a $6 million bond to provide funds for park acquisitions and a survey of

77. Newton Drury

potential park sites by Frederick Law Olmsted, Jr. It was no coincidence that in 1928, when the State Park Commission was promoting the State Park Bond Act, the NCSP convened in Berkeley for its annual meeting. Endorsing both the campaign and the meeting, which she was invited to attend, Pearl rallied the women's clubs in Santa Barbara to give their support. Writing to Duncan McDuffie, a distinguished and eloquent real estate developer who was influential in shaping the city of Berkeley and later served as president of the Sierra Club, Pearl suggested he might consider including the restriction of outdoor advertising on state and national highways leading to state as well as national parks to be put on the agenda.[28] She also wrote to Newton Drury ahead of the conference, offering to:

> [...] be of help in preparing material or at the registration desk. I have had doubtful pleasure in managing several convention headquarters and thought that an extra hand might be useful at the last. Unfortunately, I'm not a typist so don't count on me for that kind of work.[29]

Drury agreed, and later recalled the event praising Pearl "who's still going strong as a promoter of good works, national, state and Santa Barbara-an."[30]

With her influential network and recognized expertise, in 1929, Mather, then chairman, appointed Pearl director of the NCSP. The

78. Duncan McDuffie

delegates of the NCSP were truly eclectic, which was the source of its strength.[31] In the decade following the initial meeting of minds in 1921, the NCSP "emerged as the most important forum for debating ideological as well as administrative issues of Park development and management. It provided a broader framework for discussion than other organizations concerned with Park systems at the time."[32] Like the National Parks, preserving natural scenery and providing for outdoor recreation became the agreed-upon function of the state parks. "By allowing the definition of a state park to remain fluid and expansive, by elevating scenic quality to the status of natural resource and by arguing that the threats posed by outdoor recreational use could be curbed through educational campaigns and programs, differences of opinions were smoothed over."[33,34]

Pearl made a point of attending their annual meetings and on several occasions visited the parks by car with fellow member Harlean James, who became a lifelong friend. James believed passionately in preserving America's parks along the lines advocated by John Muir. In the retrospect of her 240-page book *Romance of the National Parks*, published in 1939, using the language of genteel conservation, she remarked:

> Looking backward over our journeys in the national parks and monuments, we can hardly forget that great elation of spirit

> which crowned our views of untamed natural beauty—that mastery of ego and transcendence of self which found us high on the mountain tops. We came face to face with the mighty living glaciers which are still grinding away at their assigned task. We took to heart the thought that the stars in their courses have achieved a speed and direction that make man-made aircraft seem like silly children's toys. We marvelled at the ingenuity of Nature in fashioning mountains, valleys, and streams, in husbanding forests, shrubs, and flowers, with their infinite variety of form and color. We thanked "whatever gods there be" for the birds and the beasts that we had seen, for it would be a sorry, silent world if mankind were here alone.[35]

It is easy to imagine Pearl sitting with James, in their car, reflecting on such beauty.

In the late 1930s, the NCSP changed its governing structure to provide for broader participation in the decision-making process.[36] A revised version of its objectives narrowed its scope to serve primarily an educational rather than a lobbying purpose.[37] The makeover of the NCSP in such fundamental ways was a consequence of Mather's death in 1930, but also a reflection of the people involved. In the early years the organization was dominated by prominent, well-connected, civic-minded citizens who saw the organization as an opportunity to provide a specific public service. Many of them, like Mather, were people of independent means who could pay their own way and help out if needed. Over time, the leadership, as well as the rank-and-file membership, adopted a less patrician and more plebeian attitude. Dominated by many state park officials actually concerned with the administration of state parks as going concerns, the NCSP seemed to lose touch with the lofty purpose with which it was born and focused instead on influencing the state park movement.

CHAPTER 14

The Garden Clubs and Conservation

As important as the state park movement was in influencing Pearl's conservation ethic and work, so, too, were the garden clubs. Establishing conservation as a national priority during the progressive era, the garden clubs had counted locally influential women among the majority of their members. "Besides contributing to environmental aesthetics," women garden club members promoted the belief that they could and should work "with nature for future generations."[1]

In 1926, Pearl joined the Garden Club of Santa Barbara and Montecito (GCSB&M), where she found a network of enthusiastic women eager to promote conservation. Water, drought, and the effect on plant material was a recurring threat to Santa Barbara's environment and beauty. Despite not becoming chairperson, Pearl is remembered by the club as "a key figure in the drive to beautify Santa Barbara through tree planting on city streets."[2]

Later, in 1931, such was Pearl's growing reputation in the clubs that Jean McDuffie, wife of Duncan and noted conservationist, member of the GCA, Save the Redwoods, and Sierra Club, recommended Pearl as an advisor to Elvenia Slosson, who was then organizing the California Garden Club Federation (CGCF; now California Garden Clubs, Inc.). Slosson, heiress to the Casper Lumber Company in Mendocino County, CA, was born in San Francisco and was a young woman when she married prominent Los Angeles lawyer Leonard B. Slosson. Ill-prepared for public life and working with women, she was reportedly not easy to work with, but she was committed to creating a strong organization. She was very creative, with a great amount of talent for writing and editing.[3]

Pearl was impressed by both Slosson and her club. At the organizational meeting on December 5, 1931, the GCSB&M joined the Federation along with twenty-two other charter members. The P&P was also granted membership because, as Pearl remarked, Slosson decided that their "peculiar kind of organization, which was not a club and didn't hold meetings for members and so forth, was eligible."[4,5]

The Garden Club of America (GCA), a national group organized in 1913, brought together garden clubs in a similar fashion to the General Federation of Women's Clubs.[6] Its mission statement specifically included conservation concerns. As the GCA developed its conservation credentials, a debate developed as to whether the group should continue to pursue horticulture "as a 'fine art,'" or to "step out into the realm of civic achievement."[7] The final agreed-upon decision was that "clubs should be at liberty to determine the needs of their own 'backyards' and act accordingly."[8,9]

The Garden Club of Santa Barbara joined the GCA in 1918 and Pearl, through the P&P, joined the GCA in 1924. Two years later, she helped organize and host the annual meeting in Santa Barbara with ninety-three delegates from the East Coast. She was invited by the GCA to join their conservation committee in 1929. She immediately read up on what they were doing and noticed that, in another community, a garden club was having a Conservation Week sponsored by the Parent-Teacher Association (PTA) and the Local Federation of Garden Clubs as part of an educational program. *Why not try it in Santa Barbara?* she thought.

In 1933, while advising a state committee on forest fire prevention for the California Chamber of Commerce, Pearl mentioned her idea of sponsoring an annual Conservation Week and was promptly asked by the state Chamber of Commerce to organize the event for California. A number of factors made this idea timely. Californians, inspired largely by the climate, had an intensified relationship to the environment and life in the outdoors; a love of nature was a common, shared characteristic. There was a vast number of enthusiastic supporters of an annual conservation program, many who were already practicing conservation and just needed a little prodding.

At the onset of the Great Depression, in response to soil erosion, dust storms, and flooding disasters, a new approach to conservation and the daily lives of Americans was initiated in the US, and supported by the president himself. As described by the National Parks Service:

> On April 5, 1933, one month after Franklin D. Roosevelt became President, he signed Executive Order 6101 (Emergency Conservation Work Act) creating the Civilian Conservation Corps (CCC). This act addressed two pressing needs, unemployment, and the repair of environmental damage, with one of the most successful New Deal programs. Employing three million men over nine years, the CCC played a critical role in FDR's strategy to conserve land and natural resources and raise public awareness of the outdoors and the importance of natural resource preservation.[10]

This program, combined with FDR's personal enthusiasm for conservation, laid a firm foundation for protecting the nation's natural bounty. The extent of the conservation projects carried on during the New Deal was more far-reaching than anything attempted before. Soil erosion control, water conservation, the preservation of wildlife, and other environmental protection activities became a part of the everyday life and activities of American citizens.[11] The importance of the work was new and inspiring.[12]

Pearl's offer from the state Chamber of Commerce to organize a California conservation week was a case in point. Interestingly, she declined, telling the Chamber that she wanted to try it first in Santa Barbara County. She later remarked that Santa Barbara was an excellent demonstration area "where you [were] able to experiment with samples of almost every governmental agency and people who respond to stimulus in many directions. We could move ahead, and we could move ahead faster. We could experiment more readily than most communities."[13]

It was while experimenting in this field of conservation that Pearl came up with a simple dictum to encapsulate the work: "Many new things in this fast-moving age make it difficult to keep pace with an ever-changing world. Let us communicate, cooperate and coordinate our efforts for good freely."[14] In the years ahead she applied the "three Cs" in all her projects.

Since Pearl had already worked in one capacity or another with all the agencies identified with conservation activities in the county, it was not necessary to set up new machinery. Acting as a bridge between the professional scientific conservation world and the grassroots networks of women's clubs and other civic organizations, she ably coordinated the work. Working out of the P&P office at 912 Santa Barbara Street, she enlisted the support of Jane Manning, a Montecito resident involved in women's club work, for additional secretarial help. Her calendar soon filled with appointments for every day of the year. Once established, the office produced an enormous correspondence and approximately one hundred and twenty-five thousand conservation leaflets were sent out each year to schools and public and private agencies.[15] Working on a limited budget, Pearl raised funds in from private individuals and companies; she thought they should appeal to those "who had made money from natural resources."[16]

Pearl had known Manning since the mid-1920s and found her "energetic, a very spontaneous, enthusiastic kind of person." In fact, she never drew breath: "She just bubbled."[17] She also never finished a paragraph in writing, which left that responsibility to Pearl. Pearl preferred to write and speak about conservation in scientific and civic terms. She rarely used the language of maternalism, because it

Plate 1. Bird's-eye view of Santa Barbara, 1877. The town was still largely undeveloped when Pearl's mother Nina visited in 1885.

Plate 2. Aerial view of Santa Barbara today. For its mild climate and enchanting location, the city has won the well-deserved recognition as "The American Riviera." 'No one person in the 20th century transformed the style and character of Santa Barbara more than Miss Chase'.

Plate 3. Pearl was an outgoing and popular student. She was also captain (1904) of a winning Santa Barbara High School basketball team.

Plate 4. Pearl had a very definite vision. It took root in 1907 when she returned to Santa Barbara from Berkeley and felt ashamed of Santa Barbara's shabby buildings, dusty streets, and lack of landscaping. Then and there she resolved to dedicate herself to making Santa Barbara a more beautiful place to live in. This page from her Berkeley scrapbook for 1907 sums it up in memorabilia.

Plate 5. The Pilgrimage. Pearl (fourth row back from front) and her 'Pilgrim' colleagues during Commencement week, May 11, 1909. In keeping with tradition, dressing in white, carrying parasols and bedecked with their class colors, they preceded through the Berkeley campus.

Plate 6. Las Terrasas, Hope Ranch, which belonged to Pearl's brother Harold, was one of the numerous gardens in the locality which Pearl was able to visit with her garden tours. Such was the success of the tours that they became an annual event, enabling Pearl to bring in tourists, school clubs and convention groups. They ran for nearly fifty years.

Plate 7. Up until her seventies Pearl was pursued by many men. John Uno Sebenius pictured here with Pearl c.1930 was a Swedish mining engineer and widower who lived in Duluth, MN. She never married. Her dedication to and love for Santa Barbara satisfied her more than any lover could.

Plate 8. Pearl took this picture of the White House during her first visit to Washington in 1930 for the conference on Child Health and Protection.

Plate 9. Standing in front of the ruins of the Residence Buildings at La Purísima Mission during the early planning phase pre- reconstruction, 1935. From left: L. Deming Tilton (Advisory Committee and Santa Barbara County Planning Commission), Russell Ewing (National Park Service Regional Historian), Daniel R. Hull (National Park Service Chief Landscape Architect for the State of California), Charles Wing (National Park Service Engineer in Charge of Federal Projects in State Parks), Pearl Chase, Ed Rowe (landscape architect and La Purísima Camp SP- 29 Landscape Foreman), Guy Fleming (District Superintendent for the Southern California State Park System), Kelly Hardenbrook (Advisory Committee and Lompoc Attorney). Pearl cared deeply about America's historic preservation. For over 35 years she served on the Advisory Committee as a member and for a while as Chairman.

Plate 10. Pearl loved to dress up for the Santa Barbara Old Spanish Days Fiesta. In the early years of the fiesta she organized and ran the Fruit and Flower Market along with a group of volunteer hostesses.

tended to lead to male accusations that women in conservation were "sentimental" and "unprofessional."

To Pearl, "conservation" was a broad term with as many different points of view on policies and practices as there were people.[18] She appreciated that each individual had a unique experience of nature. With this attitude to guide her, she herself chose to focus on the connection between nature, health, and education. She defined this complex and multifaceted subject as "an attitude of mind and a way of living."[19,20]

Conservation, she believed, could be achieved by practicing "outdoor good manners" to preserve and protect the nation's natural resources. Developing her awareness of conservation during the progressive era, she was neither a purist in the way Muir was, nor a utilitarian conservationist like Pinchot. Like Mather and Albright, she wrote and lectured on both approaches to conservation. Balanced conservation programs, she believed, "required continuous research, cooperative planning and concerted action."[21] As she wrote in 1940 to Bertram D. Blyth:

> Nature seems to hand out her gifts of good and evil quite impartially and even with the experts making endless charts which picture this and that cycle, we seem to disregard warnings and do things where and how we please. That's why this job of mine, promoting conservation education in California, seems endless and hopeful only to the extent that the new generation is being taught what the word means. While we were not trying particularly to bring home to the people what particular stake they have in the state's natural resources it is surprising how astonished some of the men and women are when they begin to figure the origin of their income and discover that it depends upon the exploitation of natural resources. We hope they will try to learn how the supply can be maintained and waste reduced so that incomes may be maintained.[22]

Her connection to California, in particular, was apparent throughout her life and work. "No state has more to preserve, more to develop, more to enjoy than California. Let us all preach and practice conservation," she proclaimed.[23] And in order to successfully improve this practice, under a democratic form of government, knowledge about conservation would best be disseminated through the process of education:

> Education is most fully useful to the man whom it has prepared to understand his environment and to live in it most happily and successfully. Such preparation can best be accomplished by centering our attention more directly on the vital problems which determine the degree of prosperity, growth and development of the community, state and nation and to the health and recreation of our citizens. This is conservation education.[24]

But this education she believed, had not kept pace with the social changes of the era. Most educators and politicians were lagging far behind public thinking on conservation and had been preoccupied with other issues considered more urgent. To be effective, conservation education needed to be adequately funded, provisioned, and taught with skill and understanding. In Pearl's view, the appointment of someone to coordinate the conservation education in the schools was an ideal worth working toward.[25]

In 1934, while organizing Santa Barbara Conservation Week, Pearl and Manning secured the cooperation of schools and individuals in formulating plans to stimulate and produce a permanent educational program for the conservation of natural resources and arouse public interest in natural landscape preservation. Every agency at the federal, state, and local level concerned with education or having an interest in the out-of-doors was invited to send a representative to outline what could be done yearly within the county to encourage conservation.[26] No agency invited to participate was "asked to go outside of its regular function, but each was urged to discover ways and means whereby those functions could be increased and to discover what contributions it could make within those functions."[27] With such a broad scope, it also appealed to all types of civic organizations and individuals interested in any phase of conservation.[28]

With the slogan "Practice Conservation Every Day" chosen, the campaign got off to a vigorous start. Pearl organized essay contests, public meetings with guest speakers, field trips, a fifteen-minute radio program with music each day, and articles in the local press. Aside from Pearl and Manning, several members of the community took a large share of the responsibility for coordinating hundreds of volunteers.[29] From the very onset, the way Pearl and her fellow workers went into action and the methods by which the forces were lined up for conservation across Santa Barbara County were of interest to people all over the country, in what one journalist termed "a second pioneering."[30]

79. CalCC leaflet

Leadership for conservation education came from many sources and organizations, governmental and private agencies, and associations outside of the schools, including the soil and water conservation districts, wildlife federation, and sportsmen's clubs. All these different agencies agreed to increase the conservation activities within their own organizations, to cooperate to the fullest with other agencies, and to use Conservation Week as a means of rousing public interest with entertaining and educational exhibits. Thus, an organizational wheel was set in motion, every agency a spoke in that wheel, turning about a common purpose.[31] The success of Conservation Week was clearly apparent in the elementary schools, where it not only appealed to the teachers but was also found to assist in integrating conservation into every kind of class.

Owing to its success, in 1934, Pearl decided she would expand the campaign on a statewide basis. She approached Helen Heffernan, thirty-eight-year-old Chief of the California state division of elementary education. Pearl regarded this progressive educator, who was a disciple of the educational reformer John Dewey, as "a superb woman, a brilliant woman."[32,33] At the Department of Education Heffernan reported to Vierling Kersey, State Superintendent of Schools, a Republican "fireball among educators, a man who bubbled in a hyphenated language of his own."[34] At the time, although he was her immediate superior, she had almost complete autonomy of the 780,000 children in 4,025 elementary schools taught by 24,000 teachers.[35] She was also in command of the state Curriculum Commission, a group made up of teachers from all backgrounds and fields which chose all the texts for the elementary schools.

Heffernan was fully committed to the idea that the school should observe and guide students' behaviour. Basic to her vision for education was a belief that all children were capable of becoming responsible citizens who would recognize the truth if their natural rationality was encouraged and allowed to flourish in publicly supported schools.[36] As a potent conservationist, she also believed in the importance of conservation education and that schools could do more to foster civic interest.[37]

After visiting Santa Barbara and meeting Pearl in 1934, Heffernan became one of the most active advocates for her work, rallying teachers to the cause. One of their findings was that most teachers in California, save for those in Los Angeles, had very little conservation education. They also learned there was scarce material for teachers to use in making conservation education as exciting, interesting, and valuable as they wished to.[38] Later in the year, in August, Pearl and Manning continued the expansion of their Conservation Week and organized a two-week nature camp in collaboration with the Santa Barbara Botanic Garden, state teachers' college, Santa Barbara Woman's Club, Garden Club, and the Museum of Natural History at Rocky Nook Park: "Camper tents, administration tents and class-room tents sprouted like mushrooms underneath the oaks."[39] Instruction was as informal as possible and consisted largely of field exploration under guidance supplemented by lectures conferences and reading.[40] The first opportunity for enrolment was given to teachers of public, private, and parochial schools of the city and county.[41,42,43]

A few months earlier, on April 16, 1934, Pearl and her colleagues agreed to establish a California-wide conservation organization to administer Conservation Week and to encourage education and activities on a year-round basis. Plans for this citizen group were completed six months later at a board meeting in San Francisco, and the name California Conservation Council (CalCC) was adopted on November 15, 1935. The CalCC had no precedent. To have reorganized Conservation Week on a statewide basis, established the two-week nature camp, and formed the CalCC, in six months while overseeing her other civic commitments with P&P—including roadside beautification, a county clean-up campaign, and her continued work with Better Homes in America—was nothing short of remarkable.

80. CalCC logo

The council was nonprofit and the work was entirely voluntary; membership was open to anyone with an interest in conservation and the fees began as low as $1. It did not aim at lobbying legislative action. Composed of government agencies; educational and scientific associations; civic, recreation, and sportsmen groups; and those organized for direct action, it is apparent why the council could not claim—and did not try—to represent the opinion of its co-operators in legislative matters. Neither its officers nor its committees could endorse or propose legislation in its name. It was, however, the council's policy to encourage, in every possible way, the understanding, observance, and fair enforcement of protective laws and regulations. Pearl believed "popular education should always follow the law-making function."[44]

The organization was quite simple, and its officers and committee members read like the who's who of California conservationists. Pearl thought it would be "nice and proper" that the incumbent state governor should act as honorary chairman of the Conservation Week Committee,[45] and, in connection with this, make an annual proclamation to encourage observance. In 1935, Frank Merriam, the Republican governor who defeated Democrat Upton Sinclair in the famously controversial 1934 gubernatorial election, accepted the role. In these early years, the CalCC would receive "quite a grandiose proclamation, complete with the state seal in gold and red ribbon."[46,47]

The executive committee included the officers and chairman, vice-chairman, and secretaries. A distinguished group of counsellors from diverse fields with an interest in conservation added further expertise and experience. Honorary president of the council was John C. Merriam, a UC-trained palaeontologist, educator, cofounder of Save the Redwoods League, president of the Carnegie Institute in Washington, and cautious political supporter of eugenics. Pearl regarded him as "a very brilliant person."[48]

Pearl appointed herself as president, a position she held for seventeen years until 1951.[49] As the influence of the council rapidly expanded in response to the government's demand for more intensive conservation education program promotion, so Pearl introduced new committees to assist her. In 1940, over 5,000 people were involved in the annual campaign.

In its first few years, the council organized conferences and meetings across the state, proving to be a successful way to reach new audiences, and published bulletins and leaflets on subjects to encourage schools in conservation best practices.[50] The majority of Pearl's time was devoted to preparing these, which she co-authored with field experts. She was able to reach a far wider audience in creating and distributing these publications than by other means.

It is difficult to measure the success of Pearl's work for conservation education except to show that each year following 1934 saw an increasing demand for her services as schools across California grew conscious of the need for and importance of conservation.[51] So notable was her achievement in the elementary schools that in December of 1940, she directed and co-authored the publication of "California's Natural Wealth: A Conservation Guide for Secondary Schools" for the California Department of Education. Embodying twelve key conservation objectives, this 124-page book was the first conservation guide of its kind in California,[52] compiled and paid for by the CalCC. Newton Drury, Director of State Parks, thought Pearl had "done an excellent job."[53]

"Environmental education," as it is called today, includes many educational approaches that were important aspects of conservation

81. Pearl's conservation guide for secondary schools

education in the early twentieth century: learning by doing, life-long learning, and many integrated and interdisciplinary efforts. Among her many collaborations, one Pearl was especially proud of was with the Soil Erosion Service (SES). She visited Washington, DC in 1933, just as Roosevelt had established the SES. As she later recounted, "To my horror they didn't have a single piece of literature. You went into this small office where this department-to-be was starting, and so when I came home I went to call on a man of national, international reputation who lived in Mission Canyon."[54]

Professor Frederic Clements was an American plant ecologist and pioneer in the study of vegetation succession who had settled in Santa Barbara. Visiting Clements's home and introducing herself, Pearl explained to him what she had seen in Washington:

> "People don't know what erosion is. They don't know what the word means. [...] I wish that you would write the ABCs of soil erosion," and he laughed at me and said, "That's a good idea." And he began ringing a bell calling his wife. She came in with a little startled look from the kitchen and said, "Well,

> Fred, what's the matter?" And he said, "Humph," and he was laughing. He said, "You know, you and everybody else says that I can't write or speak except in words of five syllables, but Pearl has asked me to write 'the ABCs of Soil Erosion.'"[55]

Clements agreed, and shortly afterward they presented the leaflet to the SES for its use.

The California Conservation Council's work was so readily accepted by federal and state agencies because it provided them with an audience they could not possibly create. Publicity was key to her campaign and her efforts received the widespread attention of newspapers across the state. As a reporter at the time noted:

> At the risk of diffusion, they have deliberately adopted the broad program. One object is to teach good manners and good conservation habits which will persist throughout the year, so that when a citizen goes into the woods or the country he will not be a menace. Thus, he becomes a conservationist by habit. So much progress along this line has been made that if a Sunday vandal was seen carrying on his car a stalk of the desert yucca blossoms, once a common sight, today he would be hooted to scorn for stealing one of the "Candles of the Lord."[56]

> Pearl thrived with CalCC because it brought her into contact with many individuals who were helpful and attracted to her work. Most of the experts and government officials at the time were men; Pearl was not concerned that the accomplishments and ideologies of these men were given more emphasis than women leaders, but she hoped that more women leaders would come through. While these men surely deserve great credit, not one of them created the conservation movement single-handedly, and it required the work of many to continue it.

Notably, between its inaugural awarding in 1928 and 1940, there were only four women among the thirty-nine recipients of the Pugsley Medal, an award given in recognition of contributions to the

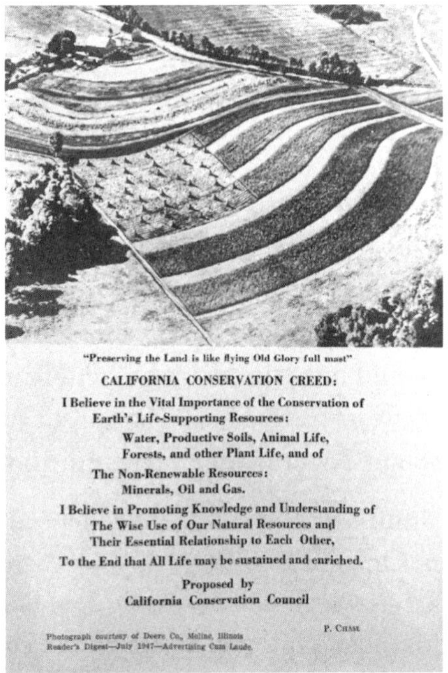

82. CalCC creed

promotion and development of parks and conservation. Pearl later elaborated on her experience in the male-dominated field, saying, "I've had to adapt, while I've been trying to educate. I have also learned not to build castles in the sand, and you go home for supper and come back the next morning and the high tide has washed out your castle."[57] While her strength lay in knowing her own mind, she also had the support of many female colleagues. Her letters to these women reveal she enjoyed the challenge and the bond it created among women, remarking on one occasion to Helen Heffernan that "life and living is still pretty exciting for us both. It would be good to exchange ideas about men and manners again."[58]

As her biographer, I am also struck by the important influence UC Berkeley had on Pearl's conservation knowledge and work in these years. As a member of the university alumni association and colleague of many of the professors, Pearl remained intimately connected to her alma mater. She believed the university was their "greatest instrument for research, education, and action in conservation fields." Many others agreed. Newton Drury once remarked, "I look upon the University of California as *the* national park university. I know Horace Albright feels the same way, and so did Stephen T. Mather."[59]

UC Berkeley had a long tradition of cooperation within conservation fields. As previously mentioned, in 1915, Stephen T. Mather and Horace M. Albright gathered a group of students at UC Berkeley to plot a future for the country's existing and evolving national parks. The result was legislation establishing the National Park Service in 1916.[60] UC Berkeley continued to put its stamp on the direction of the country's parks at national and state level. Professors Joseph Grinnell and Joseph Le Conte led early research on Yosemite's natural history, trained the first cohorts of National Park Service biologists, and connected generations of students with the parks. Ansel Franklin Hall earned a bachelor's degree in forestry from UC Berkeley in 1917. Joining the NPS, he rose through the ranks, becoming Chief Naturalist, Senior Naturalist, and Chief Forester, the first to hold that position. Working out of the NPS educational headquarters at 213 Hilgard Hall, he dispensed advice to state and local park agencies. Berkeley alumnus George Melendez Wright "started the Park Service's wildlife division with his own funds," and for many years shared an office with NPS officials on the top floor of Hilgard Hall, in what is now the Rausser College of Natural Resources.[61]

Forestry education began at Berkeley in 1914. A department of forestry was established in 1939, and seven years later in 1946, the School of Forestry as a division of the College of Agriculture began operating out of a newly constructed building. It was later named after the school's first dean, Walter Mulford, who was renowned for having been the first state forester in the nation. Under Mulford's guidance, the school "established close ties with members of the US Forest Service in California. They consulted with him and sought his recommendations on graduates suited for public service. He lived to see expansion of forestry to all regions of the United States."[62] Nearly thirty years later in 1974, the school became part of the College of Natural Resources and is now in place as the forest science division of the college's interdisciplinary Department of Environmental Science, Policy and Management.[63]

Pearl knew many of these individuals not just by name, but personally by spending time visiting them on campus. In contrast to many of the businessmen she knew and worked with in Santa Barbara, she found those in conservation especially rewarding to be with:

> It's been a great pleasure to meet these men because one of the satisfactions of working with conservationists is that they are, on the whole, a pretty grand bunch of people. In the federal services, in the early days, in the state too, the men were dedicated. They usually were not getting as much as they could get for similar exertion and knowledge and experience, but they were doing it for their country. And I found that a characteristic all these years, it's been an enriching experience to talk to, be with, and learn from these kind of persons. They were the kind of persons we meet in the conservation field, not most of them scientific specialists. They are on the whole activists. They have to do something right away with the things they know. They're experimenting both with the land, our resources and with people.[64]

CHAPTER 15

Native American Protection

Pearl's conservation efforts were not only directed at modern America's "tradition of waste", but also toward the protection of Native Americans. They were the primeval users, shapers, and stewards of the land; as described by Carolyn Merchant in *American Environmental History*, "They developed varied and sophisticated technologies for obtaining sustenance, patterns of reciprocal trade, modes of tribal governance and interpretations of the natural and human worlds. They responded to environmental catastrophes, invasions by outsiders and introductions of new technologies, diseases, and ideas through social reorganization, migration to new environments or in some cases social collapse."[1] Pearl was fascinated by these rich and differing modes of living on the land and responding to outside influences.

Pearl's initiation into the Native American reform movement came in 1923 through her connection with the Women's Club movement, which had made it their own cause. She was stirred up by the Teapot Dome bribery scandal[2] and the Bursum Bill, which confirmed white encroachment on Indigenous lands in New Mexico.[3] At the time, the Indian Bureau was persevering with its effort to destroy Indian cultures, started in 1887 with the Dawes Severalty Act.[4] Albert Fall, Secretary of the Interior, made no attempt to change this policy.[5] Condemnation of this measure and the men who proposed it spread nationwide. The campaign succeeded and the bill was turned down in Congress.[6] Leading the fight were voluntary welfare and defense associations who spearheaded humanitarian reform efforts characteristic of the progressive movement. The most aggressive and vigilant of these groups was the American Indian Defense Association (AIDA).

It was the energy, vision, and intelligence of John Collier that guided this national citizens' association for over a decade.[7,8] Educated at Columbia University and at the College de France in Paris, he developed a social philosophy that would shape his later work on behalf of the Native Americans. He believed society was becoming too individualistic, and that American culture needed to re-establish a sense of community and responsibility. Moving to California in 1919, where he worked as state director of adult education, he found his calling among the Native American Pueblos in New Mexico.[9]

Captivated by the Indian way of life, he was persuaded that the integrated social organizations at the pueblo offered an example of community life that he had not found anywhere else. These Indians maintained the attribute, lost in the white world, of communal and cooperative experience. He concluded the pueblo culture offered a model for the redemption of American society, because it concerned

83. John Collier and 2 children

itself very little with the material aspects of life. Convinced that culture was more "important than politics as a method of providing social cohesion and unity," he began a crusade to protect tribal institutions and property rights.[10]

Collier was described as "a small, stoop-shouldered man who wore glasses and kept his blond hair long and unbrushed. Smoking a corncob pipe, some of his contemporaries described him as a country storekeeper closing out the week's accounts."[11] Despite his unconventional appearance, he was quite clear about what he wanted to achieve. Hoping that he might be able to get the support of the GFWC, in November 1921 he met Stella Atwood, a fellow cultural relativist and chairman of the GFWC's Indian Welfare Committee. Her sense of humor rarely failed and she was known for her perfect comradeship, as well as being strongly influenced by the work of Helen Hunt Jackson and her book *Ramona*. Directly challenging the assimilationist approach favored by many of her GFWC colleagues, Atwood "immersed herself in the study of past legal cases involving injustices suffered by Native Americans."[12] Seeing the potential for widespread national support from more than two million newly enfranchised women voters, she convinced the executive board of the GFWC to put Indian reforms on the agenda for the annual national meeting.

With the support of the GFWC now behind his cause, in order to provide legal representation to Native Americans and promote Native American cultural autonomy at state and national levels, John Collier and a group of social scientists and writers formed the AIDA in New York on May 7, 1923.[13]

Starting in the Victorian era many Santa Barbarans revered something they called "spiritual value," which was connected in part to the Native American traditions of the Chumash, who inhabited the region long before it was settled by Spanish Missionaries. As Pearl's awareness in Indian affairs took root, she found many of her colleagues were supportive of her views. In June 1923, she helped organize a conference, sponsored by the League of the Southwest, on the Indian concerns in Santa Barbara.[14] With her many connections across the state, through the social welfare conference and her work with the Community Arts Association, Pearl invited John Collier, Mary Austin, and Walter Woehike, the pro-Indian campaign editor of the *Sunset* magazine, to speak.

During the conference, an "unusual and colorful ritual took place on the city's beach." As detailed by Robert Mullins in "Santa Barbara and American Indian Reform:"

> Two Indian representatives of the Pueblo tribes knelt in the California sand and spoke out in an ancient prayer to their mother ocean. Dressed in ceremonial tribal robes, the men, a Navajo Chief and a medicine man, offered a potion of crushed turquoise shells, flower pollen, and corn to the waters of the Pacific, and asked for good rains and a full harvest for their lands in Arizona and New Mexico. A crowd of several hundred spectators gathered on the surrounding cliffs to observe in wonder the ceremony on the shore below. After the prayer and offering, the Indians joined many of those in the crowd.[15]

The primary aim of the Indians was not to visit California in order to pray to the Pacific Ocean; they were in Santa Barbara to present their peoples' side in the controversy raging in New Mexico and Washington, DC. They "had unexpected success in Santa Barbara as their short prayer was symbolically answered."[16]

During the conference, "approximately 135 people expressed an interest in becoming members of the proposed Santa Barbara branch of the Indian Defense Association (SBIDA)."[17,18] In the same month, AIDA branches were formed in Los Angeles and San Francisco, establishing the west coast as a leader in the movement. Collier was delighted with Pearl's commitment and organizational skills, thanking her for taking the "initiative in working for Indians."[19] Atwood also congratulated Pearl for doing "a big thing for the Indian cause," and invited her to act as an advisor to the AIDA. "The time for action," Atwood wrote, "would be during the next session of congress when critical legislation would be discussed;" it would then be necessary "to pull every wire and use every bit of influence as possible."[20]

Finalizing the constitution and bylaws of the new branch, within days of the conference, Pearl held the first SBIDA meeting on June 19. The aims of the organization were to secure, for all Indians, the right to land, legal protection, health protection, modern education, and liberty of conscience.[21]

A few months after this first meeting, Pearl visited the Pueblo country of New Mexico herself. Meeting them in person, her interest in the cause of the Native American people was transformed.[22] Like Collier, she believed in securing them just treatment from the government and an end to the allotment and reservation policies. She also believed in defending Indian religious freedom and preserving their land and resource rights. Pluralism, not assimilation, characterized the approach taken by Pearl and her colleagues in the AIDA. Such a view was not only at odds with government officials but also with other conservative reform groups such as the Indian Rights Association, which advocated for the total assimilation of Indians to white American culture as the only hope for Indian survival.[23]

This middle ground taken by Pearl and her colleagues afforded Native Americans a greater degree of self-determination as a people and as citizens of the United States. Taking aim at the government she, and her colleagues, maintained that: "The property, not the person, of the Indian has inevitably been foremost in the Interior Department's consideration, and the *holding* or *transfer* of this property has taken precedence over any concern about the *development* of the property as an estate held in permanent trust."[24] The Bureau of Indian Affairs, they argued, had failed the Indian in nearly every detail of its policy and should be disbanded. "Public opinion must be activated and swung in favor of the Indian and against those who would destroy Indian culture for personal greed," Mullins details. "This was to be the reformers' goal and reason for being as private, voluntary associations."[25]

Initiating an educational campaign to raise public awareness of Native American health, education, and welfare, on July 16, 1923, Pearl invited her friend Dr. Charles Lummis to Santa Barbara to give a talk. As the president of the Landmark's Club of Southern California, founder of the Southwest Museum in Los Angeles, and a journalist, he was known for his insatiable curiosity, blazing energy, and magnetism by way of eccentricity. He was also devoted to helping Indians having lived with them as an Indian. Pearl felt she "knew him more as an Indian than anyone else I knew. Because he accentuated their feelings, because of his sensitiveness."[26] Over the following months and years, the SBIDA presented further lectures by authorities on Indian culture and government administration, distributed pamphlets and news releases about Indian concerns, and sponsored cultural events such as the showing of Indian arts and crafts.[27]

84. Charles Lummis

Pearl continued to make further visits over what she called "Indian Country," including "a delightful motor trip" across the reservations in New Mexico with John Collier and a group in September 1927. On this trip she saw Navajo, Zuni, Hopi, and Rio Grande pueblos.[28]

> We were in conference with Government officials, irrigation engineers, settlers, attorneys, the Indians themselves, and traders, and besides this met many friends of the Indians. No one can realize how different each type is in language, religion, and customs until they have had, in rapid succession, contact with many of them. The All Pueblo Council, which I attended on September 17th, was in its way quite as interesting as an assembly of the League of Nations. There were fifty-five Indians and fourteen whites, the former speaking fourteen different tongues. All of the proceedings were in English and Spanish, occasionally with interpolations in some of the Indian tongues. The meeting lasted from ten in the morning till six at night, and was as picturesque and impressive an affair as I ever attended, particularly as a great dance, in which seventy men participated went on in an adjoining street of the pueblo, and the booming of the men's voices came to us clearly at intervals. A thunderstorm with raindrops of tremendous size punctuated the afternoon's discussion. We are hoping that the report of the Bureau of Government Research, whose survey of the Indians is being financed by the Rockefellers, will bring out many of the pitifully stupid things which the Indian Bureau continues to do. I could write pages about the educational process, which, in spite of the efforts of well-intentioned teachers, proves so destructive to health and even morals. The efforts to break down tribal customs and interfere between parents and children, and the truly deplorable health conditions, which can very largely be blamed to the Indian Bureau system simply shocks one.[29]

85. Photo taken by Pearl of Mud Dance, Red Lake
Tonalea, Arizona

With her interest in housing, it is also not surprising that she was shocked by the appalling living conditions she found on the reservations:

On general principles [*sic*] I feel it is safe to say that the housing program of the Indian Bureau is very poor in most instances, if not all. Any housing project is made chargeable against tribal funds and is usually unsuited to the local needs... In some of the Apache groups, shacks have been built and the Indians have found it more healthful and comfortable to live in a tepee beside their so-called house, except in communities such as the pueblos in New Mexico and Arizona where a traditional method of repair and upkeep has been worked out most effectively by the Indians themselves. Most of the housing that I have seen for Indians consists of:

(a) Cheap and badly constructed wooden shacks which rapidly deteriorated because no funds were available for paint and repairs and the Indians had not been trained to make them. As you know, most of the Indian men feel that the home is the woman's job and if she doesn't take care of it, nobody does. This traditional belief among many tribes is a serious handicap.

(b) In certain places which have a certain picturesqueness and charm, the Indian Bureau has encouraged and commended

86. Ed Borein, A House at Laguna

> the use of corrugated iron for the houses, and you can imagine how greatly they enhance the landscape. A good example of this is at Oribai [*sic*], one of the Hopi villages.
>
> I think it would be profitable to inquire of the Indian Bureau what its housing program is, how it has been adapted to local conditions, and what the results are.[30]

In her work and travels with him, Pearl regarded Collier as a remarkable man although she had occasional misgivings:

> He was not a good administrator. I learned a great deal from him, a most astonishingly sensitive person, a feeling for animals that was bewildering for people, and so forth, and he was brilliant.
>
> One thing that I was always coaching or scolding about, he was so brilliant he could say the same things in seven different ways. And I would say, "Now? Now?" Because if he wasn't sure that he had convinced someone, he'd go over or start over again but with a different approach, but the same darn thesis.[31]

Collier credited the California branches as being of prime importance to the success of the organizational efforts amongst the

87. Ed Borein, Return of the Trappers

Pueblo Indians of New Mexico. He acknowledged that the work undertaken by the women involved was unimpeachable. In a private letter sent to Pearl, Collier mentioned and emphasized what he considered to be the most important contribution of her branch: the financial contribution.[32,33]

With her characteristic modesty, Pearl played down the significant monetary contributions that were made possible through her connections and efforts. In her view it was "remarkable that over the years so much had been accomplished with so little money, but with so great an expenditure of time and effort by a comparatively small number of 'friends of Indians.'"[34] One of the most generous of these friends was the philanthropist and benefactor William Bingham II, who, through Pearl's efforts, donated thousands of dollars to the association.

Bingham was born in 1879 the son of Charles Bingham of Cleveland, Ohio, a wealthy businessman active in cultural institutions. Little is known about Bingham's childhood, but in 1911 he moved to Bethel, Maine, where he became a patient of Dr. John Gehring, who was well known for treating nervous disorders. Bingham was very modest in his manner and living, feared publicity, and lived very quietly. In 1916 he met Marie "Auntie" Pease, who had been a live-in nurse to Pearl and Harold when they were children living at Newton Centre. Marie became Bingham's companion, secretary, housekeeper, and, on rare occasions, his nurse. In 1919 they moved to Santa Barbara along with a small entourage, including Dr. John Gehring and his wife Marian True, a divorcee from Bethel and Boston.

Bingham and Pease rented a property owned by Harold and Pearl at 2015 Anacapa Street, opposite the Chase family home at 2012. As Pearl recalled, "Before the season was out Mr. Bingham bought the property ($5,000) and two adjacent empty lots."[35] For the five years he lived in Santa Barbara, Pearl saw Bingham every day. His decision to leave the city arose for a number of reasons but mainly because there was a tendency by Dr. Gehring to have Bingham spend more time with him, which Pease deplored. Pearl always hoped Bingham would get "interested in something that was normal and 'healthy.'[36] [...] He is very suggestible and sensitive, and I think it is too bad that so much of his attention is focused on sickness and suffering."[37] Although her concern for Bingham was heartfelt, he was, in fact, extremely successful in accomplishing what he set out to do.[38]

Collier was deeply impressed with the work of the Santa Barbara IDA chapter in defending the pueblos in the early 1920s, so much so that "even if the Association never again exerted itself, it would have made a permanent contribution to Indian well-being."[39] Through hard-fought battles he and his supporters won the trust of the pueblos.[40]

The possibility of more extensive changes in federal policies toward Native Americans appeared when FDR appointed Harold Ickes as Secretary of the Interior. In April 1933, Ickes picked Collier to be Commissioner of the Bureau of Indian Affairs (BIA). Atwood told Pearl that "surely the day of miracles is not past, for this lineup in Washington is a miracle no less. Our organization must carry on, for now of all times we can be of use to John in bringing pressure to bear on Congress."[41]

It is a testament to Pearl that the SBIDA managed to keep going at a time when its finances were strained by the Great Depression.[42] At the same time, Dr. Haven Emerson, the first director of Columbia University's Institute of Public Health and president of the board of the AIDA, suggested Pearl might accept the position of Secretary of the AIDA. As a man who was easily and "usefully irritated to action, a superb and dedicated nagger in what the public barely knew to be the public interest, and intolerant of the fuzzy-minded nitwits who spoke with authority concerning matters they did not understand," this was a compliment.[43]

Pearl, however, refused the offer: "I do not feel that I am competent or sufficiently informed to be useful to the association."[44]

As Commissioner of the BIA, Collier was able to affect many significant changes from the top.[45] The most well-known change was the Indian Reorganization Act (also called the Wheeler-Howard Act) of 1934. It was ground-breaking, as it abolished the allotment program detailed in the Dawes Act and made funds available to Native American groups for the purchase of lost tribal lands.[46] It was indeed Collier's goal "to depart from earlier attempts to replicate Anglo-American patterns and encourage a form of community self-determination that would allow Native Americans to function in the modern world while retaining traditional cultural institutions."[47]

One month after Congress enacted the Reorganization Act, Pearl joined Collier and two of his sons and their wives for a two-week visit to the pueblos in New Mexico and Arizona to win support for the IRA. Describing the experience, she found soon after her arrival at Leupp she was in a new world altogether:

> I'm in a different country all right. This is the Hopi Agency, but a Navajo Boarding School. I'm housed in a comfortable

> room with bath down the hall with hot and cold water. The only charge is a 50-cent meal. Where else could you get along for $1.50 a day? A clerk and his wife from Leupp Agency met me promptly at Winslow and after lunch motored me across the plain. We arrived about 4.45, a ninety-seven mile ride, which shows that the roads are better than they used to be. We passed Indians on horseback in covered wagons and Emergency Conservation Work trucks travelling toward Keams Canyon. The meetings are held in the school auditorium a loudspeaker device carries the voices of the speakers and interpreter to four horns sticking out of windows which—Indians and some whites sit on benches or on the ground in autos on edge of sidewalk for hours. Council meetings last from 9–12 & 2–5 or 6 and Tuesday there was an Indian meeting before and after. Last night there was an evening meeting (in the latter part whites were excluded) to discuss the selling of 100,000 goats. Most are partly agin [*sic*] it from sentimental reasons because their milk has saved bottle babies.
>
> I have been asked to take several trips but think I'll go with John. He will go to Hopi land then Gallup to Santa Fe and from there he'll fly east.[48]

Putting further pressure on Collier and the work of the AIDA for Indian reform in 1933 was an ongoing feud with the Eastern Association on Indian Affairs (EAIA). Over a number of years, the conservative leaders of the EAIA and the more radical Collier had argued in public. After Collier's appointment to the BIA, they refused their support of the new administration. Rather than work with Collier, the old guard resigned, and the EAIA was forced to find a new president. Oliver La Farge was a wealthy thirty-two-year old Harvard alumnus who worked as a writer and anthropologist.[49] Unfamiliar with the feud, keen to support Collier at the BIA, and facing a collapse in its finances, La Farge changed the EAIA's name to the National Association on Indian Affairs (NAIA) in 1933.

88. Oliver La Farge

At the same time, looking for ways to pool resources and solve organizational problems, he approached the AIDA with a proposal to consolidate their two associations. Pearl, who had assumed the role of president of the SBIDA, was strongly opposed,[50] and the proposal was dropped until the spring of 1935. At that time, La Farge approached Pearl with a fresh proposal to create a new Indian Affairs Association with appropriate funding and influential leaders. Pearl agreed in principle.[51] During the summer, both the NAIA and AIDA made formal statements of their respective positions.

Pearl and the Santa Barbara branch received these proposals with scepticism. She was "against any social welfare activity" by the new association and worried that the NAIA was not concerned with the general solution of the Native American problem.[52] "She believed that its purpose should be to use lobbying pressure, national education campaigns, and such other means as to bring about administrative and legislative improvements for the Indian."[53] Writing to Pearl the following January, La Farge declared that the NAIA "had no difference that could not be adjusted in consultation" and that he agreed to phase out their social welfare activity."[54] The letter acknowledged Pearl's influence in southern California and "the importance of California Indian reformers to the future of the new Association."[55]

In October 1936, Pearl announced the merger of the AIDA and NAIA to the branch members. It was not legally consummated until the summer of 1937, delayed due to there simply not being enough money to pay for further activity.[56] The SBIDA made one further final fundraising effort in January 1937 before holding its final meeting at the La Cumbre Country Club, then owned by Pearl's brother Harold. The birth of the Association on American Indian Affairs (AAIA) was formerly announced in June, with La Farge as president. Emerson was convinced that La Farge had the "spark and spirit" they needed;[57] Pearl was less enthusiastic.

Although Pearl felt that La Farge was "wonderful, for he certainly hasn't had the help that he needed and wanted," she never developed the same affection she held for John Collier.[58] La Farge was part of a younger generation that misunderstood the progressive spirit that Pearl and Collier emulated. Describing the early years from 1922 to 1933 "as the era of kindly paternalism with the lady-bountiful desire to do nice things for the dear Indians," he had no faith that Native Americans could retain their culture, and believed that its disappearance was inevitable.[59] This is not to say he did not admire Collier's work, but that the association had grown away from much of Collier's ideology.[60]

It was no accident that the new organization dropped the active word "defense" in the name in favour of the more neutral "American Association on Indian Affairs." As La Farge saw it, the merger represented "an absorption by the National Association (NAIA) of the Indian Defense Association (IDA)."[61] In 1946, the organization became the Association on American Indian Affairs (AAIA) because, as La Farge put it, "people began coming around to the office with problems bearing upon Hindus."[62]

Shortly after the merger, Pearl and her colleagues in the Santa Barbara group organized a southern California branch of the AAIA, with members from Ojai and Pasadena, to continue the work previously pursued by the SBIDA concerned with policy at the national level and with the public educational program affecting congressional action. Pearl joined the AAIA as one of the charter members of the board of directors, but she rarely attended its meetings in New York. The association "strove to maintain efforts to stabilize the future of the American Indian through the BIA."[63,64] Collier resigned as commissioner of Indian Affairs on January 19, 1945, after twelve years in Roosevelt's administration. Writing to her "long-time friend and co-worker," Pearl remarked:

> The years of your service as Indian Commissioner marked in California by a general improvement in the attitude of the public towards the Indians; contributing to this in a very considerable degree were the splendid exhibits at the Golden Gate Exposition at San Francisco, and the many illuminating articles in magazines on Indian affairs. The character and ability of those in executive positions in the Indian Service whom we have met have been of high quality. The provisions for road building, improved housing and soil and water conservation on many Indian lands were of benefit to many. The education of Indian children in public schools has continued satisfactorily. We all regret that the California Indian Land Claims have not been settled. We realize that the direction and support of constructive thinking and progressive action on behalf of California Indians will be necessary over a long period of years.[65]

Pearl continued as an officer, president, and fundraiser of the branch into the 1950s. At the national level, she never stopped taking an interest in Native American affairs; as an educator and reformer, she worked tirelessly in the struggle for their civil rights. In 1969, aged eighty, Pearl was involved with the controversy over water allocations to the Pyramid Lake Northern Paiutes in their reservation near Reno, Nevada, that resulted from the California-Nevada Interstate Compact, or the "Bi-State Compact."[66]

CHAPTER 16

La Purísima Mission and Historic Preservation

In 1935, with her discussions of the merger between AIDA and NAIA ongoing, Pearl started work on a new project at La Purísima Mission in Santa Barbara County, one that would create a lasting legacy and bring her into contact with the Civilian Conservation Corps and the State Parks Commission.

What Collier called his "Indian New Deal" was part of a much larger New Deal enacted by President Roosevelt.[1] As Republicans, Pearl, Harold, and Hezekiah had many reservations about the New Deal, which was considered hostile to business and economic growth. In the 1936 election cycle, Pearl busied herself working as hard as she could for the Republican cause.[2]

She and her family would have rather seen less government interference. Republicans of the time, like the Chases, worried that the rapid centralization of public power threatened their traditional elites. Philanthropy had provided monied men and women voices in public policy, which federal initiative appeared to block. Moreover, the growth of public expertise promised independent professionals a lesser role as government consultants. Despite these new trends, many of their disagreements with the New Deal were partly ideological.[3] Their paternalistic assumption that people must earn social amenities clashed with the New Deal premise that social services were the public's right.[4]

Despite Republican party misgivings of the New Deal, one agency that was accepted across party lines was the Civilian Conservation

Corps. Republican reporters did not exaggerate when claiming that "attacks on the New Deal, no matter how sweeping, rarely or never extend to the CCC."[5] Part of its broad acceptance was that its best work was done "in the Midwest and New England in local areas where local Republicanism was strong."[6]

Because its measures were tangible, immediate, and obvious, it captured the popular imagination. The three million unemployed and unmarried young men aged between eighteen and twenty-six who had enrolled between 1934 and 1942 when the CCC was disbanded due to the Second World War had to work, and work hard. Living in quasi-military camps, often far from home, in the nation's publicly owned forests and parks, they earned money to send back to their needy families, received three square meals a day, and escaped from idle purposelessness by contributing to the renewal and beautification of the country.[7] These men recaptured for many people the spirit of a unique age now past, whose memory was still all-pervasive. As one newspaper declared with a hint of semi-nostalgia, "Theirs is the American way."[8]

The CCC was established by President Roosevelt on April 5, 1933. More than any other New Deal program the CCC was his brainchild and often known as "Roosevelt's Tree Army." He had a long-standing interest in conservation. The organization and administration of the CCC was a new experiment in operations for a federal government agency. The program was supervised jointly by four government departments: Labor, which recruited the young men; War, which operated the camps; Agriculture; and Interior, both of which organized and supervised the work projects.[9]

A certain number of these CCC camps were allotted to the National Park Service for development work in national, state, county, and municipal parks. The object was to conserve natural resources, preserve historical and archaeological resources, and develop recreational resources within park areas. These goals were accomplished through programs such as firefighting, archaeological surveys and excavations, ruins stabilization, road and trail conservation, reforestation, erosion control, exhibit building, research and guide services, insect control, campground developments, and construction of recreational facilities.[10]

In 1934, when it became evident that one of these camps could be stationed in Santa Barbara County, the possibility of setting up the restoration of Mission La Purísima Concepción as a project brought immediate action. La Purísima Mission was founded by Father Fermin de Lasuen on December 8, 1787, at Lompoc, one year after the founding of Mission Santa Barbara fifty-four miles to the south. It was the eleventh of the twenty-one Franciscan Missions built between San Diego and San Francisco.[11]

On December 21, 1812, an earthquake destroyed many of the Mission's buildings, and its community relocated four miles northeast next to El Camino Real. The Mission was officially re-established on April 23, 1813. Following Mexican independence in 1821, California's Mexican governors began taking the missions from the Catholic Church and distributing their lands to private individuals. In 1834, La Purísima was secularized and began its decline into ruins. Ownership came into the hands of the Union Oil company in 1903,[12] and thirty years later in 1933, the company, along with the Catholic Church, which regained title to the mission church and cemetery, gave the property to Santa Barbara County.[13]

The property was deeded to the state of California, Division of State Parks in 1934 with additional land totalling 520 acres, and was renamed La Purísima Mission State Historical Monument. It was the State Park Commission that suggested the National Parks Service establish a CCC camp at the site and undertake restoration of the Mission buildings in cooperation with the State Division of Parks. Construction of the camp began on July 18, 1934. By August 1, it was formally occupied by 320 enrolees, most of whom came from Los Angeles, along with some Chumash men, descendants of the people who originally built the mission. To the camp personnel,

89. La Purísima Mission pre-reconstruction

the task of restoring the site seemed a bit staggering, and the problems which presented themselves were many and varied. So that the work could be intelligently planned, it was necessary to formulate a definite policy of restoration. For this purpose, the State Park Commission asked a group of seven well-qualified people of Santa Barbara County to act as La Purísima Advisory Committee (LPAC).[14] Unsurprisingly, Pearl was invited to join.[15]

She was perfectly suited to her new role. Her interest in historic preservation had been stimulated during the 1910s when Santa Barbara was preserving its historic adobes. Not only had she read and collected books on the California missions and preservation, but she had met people actively involved in restoration and historical study relating to the preservation of structures. Among those she particularly admired were John Southworth, a historian and author of books on Los Angeles, San Diego, Baja, and Santa Barbara,[16] and Joseph Knowland, who was one of "the best-known figures in public life in California" at the time.[17] Following an unsuccessful bid for Senate in 1915, he purchased the *Oakland Tribune*. As publisher, he took an active interest in the development of the city of Oakland. In 1923, he joined the Associated Press and went on to be its director for twenty-nine years. Deeply interested in California, he dedicated much of his life to the preservation of California historic monuments. As a member of the Native Sons of the Golden West, he chaired the Historic Lands Committee and presided over the California Landmark League.[18] Pearl described him as "a splendid-appearing person and, of course, extremely well-trained as a presiding officer and planner of things that would catch the public attention."[19]

It was, however, her involvement with Mission Santa Barbara, constructed at the time of the country's founding, where she was able to experience preservation at first hand. To Pearl, the Mission was "one of the most widely photographed and publicized buildings in the United States."[20] Its position was "almost fantastic;" its story had to continue.[21]

After the earthquake in 1925, to raise funds for the restoration of the building, the Franciscan fathers put the open land immediately east of the mission, which exhibited features of original Indian work, on the market. Led by a group of women citizens, including Pearl, a committee was "hastily formed to raise money and purchase the property for a public park, to prevent developers from crowding houses up to the very portal of the mission."[22] As a woman already working in male-dominated organizations within the conservation field,[23] Pearl saw La Purísima as an opportunity to further her knowledge of historical preservation. She drew on her organizational and relationship-building skills in facilitating all the varying interests and was keen to both share her knowledge and to guide other women in the field.

Pearl was also eager to highlight that the institutional side of mission life was as important to the visitor as the religious. Discussing her work with the advisory committee, to preservation historian Charles Hosmer Jr., she remarked:

> And as I showed you in some of our notes, the mission system was established to supplement the civic order. The military and civil were in command at all times. The missions were not the dominant feature. They were the lasting ones because they had in one way, an architectural and a religious hold upon the imagination of the people. But I'm very much of the opinion that few people realize how wonderfully planned the Spanish occupation of California was. This wasn't just a church, it was a place where the population of the area could be served and serve, this occupying force.[24]

The purpose of the advisory committee was to formulate restoration policies and objectives, and to advise executives and the State's Park Commission on matters on which they had little time to consider in detail. Pearl believed "such a relationship can be useful in many ways, but always the advisory committee should understand the limitations of its service and be willing to remain as an advisor and not as a decider."[25]

Having defined its duties and powers, her experience told her that financial responsibility should remain in the hands of a subcommittee, which it did. No doubt she relished telling the federal government how it should spend its money on a California state historic landmark. The group had its first official meeting on March 27, at which the urgency of the project was reinforced. Between then and September 24, when they presented their first report, the committee met frequently on-site or at other locations in Santa Barbara to review the data and explore the possibilities of the restoration.

The report was comprehensive, outlining a logical policy for restoration and defining the objective of the work. It emphasized the educational aspects of the site with the preservation of the atmosphere of an authentic mission community in its natural setting. The second consideration was the recognition of its function as a state park, providing car facilities and means of recreation. The committee suggested to the NPS that they reconstruct every building that could be reproduced authentically from the evidence available at the time. Additionally, that planting should be in harmony with the surrounding landscape and the early mission planting.

Pearl thought the whole project was "thrilling"[26] and recalled later: "I remember a discussion with some pride on the part of the advisory committee that we had been told that because of the fine organization and planning work, that there seemed no prospect of a cut-off of funds and that we could plan farther ahead."[27,28]

United by the fact that La Purísima was the first mission restoration of its kind in the country and involved collaboration between local organizations and groups and state and federal agencies during the Great Depression, the committee worked at a rapid pace and were intensely excited by the project.

Asked later, how she accounted for the harmony that emerged between the national park officials and the state park officials and the experts she replied:

> Number one, they respected each other. Second, they were extremely interesting, and they were all learning something. I mean, people of that calibre are rewarded by knowledge gained in connection with work or consulting. Many of them felt that they were learning, and there was such a variety of points of view, that there was little conflict. This was a new kind of job, a bigger job, a more important job, of its kind, than most of them had been engaged in. So it was stimulating, it was rewarding and the part of the advisory committee was chiefly to maintain a social contact between these persons, as well as a semi-professional one occasionally; checking on the type of construction.[29]

In recalling the early years on the LPAC, Pearl was full of praise not just for the men in Sacramento and Washington but also for the men on the site who were "cooperative and seemed to learn a good deal."[30] Elaborating on her gratitude, Pearl explained to Hosmer:

90. La Purísima Mission site, c.1904

> [...] the thing that I have valued and admired among the men working, both as superintendents and of the project under CCC, was their recognition of the fact that they didn't know it all and that if they wanted to do a good job, they'd better get advice from those that have some special knowledge.[31]

Among those experts on the committee with special knowledge those who stood out for Pearl at this time were mission scholars and enthusiasts Edith Webb, Arthur Woodward, and Mark Raymond Harrington. Webb was an artist and photographer.[32] After her marriage to Hugh Webb in Fresno in 1901, the couple made researching the missions their life. In 1952, she published *Indian Life at the Old Missions*. Pearl felt Webb had:

> taught me as much as any of them. A teacher herself, [she] had been pleased and interested to travel up and down the state for many years, taking photographs, studying the buildings as they deteriorated. Mrs. Webb and her husband were inseparable on these trips and their notes were voluminous and extremely helpful, and always illustrated. She studied things on the ground, she read many of the diaries which had not been published, talked with the old-timers because she began a generation before

91. CCC men at work at La Purísima Mission

> 1941. She was bringing years of advice and experience, and because she was able to answer particularly the question about what was the use of these various rooms, where she had seen an olive press, or a wine press, or a fireplace or something that would seem to fit this particular situation, and she was able to, in my experience, apparently answer a tremendous amount of questions about those features. Therefore, the superintendents of the CCC camps were happy to be able to consult her.[33]

Woodward and Harrington were both provided by the NPS to give advice to the LPAC. Woodward was an archaeologist and curator of history at the Los Angeles County Museum.[34] In addition to collecting books, he also authored his own. Harrington was "curator of archaeology at the Southwest Museum in Los Angeles and discoverer of ancient pueblo structures near Overton, Nevada and Little Lake, California."[35] Pearl described Woodward as "extremely interested and very active. He had a divided interest as he was also collecting for his own museum. He helped in acquiring the furnishings and identifying the type of thing which should be hunted for and used."[36] He was always accompanied by his wife and "rendered valuable service."[37] Pearl also thought that their museums were enriched by the experience they had working at Purísima, what she described as "the finest kind of cooperation."[38]

Pearl took an interest in the CCC camp itself. "From the earliest days of the tent camp, one of the army sergeants kept a boxing ring set up. Whenever there was a squabble among the men, the disputing parties were placed in the ring to settle it after the workday ended."[39] As was in her nature, she noticed living conditions impact on those at the camp. "The most important factor determining company morale was the food served. La Purísima was fortunate to be in located in the agriculturally rich Lompoc Valley. It boasted the biggest kitchen and mess hall in the Los Angeles CCC district with a capacity of 410 men for any meal."[40,41]

Work began on the padre's residence in the summer of 1935. The policy, which received greatest emphasis, was that every effort should be made to authenticate every feature of architectural design and construction by documentary or photographic evidence, or by evidence established from study of the ruined buildings themselves.[42] As Pearl recalled, there were a series of "discoveries." New factors had to be figured every little while. Initially, the most pressing concern was the dilemma of whether to preserve or rebuild.[43]

After the mounds of eroded adobe bricks were removed, excavations around the Mission ruins revealed that the walls were unstable. Once excavation was complete, the LPAC decided to preserve the original walls and incorporate them into the new construction of the padre's residence. Since new and old had to be fitted together without any apparent break, it was essential that reproduction of the original elements should be as exact as possible. As described by Pearl:

> The NPS regional staff promoted a conservative philosophy to preserve rather than reconstruct, in order to fulfil their governmental mandate to protect the nation's architectural

> heritage and its inherent educational value. [...] This point of view was disputed by the LPAC which advocated the complete reconstruction of all structures. Their argument was based on the heightened educational value they perceived the recreated buildings would possess in comparison to preserved ruins. It was their assertion that the public could learn more about mission life from a replica than from a ruin.[44]

Fred Hageman, NPS architect, agreed. In June 1935 "he had surreptitiously instructed CCC enrolees to begin making new adobe bricks out of the rubble of the old before permission to reconstruct had been given by the NPS or the State Park Commission. Consequently, as the project proceeded, another reason for reconstruction instead of preservation became evident."[45] It was best expressed by an NPS researcher in Washington and friend of Pearl's, Dr. V. Aubrey Neasham, in a 1938 letter to Newton B. Drury.

> Its development has gone too far to arrest it in the preservation stage. A reconstructed and rebuilt group of buildings built upon mission building foundations, it has lost its historic reality. As such, its only justification is an illusion, a picture to show the public what the mission may have looked like in the days of its height.[46]

The goal was to recreate an authentic mission setting as it looked in the early nineteenth century "so that it could be interpreted to the public as a historical site."[47] At issue in the debates about the design of the buildings and the garden was the definition of "historical," and how to "balance ideas of historical accuracy with visitor needs."[48]

The LPAC members, including Pearl, were unanimous that the notion of "creating an authentic reconstruction was moot because there had been constant change since secularization and no amount of research would restore the broader landscape to its early nineteenth-century appearance."[49]

In their report to the NPS they concluded with a "rather scathing condemnation of the historical purists' objections to the garden that, 'a policy of inaction based upon fear of committing historic sin will result in a weed-covered fore-ground which in itself will be a violation of the Purísima story.'"[50] Eventually, it was agreed upon to landscape the area surrounding the Mission incorporating existing fountains at the site and develop a four-acre Mission Garden using authentic plants.

> The wrangling and rhetoric of various stakeholders reflected divisions concerning how to approach the recreation of a historical landscape for the mission but beneath the debate's surface was a shared assumption about the ultimate purpose of the space. Each group had its own ideas about the validity of the evidence, the definition of historical accuracy, and the appropriate balance of authenticity with visitors' needs, but all shared the vision of creating a landscape that celebrated early California history and conveyed nostalgia for the simple, peaceful life of mission days.[51]

92. La Purísima Mission garden by Sue Elson

On Labor Day, September 6, 1937, when the residence building reconstruction was complete, the La Purísima State Historical Monument officially opened to the public with a dedication ceremony that included a tour of the building and Mission Garden.[52]

Among other heated discussions in the years that followed, Pearl recalled the most prominent were over the Monjeríos, the building where unmarried women and girls were segregated.[53] Another important issue the LPAC debated was the actual use of the site once the buildings and plantings were reconstructed. Just before the outbreak of the Second World War, the subject of how a living museum could be developed was discussed more frequently than any other.[54] Pearl believed the issue was never likely to be solved, because "we couldn't find a way to pay people to live there and to work there."[55]

In 1941, the State Park Commission allocated $10,000 for the acquisition of additional land for the park site. At that time, the three main buildings, parts of three smaller buildings, and several units of the water system were complete. As the state prepared to take over the full-time maintenance of the complex, Pearl organized

93. La Purísima Mission after reconstruction

a committee called Old Mission Days in Santa Barbara County, its goal to plan and host an event to commemorate the founding of the county's two great missions.[56,57]

Pearl acted as advisory chairman of the committee, a position which she recalled was "very comfortable, not full of responsibility but you have your finger in the pie where it's needed."[58,59] The first Old Mission Days was a four-day event from December 4 to 7, a weekend specifically chosen because of its special significance to California Mission founding history.[60] Old Mission Days culminated at the newly restored La Purísima. It was the 154th anniversary of the dedication of the first Mission at Lompoc, and a religious ceremony was designed to emulate the original dedication ritual conducted by Padre Lasuen. As Pearl arrived at the event she was met by Charles Storke, the chairman of the advisory committee, and son of Tom Storke the *Santa Barbara News-Press* publisher. As she later recalled:

> "Well Pearl, you'll have to take over. You'll have to take over," he said. "The Japanese have bombed Pearl Harbor, and I'll have to go back as fast as I can and help get out of special addition of the paper." Because he'd heard it on the radio on his way up; it did not come out beforehand. So that was a very exciting meeting.[61]

In Storke's absence, Pearl chaired the event.

> There were no changes in the program, or the speakers and I suggested that every speaker do not [*sic*] discuss the bombing of Pearl Harbor but that the chairman attend to that and we go ahead with the regular program, because there were a lot of people, and we were all standing up. Remember that one of the disadvantages of a certain type of celebration is that you're on your own two feet for the length of the program.[62]

As the news sank in, Pearl and others were turning their thoughts from the protected past to the projected future.[63] She wrote about the event a few days later: "The outbreak of war with Japan announced on Sunday in the midst of the beautiful observance at our rebuilt Mission La Purísima Concepción, brought also the thought that what man's idealism has once created may be rebuilt."[64] Storke told her that he felt positive about the event despite the eclipsing news story. "Personally, I'm very enthusiastic over the results which were accomplished through Old Mission Days. It is unfortunate that the war broke as it did and robbed us of some of our best potential publicity."[65]

At a national level the historic sites and building survey initiated by the New Deal and the work of the CCC forever altered preservation. It was evident that the Department of the Interior now recognized the value of scholarship in the restoration process.

As one commentor noted, "Despite its shortcomings, the CCC was of the profoundest importance. It was important because of its effect on the nation's national resources and the health of its enrolees, and it is important to the story of reform in the United States. It marked the first attempt by the federal government to provide some

94. Pearl and her colleagues continued to meet after the war. Here they are inspecting the Grist Mills at La Purísima Mission in 1950

specific solution for the problems of youth in an increasingly urban society. In its makeshift, loose way it was a pathfinder, the precursor of more sophisticated programs and ideas."[66]

The recreation of the La Purísima Mission was "one of the largest historical restoration and reconstruction projects" in the United States. Pearl's greatest regret was that the state park system did so little to promote the Mission: "It has been very weak," compared to "the tremendous promotion for Hearst Castle."[67] She wondered why it was not possible to include La Purísima on the tourist route to and from San Simeon. Despite these misgivings she believed Purísima had a chance "to develop splendidly in the future."[68]

CHAPTER 17

National Recognition

During the 1930s, Pearl was becoming a Santa Barbara celebrity.

In 1935, she was proposed for city mayor. She made it clear, however, that she had no desire to accept the nomination. At the same time, she was recipient of Santa Barbara's Outstanding Woman Citizen award at a surprise lunch party with 300 guests. For Pearl, the "pleasant effects of the party seemed to multiply and increase rather than diminish with the passing of the days."[1] She enjoyed the attention but never let it overwhelm her. In 1937, she was recognized by the Grand Parlor of the meeting daughters when she was made a member of the Roll of Honor of the Native Daughters of the Golden West Reina Del Mar. This was indeed an honor, given to noteworthy women who were not born in California.[2]

Three years later, she achieved national recognition when the *Survey Graphic*[3] and *Reader's Digest*, which was the best-selling publication in America, both published articles about her and her work. She was delighted with the publicity it brought her causes. In many ways, as her fame spread, her life also changed. A letter she wrote two years later to Frank Taylor, who co-authored the article published in the *Survey Graphic*, reveals how:

> Of the more than 1,200 letters that came in two thirds sought something for the owner, or were personal notes of congratulations or approbations, some of these were from friends, possibly one hundred and fifty thought they knew me.
>
> Of the remainder, the larger number of those who asked for advice, or information, wanted to know how to get rid of

billboards. A large number of letters came from transients in Los Angeles, who objected to signs which hid the scenery. I deeply appreciate the purpose of the Reader's Digest editors in using articles about civic activities and will be glad to help them and you continue in your good work. I believe that the fact that I received the Honorary Degree of Doctor of Humane Letters from Mills College was because the articles in Digest and Survey Graphic gave the trustees the support they needed in making such a decision. I am going to San Francisco Tuesday night and will take in the UC charter day Exercises, possibly the fact that I am nominated as Trustee of UC Alumni Association may also be traced to the Degree and yours and Miss Glover's article.[4]

The funniest result was local. I knew as soon as the article was published that it would be a handicap here, really, I have never been more inconspicuous. For many months because of the attitude of one of the editors no publicity was given voluntarily to any activities of mine because the gent said we don't want to have anyone gain such a great influence. I have not thought it wise to appear before the council because the gentleman said, "We don't want to have anyone gain such a great influence." I have not thought it wise to appear before the Council because of underground jealousy developed by "National Publicity."

This spring I went East for two months as usual, to gain the latest and best possible advice as to how we might proceed in the Emergency [the Second World War] and to gather ideas from other sections and people. It was an expensive trip. On my return I was able to stimulate County Officials to action which saved weeks of time and probably secured thousands of dollars of federal services, before it was too late. Because of my support of a County Housing Authority to provide public housing in areas affected by Camp Cooke[5] the editor of Common Sense, a privately printed one-page weekly, attacked me and Mr. Preisker[6] over and over again. The first time for twenty years

> anyone had publically [*sic*] objected to my civic programs. All this and more has been interesting and enlightening. I still think you should write an article about what has happened to the people you have written about, but, YOU HAD BETTER NOT USE THE ABOVE MATERIAL.[7]

Pearl accepted the award of a doctorate from Mills College with sincere humility. She was truly grateful and appreciative toward her friend Aurelia Reinhardt, the college president, for putting her name forward. She considered it an expression of "friendly encouragement and possibly of approval."[8] As a long-standing supporter of Mills College, she was also pleased to be associated with it in this new way.[9] Reinhardt, cited her colleague as one who had "made a modern city beautiful, shown a State how to conserve and improve its human and natural resources. Had become for a Nation an exemplar of civic leadership and a proof that the ideals of a country are realities in the person of a Noble citizen."[10]

The award confirmed what people already knew: Pearl used the title selectively in her correspondence. More often the honorific was used in academic programs and conference papers that she participated in. She preferred to be addressed as Miss Chase, once remarking, "even my friends call me Miss Chase." Events were moving so fast for Pearl that it is a wonder she did not lose her way. Her friend Alice Bentz remarked, "Sooner or later the whole world will be stopping at your door asking admission. You've created such a mighty 'mousetrap,' it's no wonder the many come."[11]

Her vision kept her grounded. One of her most famous victories at the time and an outstanding example of the type of community cooperation she was capable of facilitating was saving Santa Barbara's most famous tree. A seaman visiting Santa Barbara in 1876 offered a seedling of an Australian Moreton Bay fig tree to a local who planted it near State Street. When it became as tall as a walking stick, a nine-year-old girl and her mother moved the tree to a site close to the beach on land owned by the Southern Pacific.[12]

95. The Moreton Bay Fig Tree

By the 1930s it had a branch spread of over 124 feet, making it the second-widest tree in the world as well as a champion tree. Four years later in November 1939, a series of measurements and calculations were made by the city engineer. He found that the branch spread had increased to 135 feet and that all branches covered 12,712 square feet; it would've been possible for 9,500 people to stand in its shade at noon.[13]

Pearl first suggested that the site should be made a city park in 1933. No action was taken at the time, but in October 1941 the city park board, with Pearl's persistent demands, made another attempt. The following month, Southern Pacific agreed to keep and protect the tree. Along with Southern Pacific, among those who cooperated in preserving the tree were the city park and street departments, the Southern California Edison Company, the Southern California Telephone Company, and the Santa Barbara Telephone Company, and the Native Sons of the Golden West. It was a truly collaborative effort.[14]

On September 1, 1939, Germany invaded Poland and two days later the United Kingdom, France, Australia, and New Zealand declared war on Germany. In America, the worst of the economic downturn of the Great Depression was nearly over and the nation was recovering. However, by 1941 a mood of unease hung over the country. Pearl anticipated a strange year ahead.[15] In mid-May, attending the American Association of University Women Conference in Cincinnati, she remarked that:

> The kaleidoscopic picture of the American people getting to work and of policies made and changed over-night is stirring and fascinating. Listening to speakers and audiences at five conventions, meeting twenty-eight government officials of eight departments in conferences and many socially, have made me want to help push our women a little faster into a realization of the terrific job of hard thinking and hard work ahead of them. If we don't (1) walk up and fill the volunteer jobs promptly and efficiently and (2) learn how to cook for and feed families more effectively and economically (3) keep up community morale by sustaining volunteer and civic efforts for human betterment, I am afraid women will be 'drafted' too soon as some important work will be done by the WPA (Works Progress Administration) type of worker.[16]

Seven months later, the surprise attack on Pearl Harbor caused vast changes in virtually every aspect of American life for men and women, including overwhelming support for American entry into the Second World War. After a brief and forceful speech, President Roosevelt asked Congress to approve a resolution recognizing the state of war between the United States and Japan. The Senate voted for war against Japan by 82 to 0, and the House of Representatives approved the resolution by a vote of 388 to 1. Three days later, Germany and Italy declared war against the United States, and the US government responded in kind.

CHAPTER 18

Santa Barbara and the Outbreak of the Second World War

Shortly after sundown on February 23, 1942, "the first enemy bombardment of the American mainland since the war of 1812" took place twelve miles north of Santa Barbara.[1] That evening, most Santa Barbarans, including Pearl and her father, were in their homes listening to President Roosevelt deliver one of his fireside chats on the radio. Ironically, his subject that night was the excellent state of US coastal defenses. While the president was "reassuring the American people that they were secure from enemy attack by land, sea or air, thumping sounds like far-off sonic booms rattled house windows."[2] Shortly afterward, "telephone messages from various Goleta farmers to the night editor of the *News-Press* reported that the Ellwood oilfield was being bombarded by a Japanese submarine, surfaced offshore."[3] Fortunately, there were no casualties, and the total cost of the damage was $1,000; however, news of the attack triggered an invasion scare along the west coast.

In Santa Barbara, a great spirit of communal sharing emerged during the Second World War. While hundreds of men and women enlisted, those that stayed behind felt united in that they were fighting for a common purpose. At the same time, "the long travail of war time restrictions" including blackout curtains, streetlights turned off, gasoline and tire rationing, food rationing, and cigarette shortages took effect.[4] In the early stages of the war, Pearl noted that rationing of gas and food did not cause great hardship in Santa Barbara but that many of her friends in Montecito moved into the city. Everyone noticed the increased prices of food.[5] "Don't you know there's a war on?" was a common expression. Rationing became part of everyday life, and Americans learned to conserve vital resources. They lived with price controls and dealt with shortages of everything from nylons to housing. It was far from easy. In November 1943, Pearl found herself unable to accomplish her essential work and was compelled to request double her existing allowance of three gallons a week from the gas ration board at City Hall.[6]

Pearl felt that Santa Barbara was passing through a period of rapid transition.[7] The end of the golden years, the subsequent breaking up of the great estates in Montecito, and decline of fortunes that started after 1929 had made it imperative to re-establish the foundations of the community. It was not necessary to change the spirit of the place, nor its beauty, nor its way of life, but it needed new fundamentals. The war provided many.

During the thirties, the population of Santa Barbara had not grown very much. There were 35,000 people living in the city and tourism was a dominant business. The war brought a new influx of people and sweeping changes to the area. As Pearl later recalled, "The sudden decision of the government to establish military camps in the vicinity of the town overwhelmed us and made it impossible to accommodate the people and fulfil the demands."[8]

Santa Barbara was literally overrun with servicepeople and their families, and older people evacuated from industrial centers, looking for places to live. The result was an acute housing shortage, which Pearl "expected to last for an indefinite period."[9] Where previously she had always found accommodation for friends and family from the East Coast, she now struggled. "Neither Harold nor I own any small houses," she told her cousin. "No real estate office has been given apartments or small houses to rent. It has been a question of advertising and house to house canvassing. I will put an ad in the paper and see what we will get."[10] Hotel rooms were also scarce.

With sparsely occupied land and suitable geographic conditions, many of the existing military installations were enlarged and new ones were built across California. Hundreds of thousands of troops passed through these training camps before their overseas deployment. Receiving servicemen wounded in the Pacific theatre, US military hospitals were also established throughout California. While these took the form of many different types, they all provided for the treatment of military personnel while being sick or injured. Santa Barbara was ideally located for such installations.

On December 4, 1942, Santa Barbara Airport at Goleta, which had been established in the early thirties on Harold Chase's land by his stepson, Frederick Stearns II, was taken over by the US Army Air Corps (USAAC). USAAC commissioned a Marine Corps air station to serve as a training base for numerous squadrons before they were

96. Aerial view of Marine Corps Air Station Santa Barbara pre-UCSB development

deployed to support combat operations in the Pacific. "At its peak, the station housed nearly 500 officers, about 3,100 enlisted men, and 440 women Marines."[11]

Sixty-five miles northwest of the city, Camp Cooke (now Vandenberg Air Force Base) flourished. Nine months before the attack on Pearl Harbor, the US Army acquired an 86,000-acre site of open ranch lands between Lompoc and Santa Maria in Santa Barbara County. The following September, construction of Camp Cooke was activated. In February 1942, "the 5th Armored Division rolled into the camp and soon the roar of its tanks and artillery became a part of everyday life."[12] From then until the end of the war in 1945, many other armored and infantry divisions "kept up the din," along with an assortment of anti-aircraft artillery, hospital units, and German and Italian prisoners of war.[13] The camp had a peak population of about 36,000 in June 1943; upward of 175,000 personnel were stationed at Camp Cooke during the war years.[14]

Within a few hours' driving distance of Santa Barbara were two other camps. Camp Roberts, opened in 1941 on the San Luis Obispo and Monterey County border, was one of the largest camps in the US, training 436,000 field and infantry artillery troops during the war years, and Camp San Luis Obispo which served as an infantry division camp for 1,523 officers and 19,383 enlisted personnel. On the waterfront, the city's harbour was a home base for two Navy destroyers and their dockside support facilities.

In March 1941, operations began at Hoff General Hospital, located on Hollister Avenue (now known as upper State Street), near the northwestern city limits. The hospital grounds covered 58 acres and included 102 buildings and 750 beds, which was increased to 1,141 beds by January 1945. There was a "network of more than a mile of covered sidewalks, three miles of utility lines, and a mile of gas piping serviced the installation."[15] In 1945, the peak year of service, some 6,441 patients were admitted and treated. Over the war years Hoff treated more than 27,500 military patients,[16] and the hospital was often visited by Hollywood celebrities like Bob Hope and Jack Benny.

With space at a premium, the city's large hotels including the Biltmore, Miramar, and Mar Monte were taken over for military purposes. By 1944, the War Department requestioned these hotels for use as redistribution stations. The facilities were converted by the Army into the Santa Barbara Army Ground and Service Forces Redistribution Stations. The hotels, along with other facilities and attractions throughout Santa Barbara, were used as a place of relaxation for returning soldiers from the war before they were reassigned.

According to local historians, "the men played golf at Montecito Country Club, swam at Miramar and Coral Casino, fished in the channel, and shot arrows at the archery range near the Cabrillo Pavilion." By June, Santa Barbara's beaches were "Bustin' Out All Over" with the sunbathing wives of returnees. Guided horseback rides along miles of Santa Barbara and Montecito bridle paths, as well as sightseeing tours via bicycle, were popular.[17] As described in the *Montecito Journal*:

> Wives were allowed and encouraged to join their husbands, though their spouses stayed for free, the wives had to pay $1.25 a day for the room, three meals and a linen charge. A popular feature of the Santa Barbara stations was the daily "Cheers and Gripes" session held at the Biltmore where the men—anonymously and without retribution—could sound off about anything they wanted to, including "unfair officers."[18]

As the social and cultural institutions of the city changed during the war, so did the economy. With the establishment of the draft and an upsurge in war-related manufacturing, Santa Barbara reached full employment for the first time since the onset of the Great Depression in 1929. Across California, moreover, agriculture producers fed the allied troops around the world. Most of the state's manufacturing was shifted to the war effort, and California became a major shipbuilder and aircraft manufacturer.

As employment rose, "the need for labor opened up new opportunities for women and African Americans and other minorities."[19] Employment in aviation drew over one thousand five hundred Santa Barbarans, more than half of them women.[20] Millions of Americans left home to take jobs in war plants that sprang up around the nation. Economic output skyrocketed.[21] Having spent most of the Great Depression discouraging women from seeking employment, the government now encouraged millions to enter the workforce for the first time: "Middle-class matrons answered the call along with sheltered ingenues, some becoming riveters like the iconic Rosie."[22]

In their military service and wage-based employment, women helped generate crucial changes and challenges. Volunteer work was equally important in fostering female self-esteem and independence, and ultimately in winning the war on the home front. In Santa Barbara, women volunteered in different ways and had different motives. Collectively, they served to create a feeling of community and patriotism. At a time of intense population mobility, volunteerism served as a uniting factor for those that moved to the city. Voluntary efforts increased morale and enabled citizens to feel

97. Rosie the Riveter

intimately connected and involved in the war effort. Pearl did not have to work very hard to find willing female volunteers—many rushed forward to help. She was able to secure and maintain volunteer cooperation by "a never-ending educational campaign and continuing effort to prevent lowering of standards."[23]

Pearl believed that Santa Barbara should go all out to support the servicemen and their families in the realm of morale work. Having conducted her garden tours during the Great Depression years, she found rationing prevented her from continuing in 1942. Inventing something new, she reorganized her garden tours committee and contacted some of the garden owners who had previously opened their properties.

The Garden Hosts of Santa Barbara started on May 3, 1942, and organized parties for officers, their wives, and servicemen in some of the finest gardens to be found anywhere on the Pacific coast. Every Sunday afternoon through the war, and until all the personnel disbanded in 1946, Pearl and her local volunteers, many of whom had sons or husbands that had enlisted, arranged garden parties to give the servicemen, their families, and their guests an opportunity to become acquainted with those of other military concentrations in the district and with citizens of Santa Barbara.

98. Garden Hosts and Soldiers

At the impressive Montecito estates, generals, admirals, lieutenants, and commanders from camps Cooke, Roberts, and San Luis Obispo, and the Santa Barbara naval base met with city leaders and philanthropists. Pearl felt it was "extremely important to make local residents feel that these visiting military were nice people, and pleasant to meet, and maybe a little bit different and maybe a little exciting."[24]

Realizing that the officers wanted more entertainment than a visit to a garden, Pearl integrated them with beach parties and tea dances often followed by supper. She gathered a committee of experienced hostesses and young ladies who, after a great deal of telephoning, secured attractive young women to drive cars and entertain the officers at Hope Ranch Beach, the Coral Casino at the Biltmore, or the El Paseo restaurant. To Pearl, it took "a lot of scheming!"[25] As she later recalled:

> The hostesses were young women and some of them were married, because some of the visiting officers were married, too, and I never expected to have women enough to equal the number of officers that came. Because many of the men just wanted to sit around and look and talk and not dance very much. But we provided coffee and cakes and sandwiches and punch, and the men could buy drinks at the bar, but none of the women, no matter if it was a general's or admiral's wife or younger person, could go into the bar or have a drink during the time of the tea dance. I introduced a good many young people to their future mates, not intentionally, but coincidentally and out of it got several godchildren.[26]

Over the years these events proved very popular. Among the thousands of men and women entertained by Pearl and her volunteers, Joe Foss, the leading marine fighter ace who later became governor of South Dakota, president of the National Rifle Association, and the first commissioner of the American Football League, was a regular. Another was Major General Jack Heard, a pioneer

99. Joe Foss

in military aviation and recipient of the Medal of Honor. He and Pearl became good friends, especially after she rescued his daughter's wedding when a blackout was ordered, and the caterer could not go to the camp. She also got to know Major General Albert E. Brown, who, after several months at Camp San Luis Obispo, served with distinction as commanding general, 7th Infantry Division during the Aleutian Islands campaign. He was later awarded the Legion of Merit, Bronze Star, Legion of Honour, and Croix de Guerre. All of these initiatives relied on private funding, which Pearl and her committee organized.

The United Service Organizations (USO) also had a presence in Santa Barbara. It was formed through presidential order on

100. General Albert E. Brown

February 4, 1941 and worked in partnership with the Department of War. The organization was incorporated in New York state as a private, nonprofit organization, supported by private citizens and corporations.[27] The USO became the largest entertainment organization in the world: clubs or canteens were established in more than three thousand communities across the US and became a home away from home for many military men and women and workers in wartime industry.

It was reported that the USO was Pearl's "pet,"[28] a corporation which she considered "excellent."[29] The USO was located at 740 State Street in what was called the La Placita building ("the little plaza").[30] Pearl refurbished the building and arranged for a lounge upstairs for the women, but they, however, preferred to be downstairs with the rest of the service personnel. No food was served at the USO, but it was a popular place to meet. In October 1942, approximately 13,400 men were entertained. Pearl made sure that the furnishings were "utterly magnificent, including many rare antiques loaned from local collectors."[31] It did all the things the USO did in any other city but on a more magnificent scale. Pearl was known to visit the building regularly, and as one reporter noticed, she "would pause to empty ashtrays, readjust curtains, and straighten magazines and books."[32]

While the enlisted men were having a "swell time," she also arranged, and had great fun doing it, for an officers' club at the El Paseo.[33] Pearl recalled that it comprised a "big lounge, a small room where they could go to sleep and a bathroom." It was very convenient:

> because the men could come in and they could watch the floor show, they could have food sent up, or they could go down and eat on the floor; and there didn't have to be any hostesses, and there didn't have to be anyone looking after it. We changed magazines and flowers once a week, and if the flowers got dead, the boys at El Paseo would throw them out, but it was also self-running.[34]

Again, the furniture was sourced from locals. Apparently, "when the furnishing seemed incomplete, she made an upscale antique dealer wax patriotic and lend certain treasures for the duration. She herself provided luscious draperies."[35]

Pearl also found a room for the officers' wives so that they were not neglected, as Pearl experienced when with General Heard. Known for his love of chocolate ice cream, Pearl recalled how soon after the club opened, General Heard invited Pearl to join him. While enjoying his carton of ice cream and talking to Pearl, he forgot that his wife was waiting in a car outside.

The spirit of volunteerism that Pearl facilitated through her wartime efforts was mirrored by the American Red Cross (ARC) and the American Women's Voluntary Services (AWVS), both active in Santa Barbara at the time.[36,37] Many of these volunteers included club-women from the city's elite families, such as Gertrude Chase, Pearl's sister-in-law.[38] Seeing society women of unimpeachable background, who until the war had never soiled their hands, volunteering as dish-washers, sandwich makers, fountain clerks, tidy-uppers, menders, and painters in wealthy, patrician Santa Barbara did not go unnoticed.[39]

While the Santa Barbara press was supportive, in a few other communities across the nation, these women were criticized for their "charity bazaar" approach: "Images circulated of the 'rich snob' who sat at a booth for a few hours a week but remained oblivious to real sacrifice."[40]

Interestingly, as modern women pushed to break more and more glass ceilings in business, politics, and the professions, women's clubs ceased to be key venues for women to develop their organizational and leadership skills. Club work did continue, meeting community needs and war relief efforts during the Second World War, but clubs did not continue to attract the numbers of women they had prior to the 1920s. Part of the problem was that they could not maintain a high standard of program, since transportation, rising travel costs and higher fees made it impossible to secure high-class talent.

This did not stop Pearl, from, in 1941, joining one of the oldest women's organizations in Santa Barbara. The Little Town Club was, and still is today, an exclusive, members-only club, located in a stunning George Washington Smith-designed building in the center of the city. It had "served as a meeting place for 'women with similar tastes and backgrounds' since its founding in 1914" by Helen Park, a family friend of the Chases.[41] As her network grew and tastes changed, Pearl took advantage of the convivial atmosphere to entertain guests at the club. Among other members Pearl knew well, Gertrude Chase went to the club every weekday to meet friends for lunch and play bridge. After the outbreak of war, Pearl found many of her willing volunteers from among the club's members.

In November 1942, Pearl organized a lunch at the El Paseo for a friend whose husband was away on her birthday, and invited four other women with birthdays in the same week.[42] Discovering that they shared more than simply the same Scorpio zodiac sign and had similar attitudes to public service, the lunch kicked off an annual tradition and what became Pearl's favourite women's group, which she aptly called the "Scorpio Club of Santa Barbara."[43]

Each November, Pearl would invite the women members who qualified because they were giving public service in one field or another to the community and were born between October 23 and November 22 to join her for tea. They would meet in a member's house, eat birthday cake, and celebrate their annual party. Members were expected to bring a fifty-cent gift and a card to exchange with another member so that everyone received something. It was customary that they would read their horoscope, and then each member would report on their activities for the year and their plans for the next. Meeting in this way once a year, it was meant to be a fun, enjoyable event. As one member reported:

> Even fun and games Pearl made meaningful. The club motto was "Work and Serve." She believed serious work should always

> contain some pleasure. Whenever she attended a meeting of any sort, she would bring a bag of goodies to share.[44]

As the years passed, more and more prominent civic-minded women leaders were invited to join the club and attend the annual party.[45] Doctor Charlotte Elmott, a noted educator who enrolled in 1949, remarked after one get together:

> This has been one of the organizations which provides pure joy—association with wonderful people who can look at themselves with a chuckle but at the same time contribute greatly to our community. Pearl's "conversations" revealed how many marvellous things you have done and are doing. I wonder how many other communities have so effectively had the service of women. It would be wonderful for Pitzer College if I could import all of you to that campus next November as symbols of what a group of women can accomplish both as volunteers and as working women who get paid for it. I hope always that our American culture can provide for women so that the "free" volunteer—free to work in so many ways—can contribute to our American way of life as you have contributed to the good life for so many.[46]

Whether as a member of the Scorpio Club or volunteering for the war effort, Pearl wanted everyone to have a good time in a meaningful way: "By stretching and reshaping gender stereotypes, norms and roles, the Second World War and the women who lived it laid solid foundations for the various movements that later swept the United States and gripped the American imagination in the second half of the 20th century."[47]

The Second World War did more to change the character of Santa Barbara than any other event in the twentieth century. Life would never be the same.

CHAPTER 19

The Second World War, Education, and University of California, Santa Barbara

Pearl believed that Santa Barbara's finest assets were its city-owned waterfront and its schools,[1] so much so that she went out of her way to help both during her life. In 1943, she worked to get Santa Barbara State College into the University of California system, along with Thomas Storke, the newspaper baron,[2] and two other Santa Barbarans in the state legislature: Alfred W. "Bobbie" Robertson, the Democratic state assemblyman, and Clarence Ward, who represented the Santa Barbara district in the state senate. The project was one of immense personal satisfaction. As she later remarked:

> There is hardly a day that passes but what I am consulted or consulting about some university matter.
>
> I have worked frightfully hard, Saturdays, Sundays, and nights. So many nights until the 10:30 or 11:15 mail train

101. Clarence Ward

> that it was just good luck that I was not caught down here by a blackout. One time I quit at 2 a.m. There was so much to do and so many of my former experienced helpers were on special war duty that it seemed to keep piling up.[3]

Pearl's commitment to the project was partly driven by a personal goal to merge her former teacher training college, the Santa Barbara State Normal School, (then known as the Santa Barbara State College (SBSC)), with her university, the University of California. She felt indebted to both of these institutions. She considered herself one of UC's "most admiring alumna and most faithful 'public relations.'"[4]

> Patriotism is being felt, discussed and demonstrated to a far greater degree than in normal and peaceful times. Love of Home, of State and Country is for us, in a peculiarly personal way, tied in with affection for our University of California. This love is not a blind or instinctive devotion but is founded upon gratitude to the university for its aid and guidance, its teaching and inspiration during student days. Our love is stimulated by respect for its traditions, pride in its continued and increasingly usefulness and faith in its leadership.[5]

The urge to make a bid to join the University of California was first discussed in 1935, at the same time that a liberal arts program was instituted at SBSC. A similar suggestion had been made in Los Angeles in 1919, and ten years later, the southern branch of the University of California at Los Angeles opened its gates with 5,000 students starting classes at the Westwood campus. The school's development had exceeded all expectations.

Santa Barbara thought it could do one better. Preparatory conversations were given added encouragement as the liberal arts program grew. At the inset of war, 50 percent of the students were majoring in subjects other than education. The success of the school was largely due to Dr. Clarence Phelps, a doctoral student from Stanford

102. Clarence Phelps

who joined the school as president in 1918. He was an exceptional college administrator with ambitions to grow the school. In 1932, despite the Great Depression stopping further building, Phelps promoted the purchase of a 44-acre site on the Mesa overlooking the city beach for $75,000. Pearl was always glad of this.[6,7]

As described in Roger L. Geiger's *American Higher Education since World War II*, the effect of the war was felt across the academy over the course of many years:

> The war experience on college and university campuses passed through four phases. For the first year, institutions and their students largely waited in grim but resigned anticipation; the next year was the high point of war-related activities on campuses as government programs kicked in and civilian students were called away; wartime programs were then abruptly curtailed as trainees were mobilized for combat; and institutions hung on during the final year, enduring growing hardships but looking forward to a happier post-war world."[8]

SBSC lost most of its men students and faculty at this time.

Although Pearl and Storke and others were proud of the ranking the state college commanded in California educational circles, they still believed there should be a place for it in the more

103. Thomas M. Storke

research-oriented university. They felt that the cultural background of Santa Barbara offered a real asset to the university family and that no other community in the West had so much to give. It was with this feeling that Pearl, Storke, Robertson, and Ward began a campaign to convince the legislature, the state school authorities, and the Regents of the University of California that Santa Barbara should join the UC family.[9] As Storke remarked, "it was a long and difficult fight."[10]

Up until 1943, several bills put before the legislature had failed. Under the Republican governor, Earl Warren, the situation changed. Warren had for many years shown a personal interest in Santa Barbara and its college. He often attended the annual Santa Barbara Old Spanish Days Fiesta and was known personally to many leading citizens.[11,12] Pearl thought highly of him having known him at Berkeley as one of her brother's friends.[13] As governor he embodied "the middle-class California Dreams of the 1940s and early 1950s; the family, the home, the lawn, the dog, the middle-class success."[14]

In 1943, Robertson succeeded in getting the measure (AB 956) passed by the legislature, which Warren promptly signed on June 8. The bill authorized the UC Regents' power to take over and operate the college and its properties. The next step for Pearl and her colleagues was to sell the idea to the Regents.

104. Earl Warren

On hearing the news, Pearl immediately thought of Ednah Rich Morse, former principal of the Normal School, and hoped she would help to "work out a plan for the future which would develop all the active forces of cooperation and latent possibilities of the community and the college."[15] There was in fact strong opposition from some parts of the community including the college itself. One of the staff recalled:

> Many of the faculty weren't too anxious to become a part of the university because we enjoyed being a state college. We liked the set up for a state college. And we thought that being under the university would change us so radically that it would not be the same. So, we were opposed to it in many ways. We rather wanted to stay like a college where you knew everybody and you didn't have quite so many restrictions and so on that apparently we'd have under the university.[16]

There was also strong opposition from the state Board of Education who were reluctant to lose a campus from their control and from some of the Regents and faculties of Berkeley and UCLA who feared that a forced amalgamation of Santa Barbara might set a precedent for other legislated transfers of state colleges to the university.

In 1943, while Pearl was campaigning in Santa Barbara for the smooth transfer of SBSC to the University of California, the matter

105. Santa Barbara State College property on the Mesa

was also referred to a standing committee of the twenty-two UC Regents, with Chester H. Rowell as chairman and a strong academic committee to advise President Robert Sproul and the Regents, consisting of five deans, and four professors from the university at Berkeley and Los Angeles.[17] Officers of UC made their independent investigations, and after months of careful consideration in October, the Regents cast a three to one vote for the new campus.

Pearl was credited for getting the Regents' acceptance with an "able presentation."[18] Storke referred to her as "The mother of Santa Barbara College."[19] Using all her skills of persuasion, she sold the wonders of the city to the Regents, describing its unique location, colorful history, famous landmarks, and a convincing interest in sound planning, good architecture, and gardening, all contributing to its charm. She emphasized that the community had a continuing and a substantially supported regard for the health and welfare, cultural and recreational institutions that contributed to the development and happiness of the people. These institutions, she added, were equipped and staffed to supplement the college. Finally, she made the point that since it had no ambitions to become a commercial or industrial center, the city leaders, for several generations, had furthered educational and recreational activities.[20]

On July 1, 1944, the Santa Barbara College of the University of California (SBCUC) became part of the largest university in America and at the time, along with Los Angeles, Davis and Riverside, subordinate to administrators at the Berkeley campus.[21] On Monday, September 11, the college first opened its doors as part of the university.

Originally, the Regents envisioned a small, 2,500-student liberal arts college, a so-called "Williams College of the West," at Santa Barbara.[22] Robert Gordon Sproul, who made this comment, was not a faculty man. He had done no graduate work but was a no-nonsense administrator.[23,24] Sproul had two well-known attributes: his booming voice, and his fabulous memory for people.[25] Pearl thought he was a "wonderful man."[26] He believed that Santa Barbara would have the most beautiful college campus in the world.[27]

In Santa Barbara, the decision was well received by the general public. With Storke's influence, the *News-Press* gave it glowing

106. Robert Gordon Sproul

reviews. Some members of the community, however, were surprised by UC's decision, and thought the acquisition was due to political pressure rather than academic merit.[28] In the years that followed, Pearl was instrumental in changing people's attitudes.

Since graduating from Berkeley, Pearl had made full use of the network afforded by the California Alumni Association (CAA). During the late thirties, as the idea of bidding to join the University of California developed, Pearl became a more active participant. She was determined to find "ways and means of using Alumni interest more effectively."[29]

In January 1942, she was elected as one of twelve councillors. Paul Yost, a UC Berkeley 1908 graduate and Los Angeles-based banker, was elected president.[30] He had great respect of Pearl and relied on her input, writing to her: "No one else who knows as much about what has been going on or is so closely in touch with the leadership in the county in all such matters as you are."[31,32] Open to all former students and based in Berkeley, the nonprofit organization was involved in fundraising, scholarships, and fostering rewarding connections to the university, fellow alumni, and current students.

At the first meeting after the Regents obtained power to operate Santa Barbara College in 1943, the CAA appointed a committee, with Pearl as chairman, to begin and maintain contact with the college and prepare a plan for future cooperation.[33] In November 1944, the CAA passed a motion to invite Santa Barbara College to affiliate with their association; in March 1945, the college accepted the invitation. It would be another eleven years before the UCSB Alumni Association incorporated under the laws of California as a nonprofit, charitable organization and became the publisher of the USCB Alumnus publication that continues today.[34]

In 1944, Pearl was appointed to serve on another CAA committee on dormitories along with Herman Phleger, who graduated from Berkeley in 1912 and worked as a successful San Francisco attorney specializing in international law. It was no coincidence that both

Phleger and Pearl were selected: as undergraduates, they had been involved in the drive to bring dormitories to the Berkeley campus. As Phleger later recalled:

> We were never successful in getting one. It was three or four years after I graduated that Philip Bowles, who was a Regent of the University, gave the money for Bowles Hall, and as I remember it, it was shortly after that that Rockefeller gave the money for International House.[35]

As it was then, so it continued to distress Pearl that in 1946, no local Santa Barbara committee had received support from the university in raising funds for dormitories or a student union. She wondered if the university should not have a specialist on its staff for this kind of work. "Money raising is a business," she commented. She knew, only too well from personal experience: "During the past thirty years I have been called upon to advise dozens of presidents of colleges and other organizations as to where they could raise money in Santa Barbara." She hesitated to start any program herself unless she was assured of help from the university or alumni association which would make certain that maximum results could be obtained.[36]

Despite her irritation over the lack of dormitories, the university was providing assistance for the transition. At the beginning of June 1944, the UC Santa Barbara College Planning Advisory Committee was formed with Pearl as chairman.[37] The nine-member group was particularly concerned with the style of architecture.[38]

The committee's work took on a new urgency when President Roosevelt signed the G.I. Bill into law on June 22, 1944. Designed to provide a range of benefits to returning war veterans, Title II of the bill, referred to as "educational and training opportunities," was one of its most popular offers. It provided tuition, subsistence, books and supplies, equipment, and counselling services for veterans to continue their education in school or college.

By 1946, California campuses were brimming with young men and a lesser number of young women wearing mix-and-match amalgams of military, coed, and "Joe College" attire.[39] By September 1947, for example, 43 percent of the entire UCLA student body was comprised of returned veterans on the G.I. Bill.[40] Although the bill bolstered the finances of American colleges and universities, it also put a strain on available space.[41]

It was not only veterans who created the education boom. A younger generation of grammar and high school students in California were filling overcrowded classrooms as cities and towns could not build schools fast enough or employ enough teachers to keep up with the population boom.[42] After 1945, higher education served an ever-growing portion of the population. The number of degrees awarded by US colleges and universities more than doubled between 1940 and 1950, and the percentage of Americans with bachelor's degrees, or advanced degrees, rose from 4.6 percent in 1945 to 25 percent a half-century later.[43] As Geiger describes: "Academic knowledge underwent even greater growth, as did its assimilation into American society. As the impact on American life and culture became more apparent, so did the salience of colleges and universities for American society."[44]

With encouragement from Sproul, in the summer of 1944, Storke and Harold Chase paid $40,000 to buy a tract of 25 acres on the Mesa next to the college which they held for the university. When proceedings were completed, by which the university could take title, they delivered that for what they had just invested, and the Regents pledged that the university would use the campus for a cultural and educational center, and would not dispose of the property for any other purpose.[45]

During 1945, while plans for the new campus on the Mesa were postponed pending the settlement of a threatened lawsuit against the university by the state Board of Education, Pearl and her committee began developing a master plan for SBCUC, including approach roads, new rights of way for streets, and subdivisions and easements for utilities.[46] By late 1947, not much had yet been achieved, while college, community, public agencies, and city officials deliberated. Pearl enlisted the support of her friend L. Deming Tilton, a former Santa Barbara planning commissioner, and pressed for him to work as a consultant to the city and take the project forward. While activity on the Mesa stalled, the educational program of the college was continued at the Riviera campus.

The constraints on construction, the change in management, and the Regents' desire to keep the college small, led to the retirement of Provost Phelps in 1946. He was replaced by J. Harold Williams, a Stanford graduate who had joined UCLA in 1924, becoming a professor in education and psychology in 1929. Like Phelps, he was an able administrator: his intimate knowledge of the University of California was of great help to the institution at Santa Barbara, newly incorporated into the complex system. He made a favorable impression on Pearl, who reported to Sproul, "he is getting along well and impressing many with his courteous and business-like way of meeting faculty and student problems."[47,48]

Additional space was not the only resource required for the influx of students; of equal importance was additional housing. To resolve this, a Veterans Village was established on the site of the Hoff Hospital. No longer needed by the Army, the hospital was turned over to the Federal Housing Authority early in 1946. The city acquired seventy hospital buildings in May 1946. Thirty-five units were to be used for city housing, and thirty-five for Santa Barbara College students.[49] Many local residents had the memorable experience of starting life in Santa Barbara in one of these barracks-conversions. By March 1947, conditions had deteriorated, and Pearl was forced to write to Williams that:

> Investigation has shown a distressing lack of discipline both the dormitories and the cafeteria. It seems evident that the veterans, many of whom find it hard to study, are seriously disturbed

> by the unrestrained and almost continuous roughhouse of the young non-service students. The rules have presumably not been explained recently, approved by the students, or enforced with their help. Apparently the conditions are such that, with separate dormitories, one house mother can properly supervise only one dormitory while at present one is asked to supervise two men's or three women's buildings. (During the first semester, there was no house mother for the women so that practices were followed which it is now difficult to eradicate.) The number of men in the Village makes it particularly difficult for girls who are away from home for the first time.[50]

The matter was referred to Sproul, who appointed a committee of college officials to investigate. Contrary to Pearl's findings, they reported that conditions at the Village were not such to warrant the criticisms.[51]

On October 3, 1947, Sproul visited Santa Barbara College for himself and told the assembled students, "This great enrolment is certainly an effective reply to the Kremlin's charge that capitalism exploits the masses, for here the poor as well as the rich have the opportunity to go to school."[52] Three days later, Sproul was featured on the front cover of *TIME* magazine alongside the question, "Is everyone entitled to a college education?"

That evening in Santa Barbara, Sproul, Pearl, and other city leaders watched the SBCUC Gauchos football team play Pomona. As Pearl later recalled, "We never saw the ball, and the electric lights looked as though they were smoking so thick was the fog. President Sproul admitted he had never tried to watch a football game through a cloud."[53] Pearl might have felt that developing the university at the Mesa was also in the fog. However, as Storke later wrote, "Once again Santa Barbara's 'Guardian Angel' came to our aid."[54]

In 1948, the 410-acre site of the Marine officers' training base adjoining the airport at Goleta, nine miles west of the city, was declared war surplus. As Storke later described: "The war assets

107. Goleta and Isla Vista pre-UCSB

administration offered to sell their site with its buildings, paved roads, Olympic size swimming pool, and other improvements for the sum of $1. The Regents accepted the sites in the new campus."[55] Officially opened in September 1954, the site was very beautiful, with more than a mile of shoreline. The barracks and other structures and facilities had been "renovated and adapted for instructional and dormitory uses. Two new permanent buildings were completed: the library and a science building."[56]

According to the campus history pages as derived from Verne Stadtman's Centennial Record, the University of California History Digital Archives has remarked:

> Of the ninety-nine Marine base buildings originally on the site, the University continued to use forty-two in the mid-1960s. The others were razed to make room for new roads and structures. Twenty-five permanent buildings were occupied, and five more were planned to be ready by spring or fall, 1966. Two hundred additional acres were subsequently purchased. Dormitory accommodations on campus were available for

> 2,062 students; 250 University-owned apartments for married students were available off-campus.[57]

This left the university with surplus buildings and land at the Riviera and Mesa campuses.

As I was researching papers at UC Berkeley's Bancroft Library, I came across a fascinating memo to Sproul sent by George Pettitt, secretary to the UC president. It is revealing of Pearl's perseverance at this time.

> Last Sunday morning I had a brief twenty-minute telephone call from Miss Pearl Chase, while my breakfast hotcakes were getting cold on the table, which I believe should be reported to you for information—the telephone call, not the hotcakes.
>
> Miss Chase talked so fast that I was not able to keep track of all of the points she raised, but I would summarize them as follows:
>
> 1. Miss Chase believes that conservation and recreational developments for the city of Santa Barbara require active cooperation from the University of California.
>   a. In plans for disposing of the Mesa site.
>   b. Development of recreational areas along the coast between Goleta and Santa Barbara.
>   She would like to discuss these problems with the President, and I suggested that she write a letter, putting down her thoughts.
> 2. Miss Chase is particularly interested in the canyon which traverses the northwestern portion of the Mesa site. I gather that in her opinion this canyon could be separated from the rest of the site in any sale plan without greatly decreasing the developmental value of the site for some other use. She believes that the canyon would be of greatest value to the city of Santa Barbara as a sheltered recreational area adjoining the beach.
> 3. Miss Chase has some sort of an involved deal concerning the athletic stadium on the beach. I couldn't follow her

> presentation too closely but my understanding was that the University might purchase the land which it now leases from the city in order to provide funds for further development of that immediate area.
>
> 4. Miss Chase mentioned a strip of land which lies between the Shore Highway and the beach, the ownership of which she felt should be vested in the public and the development of which should be for recreational purposes only.
>
> There were other involved points but I had my mind on the hotcakes, and spent most of the twenty minutes trying to persuade Miss Chase that it would be better to put her thoughts down on paper.[58]

In 1959, Santa Barbara Junior College took over the Mesa campus, and the site's industrial arts building was renovated to become the administration building for the newly renamed Santa Barbara City College. Pearl actively supported the move.

She was less keen, however, that the Riviera campus (today's Riviera Park) should remain a permanent site for SBCUC. It lacked ground space for athletics and physical education, and its buildings represented a large investment, difficult to duplicate. A large enrolment of students would, over the years, increase the traffic and parking problems of a fine residential area already seriously affected by existing conditions.[59] The university kept the Riviera campus intact until 1962 when it was purchased by the Santa Barbara school district for $119,349. A few years later, when the city changed the zoning classification for the Riviera, the school district sold the site for $330,500.[60,61]

In 1953, Santa Barbara-based architects Soule and Murphy were replaced with Pereira and Luckman, a Los Angeles-based architectural firm. William Pereira and Charles Luckman were well known as community master planners. They were asked by the UC Regents to create a master plan for the greater Goleta valley. Creating their master plan, it included an "urban revitalization" infrastructure program for Isla Vista and Old Town Goleta, a town center (with City Hall and other administrative facilities) at Storke and Hollister, and greater connectivity between UCSB and the surrounding community.[62] However, housing continued to be a problem during the early 1950s; there were still not enough "apartments and rooming houses in the area surrounding campus, [which] meant that a large portion of the students lived in Santa Barbara and commuted to the Goleta campus."[63]

The 1954 relocation was a fundamental step in the creation of the present-day UCSB, but the move to Goleta was not welcomed by all at the time. As one historian noted, "It would have been difficult to find a more physically isolated college in American higher education. The campus itself was a bleak, dusty, weed-grown place."[64] In 1954, there were 1,883 students at the campus. But California was growing by leaps and bounds.

As chairman of the Planning Advisory Committee, Pearl's views on the design of the new campus carried weight. She went to great lengths to emphasize the details that mattered most:

> The spacing, color, handling of outdoor areas, lines of communication and planting are particularly important. The consideration of the effect of the design of the Campus, and the climate, upon the persons using the Campus, are important both from a sociological and physiological point of view. The scale and design should be such as to inspire the personnel, but not be dogmatic or fixed.[65]

As the date for the opening of the new campus approached in the fall of 1954, Pearl, a bit like a mother hen, continued to press for appropriate accommodation. Two of the eight sororities were losing the leases of their houses, and what they were going to do next was undetermined. There were no large houses in the Goleta section; Kappa Alpha Theta had a lease in Santa Barbara until the following year which could accommodate seventeen girls, but they were losing their House Mother. As a member of KAT, Pearl took it upon herself to find a replacement for the $100-per-month job and solve the difficulty, "if sororities are both willing and able to build on lots assigned to them on the new campus by the regents."[66]

She also took charge of planning for the student accommodation at Santa Rosa Hall. The hall opened in 1955 and "allowed the students to live and eat in new buildings, not the repurposed 'temporary' Marine barracks and mess hall." It was built specifically to house "female students since at the time it was considered improper for young female students to live on their own in apartments or rooming houses."[67]

On March 28, 1955, the program for the dedication of the new campus and the inauguration of Provost Clark Kuebler took place simultaneously. Kuebler, had received his AB from Northwestern University and PhD from the University of Chicago.[68] A professor of classics, he came to Santa Barbara having previously served as president of Ripon College in Wisconsin. Pearl, who was acting as a representative of Mills College, was in her element. She described the program as:

> [...] very stirring and entirely successful. Each of the series of events proved notable. The weather was fine and those attending were therefore comfortable and could focus their attention upon the persons participating in the events. Everyone seemed to thoroughly enjoy meeting old friends and becoming acquainted with other leaders in educational and civic fields.
>
> It was a distinct honor and privilege for me to represent Mills College on this occasion. Because of the early date of the founding of Mills—1852—I was assigned the eighty-second place in the line. Several friends noted the lovely yellow and white hood of the Doctorate.[69,70]

108. UCSBC inauguration – dedication March 1955
Governor Knight, President Sproul, Regent Dickson,
Provost Kuebler

While the proposed college community was being developed at Isla Vista and the "great open space West of Goleta" on land owned by Storke, Pearl felt it was extremely important that the available areas between the university and Santa Barbara were properly planned and guided in the improvement.[71] She foresaw that very great changes would take place in this area in the years to come.

In 1958, the Regents revised the academic plan, increasing the capacity of the university to 10,000, renaming the institution the University of California, Santa Barbara, and directing that it be developed as a general campus of the university. In 1960, the planned maximum was increased once more to 15,000, and in February 1967, yet another revision in the academic plan provided for a new enrolment ceiling of 25,000 to be reached in the mid-1980s.

CHAPTER 20

The End of the Second World War

On May 8, 1945, both Britain and the United States celebrated Victory in Europe Day (V-E Day). Cities in both nations, as well as formerly occupied cities in western Europe, put out flags and banners, rejoicing in the defeat of the Nazi war machine.[1] On August 14, US President Harry S. Truman broke the news of the allies' victory over Japan. Later, at midnight, Britain's new prime minister Clement Atlee confirmed it, saying: "The last of our enemies is laid low."[2] On September 2, formal surrender occurred aboard the battleship USS *Missouri* in Tokyo Bay, officially ending the Second World War.

By the summer of 1945, Americans had been living under wartime rationing policies for more than three years, including limits on such goods as rubber, sugar, gasoline, fuel oil, coffee, meat, butter, milk, and soap. Meanwhile, the US government's Office of Price Administration (OPA) had encouraged the public to save up their money, ideally by buying war bonds, for a brighter future. With the war finally over, American consumers were eager to spend their money on everything from big-ticket items like homes, cars, and furniture to appliances, clothing, shoes, and everything else in between. Many things were looking up: "Driven by growing consumer demand, as well as the continuing expansion of the military-industrial complex as the Cold War ramped up, the United States reached new heights of prosperity in the years after World War II."[3]

After the war, many of the servicemen who had recuperated in Santa Barbara returned to stay. The population surged by 10,000 people between the end of the war and 1950, and construction activities gained momentum. This burst of growth had dramatic consequences for the local economy and infrastructure; Pearl thought such growth had also "increased the need for maintenance of controls which are fair to all."[4]

While much of the new development was directed toward the construction of residential housing located on the outskirts of the city, commercial development had also become an increasing factor. Pearl found herself called upon "day in and day out for advice and information by individuals and public officials on all sorts of subjects but particularly on zoning, tree cutting, parks, planning, parking, historical matters, billboards, signs and employment."[5]

Even with its problems, she still hoped Santa Barbara would remain beautiful. However, she worried that the business section of the city was in danger of losing the architectural harmony that so impressed visitors and residents. In 1946, the Chamber of Commerce, which the Chase family still strongly influenced, "decided that architectural harmony was 'essential in the Santa Barbara business areas to promote the economic and cultural welfare of the community, and that a return to community architectural supervision of the business district would be desirable and beneficial.'"[6] Polling its members, the Chamber found that ninety-five percent of them as well as fifteen civic organizations were in favour of both re-establishing an appropriate regional type of architecture and adopting an ordinance that would secure architectural supervision of the business district. The city council took a similar view, and on January 9, 1947, they adopted Ordinance 2121, reforming the Architectural Board of Review along the same lines as the Ordinance of 1925.[7]

Pearl was an important supporter of the new board. Despite all her efforts, however, she could not prevent State Street from slipping back toward becoming another "Main Street." As she informed the mayor in 1948, "We urge you to maintain and demonstrate your continued interest in re-establishing Santa Barbara's dwindling reputation for a distinctive architecture."[8] Her advice may as well have fallen on deaf ears. A new generation of architects influenced by the modern movement settled in Santa Barbara. Many of them took note of the many old buildings in the city and expected that they would be torn down, generating plenty of opportunities for "flat roofs."[9] They forecast correctly.

"By the mid-1950s the architectural character of the city began to change because of the increasing loss of older structures to make way for new development."[10] According to a member of the Architectural Board of Review, "Pearl was like the boy at the dyke, holding back the flood of bad and indifferent architecture with one hand while pursuing an educational programme to win support for the principles established so long ago with the other."[11] Pearl was undaunted, and over the following years she persisted in challenging the status quo. In 1957, the city adopted a fully revised comprehensive zoning ordinance and later, in 1964, adopted a new General Plan.

CHAPTER 21

The Mid-Century and Conservation Education

While the world was at war, Pearl's work with the California Conservation Council (CalCC) took on a new significance. Wartime planning was paramount, and stress was placed on the conservation of human energies as well as natural resources.[1] Conservation was closely linked to the war effort: "We have a war to win! Practice conservation for victory, for your country, for your children,"[2] and, "It is as important to work for conservation in wartime as in peacetime," became campaign slogans for the council.[3] America, and particularly California, Pearl stressed, was:

> [...] an arsenal of the "Democracies." In winning this war, this arsenal will be greatly depleted. After the war, we must maintain our strength as a nation on a smaller reserve of resources. Waste must be eliminated, our people must be trained to utlilize these resources and their products with greater efficiency, so conservation should become the watchword for tomorrow.[4]

With so much to do and so many of her former experienced helpers away on war business, Pearl worked tirelessly. As her commitments grew, she found herself in a constant state of exhaustion. Fortunately, her workload was eased when, in February 1943, an Irish woman walked through her door, looking for extra work: Patricia O'Neill Mountfort, widow of British portrait painter, Arnold G. Mountfort. Pearl wrote of her, "After her husband's death [in 1942], she needed help, she needed guidance, she needed a little

109. A blurred picture of Pearl with her secretaries, Patricia Mountfort on left and Mildred Orpet on right

money, and she began by wrapping packages and making conservation things, and she had a typewriter with three languages on it and she learned to do pretty well on the one with just English."[5]

Taking over responsibility for the CalCC, the garden tours, and Pearl's work with the Native Americans, Mountfort made many friends who thought of her as "a diminutive picture of unflagging energy and good cheer."[6] A descriptive name given to her by Navajo Indians who adopted her into their tribe was "Little White Cloud – All Alone."[7] She became one of Pearl's fiercest defenders and greatest supporters, guarding the office and, on many occasions, putting Pearl's name forward for awards and recognition.

In 1943, Pearl took an ambitious step of developing a comprehensive program for conservation education in California. She imagined it would be "most helpful and timely."[8] She was especially focused on making people aware how closely their wealth was tied with the conservation of natural resources. Moving away from nature study, which appealed exclusively to man's sense of beauty and wonder, she aimed to raise awareness, not only of nature but also its relationship to man's economy. She believed the "business of conservation education is a very serious matter if the income of the people of California is to be maintained at present levels."[9]

First, she had to secure the endorsement of educational organizations throughout California.[10] In late May, Pearl travelled to San Francisco and Sacramento to meet with leading conservationists and state officials to present her program for conservation education.[11] She believed the outcome "will be one of the most interesting and useful which we have been able to further through the California Conservation Council."[12] Successfully convincing the California Committee for the Study of Education, they established a subcommittee on conservation education with Pearl as a member.[13] The committee spent six years on the project and went through several personnel changes before reporting their findings in 1949. The following year, the California Department of Natural Resources, in cooperation with the Department of Education, published the work. Entitled *The Guidebook for Conservation Education*, it was heartily endorsed as an expression of basic policy and approved educational direction for the schools of California.[14] Directors of both departments[15] urged teachers to take note of the work and "to appreciate the philosophy expressed there."[16] This philosophy, summarized by Pearl at the end of the book, still holds true in many ways: "Progress depends upon an aroused public opinion on the responsibility of this generation to pass on our natural resources in such condition that the economic welfare of the next generation is assured."[17]

Pearl was convinced that matters should not be left to public officials or legislators alone, and that "while we work with them and include them in our boards and in our discussions and our programs, to have continuity and long-time friendliness it is better to have citizen leadership."[18]

Although great strides were made in the years leading to the development of environmental education programs in the public schools in the 1960s, in 1950, when the work was originally published, the general consensus was that conservation education had limited classroom value. The traditional approach was to "teach the facts," assume that people would "get the facts" about resources concerns, and become concerned themselves. This proved challenging. However, while California was not recognized as being in the top ten states for conservation education, it was the only state that had made conservation a year-round program. Pearl and the CalCC could take credit for this. In 1953, the Conservation Education Association was formed to support the many educators working in the field.[19]

Alongside conservation education work in California's public schools, the CalCC also provided consultation services. On one occasion, these services proved useful to Dr. Aubrey Neasham, a 1926 UC alumnus and National Parks Service regional historian, for a collaborative project with the University Extension, to promote a three-day institute on conservation at UC Berkeley the following December.[20]

110. CalCC leaflet

The CalCC was already affiliated with both the NPS and the University Extension. Putting forward the names of seven people she knew were associated with the CalCC for a planning committee, Pearl quickly established a plan for the institute.[21] However, in July, the project collapsed after the University Extension pulled out. Pearl was "very much surprised and disappointed" that after all the talk, it was called off.[22] The fact that the institute did not happen is less important than the reasons why: among those in the faculty to oppose the program, Emmanuel Fritz, Associate Professor of Forestry, summed up the views of his colleagues:

> The term "conservation" is in bad repute. It is a catchy term, and everyone is naturally for its general purposes but so much sentimentalism and emotionalism has crept into it that the term has fallen into disrepute. We have had conservation meetings every year but for the life of me I can't see that they accomplished anything of any lasting value. I believe there is a real need for rounding up people interested in conservation in one way or another sometime soon. Whether 1946 is a propitious time I can't now say. We are still too unsettled and still worrying about Russia, of [the Office of Price Administration], of atom bombs, etc.
>
> The program as outlined with principally national and state Bureau heads as speakers is all wrong in my opinion. What about the people who own the resources? The fact that this or that resource should never have been surrendered to private ownership has nothing to do with the problem the cold fact is that they are privately owned. Consequently, the rights and interests of these owners must be recognized and the owners should be invited.
>
> It is a mistake to shed crocodile tears about natural resource management within conservation circles and then pull a gun on the owners. Much better results can be attained, I feel sure, if those who as impartial students have studied the natural resource situation will get together with owners and public

> officials to discuss the situations dispassionately without rancour and without threats. If the owner group is not made part of the Institute their opposition and animosity will be a natural consequence and forever thereafter a serious hurdle.[23]

Pearl did not disagree with this sentiment; she believed that the conservation movement needed new impetus.[24]

Although the Institute never took place, CalCC continued to collaborate with UC and many of its future presidents were associated with the university.

During 1946, while making every effort to keep local and state organizations and the public informed of CalCC and its work relevant, Pearl created the CalCC Honor award. The aim was to recognize outstanding efforts and activities on the part of volunteer and part-time conservationists, and of those whose profession or occupation was in some educational or natural resources field. Five years later, a Merit award was added for educators and professional workers. It proved a notable success: the roster of recipients included some of the most well-known names working in conservation across America. Interestingly, the highest percentage were

111. CalCC leaflet

native Californians. This was not nepotism, but due to the variety and extent of responsibility which they managed in California.

Such was Pearl's influence and reputation that she was invited to address delegates at the Mid-Century Conference on Resources for the Future at Washington[25] in December 1953. She remarked:

> If anything is at the grassroots, it is the schools. I feel we should study and appreciate the importance of properly trained teachers, not only in the science field but in the social studies and in the vocational fields, agriculture, and so forth. I believe that where industry and state and federal agencies have realized the importance of teacher training in the conservation education field they have profited from the cooperation of the volunteer or civic groups in obtaining a wider field for understanding of the problems.[26]

By 1950, every Californian community had a number of important civic and conservation organizations which had no state affiliation and could only be reached through the CalCC. In counties across the state, Conservation Week committees were the nucleus of year-round county associations or councils. In these communities, farm advisors, forest officers, park administrators, and citizens' groups testified that as the demand for educational materials and services increased, their work was made simpler and more effective because of the local organization and greater citizen cooperation.[27]

Paradoxically, interest in CalCC had developed so rapidly that it had outgrown the capacity of the central machinery to keep pace with it. It was at a crossroads, and Pearl was hopeful that its supporters would rally together and suggest how it could best serve the developing needs and opportunities for conservation in California. Since it had been established in 1934, its work had been entirely voluntary. With a full-time secretary and three part-time volunteers, Pearl had exhausted all their energies to encourage local communities in California to "develop their own initiative and leadership."[28]

After seventeen years as president, she decided there was need for a change in program and she was not the person to engineer the new developments working from Santa Barbara. To get things done required personal contact with leaders and community organizers, and most of the ones she knew and relied on in the conservation field were based in the Bay Area and Sacramento. It was decided to split the state into North and South divisions. Desirous that the president should oversee the North, she stepped down from that role and appointed Aubrey Drury, brother of Newton. A UC alumnus (class of 1914), Aubrey had cofounded the Drury Brothers advertising and public relations agency before joining Save the Redwoods League to manage their affairs.[29] Pearl hoped his devotion to the cause would find a wider field, and his specialized knowledge and abilities would be of great value.[30] She continued as vice president and operated the office for southern California with Mountfort at 912 Santa Barbara Street.

On January 28, 1951, while Pearl was reshaping the council, her father, Hezekiah died quite suddenly of heart failure at age eighty-nine. Both she and her brother Harold were with him at the time of his death. Pearl was pleased that her father was spared a long period of suffering.[31] The following day, a private funeral was held

112. Hezekiah with Pearl

113. Hezekiah Chase
by Clarence Mattei

at their Anacapa Street home before his body was taken to Santa Barbara cemetery for cremation. He was interred at a family plot overlooking the ocean with the backdrop of the rising Santa Ynez Mountains. Nearly all his possessions and the bulk of his estate were left to Pearl, who decided to stay at the family home. His legacy was summed up in an obituary:

> For nearly half a century [Hezekiah] devoted his best energies and thought to the upbuilding of his community. He was known throughout California for his integrity and important dealings. With Mr. Chase the "other fellow's" problems always came first, and his generous hand was ever ready to help those in need—to an extent known only to himself and those who benefitted by his friendship and kindness.[32]

As new technologies, ambitious national purposes, and changing popular beliefs were transforming America's natural environment, the CalCC, under Aubrey Drury's leadership, began to shift its focus from material things to immaterial values. Pearl, quoting the conservationist Seth Gordon, proclaimed: "In this whole conservation program we know that our worst problem is *people*. Not how to manage the forest. Not how to manage our wildlife and all the other things. But how in the world to get the people to appreciate the things we are talking about."[33]

In February 1954, Pearl and then president, Professor Woodbridge "Woody" Metcalf,[34] decided to incorporate the CalCC as a nonprofit educational corporation with long-established activities as well as two new activities to reflect the growing interest in research and development of educational programs on conservation and wise use of both renewable and non-renewable natural resources. It was a tremendous achievement and secured its future for another generation.

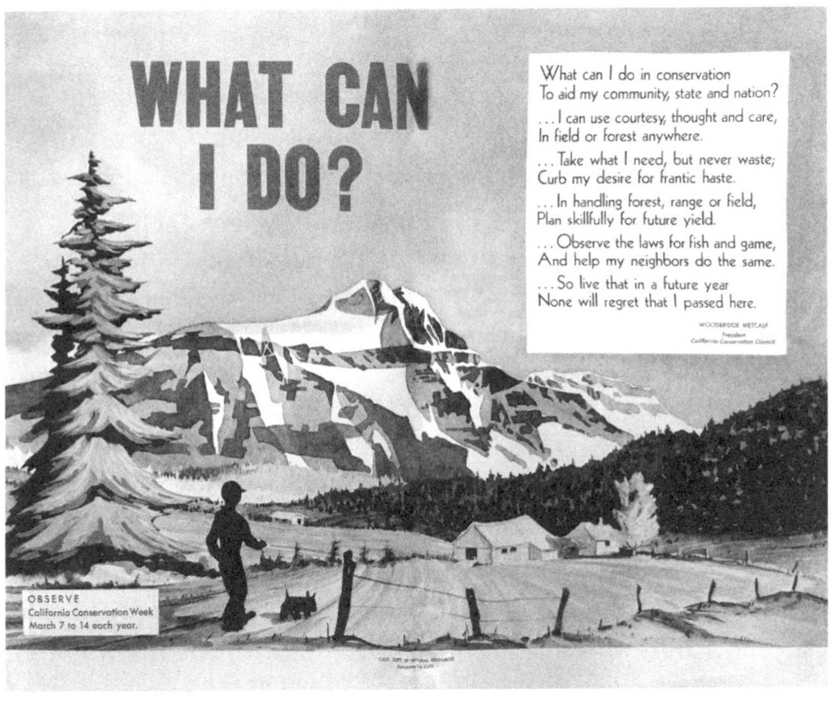

114. California Conservation Week leaflet

CHAPTER 22

Save the Redwoods League and the Sierra Club

The 1950s was a decade of growth and abundance in California and this engendered a persistent note of optimistic boosterism in public discourse.[1] Kevin Starr, California historian has remarked:

> Economically, this growth was at once the result and the symbol of the take-off era of what many economic historians have described as the single greatest arc of rising prosperity in American history and, quite possibly, in all of modern history as well. An unprecedented abundance connected to growth characterized California in these years and would continue to do so for the rest of the century. In these years the national experience and the California experience became, increasingly, a converging phenomenon.[2]

Along with this rapid growth came problems. As dam builders, loggers, miners, and highway builders increasingly targeted wilderness areas, conservationists realized they would soon have to go on the offensive.[3] Part of this was driven by the scientists who began to acknowledge the importance of protecting land, simply because allowing nature to remain untouched could benefit the future of the environment by preserving biodiversity and protecting species of trees, plants, and animals. In the years that followed, conservationists could not ignore the necessity of statutory protection of wilderness.[4]

Collaborating with the California State Parks (CSP), the National Conference on State Parks (NCSP), the Izaak Walton League, the

Audubon Society, Save the Redwoods League (STRL), and the Sierra Club (SC), Pearl played an important part in shaping this dialogue.

During the Second World War, CSP experienced a quiet period. Some parks closed for use for war exercise, and attendance was lower at the remaining parks owing to rationing and the subsequent decrease in travel around the state. This was only a temporary lull, and by the end of the war the parks saw a huge surge in use. President Dwight Eisenhower's famous interstate system made cross-country travel a reality for millions of Americans, and the national and state parks benefitted as a result. However, as administrators struggled to meet the rising demand of tourists, they had to grapple with a philosophical question about the very nature of these lands, one still relevant today: do parks exist to preserve nature, or to make that nature accessible for everyone?

In 1946, while the NCSP made an eleven-day Pacific coast pilgrimage from Los Angeles to Portland, opposing sides of the recreation issue began to form within the state park ranks. As described by Ney C. Landrum in *The State Park Movement in America*, in 1947:

> "The NCSP took it upon itself to set up a committee on state park standards, facilities and services to develop some guidelines on this sticky area." The report "acknowledged the legitimacy of outdoor recreation but held that the more active forms should be provided for in separate types of areas other than the scenic or natural state parks, preferably located closer to centers of population." Further work and committees studied the "preservation versus use" issue during the 1950s. However, most of the recommendations were "relatively innocuous and did not generate too much controversy although overdevelopment was frowned upon." What no one denied was that America's state parks would have a major part in the effort to meet the country's burgeoning outdoor recreation demand.

> Most state parks were ill-prepared to assume their share of responsibility. To achieve their potential, traditional state "park" programs would also have to become state "outdoor recreation" programs.[5]

In California, Save the Redwoods League, under the leadership of Newton and Aubrey Drury, had maintained a close partnership with the state parks. It was their wish to create parks that touched the lives of ordinary people. Given her close relations with the Drurys, it was unsurprising that Pearl was elected a councillor of Save the Redwoods League in 1953.[6,7] The goals of the STRL were to save as much as possible of the two million acres of redwoods that remained in private hands along California's coast, and "to foster and encourage a better and more general understanding of the value of the primeval redwood and other forests of America as natural objects of extraordinary interest to present and future generations."[8] Its strategy was to raise the funds to purchase the land from its private owners and then give these holdings to the state to be made into parks: "The League engaged in an extensive national public relations campaign and solicited donations from wealthy individuals across the United States."[9]

Pearl's first visit to see the redwoods was in 1908, to the San Lorenzo River watershed with a group of women from Berkeley. She recalled swinging in "great comfortable hammocks;"[10] she thought the giant trees possessed "a magnificent dignity as well as a tranquil charm." She marvelled at their height, size, and strength; their resistance to fire, to insect pests, and diseases; and their abounding vitality.[11,12]

Quoting Edwin Markham, the poet and native Californian, she remarked:

> These great trees belong to the silences of the millenniums. Many of them have seen a hundred of our human generations rise, give off their little clamours and perish. They chide our

115. Pearl standing by a redwood tree

> pettiness they rebuke our impiety. They seem, indeed, to be forms of immortality standing here among the transitory shapes of time.[13]

She joined the League as a member in 1927 at the same time that STRL helped to establish the California state park system.

In 1930 the Garden Club of America (GCA), of which Pearl was a member, partnered with the STRL to purchase four parcels of land containing 2,552 acres from a timber company in Humboldt Redwoods State Park.[14] The property which was protected from logging and incorporated as the Garden Club of America Grove in 1931, was formally dedicated in 1934. Pearl, as a member of the GCA Redwood Grove Committee that facilitated the purchase took great pleasure from the work. She later wrote an article for the *California Arts and Architecture* magazine[15] on the GCA Redwood Grove entitled "A Gift to California."[16,17]

Over the following years, Pearl continued her fundraising activity for the STRL through the local, state, and national garden clubs. One of her publicity methods was to enclose a redwood trees card in her letters whenever possible. She explained, "I hope I have made a number of new friends for the Redwoods League in this way. We, who know and love our beautiful trees so much, have to remember that there are still many people who have never seen them and have no true idea of their grandeur and beauty."[18]

On April 3, 1937, Pearl and her League colleagues saw the redwood officially recognized as California's state tree. Although they might have been accused of bias, they felt "no tree could better represent the Golden State" and were quick to publicize the fact."[19]

Pearl remained involved in protecting further tracts of redwood forest for the rest of her life.[20,21] She enjoyed her association with STRL, particularly admiring its work because it did such a fine public relations job it made "the world of cooperators comparatively easy."[22] Feeling privileged to be a member of the council and to follow, step-by-step, the growth of the organization and its wise use of the funds placed in its hands, she remarked, "Raising almost $1,000,000 a year over a long period of time makes the League an outstanding example of fine programming and management."[23]

During her visits to San Francisco, it was not unusual for Pearl to make a four-minute walk from the STRL Office at 114 Sansome Street south to the Sierra Club office in the Mills Building on Bush Street. She officially joined the Sierra Club in 1936. Founded in San Francisco on May 28, 1892 by John Muir, the Scottish-American preservationist, the club aimed at sponsoring wilderness outings in "the mountain regions of the Pacific Coast."[24] However, through Muir's advocacy, the club participated in political action to further nature conservation.[25] In the early twentieth century, the club built trails and park buildings, and vocally opposed damming and grazing on some public lands. The club worked closely with the California state parks and supported outdoor recreation programs. Starting in the mid-1930s the California Conservation Council (CalCC) collaborated with the Sierra Club, as it did with many other citizen conservation groups. Despite knowing many of the Directors Pearl did not sit on the club's committees or on the board; she offered her support through the CalCC network, to foster the club's campaigns and literature. In turn, Sierra Club officials participated in Conservation Week and supported her year-round efforts in conservation education.

In 1949, a Santa Barbara-based hiking group started to consider becoming a unit of the Sierra Club. The nearest chapter at the time was in Los Angeles County. A meeting was organized at the Montecito School for Girls,[26] at which Pearl was present. She felt strongly that Santa Barbara seemed "to need advice without end as to how to live near and enjoy our natural forest."[27] That night, it was decided that they join the national club as the Santa Barbara group of the Angeles Chapter of the Sierra Club.[28] Pearl felt that that the new group could be an important and a continuing good influence upon the cause of conservation.[29] Addressing the newly formed team, she said the Sierra Club, "since its beginning[,] has included in its membership men and women who both saw the need for conservation in this country and were able to make others see the need through their work, enthusiasm, and teachings."[30,31]

In 1952, David Brower, a native Californian who attended UC Berkeley before joining the Sierra Club and working his way up, was appointed as the first Executive Director of the Club.[32] In April 1956, he visited Santa Barbara to give a talk to the renamed Los Padres chapter. He and his wife Ann stayed overnight with Pearl at 2012 Anacapa Street. A man of multiple talents, Brower was a master of persuasion. As leader and principal strategist of the club he was credited with inventing modern American environmental activism.[33] Pearl was charmed by him.[34] In his "splendid" talk, he referred to the two kinds of conservation: "The wise use and budgeting of resources for their commodity value, and the preservation, without exploitation, for monetary gain, of some of our best natural, beautiful world."[35] He then discussed "the new force now emerging—the conservationist force."[36]

Pearl was drawn to the dynamic nature of the Sierra Club. Unlike the conservative approach to wilderness preservation taken by the

STRL, the Sierra Club actively fought with state authorities against development in parks and forests. The Sierra Club, with Brower's lead, brought about the September 1964 passing of the Wilderness Act.[37] In the years that followed, the club found its voice in promoting a shift from resource conservation to a more preservation-based approach and the birth of the environment movement

By the end of the 1950s, Pearl had built a formidable reputation, and her value was recognized at national, state, and local levels. Pearl was modest about personal publicity and persistently refused to have her photograph taken, but she enjoyed being valued for her work. As I worked through the archive at UCSB I was impressed at the significant number of awards she received during her lifetime. Unlike many who might frame them in their office or home, Pearl chose to file hers away among her papers. As her biographer I am keen that her achievements are recognized. Taking the mid-century as an example, the long list of awards and tributes she received is notable for the variety.

Among the most remarkable:

- In 1949, the Garden Club of America awarded Pearl the Frances K. Hutchinson Medal for "far-reaching and inspirational leadership in conservation."[38]
- In 1950, the National Conference of Social Work gave her lifetime membership. The same year, the *LA Times*, under the management of Dorothy Chandler, started the "Women of the Year" awards to honor achievements in science, religion, the arts, education, government, community service, entertainment, sports, business, and industry. Pearl was among eleven Southlanders honored in the inaugural year.[39]
- In 1951, the Shoreline Planning Association of California awarded her a certificate of merit.
- In 1952, she received Honorary Life Membership of the California Congress of Parents and Teachers for active leadership in conservation.[40]

- In 1953, the California Fire Prevention Committee awarded Pearl a plaque for efforts to help prevent forest fires through education.[41] She also received a national Nash Motors Company award for her work in conservation.
- In 1954, the Santa Barbara Advertising and Merchandising Club made her an honorary member.[42]
- In 1955, the Santa Barbara chapter of the American Institute of Architects elected Pearl their first honorary associate.[43]
- She was awarded Woman of the Year of Santa Barbara for 1956 by the Santa Barbara Advertising and Merchandizing Club for her continuing efforts above and beyond her regular assignments in furthering the progress, development, and welfare of the city. She was the first woman from the community to receive the award.[44]
- In 1957, the California Recreation Society awarded her for her outstanding work. She was only one of two people to receive the award outside the field, the other being Newton Drury.[45]
- In 1958, the Citizens Adult Education Advisory Council presented Pearl with a sculptured plaque of her profile for her inspirational leadership in the city's adult education program. The Izaak Walton League gave her a tribute award for long and continued service.[46]
- In 1959, the Falcon Club of the US Airforce Academy in Colorado Springs gave her honorary membership for services to their institution.[47]
- In 1960, she was made an Admiral in the Lone Star Navy signed by King Neptune and Davy Jones, and received a certificate of merit from the Western Chapter of the National Shade Tree Conference.[48]

Each award meant something different to her, but the 1959 award of an honorary PhD from UC Santa Barbara was particularly special, given that she had done more than any other person, save for Tom Storke, to bring the university to Santa Barbara.

116. Pearl at the 1958 Adult education program awards. She stands alongside local attorney Francis Price

On September 18, 1959, the university bestowed on Pearl its highest award: an honorary Doctor of Humane Letters. Clark Kerr, who succeeded Robert Sproul as president of UC in 1957, personally recommended Pearl to the Regents for consideration for the award. Like her, he came from a background of Anglo-American probity.[49] Pearl was the first woman to receive an honorary degree from the new university.

Dozens of colleagues and friends sent congratulations, citing the honor as a well-deserved recognition of her accomplishments. It was all the more remarkable given the barriers women still faced in most professions.

CHAPTER 23

The Santa Barbara Presidio and Historic Preservation

The early sixties witnessed the birth of what President John F. Kennedy envisaged as "a new frontier: a frontier of unknown opportunities and perils, a frontier of unfulfilled hopes and threats."[1] This new frontier was not a set of promises, but a set of challenges. An unanticipated beneficiary was the movement to preserve the nation's historic resources. Across the nation, private organizations and individuals were assuming greater responsibility for their past.

In 1961, Jane Jacobs, an American-Canadian journalist, author, theorist, and activist published *The Death and Life of Great American Cities*. This influential book was "the first major effort to repudiate the urban renewal and Modernist planning efforts that were in vogue at the time. She trumpeted the vibrancy of traditional neighborhoods."[2]

Pearl had been formulating ideas along similar lines for a number of years. With her influence in both the public and private sector, she now saw an opportunity for Santa Barbara to preserve and restore its deteriorating Presidio, the last fortress in California that was built by the Spanish in 1782, which occupied a full block in downtown.

As the population within Santa Barbara grew and the development of outlying regions and highways to support them went forward, Pearl felt they had "never known a period of such development of this area."[3] In her opinion, comprehensive planning was an increasingly vital concern. Zoning and subdivision ordinances became the accepted way of dealing with the steadily worsening problem of adequate housing, and with new annexations to the city in the 1950s and 1960s. Moreover, new highways had bypassed, and in many cases demolished, landmarks where too little interest had been shown in preservation.[4] Santa Barbara was one of many communities across America with historic buildings facing these challenges and Pearl kept a close watch on the efforts of other cities to enact and implement historic zoning ordinances.

After the 1953 Louisiana Supreme Court decision to uphold a New Orleans architectural control ordinance which sought to preserve the Vieux Carré section of the city, Pearl was encouraged to believe that an ordinance might be legally valid in Santa Barbara for the Presidio characterized by Spanish Colonial architecture.[5] To bring her vision to life, she needed the cooperation of all members of the community. In lectures, presentations, and exhibitions, she continued to stress the important role of local citizens in planning, which she had started in the 1920s. She believed that citizen understanding of all problems involved were necessary to the success of the planned development of Santa Barbara.[6]

In 1957, the city's second comprehensive zoning ordinance went into effect, the first dated from 1930.[7] In 1958 Pearl rallied all those in the community interested in city planning to discuss and agree on principles of "zones of preservation."[8] Among those interested in this cause was Edwin William Gledhill, "the guardian of Pueblo Viejo." Having served as an early director of the Santa Barbara Historical Society,[9] in 1956 he became director of the Santa Barbara Historical Museum and served as curator of its collection. In August 1958 he proposed the idea of "El Pueblo Viejo" ordinance for the downtown district.

At a meeting on September 19, agreement was reached between representatives of public agencies and organizations as to what was considered "reasonable and desirable" regarding preservation of historic areas.[10] With Pearl's support, a coordinated effort was made in the following months to assist Gledhill and the historical society in passing the ordinance. In 1959 state legislature empowered local governments to establish zoning regulations to protect historic structures and Santa Barbara adopted their "El Pueblo Viejo" ordinance. Passed in March 1960, it prohibited the demolition of any adobe or building of "special historic or aesthetic interest or value," in that area.[11]

In May 1960, two months after the passage of the El Pueblo Viejo ordinance, city council created the Santa Barbara Advisory Landmarks Committee (SBALC) to carry out the necessary inventory of historic sites and structures, and to determine which public and private buildings were of architectural and aesthetic significance. It consisted of nine mayoral appointees, including Pearl and Gledhill.[12]

While Pearl was determined that all buildings in the zone should be safeguarded, she was especially keen on the Presidio, a military fort founded by the Spanish on April 21, 1782, which she considered had inestimable value as an educational attraction.[13,14,15]

The Presidio area never became a fashionable Anglo-American residential district and remained part of the Hispanic community. Although the descendants of the original settlers adopted many Anglo-American traits, they continued to maintain a cohesive Hispanic culture until after the Second World War when the downtown area was commercialized. At the heart of the Hispanic community and near the former Presidio were Santa Barbara's Japanese and Chinese immigrant communities. They lived an almost entirely segregated existence with their own restaurants, joss houses, groceries, and churches.[16]

The story after the war was one of commercial expansion in which residences were replaced with office buildings and many families left. However, Pearl was determined that the Presidio should not be lost to modern city development.

The P&P had followed the growth of the site since the 1920s, when the Community Arts Association took over numerous buildings in the vicinity including some of the original adobes. In 1947, she successfully encouraged a celebration of the founding of the Presidio as part of the California Centennial; five years later, she organized Santa Barbara's 170th birthday celebration on the founding day of the Presidio.

As the "back to the city" movement developed in Santa Barbara, so, too, did its accompanying focus on downtown revitalization. Pearl was determined that the Presidio should be the focus of this cultural revival. Envisioning how it would be financed and operated, she was convinced that its future would be most secure as part of the state parks system.[17] Her timing could not have been more opportune, as the CSP, State Park Commission, and NPS were all revising their strategies beyond simply protecting areas of recreation and scenic value. Alongside the movement to conserve natural resources and wilderness preservation, the historic preservation movement found new impetus.[18]

Stirring this impetus were the Gold Discovery and Gold Rush centennials of 1948 and 1949, the 1949 appointment of the State Historical Landmarks Advisory Committee to advise the State Park Commission on matters relating to historic sites, Newton Drury's 1951 appointment as chief of the division of beaches and parks, the 1953 appointment of Aubrey Neasham as supervisor of the newly created history section of the California division of beaches and parks.[19]

In 1955, Pearl started "quietly working to acquire all the information possible including photographs, maps, and written records concerning the Presidio;" only two rooms from the original fort had survived.[20] She took advantage of the resources in the Mission archive as well as the advice, interest, and knowledge of both Father Maynard Geiger, the archivist, and Aubrey Neasham, whom she knew personally. However, her project was a step into the unknown.[21]

Undaunted, she began a voluminous correspondence with the state division of beaches and parks, city and county government, and local organizations. Acutely aware that downtown property prices were rising and that key lots could change hands, which would make the project impossible, Pearl set about understanding how local interests should be best organized and channelled. Strong public support for the project was shown from the first announcement of the idea of bringing the Presidio into the state parks system. As described by what is now the Santa Barbara Trust for Historic Preservation (SBTHP), "In July 1956, Newton Drury suggested the formation of a private foundation to secure properties within the Presidio area as a holding action until State funds should become available for acquisition and development of an historic park."[22] The idea of a historical preservation trust took root to "be used separately or in combination for the establishment of such a park."[23]

Women had played an important part in the historic preservation movement in the US since the mid-nineteenth century.[24] Whereas in the early years much of their work was done through all-female organizations as amateurs, by the 1950s, while that amateur tradition continued, women had moved into the professional ranks of historic preservation.[25] No one would argue Pearl was not among their ranks. Confident of her own abilities and aware of the challenges ahead, she saw the project as an opportunity to show how historic preservation could work as a tool for community redevelopment and reinvestment, to encourage tourism, and to illustrate how women's leadership could manifest itself.

As with all her work, the educational role was paramount. The multifaceted nature of the task also meant teamwork was essential; no one, she believed, could be an expert on everything. Unlike her previous preservation projects with the missions, the Presidio was almost entirely her own idea, and she provided the funds in the early years. Her goal was to preserve one aspect of Santa Barbara's cultural history. It was not intended as a return to a more innocent past, but rather as a means of discovering the city's identity.

On March 15, 1957, Pearl attended a State Park Commission meeting in San Francisco, where approval was given for a feasibility study of the Presidio. At the same time, she formed a Presidio project committee of nine members, including her brother Harold. The city and county planning departments undertook independent feasibility studies of the site.[26]

On June 18, 1958 a ceremony was held at the Presidio. Joseph Knowland, Chairman of the State Park Commission unveiled a handsome bronze plaque with the inscription

"California Historical Landmark No. 636 Plaque placed by the California State Park Commission in co-operation with the city of Santa Barbara, the Grand Parlors of the Native Daughters and Native Sons of the Golden West, the Santa Barbara Historical Society, and the Boy Scouts of America." During the ceremony Pearl spoke of her hope of preserving the site indefinitely.[27]

117. Royal Presidio Ceremony, June 1958, with Joseph Knowland speaking, Mrs Ben Dismuke standing and Pearl seated to her left

In 1959, Drury was succeeded as chief of the division of beaches and parks by Charles DeTurk, a likeable professor of park management at Sacramento State College.[28] That October, Pearl, who had known DeTurk for many years, having met him at the National Conference of State Parks, invited him and other representatives from the division to see the Presidio for themselves. They were not only interested in the site, but DeTurk also advised the board of supervisors to waste no time in making plans for the future acquisition and development.[29] In 1960 Neasham published a three-year study of the State's recreation needs under the title: California Public Outdoor Recreation Plan. The plan contained "a report on California's history, routes and sites with an emphasis on the importance of the preservation of historic sites for their educational and commercial value."[30] Pearl was one step closer.

A resolution restating the city's interest in a plan for a historic park and beautification project in the heart of El Pueblo Viejo was adopted and sent to the State Park Commission. The Commission, meanwhile, was gathering information for a proposed bond finance program of park development throughout the state. It was reported that if and when the Commission decided to proceed, "Santa Barbara official bodies and interested private citizens would find many ways in which to assist and augment it."[31]

On January 21, 1962, the first organizational meeting to promote incorporation of the Santa Barbara Trust for Historic Preservation was held. Shortly before, "Articles of incorporation were filed with the office of the California Secretary of State on January 17, 1963, and the first board meeting was held the following day."[32] Pearl, who was elected as the trust's first vice president, was largely responsible for the appointment of the officers and trustees.[33] The goals of the SBTHP were: "The cultivation of knowledge, appreciation and civic pride in buildings, sites and areas of historical significance, and encouraging and assisting in the preservation, restoration and beautification of the real and personal property of every nature and description, including but not limited to the Royal Presidio."[34] Although reconstruction of the Presidio as a State Historic Park (SHP) was a primary aim of the trust, it was also dedicated to preserve, rehabilitate and restore historic sites buildings and objects of historical interest in the county.

Incorporated as a nonprofit, tax-exempt California corporation, Pearl declared the SBTHP was "in no way set up to usurp any of the duties of other local organizations such as the Santa Barbara Historical Society, and the regional historical societies in the county."[35] She reminded the incorporators the site would serve as a "Great tourist attraction, and could be utilized for recreational and educational purposes. But the project was not intended to serve purely as a museum and there was a need to focus public attention on the reconstruction plan and its value to the community."[36]

Part of the urgency in forming the trust in late 1962 and its initial objective was the acquisition of the El Cuartel, the Guards House. This one-story adobe located in the Presidio area was constructed in 1788, and was the oldest adobe in Santa Barbara and second oldest in California. It was one of only two adobes remaining from the original Presidio.[37,38] The SBTHP acquired El Cuartel for $27,500. It was Pearl's aim that El Cuartel would be offered to the Department of Parks and Recreation as the first unit of the State Historical Monument, hoping it would be used as a hospitality center for visitors. As one reporter at the time noted, "In these matters her great enthusiasm usually wins out so that's probably what will be very appropriately."[39]

While Pearl forged ahead with her Presidio work, "in 1964 the Santa Barbara City Council adopted a General Plan for the city. The plan showed a reconstructed Presidio as part of the city's Master Plan. In the following year, the Santa Barbara County Board of Supervisors declared its support of a reconstructed Presidio by passing a resolution similar to the one adopted by the Santa Barbara City Council."[40]

118. El Cuartel, c.1958

In January 1966, the offer of El Cuartel to the State Parks Commission was accepted, and the following May it was deeded to the state of California as a historic monument.

At the same time, the federal government was renewing its role as an active preservation advocate. In 1965, President Lyndon B. Johnson, who had served as president since the assassination of President Kennedy in 1963, convened a special committee on historic preservation funded by the Ford Foundation. In the presidential campaign of 1964, he "wanted a catchy slogan."[41] He unveiled his slogan "in 'The Great Society,' which encompassed movements of urban renewal, modern transportation, clean environment, anti-poverty, healthcare reform, crime control, and educational reform."[42] This new consciousness fostered an alliance between conservationists and environmentalists, and a growing awareness of the nation's historic resources. The special committee produced a report titled *With Heritage So Rich*, which became a rallying cry for the preservation movement.

On October 15, 1966, Congress passed the National Historic Preservation Act. As detailed by the National Park Service, "It was the most comprehensive preservation law the nation had ever known. The act established permanent institutions and created a clearly defined process for historic preservation in the United

States."[43] No longer was preservation to be dominated by the state: "With the introduction of federal programs and with the granting of funds predicated on the implementation of an approved state preservation program, the impetus for preservation shifted away from Sacramento to Washington."[44]

The law required individual states to take on much more responsibility for historic sites in their jurisdictions. Each state would now have its own historic preservation office and was required to complete an inventory of important sites.[45] In California, the Department of Parks and Recreation "was given responsibility for the new federal mandates."[46,47]

By the feast day of Saint Barbara on December 4, 1966, the trust's repairs were completed and El Cuartel came under the operation and maintenance of the state division of beaches and parks. Private subscriptions covered the $37,000 cost of bringing the property back to life. The trust could then turn its attention to the next major step in its goal of Presidio restoration. The previous November, the group started trying to acquire the site of the Presidio Chapel.[48] Pearl and her colleagues were realistic, recognizing that the trust lacked sufficient funds to accomplish this on their own. To overcome this obstacle, in 1966 they developed a strategy to combine the trust's unique capacities with the power and resources of state government by "creating a model private-public partnership between SBTHP and the department" of Parks and Recreation.[49] This strategy is detailed in "Interpretation Master Plan: El Presidio de Santa Barbara State Historic Park:"

> Under this strategy SBTHP would acquire properties on and around the site of the original Presidio and deed them to the department to become part of a new State Historic Park. An enabling law passed by the State Legislature granted SBTHP the privilege of operating, maintaining, and staffing the park on behalf of the California State Parks. In addition, SBTHP raised funds for the property acquisitions and to carry out major

archaeological excavations, historical reconstructions, museum installations, and ongoing education programs related to the Presidio. Rental income generated from the various properties acquired within the park including parking lots and commercial buildings was given by the State to help the trust support its operations.[50]

Pearl considered the restoration of the Chapel to be "the finest possible memorial to the early founders of our beloved Santa Barbara."[51] There were many other members of the community, old and new, who agreed and were willing to give support to the project. Owing to the political constraints and funding requirements, Pearl saw the work as a step-by-step project;[52] she enjoyed the fact that "the more we learn, the more we want to know!"[53]

The chapel site, which was in ruins, was partially built over with a Buddhist temple. In preparation for the eventual reconstruction, this was immediately torn down. Archaeological work began in 1967, led by UCSB students, instructors, and volunteers. Among those to spend many weekends at the Presidio were Bill Luton, Jr.

119. Cañedo Adobe at El Presidio de Santa Barbara Historic Park after reconstruction

and his father, who owned KEYT, Santa Barbara County's first TV station, several Ford dealerships, and other businesses. "It was very much a working board because they did not have a lot of paid staff to do things," Luton told me. "Miss Chase was hands on to a big degree. She didn't just sit and have the ideas. She put her work with it."[54] Pearl inspired strong feelings among her volunteers. She was universally praised for standing almost single-handedly as a bulwark against the intrusion of forces that would have completely changed the character of the city.[55]

At its February meeting in 1968, the California State Park and Recreation Commission classified the Presidio project as "Presidio de Santa Barbara State Historical Monument." The following June, "the Commission adopted the Spanish article 'El' as part of the unit's name. In May 1970, the Commission dropped the words 'Historical Monument' from the project title and added 'State Historic Park.'"[56] Pearl remained a vice president of the SBTHP until 1972.

On November 16, 1968, Pearl was given a surprise eightieth birthday party. More than two hundred and fifty people of a grateful community attended. She received a message from President and Mrs. Johnson and a letter from Governor Reagan. Looking her best in a blue gown with her signature orchid corsage, she cut a huge birthday cake with a masterpiece sugar icing painting of the Presidio alongside the message, "Congratulations and best wishes to a Great Lady from her countless friends and admirers." Daniel Grant, county supervisor, spoke admiringly of the cake, to which Pearl responded with a question: "Yes it's beautiful. But tell me, Dan, what are you doing about putting utilities underground?"[57]

In the same year the SBTHP was formally established, Pearl retired from active leadership of the California Conservation Council, which she had managed since 1933. Changing her role with the council, she became its honorary president, remarking that "there will always be work to be done by good conservationists!"[58]

CHAPTER 24

Civic Beautification

As a conservationist, Pearl adapted wholeheartedly with the changing environment brought about by the Kennedy and Johnson administrations. The early sixties saw a shift in emphasis from resource efficiency to that of quality-of-life issues.[1] Aimed at halting the rapid deterioration of America's environment due to urban blight, uncontrolled waste production, and unplanned development, this new consciousness encouraged new thinking in conservation circles. There was not, as of yet, what could be called an "ecological" or "environmental movement." Citizens became concerned with "saving wild lands and scenic rivers for fishing and fish habitat rather than damning rivers for irrigation projects. They became concerned with the health effects of pesticides and polluted air and water as opposed to maximising crop and timber yields."[2]

In 1962 a new feminine voice made herself heard. The work of Rachel Carson "focused public concern on whether American technology and its influence on national politics was threatening the general health and safety of the nation's people and the future of the land itself."[3] Silent Spring was a landmark in the emergence of the modern environmental movement. Like millions of other Americans, Pearl was deeply impressed by her book.

During President Kennedy's administration, the federal government took greater responsibility than at any previous time to exercise its authority on issues involving conservation and preservation. The development of policy in these fields increasingly became the province of the national government. Kennedy was instrumental in the adoption of the idea of an expanded federal role and a higher level of funding, and the Johnson administration extended this legacy even further.[4]

One aspect was an expansion of conservation policy. Congress's participation was vital, and "played a major role in passing legislation, while the executive branch implemented the policy that [it] created, exhibiting a considerable ranch of discretion in how the policy was applied."[5] When Johnson became president, he and his wife Lady Bird were influenced by Stewart L. Udall, the politician and federal government official who had worked with President Kennedy as Secretary of the Interior.[6] He "brought energy and a commitment to conservation to the Interior Department."[7] In 1963, he wrote *The Quiet Crisis* prefaced by President Kennedy. The work brought him national recognition in conservation circles, and Pearl in particular felt he had achieved a leadership in conservation which few others in his position had ever attempted.[8]

Johnson, who saw himself carrying forward FDR's tradition of support for natural resources and extending the Kennedy legacy, relied heavily on Udall's advice. On September 3, 1964, on the occasion of signing the Wilderness Act, Johnson told Americans, "The significance of this occasion goes far beyond these bills alone. In this century, Americans have wisely and have courageously kept

120. Lyndon B. Johnson

a faithful trust to the conservation of our natural resources and beauty. But the long strides forward have tended to come in periods of concerted effort."[9]

President Johnson "wished to unify America, polarized as it then was by race and inequality, around stewardship of its immense beauty. And he was clear: the beautiful land he dreamed of was not meant to be a luxury for the fortunate, but a birth right for every American."[10] In November 1964, he easily won re-election and received a mandate to promote the quality-of-life aspects of his Great Society program. Over the following four years he and Lady Bird made conservation and preservation of natural beauty a passionate aspect of their work. The beautification program that developed helped lay the foundation of the environmental movement of the 1970s and 80s.

Lady Bird's "interest in natural beauty propelled her towards the beautification of her surroundings and with tremendous backing from her husband she made it her own."[11]

She wrote in her diary on January 27, 1965, "Getting on the subject of beautification is like picking up a tangled skein of wool. [...] All the threads are interwoven, recreation and pollution and mental health, and the crime rate, and rapid transit, and highway beautification, and the war on poverty, and parks, national, state

121. Lady Bird Johnson

and local. It is hard to hitch the conversation into one straight line, because everything leads to something else."[12] Indeed, it's very clear from her writings that her interest remained strong, as she later remarked: "Beautification, prissy word though it may be, became the business of the politician, the businessman, the newspaper editor, and not just the ladies over a cup of tea."[13]

In 1964 with the president's direction, "staff member Richard Goodwin put together a task force on Natural Beauty with Charles M. Haar, Professor of Law at Harvard University as chair."[14] With this, Lady Bird "launched her beautification efforts through [the] group. The task force urged the federal government to focus on natural beauty and national programs for the preservation of landscaping and open space. This meant regulating billboards, cleaning up junkyards, rehabilitating city parks, and making national parklands more useful to citizens."[15]

The following February, President Johnson delivered a special message to the Congress on Conservation and Restoration of Natural Beauty in which he said, "A growing population is swallowing up areas of natural beauty with its demands for living space, and is placing increased demand on our overburdened areas of recreation and pleasure." The solution was "a new conservation that would emphasize restoration and innovation."[16]

He asserted that the nation could "introduce, into all our planning, our programs, our building and our growth, a conscious and active concern for the values of beauty."[17] Specific programs included highway beautification, clean-air legislation, and an array of other conservation measures. Plans for a White House Conference on Natural Beauty, to meet the following May were announced on March 12.

On May 24 and 25, the conference, commonly known as "Operation Ladybird," was held at the state department under the chairmanship of Laurance Rockefeller, the businessman, financier, philanthropist, and son of John D. Rockefeller Junior. Mrs.

Johnson opened the conference, and the President made the closing remarks.

It was reported that many Americans, unfamiliar with conservation issues, "mistook the conference to be a search for a new Miss America or new varieties of roses."[18] Pearl was one of 800 delegates from across the nation invited to the conference which consisted of fifteen discussions by panels of citizens, technical experts, representatives of industry and labor, and government officials. Over three thousand applications were received by the organizers. Pearl was one of forty-eight delegates from California, the only one from Santa Barbara.

Representing the Roadside Council on the scenic roads and parkways panel, she called attention to roadside rests. Her recommendations were presented to the President at the final session at the White House. According to Pearl:

> It had been raining all that morning and we were told at noon that the last session would have to be called off. But then at 2:30 the rain subsided, and word came that Mrs. Johnson wanted to hold the reception after all. Well, we all piled into big black buses that took us to the White House, where the 1,000 chairs and a platform were set up on the lawn waiting for us. Hundreds of pink potted geraniums had been put out especially for the occasion. No sooner did everyone settle down than it started to rain again and there was only one solution. We all were told to go into the White House. As we all jammed into the beautiful East Room who should come down the Stairway but President Johnson who had just got up after a short rest. He started shaking hands with everybody which made his guards frantic. Everybody jammed into the beautiful East Room with about 200 standing out in the Hallway. A loudspeaker was set up, the refreshment stands were moved in, and the program went on as scheduled. It was a beautiful piece of impromptu organizing. President Johnson indicated in his talk that he intended to ask

congress for legislation prohibiting billboards along federal-aid highways, except in commercial and industrial areas.[19]

Pearl was pleased with the conference which she thought was "as well organized as any she had seen."[20] So was the president and his wife. He hoped it would help stimulate and guide a truly national effort, at every level of American life, to ensure that all our people can find their lives enriched by the beauty of the world they live in.[21] It has been suggested that it "represented a major transition—a bridge from the traditional conservationism to the new environmentalism, and the start of something grand."[22] It certainly gave a new life to the California roadside reform movement, which, since the end of the 1930s and the victory for county zoning, had fought a tough battle against the billboard barons and their supporters.[23,24]

Through letter writing, petitions, lobbying, and education, Pearl and her colleagues took satisfaction in their achievements. However, the women still faced tired clichés pronounced in belittlingly sexist terms with which they were "cast as educators, civic conscience, and maternal protectors of a nation in need of tidying."[25] After the Second World War when highway construction and plans for a national system of interstate and defense highways resumed, so did reform efforts driven largely by state roadside councils.[26,27]

In 1956, President Eisenhower's Federal-Aid Road Act, which authorized a 41,000-mile system of highways funded by the federal government, was envisioned as a solution to the swollen ranks of motoring Americans. Designed to keep traffic moving safely and at a constant speed, it made no provision for controlling billboard blight or "gently curving country roads with unfolding picturesque views."[28,29]

As state after state tried to enact standards and controls on billboards—usually failing—Pearl and hundreds of other women in garden clubs and roadside committees lobbied their state senators. Pearl had no objection to the long-range planning, engineering and construction record of the California state division of highways. She believed, however, the legislature should be persuaded to protect the enormous investment of the people's tax money by adopting measures to control outdoor advertising and other distracting ugly uses of the roadside.[30,31] Despite their efforts, little was done.

The situation changed, however, in 1965 when the president, who had previously opposed billboard restrictions and had used them for his own campaigning, spoke out in support of highway beautification. Wanting to "make sure that the America we see from the highways is a beautiful America," on October 22, 1965, Johnson signed the Highway Beautification Act. It was nicknamed "Lady Bird's Bill" and described as "a frivolous frill, and a woman's 'whim'" by some senators. Interestingly, the roadside reformers were afforded no role in helping to shape legislation and had scant contact with members of the administration.[32,33]

Despite the president and first lady's energy, the industry was never threatened by the new act and even offered to support it, "knowing well from meetings with White House officials that the bill included the provisions it desired."[34] They even succeeded in having an amendment passed that assured "just compensation" to be paid to all billboard or property owners whose billboards were removed as a result of the act. For roadside reformers this was humiliating, as it meant the defilers of the landscape were now paid to keep from polluting, rather than being fined for having done so all these years."[35,36] Support by roadside reformers "was half-hearted."[37] Helen Reynolds of the CRC noted:

> The roadside beauty lovers—roadside councils, garden clubs, conservationists, etc.—were split into various segments. Some cold-shouldered the bill entirely, some supported it but with reservations so severe it appeared closer to opposition and others recognized a step-in advance and set to work to give it what backing they could.[38]

Pearl was among the latter group. "Everyone, however, found it difficult to stomach the just-compensation clause."[39]

Santa Barbara, with its existing restrictive policy, was less affected than other communities; however, Pearl worried about the remarkably new and quite dreadful ways of advertising on highways then in practice which threatened the city and county. She continued to work for stronger state regulations and hoped that Santa Barbara would "maintain its integrity and standards."[40,41]

Inspired by the national beautification movement, a Santa Barbara-based group of dedicated activists and citizens decided to form an organization to stimulate community interest and action toward the enhancement of Santa Barbara's beauty as a complement to government and private activity. In the summer of 1965, they approached Pearl for her advice and participation, which she was only pleased to offer. She insisted, however, that Santa Barbara should be in the organization's name.

On September 9, the newly formed "Santa Barbara Beautiful" met to begin an effective program for city beautification. All civic groups and private citizens were urged to take part. At this meeting, Pearl offered a quotation from Abraham Lincoln: "I like to see a man proud of the place where he lives." She said she felt a motto could help to crystallize community thinking and stimulate interest. Thus, the idea for Santa Barbara Beautiful took root.[42]

The nonprofit civic organization led by volunteers dedicated to beautifying the city was formally inaugurated at a dinner on September 15. By the following September, Santa Barbara Beautiful had grown from nine to seventeen board members, and Pearl continued to offer her advice.[43]

Across America, the "Camelot years" of the early sixties saw widespread improvement in economic and social terms. After President Kennedy's assassination, a new period, "redolent with the emergent energies and transformation of the Age of Aquarius," took root.[44] The launch and implementation of the Great Society resulted in "the most dramatic decline in poverty over such a brief period" in the twentieth century.[45] During my research, I discussed this period in American history with Professor Emeritus of History at UCSB, Elliot Brownlee. As one of the foremost economic historians in the US, I listened intently as he remarked, "It was really rather phenomenal, and its success is kind of forgotten about; lost in the Vietnam war."[46]

California passed New York state in 1962 as the most populous state in the nation. Two years later, the Free Speech Movement erupted on the UC Berkeley campus. In June 1965, Major Edward White II opened the hatch of the Gemini 4 and stepped out of the capsule, becoming the first American astronaut to walk in space. Pearl, who had been born at a time before the idea of placing stop signs at road junctions, remarked: "Hurrah for the Astronauts and the USA."[47] America was in its ascendancy, and for those Americans making it so, it was great place to be.

CHAPTER 25

Environmental Action

Pearl started the new year of 1967 discussing horoscopes with Tom Storke. Of course, their predictions were focused on the growth of Santa Barbara and its beautification. Architecturally and environmentally the city was facing the new challenges of high-rise construction and pollution. "Like a balloon, the ideology of 'progress,' of upward and onward," was about to burst.[1] Pearl was more determined than ever to take responsibility for tackling the environmental problems and protecting quality of life against unrestrained growth.

As a nation, America was indeed ascendant, but it was also a country on edge. Movements that had been building for years—civil rights, the peace movement, women's liberation, the youth movement, and others—were close to exploding. In 1967, protests erupted around the world; specifically in Santa Barbara, UCSB students expressed their vehement anger toward US foreign policy through a series of violent protests causing thousands of dollars-worth of property damage in Isla Vista and the temporary shutdown of the Santa Barbara Airport. These protests sent an unfiltered message to the government: that they would be held accountable for their decisions, no matter what the cost.[2] Pearl was not directly caught up in the protests, but she understood the issues and felt sympathy with those struggling to be heard.

Pearl's life was dramatically affected by the death of her secretary, Patricia Mountfort,[3] on April 17, as well as her brother Harold's crippling stroke the following month.[4] Over the following years, his attorney and his loyal secretary of over fifty years took care of routine business matters, while Pearl took care of everything else. She read his personal mail for him, answered his personal correspondence, and kept a record of the growing list of friends who wanted to be updated of his condition.

On February 15, 1970, Harold suffered another massive stroke and remained unconscious until he died on April 26 at his estate in Hope Ranch. He was seventy-nine. On May 4, an intimate funeral service organized by Pearl was held at Episcopal All Saints-by-the-Sea Church in Montecito.

According to America's *Who's Who* at the time, Harold held fifty key positions in national and civic organizations. He received dozens of tributes praising his unselfish devotion to duty. Among those, the *News-Press* detailed:

> Santa Barbara has lost one of its greatest citizens. He was noted as a real estate developer, civic leader, sportsman and conservationist. But most of all, perhaps, he will be remembered for his innumerable benefactions to his beloved Santa Barbara. Through many decades, he could be counted on for leadership or support of projects important to the progress of this unique community. Cottage Hospital is only one of the institutions to which he devoted himself, but his service to it was typical. He became a director in 1927, served as president from 1958 to 1965 and as Board Chairman to the time of his death. The $4,500,000, five-story Chase Wing, completed five years ago, was named in his honour. Relatively few Santa Barbarans know, probably, that he was the man who quietly raised millions of dollars for recent hospital construction. Indicative of his wide-ranging interests was the fact that he was president of the Santa Barbara Museum of Natural History from 1952 to 1966 and a benefactor and charter patron of the Santa Barbara Museum of Art.
>
> Hope Ranch Park, which he and his wife developed, will serve as one of many lasting reminders of his vision. It is a dramatic

122. Harold S. Chase

> illustration that the beauties of nature can be preserved through careful planning of a residential area.
>
> It is impossible to catalogue or measure the value of the accomplishments of this gentle, noble man. But this much is sure—all Santa Barbarans are indebted to him.[5]

Harold's estate in Hope Ranch was sold to Fess Parker, an actor and real estate developer. Pearl mused how interesting it would be to compute how many people had had the pleasure of strolling through the grounds over the years with her garden tours.[6] The H.G. Chase office in State Street was permanently closed. Pearl liked to say, "My fond brother has done more for Santa Barbara than I have."[7]

In November 1968, Pearl was invited by George Hartzog, director of the NPS, to attend the dedication of the Redwoods National Park and hear Lady Bird Johnson speak in Bald Hills. She could not make the journey north, as she was occupied with local conservation affairs in "some of the most remote, wild, and rugged landscapes of California's central coast region found in the backcountry of Santa Barbara," twelve miles north from the city, in an area known as the San Rafael Wilderness.[8] In the early sixties, this area, famous for condors and one of the richest assemblages of Native American pictographs, was at risk from recreational motor bikes running up and down the trails. After the Wilderness Act was signed by Johnson in 1964, the Forest

Service was required by law to review the suitability of all existing primitive areas in the country for possible designation as wilderness.

By coincidence, the San Rafael Primitive Area was the first to be reviewed. The area captured widespread attention, and two books, *California Condor: Vanishing America* by Dick Smith and Bob Easton, and *Rock Paintings of the Chumash* by Campbell Grant, highlighted the need to further protect the area. After completing its report in 1965, the Forest Service suggested protecting an area of 110,403 acres.[9] Local residents, who had formed an ad hoc committee for the San Rafael Wilderness, called the "Citizens Committee," promoted a larger area covering nearly 150,000 acres.[10]

Pearl knew this land, and had been advocating for its protection since the 1950s. She was eager to help the Citizens Committee. At different times after the Second World War oil and gas leases were issued and the Forest Service proposed opening and paving the roads to accommodate an intensive development plan including a ski resort.[11] Although nothing came of the proposals, in 1964 when construction of a road along the Sierra Madre ridge was resurrected, Pearl wrote to regional forester Charles Connaughton, requesting the Forest Service postpone the scheme:

> The Forest Service knows better than any other Public Agency, and has frequently reported and pictured the dreadful disorder, damage and destruction, that a few people can create in a few hours in our forests and parks! Please don't build the road now! Keep people out of the Upper Sisquoc, and that includes me because I can't walk or ride the trails or use a tote-goat. I have to use a motor car.[12]

The question of the size of the San Rafael Wilderness area reached a boiling point on November 8, 1965 at a Forest Service's public meeting in Santa Barbara, which Pearl described as "history-making."[13] The overwhelming consensus of the fifty-seven speakers was that the area should be protected, with a great majority supporting the larger citizen proposal:[14] "The Forest Service received more than six hundred letters during the thirty-day public comment period following the hearing."[15] The *Santa Barbara News-Press*, the *New York Times*, and the *Washington Post* all supported the citizens wilderness proposal.

Quite by accident, while interviewing Kellam de Forest in 2019, I met Anne Eissler, whose husband, Fred, spoke at the hearing. Like her husband, Anne was also a passionate conservationist. She was highly respected by Pearl and played an instrumental role in many Santa Barbara area environmental, planning, and preservation issues from the 1960s into this century. As we chatted over my soup and her luncheon dessert at the Woodglen retirement home, the popular conservationist turned to things Miss Chase. She told me a story of how in 1965, shortly before the Forest Service public meeting, she, Fred, and Miss Chase, as she liked to call her, "drove up to the Sierras for a conservation meeting squeezed together in a little Chevrolet pickup." Stopping at a gas station, she recalled how Pearl, then aged seventy-seven, enjoyed herself, climbing out of the pickup and saying how traveling in this way was a good thing. She remembered Pearl as a great sport and a strong woman.[16]

According to Bob's son, Robert Olney Easton, noted author and later one of Pearl's executors, "Pearl was the last to testify at the hearing. I didn't quite know what she was going to say. Pearl seldom gave herself away beforehand, and she never took sides politically in public but you could often tell where she was going to stand."[17] When Pearl testified, she urged citizens to "get the most land you can."[18] Robert recalled, "This was kind of hard for her because she worked very closely with the Forest Service for a number of years, and continued to do so—but in this issue she went with us."[19]

As public support over wilderness preservation grew, the Forest Service expanded its wilderness recommendation to nearly 143,000 acres, a 30,000-acre increase over its initial proposal. In February 1967, the San Rafael Wilderness legislation was introduced in the

Plate 11. The Chase family in 1944. Hezekiah, Pearl, Barbara (Lansdowne), George (Lansdowne), Gertrude Boyer, with Caroline and Charlie. Pearl was devoted to her niece Barbara. She was extremely proud of Barbara's 1938 marriage. George was the godson of King George V and stepson of John Jacob Astor. Pearl described him as "charming, smart, attractive looking with good sense and a fine Scottish-English inheritance".

Plate 12. Redwoods in Muir Woods National Monument. Pearl thought the giant trees possessed a magnificent dignity as well as a tranquil charm. Working with Save the Redwoods League and the Garden Club of America she tried to protect and restore them.

Plate 13. El Presidio de Santa Barbara State Historic Park. The primary authority in the reconstruction and preservation of the site (Santa Barbara's 18th century birthplace) is the Santa Barbara Trust for Historic Preservation which Pearl founded in 1963. She supported its efforts all her life.

Plate 14. From left, Mayor Don MacGillivray, Pearl Chase, Mike Pahos, City of Santa Barbara Parks Superintendent, a representative of the US Junior Chamber of Commerce. Inspired by the national beautification movement of the 1960s, Santa Barbara Beautiful was founded with some help from Pearl. She continued to support their work towards community interest and action towards the enhancement of the city's beauty.

Plate 15. Clearing storm, San Rafael Wilderness, Los Padres National Forest. During the 1960s a citizen committee enlisted the support of Pearl to protect 150,000 acres. During the late 1960s with perseverance and publicity, they won public support, and the Forest Service expanded its wilderness recommendation to nearly 143,000 acres, a 30,000 acre increase over their initial proposal.

Plate 16. Alice Keck Park Memorial Garden, Santa Barbara. In the late 1960s Pearl set about defeating the city 'establishment', then predisposed to permitting high rise buildings in the city. She led a community uprising and a lawsuit and won the battle. A few years later Alice Keck Park, a one-time resident of Santa Barbara and friend of Pearl's, bought the site from the developers and gave it to the city as an open space.

Plate 17. University of California, Santa Barbara campus today. A UC Alumnus (class of 1909), Pearl was determined that Santa Barbara should join the then growing university system. In 1944 with intense lobbying, she and other city leaders persuaded the State Legislature, Governor Warren and the Regents of the University to move the Santa Barbara State College over to the UC system. She continued to work for the university on planning matters. In 1958 after securing a 400 acre site at Goleta, the Regents established Santa Barbara as a general university campus.

Plate 18. Vernon Cheadle, Chancellor of UCSB, Pearl Chase and William Penn Mott, Director of the California Department of Parks and Recreation (later Director of the National Park Service), at the inauguration of the Pearl Chase Garden at UCSB in 1972. UCSB had formerly awarded Pearl an honorary doctorate in 1959. Cheadle liked to refer to Pearl as Santa Barbara's First Lady. He felt her continuing interest and support for the university was one of 'our greatest assets'.

Plate 19. Pearl once remarked, 'My whole object in life was to make people happy. I started in public health because unless you are healthy you aren't happy. Recreation is necessary to provide a balanced life. From there to housing because the home environment is vitally important. Then into the business of enjoying what you look at. To teach people to see what they look at is one of the most difficult things to teach.'

House, while companion legislation was introduced in the Senate, passing in both. During the signing ceremony at the White House on March 21, 1968, President Johnson remarked:

> I want so much to protect and extend the legacy of our land. I want so much to take the pieces of our birthright that we should never have lost—and reclaim them, restore them and return them to the American people. San Rafael is part of that work.... Wilderness parks should be a part of the America of tomorrow—the kind of America that we think we are building today. I am very proud to sign this bill. I believe that it will enrich the spirit of America.[20]

The 1960s saw intense public interest in preserving California's wildlands from encroaching development. By a 1.5 million plurality vote, Californians approved a $150 million bond act in 1964, which allowed acquisition of new state park lands including Point Mugu and Ed Z'berg Sugar Pine Point. In 1965, Pearl was invited by Lawrence Stuart, the president of the National Conference on State Parks, to serve on the conference's nominating committee. She graciously declined: "I'm flattered, however I hasten to decline the honor. With the knowledge that you can surely find another friend and co-worker who will be in touch with the younger generation and will be readily recognized as a leader in the new and expanding program of Parks and Recreation."[21]

Pearl felt "the old conservationists should be gratified to see how quickly and rapidly some attitudes and programs have changed. Thank Heaven many of them for the betterment of our people, our land and waters."[22] Among her generation, Pearl was a few steps ahead of her colleagues. In a 1979 interview given by Helen Baker Reynolds from the CRC, Reynolds recalled, "I remember Pearl Chase at a convention meeting one day saying to an assembled crowd, 'Has anyone of you ever heard the word ecology?' And everyone a total blank. Can you imagine today?"[23]

As the world of conservation and preservation was intensifying, a gradual transformation in the style of leadership was taking shape. Whereas before, organizations were managed by leaders like Pearl, with a highly personal style of leadership, the new leaders were men and women experienced in managing complex enterprises. It was no longer so straightforward for Pearl to visit department heads based in Sacramento and sit around their desks, take advice, and discuss projects.

Furthermore, at a time when the nation was deeply committed to a very expensive war in Vietnam and the civil rights movement was gathering speed, the American public began to question the way they lived their lives. Many decided to place less emphasis on work and more on home, family, leisure, and on the quality of those non-work activities. One aspect of these new values and objectives was to insist on a higher quality of one's surrounding environment: the air, water, and land. This interest in pollution was quite new and had not been part of earlier conservation activities.[24]

The environmental movement which began to take shape in the late 1960s was popular and mass based. It was closely tied to the women's movement.[25]

By November 1968, when Richard Nixon, Republican presidential nominee, won one of the closest presidential elections in US history, Johnson had signed nearly three hundred conservation laws to address air and water pollution and protect national parks. While these measures were modest compared to the environmental policies of President Nixon's administration in the early 1970s, the achievements of the "Great Society" were critical in the evolution of the environmental movement.[26]

On the eve of the election, red, white, and blue decorations accentuated parties in the Santa Barbara area. Pearl joined her Scorpio Club friends for tea as Nixon fought an extremely close election. The key states proved to be California, Ohio, and Illinois, all of which Nixon won by three percentage points or less. He was sworn in on a cold, cloudy day, January 20, 1969, on the east portico of the US Capitol, by another California Republican and friend of Santa Barbara, Earl Warren. Although both men were all smiles for the cameras, they had been waging political war against each other for decades.[27]

CHAPTER 26

Get Oil Out

On January 28, 1969, eight days after President Nixon was inaugurated, a blowout on an offshore oil drilling rig operated by Union Oil, five and a half miles off the coast of Santa Barbara, caused the then largest oil spill in the nation's history. Two days later, word of the spill finally reached far-off Washington, DC, and the Nixon administration and Walter Hickel, new Secretary of the Interior, were quickly introduced to environmental realities at the national level.

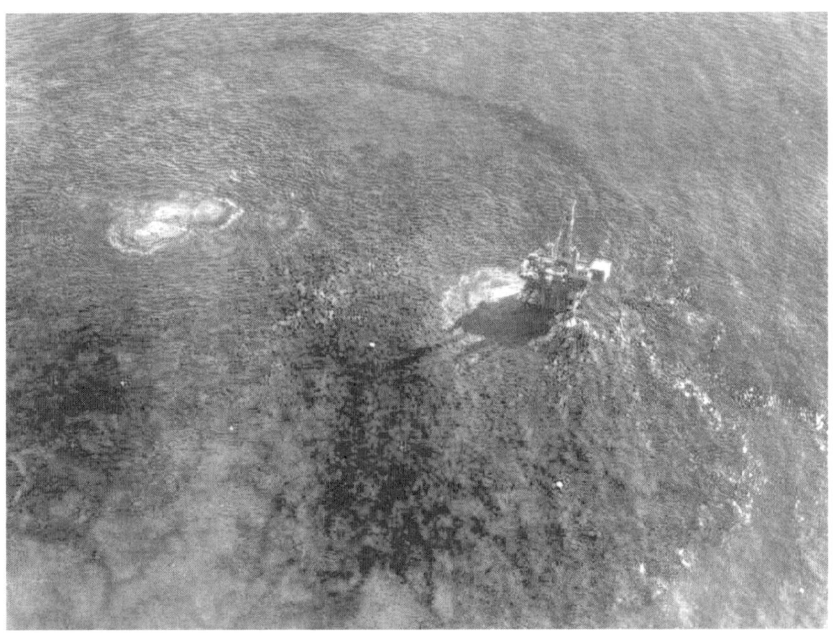

123. Aerial view of the Santa Barbara oil spill

Figures vary, but it is estimated that before it could be stopped on February 7, 80,000 barrels, or 3 million gallons, of crude oil spilled into the channel and onto the beaches of Santa Barbara County. At its worst, "its maximum size covered 660 square miles, and thousands of sea birds and animals perished as a result of the contamination."[1] The national media attention waned after the spill stopped, but at the local level, coverage remained heavy.

On February 8, Governor Reagan declared the Santa Barbara beaches a disaster area. For months, oil contaminated the area's beaches. Birds continued to die; the first month after the spill saw the greatest number of oil-covered birds being brought to the rehabilitation centers. The *News-Press* was one of the most informed and outraged newspapers to report on the disaster.[2] Among the reports, the paper kept a daily tally of the number of oil-covered birds;[3] neither local officials nor "Union Oil, the owner of the rig, [...] ever completed a census of dead birds found on the beaches."[4] But 3,686 birds were estimated to have died because of contact with oil.[5]

Hundreds of volunteers, many of them UCSB students, worked onshore catching and cleaning birds and mammals, while an army of workers used skimmers to scoop up oil from the ocean surface. Airplanes were used to drop detergents on the oil slick to try to break it up. The clean-up effort took months to complete and cost millions of dollars, having a detrimental effect on tourism in the area for many months;[6] the only tourists were those coming to see the devastation for themselves.

Wrestling with the aftermath, "the anguish felt by local residents trying to cope with the disaster transformed people into activists working to protect the environment."[7] Among them was James "Bud" Bottoms.[8] A former president of Santa Barbara Beautiful organization and an avid outdoorsman, he loved to fish, scuba dive, hunt, and camp. During the crisis, "he made himself everywhere."[9] One of his most quoted remarks was, "You go to the beach and you couldn't hear the waves. All the ocean was black. People just stood their

124. In this February 5, 1969 image, clean up crews rake and shovel oil soaked straw on the beach

crying. We figured it was all over for Santa Barbara."[10] Determined it would not be, in the first few days of the spill, Bottoms, along with two colleagues, formed a grassroots organization called Get Oil Out! Or "GOO!."[11] GOO! battled for the government to stop drilling in the Santa Barbara Channel. Pearl liked Bud and became something of a mentor to him. She offered GOO! her support, not simply because she believed in their cause, but also because she took an interest in young people who were standing up for what they believed in. According to one Santa Barbaran, "She was a sort of activist emeritus" whose name carried significant weight and whose voice was authoritative.[12] As Bottoms later recalled:

> She was encouraging and would back me up on these at times controversial matters. She was quite a lady. She would not hesitate to call me. She might talk an hour! I used to lay the phone down, and I could still hear her talking because you

125. Pearl sitting on the porch at 912 Santa Barbara Street with her secretary Marie Harvey

> could not get a word in edgewise, nor did she want to hear anything from you. She just wanted to report. So I would set the phone down and every once in a while concur with her, to let her know I was still there.[13]

Pearl disliked oil development in Santa Barbara. It was controversial from the earliest days.[14] In 1928, Hezekiah, Pearl's father, sold Ellwood Cooper's ranch twelve miles west of the city, where the new owners not only struck oil, but had a significant gusher, initially producing 1,316 barrels per day. The Ellwood Oil Field was important to the economic development of the Santa Barbara area; the discovery triggered a period of leasing and wildcat well drilling[15] in the Santa Barbara area, but when oil was discovered on the Mesa Oil Field, a hilltop location overlooking the channel within the city limits, it proved controversial. Bracketed on east and west with oil fields, Santa Barbarans and tourists were deeply unhappy to find oil

126. Oil derricks just off shore at Summerland in the Santa Barbara suburbs in 1915

in the city limits. An eastern visitor remarked, "With one hand you spend millions for the sake of beauty and scenery, with the other you destroy by the stroke of a pen just as magnificent beauty *forever*."[16]

In January 1929, Pearl, along with most other Santa Barbarans,[17] fought back against oil developments in the city. She was adamant that it would damage the future of the city, and as property values plummeted, advised the city council to proceed "very carefully before making decisions in matters which affect the interests of land-owners of the entire city."[18]

Despite their efforts, there was an ordinance at the time specifically allowing drilling on the Mesa. Subsequently, "oil derricks sprouted on the hilltop within easy view of the harbour, on narrow town lots intended originally for houses. The oil derricks only went away when production on the oil field abruptly declined and ended in the late 1930s."[19] However, interestingly, the field was not particularly profitable.[20]

In 1933 when it was suggested that an oil refinery be constructed within the city, Pearl, again along with most of the town's citizens, went on record against the idea, reminding city council: "Santa Barbara's greatest asset is to continue to be a city of homes known for its splendid recreational and educational facilities and we believe that the allowing of oil refineries within our city would be most detrimental to the entire community."[21]

This time, she succeeded.

Improved technology gradually allowed drilling farther and farther from shore, and in 1938 the California State Lands Act legalized oil leasing in state tidelands out to a three-mile limit.[22] In 1953, Congress passed the Submerged Lands Act, which granted states ownership of all oil within three nautical miles of the shore; oil found beyond that point belonged to the federal government.[23] Pearl thought the reappearance of the pressure to drill was the worst thing facing Santa Barbara at the time.[24,25]

Development of leases in the federal waters outside the three-mile limit was next. The first lease sale took place on December 15, 1966, and a little over a year later in February 1968 leases went up for sale totalling $603 million.[26] Local hostility was increased by the need for processing plants for handling offshore production. In many cases, Santa Barbarans defeated the proposed plants but opponents of oil development failed to stall the tide as companies moved their facilities to neighbouring Ventura county.

The 1969 oil spill amplified this anger to heretofore unimaginable levels. GOO! channelled the public outrage and showed what grassroots activism would do to create awareness and change on the planet. It succeeded because it reduced things "to that kind of bumper-sticker level, which you really needed if you're going to be communicating with large crowds."[27]

Bottoms decided to write up a petition banning offshore drilling. Pearl believed that individual letters and cards were far more effective than petitions, and this method proved highly effective.[28] Within months GOO! had collected more than 100,000 signatures on anti-oil petitions. In early 1970, "an attempt to deliver 200,000 signatures to President Nixon at his 'Western White House' in San Clemente was thwarted by presidential aides."[29]

127. Richard Nixon walking on the beach after the oil spill, March 21, 1969

On March 21, President Nixon visited Santa Barbara to see the blotted coastline for himself. Observing the polluted water from his helicopter, he later strolled the beach in his formal suit, kicking the cleaned-up sand with his shiny black Oxfords as his entourage and the press swarmed around. After meeting clean-up workers, he told the assembled reporters, "What is involved is the use of our resources of the sea and the land in a more effective way, and with more concern for preserving the beauty and the natural resources that are so important to any kind of society that we want for the future. I don't think we have paid enough attention to this."[30]

Environmentalists were sceptical of the new president's assurances; Nixon had almost no record on the environment and had barely mentioned the issue during his campaign.[31]

If the spark to the national environment movement was Rachel Carson's Silent Spring in 1962, the first resistance to environmental theft came in 1969 with the Santa Barbara oil spill.[32] The spill blackened not only the channel but the reputation of the oil industry.[33] Over the following months and years Nixon proposed an ambitious and expensive pollution-fighting agenda to Congress, and went on to create the Environmental Protection Agency (EPA) and the National Oceanic and Atmospheric Administration (NOAA).[34]

128. Richard Nixon talks with workers cleaning up the beach from damage caused by the oil spill

Shortly after the federal government passed the National Environmental Policy Act (NEPA) in 1969, the California Environmental Quality Act (CEQA) was signed into law by Governor Reagan. In the same year, the California State Parks Foundation (CSPF) was founded by director of the CPS, William Penn Mott, Jr., as an independent nonprofit membership, "organization dedicated to protecting, enhancing and advocating for California's" magnificent state parks.[35]

One of the most remarkable outcomes for the global environmental movement was Earth Day. According to Denis Hayes, an environmental advocate and coordinator of the First Earth Day:

> Senator Gaylord Nelson [The Democrat Senator from Wisconsin] was flying from Los Angeles up to Seattle for a meeting while the spill was going on. He was horrified by the extent of it from the plane window. So Santa Barbara played a key role in prompting him to develop the idea for Earth Day. In the run-up to the protests of the war in Vietnam, and the early

> days of the civil rights movement, there had been teach-ins on college campuses. He thought that would be a useful thing to do for conservation issues broadly.[36]

Gaylord announced the idea for a teach-in on college campuses to the national media, and persuaded Peter "Pete" McCloskey, a conservation-minded Republican congressman, who represented San Mateo, to serve as his co-chair. They recruited Denis Hayes to organize the campus teach-ins and chose April 22, a weekday falling between spring break and final exams, to maximize the greatest student participation.[37]

In April 1970, Earth Day inspired twenty million Americans to take to the streets, parks, and auditoriums to demonstrate against the impacts of 150 years of industrial development which had left a growing legacy of serious human health impacts. Later, in 1990, Earth Day went global and today is widely recognized as the largest secular observance in the world, marked by more than a billion people every year as a day of action to change human behaviour and create global, national, and local policy changes.[38]

CHAPTER 27

Building Heights

When attention on Santa Barbara was overshadowed by oil development, another issue of major importance to Pearl, her vision, and the future of the community, was the prospect of high-rise buildings.

She had worried about this question since 1962 when she organized a series of meetings on "Planning for Growth in Santa Barbara County." While much of the discussion revolved around the topic of roads and route US 101, the panellists touched on high-rise.[1] Santa Barbara had a long history of limiting building heights.

It began with the Santa Barbara City Planning Commission, created in 1923. The following year, a building zone ordinance was adopted which permitted six stories and eighty feet in commercial and manufacturing zones. After the earthquake in June 1925, the new building code and zoning ordinance were put to an unforeseen amount of use. On June 26, 1930, "the first 'comprehensive' zoning ordinance was adopted by the city council. The maximum height was four stories and 60 feet in the commercial zones and three stories and 45 feet in family zones."[2] These regulations were still in effect in 1962 when the question surfaced at Pearl's meeting. Despite a limiting ordinance in place, the then director of planning for the city, said that if high-rise structures were permitted, they would be constructed. While the issue did not go away, the General Plan, adopted by the city in 1964, called for carefully formulated regulations if multistorey buildings were to be considered. In the years that followed, the question was settled by a series of events which polarized the community and brought Pearl into the local limelight like never before.

In August 1967, Jacob Seldowitz, owner of El Mirasol Hotel, proposed to the city council "to demolish the old hotel and build a nine-story 'low-rise' hotel with underground parking for four hundred cars and auditorium for 2,500 people."[3] To launch his proposal publicly, he "invited over a hundred leading citizens to discuss the project. All but five people voted for the development."[4] Pearl, who "truly believed" that Seldowitz was "a little crazy, but that makes him all the more dangerous," was against.[5] She stated, "You have skirted the objection of Santa Barbarans to the term 'high-rise' by calling your nine-story projections 'low rise.' I doubt that this artful dodge will be accepted in the manner proposed."[6] The architect for the project argued "that beautification alone was not enough to preserve the health of the community," and that "if nothing was done to upgrade the central area, in 15 years all that will remain is a rather shabby portion of Old Town."[7] So began "a typical Santa Barbara style controversy as opponents and supporters of the plans marshalled their resources."[8]

Pearl's resources at this stage were formidable. Aged seventy-nine, with over forty years' experience leading the P&P committee, there was almost no aspect of planning, architecture, and landscape architecture in the design of an urban area with which she was not familiar. Determined Santa Barbara should remain a demonstration area where "good planning and common-sense reigns,"[9] Pearl set about defeating the "establishment" in an ill-begotten scheme.[10]

She had more than simply a professional interest at stake—she had a personal attachment to the El Mirasol. The property had been the private home of Mary Herter, a family friend of her parents'. Her son, Albert, and his wife, Adele, were close friends of Pearl's. After Mary's death in 1913, the property was converted by Albert and Adele into the El Mirasol Hotel. In 1920, they sold the property and it passed through a succession of different owners until in December 1966, two consecutive fires destroyed the entire attic of the west wing of the house.

129. El Mirasol as Pearl would have remembered it in 1916

In October 1967 Seldowitz appeared before the Planning Commission for a zoning change from R-3 (apartments) to R-4 (apartments-hotels-motels).[11] At the same time, "he sent out a voluntary survey to which 225 people responded with 85 percent in favour of the nine-story hotel."[12] Sixteen letters of opposition, including one from Pearl, and a petition with 261 signatures opposed the request.[13] Pearl personally funded the legal costs for wording the petition.

The Commission denied the application, as it had done the previous year, when the Biltmore applied to build an eighteen-story hotel on their site in Channel Drive. Writing to her friend Katharine Dexter McCormick, the widow of Stanley McCormick of the Riven Rock Estate in Montecito, who also knew the Herters, Pearl remarked, "I hope this note will be a cause for some thanksgiving."[14]

Despite having his plan turned down, Seldowitz won a partial victory when he was given permission to tear down the hotel and its bungalows. That should have been the end of it, but the property was acquired by El Mirasol Investment Company (EMIC). This company was composed of twenty-eight city and non-city civic and business leaders including many of Pearl's associates including Thomas Storke.[15] To these investors the project was novel and interesting. They also felt that no one had a right to say how high a building should be. This was viewed as infringing.[16] The general partners were William Cress "Bill" Alexander[17] and Jerry William Beaver.[18,19]

In September 1968, with an investment of over $500,000, they proposed building an eleven-story condominium complex of 162 units. This was eight stories higher than that permitted in the area.

It was clear to Pearl that she was going to need help to organise another campaign and publicity when, as she wrote, "the air and papers will be filled with political hash."[20] As public involvement in the controversy increased, she founded a citizens' group called Save Our City (SOC). It served as a focal point for community support. Protest petitions flooded City Hall. In November the EMIC withdrew their variance appeal, stating they wished to revise the plans. In the meantime, the local chapter of the League of Women Voters joined the dispute along with several neighborhood groups in the call for a city policy on building heights.

A few weeks later, EMIC "applied for a variance to construct two high-rise condominiums of nine stories, 107 feet tall, each which were referred to as 'medium-rise.' This application was also withdrawn pending preparation of a high-rise ordinance for the city."[21]

Meanwhile, EMIC placed advertisements in the *News-Press* claiming "the project would bring $8 million in buying power" to the city, and that those who opposed it were a vocal minority that did not represent Santa Barbara.[22] Among those directly affected by the project were a couple who lived opposite the site and were petitioned by a man working for EMIC. Recounting their story years later, Penny and Terry Davies recalled:

> One night there was a knock on our front door. A man who we did not recognize had a petition that he was circulating around our neighborhood. It was supporting two high rise condos. When we inquired who was behind this project we couldn't get an answer. We knew this was a big mistake, having seen other towns that had been destroyed by high rise buildings. We felt

> helpless and didn't know what to do then a friend mentioned Pearl Chase. We had no idea what we were in for. We called up Pearl Chase, who lived in the neighborhood, and told her about the petition.
>
> "I'll be right over," she said. When she came to our door, we knew here was a greater presence than the small white-haired lady who stood before us. She immediately took charge. She confided to us this project was a "kick in the stomach by her friends." In our battle to keep Santa Barbara low-rise, we attended endless council meetings under her direction, and tried to inform the public using her media savvy. To see Chase in action with the City Council, very clearly making her viewpoint known was a lesson in power projection."[23]

Writing about the controversy to the author Irving Stone, Pearl explained at the time: "I have had to use all the psychology and knowledge of community organization that I have gained in many years of work with little and big problems and politicians. In planning, they go together."[24]

As detailed in the *News-Press*, the controversy "embodied all the drama of community dynamics one could imagine. Well-established business and political interests versus determined citizens and a select number of design professionals, electrifying public hearings before the City Planning Commission and City Council, numerous neighborhood strategy meetings, petitions and mailouts."[25] In January 1969, public meetings were held on the planning department's ordinance draft and the following month EMIC's application was refiled. A month later, the Planning Commission "voted 4-3 to deny the variance explaining that the four stipulations for a variance had not been met. EMIC immediately filed an appeal, confident of their standing with the public. For the city council, the die had been cast."[26]

On March 25, 1969, the council overruled the Planning Commission, "granting the variance on a 4–2 vote. However, the motion did not contain findings that the four required variance conditions had been met."[27] According to Penny and Terry Davies:

> When we heard that the City Council was going to give a variance to the builders, we were shocked. We decided to advertise and ask for public financial support to take our case to the courts. We asked for money for our legal fees and the people of Santa Barbara responded enthusiastically. One woman wrote to us that she was postponing her kitchen renovation and sent the kitchen money to Save Our City.[28]

Pearl and SOC instructed John Marshall Sink, a respected attorney, to act for the opposition.[29] Organizing themselves for the next stage of the battle, SOC appealed to the courts and on April 9, local superior court judge and former mayor, John "Jack" T. Rickard "signed a stay order prohibiting start of construction."[30]

By this time, a large number of new citizens had joined the group eager to protect their environment and the community's special character.[31] On May 8, Superior Court Judge Harold Underwood, on loan from Trinity County, took the issue under submission. Two months later, after a nail-biting period waiting for Underwood's decision, it was all over: on July 10, the judge ruled that the city council, by approving the project, had violated the city's General Plan. The city council was ordered to rescind the order of variance.[32] The ruling left Pearl and her colleagues feeling a mixture of euphoria and relief; she was very happy, and her colleagues were proud to have worked with her.[33]

On July 18, EMIC accepted the ruling and Alexander and Beaver informed their investors that they planned on selling the property and returning their investments. However, this was not quite the end of it for Pearl and those others who had been opposed to the height variance. She understood that although they had won on this occasion, the issue was going to return over and over as new projects were developed unless the matter was resolved.[34]

Undoubtedly, the incident damaged Pearl's relations with the city's establishment, especially Tom Storke, who remarked at the time that Pearl was "the kiss of death."[35] However, it was also a sign the times were changing and that the "old establishment" was no longer as dominant as in former years. The community was developing other power centers for activism, and for getting things done in the community; it was no longer simply a matter of who you knew and convincing them. While there was still a place for the establishment and they still carried plenty of power in the city, they were not as powerful as in earlier years.

Storke was disappointed by the ruling, though he did not live to hear the 1972 ruling regarding the variance, as he died of a stroke on October 12, 1971, at ninety-four. Although he had sold the *News-Press* in 1964, he continued to act as consulting editor and publisher emeritus of the newspaper at the time of the El Mirasol controversy. Despite her victory, Pearl paid a huge price for breaking her lifelong rule against fighting political battles in public. Shortly after the ruling was made, an anonymous letter was received by the Corporations Office of the Secretary of State in Sacramento asking for the records of P&P's filings. When it was discovered that she had not been paying her correct dues for a number of years and was in breach of the tax code, the P&P lost its nonprofit status, its tax deductibility, and its source of funding. Sadly I have been unable to discover what her 'correct dues' were or how this unfortunate matter occurred. What I am certain of, however, is that Pearl would not have intentionally paid too little tax. While some individuals continued to support her projects for the benefit of the city, she lost many others.[36]

It was the only occasion when those that knew her saw her completely dejected and down.[37] At eighty-three, it was a cruel blow, and she never fully recovered. With its reputation damaged, the P&P continued but did not have the infusion of funds it relied on to do its work effectively. There is no record of where the letter came from. She had a reputation as a dragon slayer and over many years had challenged some of the most powerful interests in the city and state, but it was customary in those days that people agreed to disagree without ill will. It was a sign that the stakes were higher, and the game was nastier.

Pearl closed her office at 912 Santa Barbara Street in 1973 and continued to work from home as a private citizen. It was the end of an era—however, the ultimate victory was hers.

In the summer of 1969, the old El Mirasol Hotel buildings were demolished. Soon after, in 1970, the Museum of Art acquired the site and planned on building a new museum, but money for the project was not available. Over the following few years, various ideas for development arose but none came to fruition. Finally, on December 9, 1975 "the city of Santa Barbara received an early Christmas present when an anonymous donor gave the entire site to the city for a park."[38]

The donor's identity remained a mystery until her death in 1977, when it was revealed to have been Alice Keck Park, a one-time

130. Alice Keck Park Memorial Garden, Santa Barbara

resident of Santa Barbara. Park was the daughter of William Myron Keck, the founder of Superior Oil Company and had a family connection to the Herters and the site. The silent intermediary helping to facilitate the donation was Pearl. Keck insisted that Elizabeth de Forest, who Pearl had known since the early 1920s, was hired to landscape the memorial garden. In 1980, the Alice Keck Park Memorial Gardens became a reality,[39] now generally considered a local "crown jewel" in Santa Barbara.

CHAPTER 28

Final Years and Widespread Appreciation

All of Pearl's concerns centered on her desire to have a healthy and happy environment. In her final years, she continued to pursue this vision through advanced planning, environmental education, historic preservation, and ordinary, everyday cooperation. As people began to understand and agree with her vision, she received widespread appreciation.

Speaking with the historian Charles Hosmer, Jr., in 1971 she explained:

> My whole object in life was to make people happy. I started in public health because unless you are healthy you aren't happy. Recreation is necessary to provide a balanced life. From there to housing because the home environment is vitally important—order and keeping it repaired. Then into the business of enjoying what you look at. To teach people to see what they look at is one of the most difficult things to teach.[1]

The Santa Barbara oil spill and the high-rise debate created a new sense of urgency among local citizens. At UCSB, faculty joined together to launch a formal Environmental Studies Program led by Professor Roderick Nash, America's foremost wilderness historian.[2] In Santa Barbara, the Community Environmental Council (CEC) and Environmental Defense Center (EDC) were established. Pearl was invited to join the CEC in 1972 to fight another development project, a $72 million proposal by the Southern Pacific and Hyatt Hotels to develop a thirty-two-acre site on the Santa Barbara waterfront and build a 1,000-room hotel and a 2,000-person conference center.

Such was her influence that the CEC found having Pearl's name on the letterhead helpful. According to Paul Relis, the CEC executive director who led the opposition campaign, the development would have been about the size of the entire downtown core. "Determined not to reject the proposal out of hand," the East Beach Committee, as they called themselves, with Pearl as honorary chairman, countermanded with a proposal of their own.[3]

Planned in harmony with Santa Barbara's quality and aspirations, while satisfying its economic needs, this was received with enthusiasm. On August 8, the Southern Pacific's developers announced a new plan.[4] According to former city Mayor Sheila Lodge, "If CEC hadn't existed, and that group of Lower East Side residents hadn't come to it, and if its twenty-something [year old] co-director hadn't become engaged in the issue, Santa Barbara might have been cut off from the waterfront."[5]

On a sunny afternoon on April 23, 1972, UCSB dedicated a portion of the campus on the banks of the lagoon as "Pearl Chase Garden" in tribute for Pearl's pioneering contributions to conservation, Santa Barbara's historical heritage and the beauty of the city. The ceremony was officiated by Chancellor Vernon Cheadle

131. East Beach Park, Santa Barbara today

132. Pearl speaking at the dedication of her garden at UCSB, April 1972

and his wife.[6] Among the 200 friends invited, William Penn Mott, Jr., director of the California Department of Parks and Recreation represented the state; Mayor Gerald Firestone, the city; and Eileen Kadesh, the UCSB student body. Paying tribute to Pearl on behalf of the students, Eileen remarked:

> With the dedication of this open space here today, I would like particularly to thank Miss Chase for the three years of pleasure I have had in Santa Barbara. Since my freshman year at UCSB, I have found Santa Barbara a unique and exciting community and one in which I have been proud to call home. During the first part of my stay at UCSB, I came down to this lagoon area every day to acquire some peace of mind and inspiration after the tension of everyday campus life. I find it especially fitting that we dedicate such an area of beauty and lasting tranquillity to Pearl Chase a woman who has certainly been a friend of nature and earned this title.[7]

Pearl's vision resonated across all ages. She was thrilled and humbled to have a garden dedicated in her name although in her characteristically modest manner she hoped it would be known as the Lagoon Garden. She found the area to be a wonderful asset to the campus and was gratified that the university planned to keep it

133. A view of the Pearl Chase Garden UCSB, April 1972

as an open space with its rolling lawns, towering eucalyptus trees where blue herons nested, and natural views across the rolling waves of the Pacific where the evening sun set.[8]

Pearl's relationship with the University of California, since her admission to Berkeley in 1905, had been one of the most fulfilling and rewarding aspects of her career. For her services to the UC family, she had been awarded an honorary doctorate by UCSB and Alumnus of the year by the UC Santa Barbara Alumni Association. Interestingly, while some of her UC contemporaries including Newton Drury had many reservations about the direction of the University in the late sixties, Pearl remained strongly supportive. In 1968 Irving Stone, the author, who was editing a book for the UC centennial called *There Was Light: Autobiography of a University: Berkeley, 1868–1968*, invited Pearl to submit a chapter on her Berkeley years. She wrote a draft and asked Horace Albright to review it. Unable to make herself finish the chapter because she felt "it showed what a different attitude her generation had towards the University and each other," she never submitted the work.[9] Such loyalty had changed over time; a few years later, she admitted she made a mistake in not submitting her chapter as Drury did, which Stone rejected.[10]

Despite refusing to have her own biography written because "she did not want to look back," history was one of her primary interests.[11] "Chase drew her strength from the good deeds of the past and saw no reason why they should not continue through herself. She felt that having a history and maintaining tradition was essential to the health of the community."[12] She believed that "history brought tradition, tradition brought with it a sense of pride, pride led to responsibility, responsibility led to concern, concern led to action, action led to justice in achievement and that through communication, coordination that which blesses one would bless all."[13]

Given that so many of her records were of concern to the fabric of Santa Barbaran life, Pearl was determined that the bulk of her public and private papers should go to the special collections at UCSB for the benefit of all. "Records of fifty years are precious in spots!" she once remarked.[14] By 1969, it horrified her to see the quantity and variety of her papers uncatalogued and stored in multiple places.[15] She was encouraged in this project by Vernon Cheadle, who arrived at UCSB with a vision to change the landscape of the university. To Cheadle, "universities became great because of investment in faculty, and he believed this from the moment he arrived at UCSB."[16]

Growing the special collections was very much a part of Cheadle's project. Referring to Pearl as, Santa Barbara's first lady, he was impressed by her will to serve, her breadth of vision, and power of initiative which had been brought to bear on almost every phase of community life in Santa Barbara.[17] He recognized that her continuing interest and support for UCSB was one of "our greatest assets,"[18] writing to her:

> You have provided moral support in our most trying times for which all of us in the university and its community are

> continually grateful. As a result of your life-long commitment to our beautiful city, Santa Barbara's been able to retain its charm and uniqueness. As I recently heard one of our community members say recently "every city needs a Pearl Chase."[19]

Pearl had enormous respect for Cheadle, "whose friendliness was so evident."[20] With his good sense of humor and integrity, she also believed him when he told her that her collection of papers were indeed important, and that UCSB would offer assistance with them.

In early 1970, Cheadle introduced Pearl to the library staff and the department of special collections. After further discussion it was agreed that the library would assign one of their manuscript cataloguers to the project. The library agreed to pay up to nineteen hours per week. All other costs would be met by Pearl, including transportation of the records.

Pearl was adamant that her papers should be called the "Community Development and Conservation Collection" rather than as was customary the Pearl Chase papers. She was also keen that it should be recognized that she established the collection at the university. Divided into two equal parts, including personal papers, her hope was that other organizations and individuals would wish to contribute to its growth. As she told her grandniece at the time, "I am trying to include some records of the splendid achievements of your grandfather Chase."[21]

Michael Heskett, a PhD student working in special collections, began work in August 1970. One year later, Pearl realized that the project required greater input, and she provided further funding for another assistant, PhD student Robert Mullins. Pearl enjoyed working with the students who kept her updated with bimonthly letters on their progress. She felt that "it [was] a super kind of scholarship for the young men, and [a] valuable addition to UCSB Library for use of students and others interested in studying and writing about the subject fields in the collection."[22]

134. Pearl with UCSB special collections librarians, Wally Brem, Donald Davidson, and Robert Mullins

The students felt that the unflagging support in both materials and funding that Pearl gave to the library would be remembered as one of the most significant of her very important public services. She was, as Michael Heskett described, "providing an immensely valuable archive in the fields of conservation, community development and human welfare, that if properly arranged will be of inestimable aid to scholar and layman alike."[23] Key, in their opinion, was having the collection organized so that it could be used.[24] This took a further seven years to complete. At that time, the collection was known as one of the largest collections of a private individual and their work of its kind in an American university archive. Helping to grow the collection further during the following years, a few other organizations and individuals donated their records. Under the supervision of Rosanne M. Barker, special collections manuscript curator, the collection was estimated to measure 1,100 linear feet, or 2,200 document boxes. According to Barker, "[Pearl] realized that her work was important, that its value would transcend time."[25]

On December 4, 1971, Pearl's place in history was further secured when a gift was made to the Santa Barbara Trust for Historic

135. Pearl among her own papers at UCSB special collections research department

Preservation: the Casa de la Guerra and El Paseo shopping complex, then valued at $2 million. Irene Suski Fendon donated the property in honor of Pearl, she said, and as a memorial to her late husband. The gift, which was described as one of the of the greatest philanthropic gifts in Santa Barbara's history, expanded the trust's existing operations dramatically. Pearl stepped down as a vice president of the SBTHP in 1974. It was financially secure and had made steady progress in acquiring properties at the Presidio site. Its future appeared bright.

In early May 1973, Pearl went to Washington to receive an award from the National Trust for Historic Preservation (NTHP) at its third annual luncheon at its headquarters, the Decatur House. Three days before the luncheon on May 5, President Nixon, who was embroiled in the Watergate scandal,[26] signed a proclamation designating the week of May 6–12 as National Historic Preservation Week. In his proclamation, he stated that, "Americans more than ever before need a lively awareness of our roots and origins in the past on which to base our sense of identity in the present and our directions for the future."[27] Informed about Pearl's association with the NTHP, the president instructed one of his staff assistants to send her a signed copy of this proclamation.[28]

Later that week on May 8, Patricia Nixon was guest of honor at the luncheon and presented the National Trust awards at Decatur House. Pearl was one of six recipients chosen for an award for her service to historic preservation and ecological planning in Santa Barbara and throughout California, and the only recipient from the West, largely due to a recommendation from Horace Albright. Pearl, who was not supposed to make a speech, could not keep quiet. According to a Santa Barbara reporter, Pearl was in her element:

> "I just want to say," [Pearl] started right in some distance from the microphone, "how proud we are of Mrs. Nixon and her husband because they're Californians. We admire Mrs. Nixon's courage and manners and delightful sense of friendship she gives wherever she goes."
>
> Mrs. Nixon grinned and took Miss Chase by the shoulders and gently pushed her in front of the microphone.
>
> At that point Miss Chase gave up her appreciation of Mrs. Nixon and started to push preservation. "It's a matter of good housekeeping. Pick up, change and improve after you. My pollution solution is simple: get rid of anything which offends your eyes, ears, nose and mouth." Miss Chase got a standing ovation from the crowd.[29]

136. Pat Nixon

It was nationally reported that "tears came to Mrs. Nixon's eyes when Dr. Chase said, 'The people of California were very proud of this lady.'"[30] And for Pearl, she later remarked that this trip to Washington was the highlight of her career.[31]

Because of her speech, albeit brief, Pearl received an astonishing amount of publicity, which resulted in a deluge of letters and people wanting to know her. She responded to the attention with her typical humility: "I don't deserve and really regret this attention but deeply appreciate the goodwill that has been evidenced."[32] Pearl's popularity ensured that the directors of Santa Barbara's Old Spanish Days Fiesta Committee chose her to be the Grand Marshal of the El Desfile Histórico ("Historical Parade") in August 1973. Seated in an open carriage, Pearl's fiesta adventure proved to be a pleasant and enjoyable experience.

The streets were lined with flags and everyone smiled. Strolling organ grinders with their monkeys walked amongst the enthusiastic crowds. Every shopkeeper dressed in Spanish and Mexican attire. Horses, especially golden palominos, trotted down the street, beautifully adorned in silver saddles and trim. Fiesta was a community affair; it was a delightful experience with vivid costumes, music, and spirited dancing. As Grand Marshal, Pearl wore a yellow- and blue-colored embroidered shawl and a high comb for her full head of white hair.[33]

Santa Barbara went one step further in honoring Pearl when, in the spring of 1978, a group of individuals banded together to commemorate Pearl and her brother Harold.[34] They were surprised that there was not one thing—no monument, no street, no park, nothing in Santa Barbara—that bore the Chase name. Forming a steering committee, they asked the city council to change the name of Santa Barbara's Palm Park to Chase Palm Park. Where land met water, the ten-acre, oceanfront park had stunning views and amenities for the community. Its stately palm trees were the subject of postcards. As "a fitting tribute to a brother and sister who saved the beachfront from development for the enjoyment of future generations to come," the city council approved the committee's request and the park was renamed in May 1978.[35] Pearl was delighted; she thought the East Cabrillo Boulevard and its bordering parks was one of the great scenic and recreational assets of the city: "Palm Park provides one of the most attractive roadside rests in California."[36]

Pearl spent her final years surrounded by friends, feted by her community, and honored by her state and country. With sufficient income from her family and the assistance of a devoted housekeeper and secretary, Pearl remained at 2012 Anacapa Street. She continued to attend committee and public meetings up until her final days with boundless energy and dedication. As one of her contemporaries remarked:

137. Bust of Pearl by Bernice Adair, 1978

> To those that knew her she appeared to have an insight to what the future would hold. Miss Chase was always right. Sometimes I wouldn't believe her then lo and behold it would turn out exactly the way she said it. Perhaps this was due to her ability to see the whole picture, to perceive the interrelatedness of all things. She was able to see things holistically.[37]

CHAPTER 29

Death

On Wednesday, October 24, 1979, after two mild strokes, Pearl died quietly at home, three weeks before her ninety-first birthday. Within hours of her passing, the community rallied together in a quite extraordinary manner. The media was well-prepared for Pearl's passing. The *Santa Barbara News-Press*, which had done so much to support her activities, was the first paper to announce the news. It was also reported on the radio. City flags were flown at half-mast.

The following day in-depth obituaries and notices were published. In the *News-Press*'s piece:

> The death of Dr. Pearl Chase at age 90 has ended the life of one of the most remarkable women in the modern history of California. A particularly strong-willed, intellectual, and dynamic individual, Miss Chase utilized the force of her strong character to make Santa Barbara a better place. She did this in many ways. The diversity of her civic causes became legendary many years prior to her death. It is difficult, in fact, to imagine this community without her imprint. In a community that has had perhaps more than its share of public benefactors with regard to both time and money, Pearl Chase had exceedingly few peers.[1]

The *Los Angeles Times* devoted a full page to Pearl under the title, *Woman Who Shaped Image of a City Dies*.[2] The article commented, "Miss Chase was recognised throughout the country for her leadership in public health, education and conservation efforts."[3]

At the same time as the press paid tribute to Pearl, numerous organizations she had worked with passed resolutions and posthumous awards honoring her.[4] The Santa Barbara Landmarks Advisory Committee remarked, "The good works of Dr. Pearl Chase will continue to inspire and guide the committee in its future efforts to safeguard and enhance the unique quality of Santa Barbara's abundant historic and architectural resources."[5]

Community and civic leaders were quick to offer their own tributes to her. Vernon Cheadle, Chancellor Emeritus of UCSB remarked, "I have never seen her equal in the combination of thoughtful planning for and persistent zeal in reaching environmental goals."[6] Hal Conklin, a director of the Community Environmental Council who was acting city mayor pro tempore,[7] made a similarly poignant tribute:

> No one person in the 20th century transformed the style and character of Santa Barbara more than Miss Chase. The Spanish motif of our buildings, our architectural standards of excellence, our structures of world-wide repute such as the Santa Barbara Courthouse, our magnificent waterfront boulevard and Chase Palm Park left uncluttered from commercial development, as well as the miles of lush vegetation which have made our city world renowned as the "jewel of the Pacific" were all due to her strength and perseverance. In a world which continually views change as suspect and not "cost-effective," Miss Chase challenged us all to view the world as a grand dream. Beginning in the early 1920s her ideas rose like the phoenix from the rubble of a devastating earthquake in 1925 to create Santa Barbara as we know it today. To paraphrase the words of George Bernard Shaw we see things as they are and ask "why," but Miss Chase dreamed things that never were and asked, "why not?"[8]

Pearl remained a true visionary to the end. By her own wishes, she was cremated within twenty-four hours of her passing, and on Friday October 26, after a short private service attended by family and friends, she was laid to rest next to her father and brother in Santa Barbara cemetery. The burial plot was spectacular, overlooking the ocean and shaded by pine trees.

While the city and state continued to pay tribute to "the most important woman in this century in Santa Barbara",[9] some of Pearl's closest friends and her great-niece, who was then living in Montecito, discussed a memorial service.[10] Pearl had not given any instructions for the service, but her friends were certain she would appreciate it. In a fantastic upwelling of love for their friend and mentor, they met at 2012 Anacapa and planned the November 2nd memorial service at Mission Historical Park in meticulous detail. They wanted it to be inclusive, as Pearl herself was, and meaningful.[11] It was. Leaving Mission Historical Park after the service that sunny afternoon, they congratulated themselves on bringing together so many of her friends and colleagues. Her death had united them in a single purpose: to keep her memory and vision alive. A few days later, Pearl's will was published, revealing that she was as generous in death as in life.

Her estate, which included mostly property, was valued at $497,575.72. Twenty-five organizations, including the Association on American Indian Affairs, Mills College, the USCB scholarship fund, the Santa Barbara Foundation, and the SBTHP, received payouts ranging from $2,500 to $10,000.[12]

In a letter to the *News-Press* editor, one of her colleagues, wrote:

> Pearl Chase is gone, but she is still with us in spirit. Every organization with members who feel respect and love for Pearl Chase and her deeds in behalf of this city, should make an effort to do their own thing to perpetuate her memory for future generations. Santa Barbara is unique because of Pearl Chase. What greater tribute to her honor, than to have so many public places of recognition in this city, that a visitor in the year 2079 will ask, "Who was this woman who is so revered?"[13]

The bounds of Pearl's posthumous reputation were established in this way. In death, Pearl was elevated to the sainthood of Santa Barbara. As the city's foremost civic advocate, she was placed on a pedestal and a legend developed around her and her memory.

Within a very short while of her death, it became common for citizens addressing community meetings and city projects to ask the question: "What would Miss Chase have done?" As people searched for the answer, it became harder to understand who Pearl was as a person; in fact, very often, as was the case with East Beach, she was given more credit than she deserved and, similarly, in the field of conservation, much less.

CHAPTER 30

Pearl's Girls

Such was Pearl's influence that even today her legacy remains strong. Among those who deserve much of the credit for keeping Pearl's memory alive, "Pearl's Girls" were the most dynamic. Devoted, enthusiastic and protective, Santa Barbara residents Vivian "Vie" Obern, Sue Higman, Nancy De l'Arbre, Gloria Forsyth, Julia Forbes, Joy Parkinson, and Mary Louise Days perpetuated Pearl's ideals and values for the benefit of the community.

The name "Pearl's Girls" was not created or used by Pearl herself but it was assumed by the community to describe these women volunteers involved in public service and leadership.[1] As individuals, they had much in common and much that was not. Like Pearl, their own accomplishments, in fields ranging from conservation to preservation to planning, would overwhelm the ordinary citizen. They all had a shared interest in history and a willingness to be activists. They cared about the community and its people in an educational sense. All of them credited Pearl for changing their lives and teaching them leadership skills.[2] Her motto of the "Three Cs: Communication, Cooperation and Coordination" became theirs. Among their most notable achievements collectively was their leadership at the Santa Barbara Trust for Historic Preservation.

Vie Obern, who was closest to Pearl, recalled:

> One thing Pearl taught me was to carry a big bag. Out of that bag she could pull literature and a job for you to do on some important project. There was quite an assortment of jobs to be

> done in that bag at all times, and I might add, one just didn't say "no" to Pearl Chase.[3]

Determined that Pearl and her brother should have a permanent memorial, they raised $4,700 to furnish one. The dedication of the native sandstone boulder bearing a bronze plaque with the likenesses of Pearl and Harold, "Honoring a sister and brother," took place on November 16, 1982.[4] Created by local sculptor Ruth Schurz and placed at the foot of Anacapa Street, two miles from their house in Chase Palm Park, the impressive memorial sits comfortably in the sun, guarding the park at the meeting place of land and water. Today, the park is a popular place for families and friends to gather, used for hosting concerts, family picnics and gatherings, play dates, and weddings.

On November 16, 1988, under the auspices of the Santa Barbara Trust for Historic Preservation, they organized a celebratory lunch at the El Paseo restaurant. Nearly two hundred people filled the

138. Chase Palm Park Monument

dining room to the fire safety capacity to celebrate what would have been Pearl's 100th birthday. "Every person in the room had shared some life-enhancing experience" with Pearl.[5] Among them, Mary Louise Days spoke of the connection between Pearl and the Native Daughters of the Golden West:

> Whenever Miss Chase needed a group of women to form an organization or a civic venture, she recruited one or more representatives of the Native Daughters. I remember one or two telephone conversations with Miss Chase chuckling over memories of gossipy tidbits of Native Daughters history. She usually made it a point to attend civic events given by the parlors; in turn, we joined in her projects. Reina del Mar Parlor has never ceased to cooperate with the city birthday pageant begun by Miss Chase and now held at the Presidio. She used to telephone me to get the historic flags hung on the City Hall balcony, to make sure our Saint Barbara would be there, and to help with the program and refreshment servers. We will always keep her memory alive in our hearts.[6]

In 1995, "Pearl's Girls" and other preservation-minded individuals, including Kellam de Forest, the son of Lockwood and Elizabeth, established the Pearl Chase Society. The initial idea was to form an auxiliary to the SBTHP. However, when they decided to create a 501(c)(3) tax-deductible organization, they needed a name, and Pearl's was the first that came to mind. It was adopted. Despite her modesty and lifelong effort to never put herself or her name first I suspect that she would have been proud of this recognition.

Santa Barbara and its many communities have developed exceptionally since Pearl's death, and the many success stories of the society, which "continues to advance and enlarge upon the founding vision of Chase,"[7] is testament to the dedication of the Board and Members. Pearl's legacy is in the open spaces and fine buildings that make Santa Barbara an uncommon American city. It is these things that residents love, visitors are drawn to, and have brought a better quality of life.[8]

Pearl's environmental work has also left an important legacy. The absence of billboards and restriction of advertising in Santa Barbara has warranted the drive between Fernald Point and Goleta as being one of the most iconic in the US. Pearl's impact on raising awareness of roadside beauty can be seen today in groups as Scenic America and the Federal Highway Administration's Scenic Byways.

The strategies and public education campaigns that Pearl organized through the California Conservation Council helped quicken the modern environmental movement by feeding public awareness of environmental issues. The extensive resources and wide network of informed and concerned citizens, built by the council, was of benefit to modern environmental organizations. Today, California is implementing some of the most comprehensive environmental education guidelines in the country. Where the CalCC pioneered, new organizations now connect education, environment, and community with a modern vision.

Pearl's contribution to the state parks system is evident in the success of La Purísima SHP and El Presidio de Santa Barbara SHP. Her memory continues to inspire action; her influence and activism as a director of the National Conference on State Parks is continued today by the National Association of State Park Directors and the National Recreation and Park Association.

Pearl's continuing legacy with Native Americans is less apparent than many of her contemporaries. The history of the movement is full of people and events that go unmentioned. By adding her voice and financial support, she helped change the way grassroots organizations addressed national, state, and regional issues. The Association on American Indian Affairs continues to provide national advocacy on issues that support sovereignty and culture.

Newton Drury mused in 1965, "Probably no other person in the United States over so long a period of years has been as effective as Pearl Chase in awakening the American consciousness to the need of conservation in all its phases."[9] Pearl's life and career prove that one person can, indeed, make a difference. I believe her legacy also offers hope to those involved in modern efforts to develop a stronger, fairer, and happier world, one in which people from all backgrounds can realize their potential. As Pearl used to say, "I'm tired of people thinking they've done their civic duty when they have signed a petition. If they really care, they better get out and do something."[10]

Let's follow her advice and get out and do something.

ABBREVIATIONS

AAC Architectural Advisory Committee
AAIA Association on American Indian Affairs
ABR Architectural Board of Review
ACA American Civic Association
AIDA American Indian Defense Association
ARC American Red Cross
ASUC Associated Students of the University of California
AWS Association of Women Students
AWVs American Women's Voluntary Services
Banc Bancroft Library
BHA Better Homes in America
BIA Bureau of Indian Affairs
CAA California Alumni Association
CAA Community Arts Association
CalCC California Conservation Council
CAP Community Arts Players
CCC Civilian Conservation Corps
CCSW California Conference on Social Work
CCW California Conservation Week
CDDC Community Development Conservation Collection
CDR Community Drafting Room
CEC Community Environmental Council
CEQA California Environmental Quality Act
CGCF California Garden Club Federation
CMC Civic Music Committee
CPS California State Parks
CRC California Roadside Council
CSPF California State Parks Foundation
EAIA Eastern Association on Indian Affairs
EDC Environmental Defense Center
EMIC El Mirasol Investment Company
EPA Environmental Protection Agency
FDR Franklin Delano Roosevelt
GCA Garden Club of America
GCSB&M Garden Club of Santa Barbara and Montecito
GFWC General Federation of Women's Clubs
KAT Kappa Alpha Theta
LPAC La Purísima Advisory Committee
Mss Manuscript
NAIA National Association on Indian Affairs
NCSP National Conference on State Parks
NEPA National Environmental Policy Act
NOAA National Oceanic and Atmospheric Administration
NPS National Park Service
NRC National Roadside Council
NTHP National Trust for Historic Preservation
OAP Office of Price Administration
P&P Plans and Planting Committee
PTA Parent-Teacher Association
SBALC Santa Barbara Advisory Landmarks Committee
SBCUC Santa Barbara College of the University of California
SBIDA Santa Barbara Indian Defense Association
SBRC Santa Barbara Roadside Council
SBSC Santa Barbara State College
SBSCC Santa Barbara County Social Service Conference
SBTHP Santa Barbara Trust for Historic Preservation
SES Soil Erosion Service
SHP State Historic Park
SOC Save Our City
STRL Save the Redwoods League
UC University of California
UCLA University of California Los Angeles
UCSB University of California Santa Barbara
USAAC United States Army Air Corps
USO United Service Organizations
V-E Victory in Europe
WPA Works Progress Administration
YMCA Young Men's Christian Association
YWCA Young Women's Christian Association
WC Wikimedia Commons

NOTES

Chapter 1

1 Editor, "City Honors Dr. Pearl Chase," *Santa Barbara News-Press,* November 4, 1979.
2 *Ibid.*
3 *Ibid.*
4 Pearl Chase, interview by Gibbs Smith, ca. 1972–1973, OH 115, transcript, Pearl Chase Oral History, Department of Special Collections, UC Santa Barbara Library, Santa Barbara, CA.
5 *Ibid.*
6 *Ibid.*
7 *Ibid.*
8 She accompanied Lillian Nordica, who later became a Coca Cola model and famous opera singer of the Gilded Age.
9 Hezekiah Chase to Nina Chase, May 23, 1893, Series V_Masterbox 722_Box 5, Folder 0, Community Development and Conservation Collection. SBHC Mss 1. Department of Special Research Collections, UCSB Library, University of California, Santa Barbara (hereafter referred to as CDCC).
10 Chase, interview.
11 Although there is no record, I suspect that either before or during her 1885 visit to California, Nina was influenced by the two most popular books about the state. Charles Nordhoff's *California for Health, Pleasure and Residence: A Book for Travellers and Settlers* promoted southern California as a health-giving paradise and a land of new beginnings. Helen Hunt Jackson's *Ramona* unintentionally promulgated a romanticized Spanish heritage, complete with its missions, priests, and lowly Indians, and provided Euro-Americans with antiquity and a sense of stability in a newly evolving California.
12 Michael R. Adamson, "The Makings of a Fine Prosperity, Thomas M. Storke, the *Santa Barbara News-Press,* and the Campaign to Approve the Cachuma Project," *Journal of Urban History* 30, no. 2, (January 2004): 189–212.
13 Hezekiah Chase to Nina Chase, June 20, 1901, V_722_5, CDCC.
14 Hezekiah Chase, "The Murray Mine," 1902, Western History, Denver Public Library.
15 Report Card, Pearl Chase, 1902, V_777_6, CDCC.

Chapter 2

1 Neal Graffy, *Historic Santa Barbara: An Illustrated History* (Historical Publishing Network, 2012), 57.
2 H.G. Chase, 728 State Street, May 1903, V_728_11, CDCC.
3 Owen, H. O'Neill, *History of Santa Barbara County, State of California, Its People and Its Resources,* (Santa Barbara, CA: Harold McLean Meier, 1939), 303.
4 Graffy, *Historic Santa Barbara,* 57.
5 Walker A. Tompkins, *Santa Barbara History Makers* (Santa Barbara, CA, McNally & Loftin, 1983), 278.
6 Thaddeus S. Kenderdine, *California Revisited: 1858–1897* (Doyleston Publishing Company Printers, 1898), 216.
7 Michael Redmon, "Phones in S.B.: When did the first telephones come to Santa Barbara?" *Santa Barbara Independent,* June 10, 2011, https://www.independent.com/2011/06/10/phones-s-b/.
8 Editor, "Local Realtors Honor Memory of H.G. Chase," *Santa Barbara News-Press,* December 12, 1951.
9 "*Zaca*," Chumashan for "quiet place."
10 Pearl Chase quoted in "How Did Beautiful Santa Barbara Get That Way?," *Sunset Magazine,* January 1975.
11 Stephen Birmingham, *California Rich: The Lives, the Times, the Scandals, and the Fortunes of the Men & Women Who Made & Kept California's Wealth* (Lanham, MD: Lyons Press, 2016), 267.
12 Nancy Schwarz, "Pearl Chase: Citizen Leader," *UCSB Environmental Studies* 192 (June 3, 1982): 7.
13 Pearl Chase to Nina Chase, September 23, 1905, V_719_2_11, CDCC.
14 Dr. Alan "Lanny" Ebenstein, "Santa Barbara High School, 1875–2000, To Celebrate 125 Years," *Noticias: Magazine of the Santa Barbara Historical Society* 46, no. 3 (Fall, 2000): 46–70.
15 Marco Farley, *The Legacy of Pearl Chase* (Santa Barbara, CA: Santa Barbara Trust for Historic Preservation, 1988), 2.
16 Pearl Chase, interview by Gibbs Smith, ca. 1972–1973, OH 115, transcript, Pearl Chase Oral History, Department of Special Collections, UC Santa Barbara Library, Santa Barbara, CA.
17 Pearl Chase to Friends of California Alumni Association, September 10, 1959, V_771_1, CDCC.

18 Henry Farnham May, *Three faces of Berkeley: Competing Ideologies in The Wheeler Era, 1899–1919, Chapters in the History of the University of California* (Berkeley, CA: Center for Studies in Higher Education and Institute of Governmental Studies, University of California, Berkeley, 1993), 7.
19 "About University of California, Berkeley," University of California, Berkeley, November 4, 2020, https://www.berkeley.edu/about.
20 Kevin Starr, *Inventing the Dream: California Through the Progressive Era* (Oxford, Oxford University Press, 1985), 224.
21 *Ibid.*
22 Alexandra M. Nickliss, *Phoebe Apperson Hearst: A Life of Power and Politics* (Lincoln, NE: University of Nebraska Press, 2017).
23 I. Natividad, "'On equal terms:' UC Berkeley celebrates 150 years since women were first admitted," *Berkeley News*, January 14, 2020, https://news.berkeley.edu/2020/01/14/on-equal-terms-uc-berkeley-celebrates-150-years-since-women-were-first-admitted/.
24 Lynn D. Gordon, *Gender and Higher Education in the Progressive Era* (New Haven, CT: Yale University Press, 1992), 2.
25 *Ibid.*, 71.
26 *Ibid.*, 71.
27 *Ibid.*, 53.
28 "Soon after Berkeley's founding in 1868, a tradition known as *class rush* started up. Freshmen would run up the hills above the campus and mark their class numerals in the hillside, and the sophomore class would try to protect the hill by rolling the freshmen back down the hill. Recognized as dangerous the university banned the event. As a result, the men of the freshmen and sophomore classes jointly constructed the Big 'C'." "Bear Traditions; Days of Cal", 4 November 2020, https://bancroft.berkeley.edu/CalHistory/traditions.html. "A plaque was emplaced with the words "In memory of the Rush, buried Charter Day 1905 by the classes of 1907 and 1908." Harvey Hefland, *Charter Hill and the Big C, University of California, Berkeley: An Architectural Tour*, (New York, NY, Princeton Architectural Press, 2001), pp. 262–265. "Since then, the 'C' has been considered legitimate prey by the athletic opponents of Berkeley who try to emblazon their colors on it."
29 Gordon, 8.
30 *Ibid.*, 25.

Chapter 4

1 Editors, "San Francisco earthquake of 1906," *Encyclopaedia Britannica*, last modified April 11, 2022, https://www.britannica.com/event/San-Francisco-earthquake-of-1906. Ron Henggeler, https:www.ronhenggeler.com.
2 Pearl Chase to Nina and Hezekiah Chase, April 21, 1906, V_767_24, CDCC.
3 Hezekiah Chase to Pearl Chase, April 21, 1906, V_745_2, CDCC.
4 Henry Morse Stephens, "The University and the Fire," *San Francisco Examiner*, April 18, 1908.
5 Pearl Chase to Harold Chase, September 26, 1906, V_719_2_12. CDCC.
6 Friend to Pearl Chase, Undated 1908, V_786_13, CDCC.
7 Harold Chase to Hezekiah Chase, August 30, 1908, V_719_2_5, CDCC.
8 Carol Jenks, interview by Ron Nye, May 15, 1975, OH 26_1_1_ # A6703/CS, audio cassette, UC Santa Barbara, Santa Barbara, CA.
9 Pearl Chase, interview by Charles Bridgham Hosmer, Jr., August 8, 1971, in *The New York Preservation Archive Project*, 63.
10 *Ibid.*
11 Pearl Chase, interview by Gibbs Smith, ca. 1972–1973, OH 115, transcript, Pearl Chase Oral History, Department of Special Collections, UC Santa Barbara Library, Santa Barbara, CA.
12 Pearl Chase to Hezekiah Chase, January 2, 1907, *Kappa Alpha Theta*, "Scrapbook of Pearl Chase, Omega Chapter, UC Berkeley, 1905–1909," Gledhill Library, Santa Barbara Historical Museum, Santa Barbara, CA.

Chapter 5

1 *Santa Barbara Yesterdays*, "Pearl Chase Biography", January 10, 1984, A3180/R7, Walker A. Tompkins collection, SBHC_Mss_19_Department of Special Research Collections, UC Santa Barbara Library, University of California, Santa Barbara, CA.
2 Michael Redmon, "Ednah Rich Morse – Educator Devotes Her Life to Higher Learning," *Santa Barbara Independent*, November 29, 2010. Although an age gap of seventeen years separated Ms. Rich from Pearl, they had much in common and became close friends. An excellent student as well as an ambitious and progressive educator not afraid to use great push, Rich often worked too hard in her desire to reach distinction. Aged eighteen, her potential was spotted by Anna C. Blake, a wealthy Bostonian and educational pioneer, who opened the first Sloyd School on the west coast, in Santa Barbara in 1891. "The Sloyd method, originally developed in Sweden, emphasized hands-on education in manual arts with a view to training the student physically, mentally, and morally." "After studying the method in Europe with her expenses paid by Blake, Rich returned to Santa Barbara and became responsible for the progress of

the school. In 1908 she worked determinedly for its next iteration as a training school for teachers of manual education, and she succeeded. It was not a prerequisite to have been to university to enrol, and in this way normal schools helped boost the number of women entering the teaching profession."

3 "Normal" derived from the French term for teacher training schools.
4 Chase diary, November 1, 1909. Quoted in Barker, 117 (see chap. 3, n. 14).
5 Michael Heskett, "The First Lady of Santa Barbara: Pearl Chase," *Soundings: Collections of the University Library*, 4, no. 2 (December 1972).
6 Pearl Chase Domestic Science Notes (undated), V_781_9.1, CDCC.
7 "The Faculty," *Olive and Gold Commencement Issue 1911* (Santa Barbara, CA: Santa Barbara High School, 1911), Mary Louise Days Collection, Santa Barbara, CA.
8 Pearl Chase to Marion Hall, May 4, 1933, V_769_26, CDCC.
9 Tompkins, *Santa Barbara History Makers*, 309 (see chap. 2, n. 5).
10 *Ibid.*, 309.
11 "How organizations and institutions started in Santa Barbara", Pearl Chase lecture (undated), CUSB-a858, CDCC.
12 Pearl Chase, interview by Gibbs Smith, ca. 1972–1973, OH 115, transcript, Pearl Chase Oral History, Department of Special Collections, UC Santa Barbara Library, Santa Barbara, CA.
13 Farley, 3 (see chap. 2, n. 15).
14 Nancy Wooloch, *Women and the American Experience* (New York, NY: McGraw-Hill, 1994), 290.
15 Nancy Schwarz, interview with Vivian Obern, "People who carry on Miss Chase's ideas," May 4, 1982, transcript, Gledhill Library, Santa Barbara Historical Museum, Santa Barbara, CA.
16 Edward S. Spaulding, *Santa Barbara Club: A History* (Santa Barbara, CA: 1954), 55.
17 O'Neill, 300 (see chap. 2, n. 3).
18 *Ibid.*
19 Stephen H. Provost, *Highway 101: The History of El Camino Real* (Fresno, CA: Craven Street Books, 2020), 3.
20 Editor, "50-Year Auto Club Members are Honored," *Santa Barbara News-Press*, November, 16, 1965.
21 California Digital Newspaper Collection, "Death Suddenly Beckons Noble Worker for Charity," *Morning Press*, 41 (295), July 13, 1913.
22 Chase, interview.
23 *Ibid.*, 11.
24 Pearl Chase to Harold Chase, Undated 1969, V_767_243, CDCC.

Chapter 6

1 Pearl Chase, interview by Gibbs Smith, ca. 1972–1973, OH 115, transcript, Pearl Chase Oral History, Department of Special Collections, UC Santa Barbara Library, Santa Barbara, CA.
2 *Ibid.*
3 *Ibid.*
4 Frank Taylor and Katherine Glover, "Blue Ribbon Citizen: 1. The Townswoman," *Survey Graphic: Magazine of Social Interpretation* (March 1940), 178.
5 Farley, 3 (see chap. 2, n. 15).
6 Chase, interview.
7 Taylor, 178.
8 Jim Little, "Mother Pearl: A Centennial Celebration for Miss Chase," *The Santa Barbara Independent*, November 10, 1988.
9 *Ibid.*
10 Pearl Chase to Mrs. A.E. Wellington, March 25, 1940, V_789_16, CDCC.
11 Chase, interview.
12 Barker, 319 (see chap. 3, n. 15).
13 Mildred Selfridge to Pearl Chase June 10, 1931, Ia_136_1_1, CDCC.
14 Hezekiah Chase to Pearl Chase August 28, 1916, V_745_2, CDCC.
15 At the time, the unlisted company employed 12,000 workers and was doing business of $30 million a year, roughly equivalent to $413,450,794 in 2023.
16 Marion Paulton (Chase) to Pearl Chase, July 24, 1917, V_719_2_8, CDCC.
17 Chase, interview.
18 Kathleen Brewster, "Miss Pearl Chase: Home Economics: The Recipe for Success," November 2013. K. Brewster Collection, Santa Barbara, CA.
19 Chase, interview.
20 *Ibid.*
21 California Digital Newspaper Collection, "Social Agency Work Topic of Conference," *The San Bernardino County Sun*, April 20, 1918.
22 California Digital Newspaper Collection, "Santa Barbara will be Mecca of Social Workers this week," *San Jose Mercury-News*, April 14, 1918.
23 Aurelia Henry Reinhardt to Pearl Chase, April 25, 1918, V_745_2, CDCC.
24 Chase, interview.
25 California Digital Newspaper Collection, "Chest Plan is discussed at Center," *Morning Press*, October, 1, 1921.
26 Pearl Chase to Ralph Hiett, November 24, 1919, V_748_5, CDCC.

Chapter 7

1 Pearl Chase, interview by Gibbs Smith, ca. 1972–1973, OH 115, transcript, Pearl Chase Oral History, Department of Special Collections, UC Santa Barbara Library, Santa Barbara, CA.
2 Kevin Starr, *Material Dreams: Southern California through the 1920s* (Oxford, UK: Oxford University Press, 1990), 258.
3 *Ibid.*
4 Gloria Ricci Lothrop, "Strength Made Stronger: the Role of Women in Southern California Philanthropy," *Southern California Quarterly*, 71, no. 2/3 (Fall 1989), 174.
5 Chase, interview.
6 Marc Appleton, interview with author, February 26, 2019.
7 Community Arts Music Association of Santa Barbara, "Through the Decades 1919/20s," May 19, 2016, https://camasb.org/2016/05/19/1920s/.
8 California Digital Newspaper Collection, "Community Art Assn. Plans to Enlarge Scope," *Morning Press*, September 25, 1920.
9 The Herters, who were both from New York, had met in Paris as art students. Before moving to Santa Barbara, they lived in the East Hamptons. "Albert's father Christian Herter had cofounded Herter Brothers, a prominent New York interior design firm. After it closed in 1906, Albert and Adele founded Herter Looms, a tapestry and textile design and manufacturing firm. Albert's mother Mary had moved to Santa Barbara in 1904 where she lived in a block-sized property called the El Mirasol ('The Sunflower'). As a volunteer at Cottage Hospital she was acquainted with Nina Chase. After Mary died in 1913, Albert and Adele moved to Santa Barbara. They converted the Mission Revival property into a discreet and exclusive hotel for the rich and famous, adorning it with art from Herter Looms. They managed the property until 1920 when they sold it to hotelier and attorney Frederic Clift."
10 Chase, interview.
11 *Ibid.*
12 The city electrical workers volunteered the difficult job of decking out the tree with 14 strings each 110ft in length with a total of 300, 25-watt bulbs and a further fifty bulbs at the top of the tree.
13 Born in Stockbridge in 1874, Hoffmann graduated from Cornell University in 1895 in electrical engineering. In 1903 he married Irene Botsford, a former Chicago debutante and daughter of the founder of the meat-packing business in the city.
14 Charlie Wasserman, "The Upper-Class Influence of Planning in Santa Barbara" (research paper, UC Santa Barbara, November 1975).
15 Mary Carroll, "A History of the Santa Barbara Botanic Garden and its Landscapes" (Santa Barbara Botanic Garden, June 2003), 8.
16 Community Arts Music Association of Santa Barbara, "Through the Decades 1919/20s."
17 Chase, interview.
18 Chase, interview.
19 Jim Little, "Happy Birthday, Miss Chase: Celebrating the Centennial of the Woman Who Is an Inspiration To Us All," *Santa Barbara Independent*, November 10, 1988.
20 Chase, interview.
21 Pearl Chase to Dr John Gardener, September 7, 1959, Ia_225_14, CDCC.
22 Pearl Chase to Auntie Pease, November 1, 1924, V_722_5, CDCC.
23 Chase, interview.
24 Lee M.A. Simpson, *Selling the City, Gender, Class, and the California Growth Machine, 1880–1940*, (Redwood City, CA: Stanford University Press, 2004) 140.
25 *Ibid.*
26 Sheila Lodge, *Santa Barbara: An Uncommonplace American Town* (Seattle, WA: Olympus Press, 2020), 30.
27 Barker, 245.

Chapter 8

1 Although the Richter magnitude scale was not developed until 1935, comparison records show that the main shock had an approximate magnitude of 6.3.
2 Neal Graffy, "The 1925 Santa Barbara Earthquake, Day 1, Part 1," *Edhat Santa Barbara*, June 29, 2020, https://www.edhat.com/news/the-1925-santa-barbara-earthquake-day-1-part-1.
3 "The Big One!," *The Story of Santa Barbara*, Santa Barbara Historical Museum, Santa Barbara, CA.
4 Harold Chase note, Undated, V_728_11, CDCC.
5 Pearl Chase, "Santa Barbara Resurgent," *Survey Graphic* 54, no. 9 (August 1, 1925), 469.
6 O'Neill, Owen H., *History of Santa Barbara County, State of California, Its People and Its Resources*, (Harold McLean Meier, Santa Barbara, 1939), 324.
7 Kevin Starr, *Material Dreams: Southern California through the 1920s* (Oxford University Press, Oxford, 1990), 288.
8 Pearl Chase, "Activities of Bernhard Hoffmann at the time of the Santa Barbara Earthquake", notes for article, undated 1960–1965, V_762_19, CDCC.
9 O'Neill, 325 (see chap. 2, n. 3).
10 Ellen K.A. Knowles, "Unifying Vision: Improvement, Imagination and Bernhard Hoffmann of Stockbridge (New England) and Santa Barbara (New Spain)" (master's thesis, University of Southern California, 2011), 154.

11 Charles Bridgham Hosmer, Jr., 13 (see chap. 4, n. 9).
12 Pearl Chase, interview by Gibbs Smith, ca. 1972–1973, OH 115, transcript, Pearl Chase Oral History, Department of Special Collections, UC Santa Barbara Library, Santa Barbara, CA.
13 Neal Graffy, "The 1925 Santa Barbara Earthquake, Day 3," *Edhat Santa Barbara*, July 2, 2020, https://www.edhat.com/news/the-great-santa-barbara-earthquake-day-3.
14 Chase, "Santa Barbara Resurgent," 472.
15 Knowles, 155.
16 Fukuo Akimoto, "The Birth of Architectural Control in Santa Barbara" (paper presented at the 12th International Planning History Conference, New Delhi, India, December 10–15, 2006), 15.
17 Paul B Israel. "The Earthquake of 1925", (Department of History, UCSB, June 1978), IV_714_3_9, CDCC.
18 Starr, *Material Dreams*, 288.
19 *Ibid.*
20 Pearl Chase, "Activities of Bernhard Hoffmann at the time of the Santa Barbara Earthquake", notes for article, undated 1960-1965, V_762_19, CDCC.
21 Paul B. Israel, "The Earthquake of 1925", (Department of History, UCSB, June 1978), IV_714_3_9, CDCC.
22 Pearl Chase to Mr C.W. Tooks, April 3, 1934, Ia_218_7, CDCC.
23 Bernhard Hoffmann to Allison Owen, November 1, 1926, Ia_213_2, CDCC.
24 Pearl Chase, interview by Gibbs Smith, ca. 1972–1973, OH 115, audio cassette tape cusb-a8578b, Pearl Chase Oral History, Department of Special Collections, UC Santa Barbara Library, Santa Barbara, CA.
25 Knowles, 161.
26 Starr, *Material Dreams*, 288.
27 Chase, interview.
28 Thomas M. Storke, *California Editor* (Santa Barbara, CA: News-Press Publishing Company, 1958), 255.
29 Pearl Chase to Dr. F.P. Keppel, September 30, 1925, 1a_213_2, CDCC.
30 Pearl Chase to Mayor Charles M. Andrea, March 4, 1926, V_758_15, CDCC.
31 David Silver, "The History of the Southern Pacific Roundhouse in Santa Barbara" (research paper, University of California, Santa Barbara, 1977), 195.
32 Irving Morrow, "New Santa Barbara," reprinted from *The Architect and Engineer* 86, no. 1 (July 1926).
33 Christine Palmer, "The 1925 Santa Barbara Earthquake," *Noticias: Quarterly Magazine of the Santa Barbara Historical Society* 46, no. 2 (Summer 2000), 43.
34 NoeHill Travels in California, "Nation Register of Historic Places in Santa Barbara County: The Santa Barbara Courthouse," https://noehill.com/santabarbara/nat1981000177.asp.

Chapter 9

1 Herbert Hoover, in *Better Homes in America: Aims and Methods* 7 (Washington, DC: Better Homes in America, 1925). "The home is the concern of all and everybody should welcome the opportunity to contribute to its welfare."
2 "Santa Barbara Divides Prize with Atlanta," *Los Angeles Times*, July 16, 1925, 10.
3 Herbert Hoover to Pearl Chase, July 22, 1925, Ia_34_8_5-11, CDCC.
4 Simpson, 144 (see chap 7, n. 24).
5 Mrs. L.B. Bridgeman to Pearl Chase, November 10, 1919. Ia_456_2_1, CDCC.
6 *Morning Press*, September 19, 1922, quoted in Barker, 261.
7 Manisha Claire, "The Latent Racism of the Better Homes in America Program," *JSTOR Daily*, February 26, 2020, https://daily.jstor.org/the-latent-racism-of-the-better-homes-in-america-program/.
8 *Ibid.*
9 Mary Louise Days Collection, "Better Homes in America: Santa Barbara a Leader in a Nation-Wide Movement," *The Western Woman* (March 1931), 30.
10 Pearl Chase to Mrs. William Brown Meloney, February 5, 1934. Ia_218, CDCC.
11 "Better Homes in America: Guidebook for Better Homes Campaigns, Better Homes Week, April 25 to May 1, 1926," *Better Homes in America* 10 (Washington, DC: Better Homes in America, October 1925).
12 Pearl Chase, interview by Gibbs Smith, ca. 1972–1973, OH 115, audio cassette tape cusb-a8578b, Pearl Chase Oral History, Department of Special Collections, UC Santa Barbara Library, Santa Barbara, CA.
13 *Better Homes in America* 10, 31.
14 Pearl Chase to L Deming Tilton, October 19, 1931, 9_14, Dr. Marian A. Johnson Santa Barbara oral history collection, SBHC Mss 90. Department of Special Research Collections, UC Santa Barbara Library, University of California, Santa Barbara, CA.
15 Pearl Chase to William Paulton, November 30, 1924, 1a_34_8_5-11, CDCC.
16 *Better Homes in America* 10, 46–50.
17 At a cost of $9,343, including the house, fixtures, garage, landscaping, and value of the lot, the Committee showed how, by using a slightly smaller floor plan permitting an addition, and by other affecting economics, $1,099 could be saved in the

construction of the house. This house was furnished at a total cost of $1,592.10.

18 *Better Homes in America* 10, 46–50.

19 *Ibid.*

20 Pearl Chase to James Ford, August 11, 1926, Ia_34_5_8-11, CDCC.

21 *Ibid.*

22 James Ford to Mrs. J.O. Knighten, July 2, 1926, Ia_34_5_8-11, CDCC.

23 Pearl Chase, "Better Small Homes in Santa Barbara" (Santa Barbara, CA: The Plans and Planting Committee of the Community Arts Association, 1926), 53.

24 *Ibid.*, 53.

25 *Ibid.*, 49.

26 Alice Van der Water, "The Garden Club of Santa Barbara: A Centennial History," *Noticias: The Quarterly Magazine of the Santa Barbara Historical Society* 60, no. 1 (April 2016), 10.

27 Esther Gwynne, "Work, Plan, and Pay to Help City," *Evening Tribune San Diego*, November 16, 1961.

28 Chase suggested the De Lockwood's start the magazine and she gave them $25 to do so. She continued to fund the magazine until it was disbanded in 1941.

29 Robin Karson, *A Genius for Place: American Landscapes of the Country Place Era* (Boston, MA: University Massachusetts Press, Boston, 2008).

30 Pearl Chase, "Friendly Gardens: Garden Tours," KDB Radio, Santa Barbara, CA: KDB, March 16, 1932.

31 Pearl Chase Memoranda re: Civic Service, July 1966, V_763_20, CDCC.

32 Pearl Chase to James Ford, July 18, 1927, Ia_35_9_1-6, CDCC.

33 James Ford to Pearl Chase, August 6, 1927, Ia_35_9_1-6, CDCC.

34 Pearl Chase to Mrs. Mabel Urmy Seares, October 11, 1927, V_752_9, CDCC.

35 Pearl Chase to Bernhard Hoffmann, December 7, 1928, Ia_214_3_1, CDCC.

36 Worn down by the politics, an undercurrent of indifference, and blatant opposition to his ideals, Hoffmann's health was suffering. Pearl, who was already chairing the committee in all but name, was his obvious successor. The following year, the forces of public opinion had risen to such a high crescendo of politics, press, and money that Hoffmann withdrew entirely from all civic involvement. He and his wife then divided their time between Santa Barbara and the East Coast.

37 Hosmer, Jr., 69 (see chap. 7, n. 24).

38 Pearl Chase, "Cooperation in Town and Country Planning", June 1929, V_788_15, CDCC.

39 Eric P. Hvolbøll, "The Santa Barbara County Planning Commission," *Noticias: The Quarterly Magazine of the Santa Barbara Historical Society*, 31, no. 2 (Summer 1985), 39.

40 Pearl Chase, "Better Homes in America 1928," Ia_28_2_5, CDCC.

41 Thirty-three houses ranging in size from three to nine rooms and in price from $1,352 to $16,000, were used to demonstrate the variety of types and range of possibility in building and furnishing a small house to make it a comfortable, convenient, and attractive home. Competitions in small house design, foundation and boundary planting, and small garden design reached every part of the county. A home builders' clinic was conducted. Additionally, 3,000 guide and budget books were printed and distributed.

42 James Ford to Pearl Chase, June 13, 1928, Ia_35_9_1-6, CDCC.

43 Pearl Chase to James Ford, July 13, 1928, Ia_35_9_1-6, CDCC.

44 Frank Watson to Pearl Chase, November 23, 1935, Ia_36_10_1-12, CDCC.

Chapter 10

1 History.com editors, "The 1930s," *History* (New York, NY: A&E Television Networks, 2010), https://www.history.com/topics/great-depression/1930s.

2 *Ibid.*

3 Walker A. Tompkins, *Cottage Hospital: The First One Hundred Years, The Centennial History of Santa Barbara Cottage Hospital* (Santa Barbara, CA: Santa Barbara Cottage Hospital Foundation, 1988), 91.

4 Richard Norton Smith and Timothy Walch, "The Ordeal of Herbert Hoover, Part 2," *Prologue Magazine* 36, no. 2 (Summer 2004), https://www.archives.gov/publications/prologue/2004/summer/hoover-2.html.

5 James N. Giglio, "Voluntarism and Public Policy between World War I and the New Deal: Herbert Hoover and the American Child Association," *Presidential Studies Quarterly* 13, no. 3 (Summer 1983), 430–452.

6 J. Schuyler Long, "The White House Conference on Child Health and Protection," *American Annals of the Deaf* 76, no. 1 (January 1931), 1–7.

7 Aparna Mukherjee, "Inventory of the White House Conference on Child Health and Protection records" [finding aid] (Stanford, CA: Hoover Institute Library & Archives, Stanford University, 2006), https://oac.cdlib.org/findaid/ark:/13030/kt6j49r12c/entire_text/.

8 Pearl Chase to Harold and Hezekiah Chase, September 27, 1931, V_721_4, CDCC.

9 Natasha Porfirenko and James Ryan, "Register of the President's Conference on Home Building and Home

Ownership (1931: Washington, D.C.) records" [finding aid] (Stanford, CA: Hoover Institute Library & Archives, Stanford University, 1998), https://oac.cdlib.org/findaid/ark:/13030/tf1w1001jf/entire_text/.

10 Robert P. Lamont, "Do Women Make Good in Uncle Sam's Service?" *Oakland Tribune*, January 10, 1932.

11 Mickey Moran, "1930s, America – Feminist Void? The status of the Equal Rights Movement during the Great Depression," *The Student Historical Journal, 1988–1989*, 20 (Chicago, IL: Loyola University) 7–14, http://people.loyno.edu/~history/journal/1988-9/moran.htm.

12 Pearl Chase to George Owen Knapp, May 19, 1931. Ia_216_5, CDCC.

13 Pearl Chase to Mildred Selfridge, September 27, 1931, V_722_5, CDCC.

14 Pearl Chase to Hezekiah and Harold Chase, September 27, 1931, V_722_5, CDCC.

15 H.G. Chase & Associates, *Daily News*, November 14, 1927.

16 Pearl Chase to Hezekiah and Harold Chase, September 27, 1931, V_722_5, CDCC.

17 Pearl Chase to Mildred Selfridge, September 27, 1931, 1a_142_7_1, CDCC.

18 *Ibid.*

19 Neil Flanagan, "Miss Harlean James Sells the City Beautiful," April 25, 2017, https://medium.com/@jg_bollard/how-miss-harlean-james-took-a-road-trip-and-created-modern-washington-1f619e787bd2. In 1935, the ACA became the American Planning and Civic Association (APCA).

20 Hosmer, Jr., 68 (see chap. 4, n. 9).

21 The National Commission on Law Observance and Enforcement (also known unofficially as the Wickersham Commission) was a committee established by the President Hoover on May 20, 1929.

22 Pearl Chase to Harold Chase, November 18, 1931, V_754_11, CDCC.

23 Pearl Chase, "Home Information Services and Centers" (presented at The President's Conference on Home Building and Home Ownership, Washington, DC: 1932), 137–238.

24 Porfirenko and James.

25 Encyclopedia.com, "Housing 1929–1941," *Historic Events for Students: The Great Depression*, https://www.encyclopedia.com/education/news-and-education-magazines/housing, 1929–1941.

26 Porfirenko and James.

27 The Bonus Army was a group of 43,000 demonstrators made up of 17,000 US First World War veterans, together with their families and affiliated groups. They gathered in Washington, DC in mid-1932 to demand early cash redemption of their service certificates.

28 Pearl Chase to Miss Winifred Pomeroy, July 5, 1932, V_755_12, CDCC.

29 *Ibid.*

Chapter 11

1 *I think that I shall never see*
A billboard lovely as a tree.
Perhaps, unless the billboards fall,
I will never see a tree at all.
Ogden Nash, "Song of the Open Road," *The New Yorker*, October 15, 1932.

2 It was known in the early years as the National Council for Protection of Roadside Beauty.

3 Founded in 1891 to promote and increase the efficiency of outdoor advertising.

4 Dan Neil, "America's Roadside Reading," *Los Angeles Times*, May 30, 2004, https://www.latimes.com/archives/la-xpm-2004-may-30-bk-neil30-story.html.

5 Gail Lee Dubrow and Jennifer B. Goodman, *Restoring Women's History Through Historic Preservation* (Baltimore, MD: John Hopkins University Press, 2003), 50.

6 Pearl Chase to Frank Balfour, January 21, 1952, Ia_223_12, CDCC.

7 Also known as the California Council for Protection of Roadside Beauty.

8 "Born in the Ojai Valley on August 15, 1896, Helen Baker Reynolds's parents arrived by stagecoach from Walla Walla, Washington to seek a cure for her father's consumption. The move was successful, and California claimed his as a convert. After high school, Helen went to UC Berkeley to study writing, and while there she met Ralph Reynolds, a medical student, and decided to leave the university to marry him." Source: Marin County Free Library, *Oral History Project*, Ehat, Carla, and Kent, Anne T., "Interview with Helen Baker Reynolds", February 28, 1979.

9 Helen Baker, interview by Carla Ehat and Anne T. Kent, February 28, 1979, transcript, Marin County Free Library.

10 Pearl Chase, interview by Gibbs Smith, ca. 1972–1973, OH 115, transcript, Pearl Chase Oral History, Department of Special Collections, UC Santa Barbara Library, Santa Barbara, CA.

11 Appendix to the Journals of the Senate and Assembly, Volume 5, Sacramento, CA, (1932)

12 "The Roadsides of California: A Survey" (New York: American Nature Association and National Council for Roadside Beauty, 1931).

13 *Ibid.*, 5.

14 Catherine Gudis, *Buyways: Billboards, Automobiles, and the American Landscape* (New York, NY: Routledge, 2004), 218.

15 Chase, interview.

16 "America 1900: Other Notable People," *American Experience* (Boston, MA: WGBH Educational Foundation), https://www.pbs.org/wgbh/americanexperience/features/other-notable-people/. Carrie Nation was a radical member of the temperance movement. She described herself as "a bulldog running along at the feet of Jesus, barking at what He doesn't like."

17 Frank and Glover, 179 (see chap. 6, n. 4).

18 *Blue Lake Advocate* 41, no. 32 (December 1928).

19 Gregory King, "Fill 'er Up!," *Santa Barbara Magazine* 9, no. 4 (Fall 1983), 24.

20 *Ibid.*, 30.

21 Pearl Chase to Mrs Calvin Funk, March 16, 1931, Ia_216_5, CDCC.

22 Nancy Schwarz, "Pearl Chase: Citizen Leader," *UCSB Environmental Studies* 192 (June 1982) 6.

23 Nancy Schwarz, interview with Sue Higman, December 1, 1982, Gledhill Library, Santa Barbara Historical Museum, Santa Barbara, CA.

24 "Categories included landscaping, improvements in landscaping, and appearance of buildings and signage. Cash prizes ranged from fifteen to forty dollars. Certificates of award were also given to all participants." Source: Redmon independent.

25 Patrick Maher was an Irish born immigrant of independent mind. He came to Santa Barbara in 1915 from Colorado. After enlisting in the US Army in 1917 and serving in Europe, he returned to Santa Barbara in 1919. By 1920 he was selling Dodge automobiles, which he continued until 1924 when he leased a Richfield station. Another followed two years later. After the 1925 earthquake, he became involved in civic affairs, serving as mayor of Santa Barbara from 1936–1945.

26 King, 31.

27 *Ibid.*, 24.

28 It also included Wallace "Wally" Penfield, a civil engineer and later director of the planning commissioner, who arrived in Santa Barbara in 1928 after growing up in Pasadena.

29 Chase, interview.

Chapter 12

1 The Directors of the CAA were unable to allocate any of their funds to the branch.

2 Pearl Chase to Adele Herter, November 1, 1930, Ia_216_5, CDCC.

3 "Lifetime of Civic Endeavor," *Santa Barbara News-Press*, October 6, 1974.

4 Pearl Chase, interview by Gibbs Smith, ca. 1972–1973, OH 115, transcript, Pearl Chase Oral History, Department of Special Collections, UC Santa Barbara Library, Santa Barbara, CA.

5 Aurelia Reinhardt to Pearl Chase, February 24, 1937, V_757_14, CDCC.

6 Pearl Chase to Mrs. Max Schott, September 25, 1946. Ia_221_10_1, CDCC.

7 Pearl Chase to Mr. William Templeton Johnson, August 4, 1932, Ia_217_6_1, CDCC.

8 Chase, interview.

9 Pearl Chase to Harold Chase, May 30, 1960, V_762_19, CDCC.

10 Pearl Chase to Santa Barbara Foundation, December 8, 1958, Ia_225_14_1, CDCC.

11 Hymy [?] Sachsen to Pearl Chase, September 14, 1914, V_748_5, CDCC.

12 Pearl Chase to Mrs. George Morgan Bacon, July 27, 1932, V_769_26, CDCC.

13 Mildred Selfridge (Orpet) to Mrs. Albert (Adele) Herter, May 4, 1932, Ia_217_6_1, CDCC.

14 *Ibid.*

15 Pearl Chase to Miss Winifred Pomeroy, July 5, 1932, V_755_12, CDCC.

16 Newton Drury to Pearl Chase, April 30, 1932, V_755_12, CDCC.

17 Pearl Chase to Dr. John Gehring, June 5, 1932, V_769_26, CDCC.

18 Pearl Chase to Miss Marion Hall, May 25, 1932, Ia_217_6_1, CDCC.

19 Pearl Chase to Carl Dennett, August 26, 1932, V_755_ 12, CDCC.

20 Pearl Chase to Dr. John Gehring, June 5, 1932, V_769_26, CDCC.

21 Pearl Chase to John Gamble, June 24, 1932, V_755_12, CDCC.

22 Mrs. Francis Price, wife of the town's leading attorney, and Mrs. Frances Linn, the librarian, did so, too.

23 Chase, interview.

24 Pearl Chase to Bernhard Hoffmann, February 27, 1931, Ia_216_5_1, CDCC.

25 Pearl Chase to Mrs. Albert (Adele) Herter, September 9, 1932, Ia_217_6_1, CDCC.

26 The music branch continued to sponsor worthwhile concerts and a community orchestra. Drama ceased to guarantee expenses of dramatic productions but continued to host theatre at the Lobero. The arts school disintegrated and closed in 1933.

27 Pearl Chase to Mrs. Albert (Adele) Herter, October 21, 1932, Ia_218_7_1, CDCC.

28 Pearl Chase to Bernhard Hoffmann, January 28, 1930, Ia_215_4_1, CDCC.

29 Pearl Chase to Mr. Siegried Goetze, June 20, 1933, Ia_218_7_1, CDCC.

30 John Frederick Murphy was a founder and director of the noted local architectural practice Soule, Murphy and Hastings. After the earthquake in 1925, this firm was closely involved in the physical

expansion of the School of the Arts campus as a complex of nine buildings bounded by Canon Perdido, Carrillo, Santa Barbara, and Garden Streets, which included 912 Santa Barbara where Pearl's office was located.

31 Pearl Chase to Mrs. Albert (Adele) Herter, October 21, 1932, Ia_218_7_1, CDCC.

32 Bernhard Hoffmann to Pearl Chase, October 15, 1932, Ia_218_7_1, CDCC.

33 Pearl Chase to Sherlie Harpham (Hilton), October 20, 1932, V_755_12, CDCC.

Chapter 13

1 "Conservation Movement." Encyclopedia of the Great Depression. *Encyclopedia.com.* https://www.encyclopedia.com/economics/encyclopedias-almanacs-transcripts-and-maps/conservation-movement.

2 Pearl Chase to Carl Dennett, August 26, 1932, V_755_12, CDCC.

3 Carolyn Merchant, *The Columbia Guide to American Environmental History* (New York, NY: Columbia University Press, 2002).

4 Pearl Chase to Mr. Charles A. Connaughton, February 22, 1964, 1a_226_15_1, CDCC.

5 Gifford Pinchot, *Breaking New Ground* (San Diego, CA: Harcourt Brace and Company, 1947), 505.

6 National Park Service, "Theodore Roosevelt and Conservation", November 16, 2017, https://www.nps.gov/thro/learn/historyculture/theodore-roosevelt-and-conservation.htm.

7 National Park Service, "Conservation vs Preservation and the National Park System," October 29, 2019, https://www.nps.gov/teachers/classrooms/conservation-preservation-and-the-national-park-service.htm.

8 Robert W. Righter, *The Battle Over Hetch Hetchy: America's Most Controversial Dam and the Birth of Modern Environmentalism* (Oxford, Oxford University Press, 2005), Abstract.

9 Nancy C. Unger, "Women and Gender: Useful Categories of Analysis in Environmental History," in Andrew C. Isenberg, ed., *The Oxford Handbook of Environmental History* (October 2014).

10 Merchant, 65.

11 Glenda Riley, "Victorian Ladies Outdoors: Women in the Early Western Conservation Movement, 1870–1920," *Southern California Quarterly* 83, no. 1 (Spring 2001), 72.

12 Cameron Binkley, "'No Better Heritage than Living Trees': Women's Clubs and Early Conservation in Humboldt County," *Western Historical Quarterly* 33, no. 2 (Summer 2002), 179–203.

13 Susan Rimby, *Mira Lloyd Dock and the Progressive Era Conservation Movement* (University Park, PA: Pennsylvania State University Press, 2012).

14 Horace Albright, *Creating the National Park Service: The Missing Years* (Norman, OK: University of Oklahoma Press, 1999), chap. 11.

15 Richard West Sellars, *Preserving Nature in the National Parks: A History* (New Haven, CT: Yale University Press, New Haven, 1997), chap. 3.

16 Rebecca Conard, Rebecca, "The National Conference on State Parks: Reflections on Organizational Genealogy," *The George Wright Forum* 14, no. 4 (1997), 28–43.

17 Riley, 73.

18 Pearl Chase to the Wakes, March 25, 1968, V_763_20, CDCC.

19 Pearl Chase to Miss Katherine Glover, September 14, 1938, V_748_5, CDCC.

20 At this time, outdoor recreation became more intimately connected with consumerism and American expenditures on recreation during the 1920s increased by 300 percent.

21 "New Era of Conservation is reported," *Santa Barbara News-Press*, n.d.

22 Pearl Chase, "Public Participation in Park Work," October 1938, 13.

23 Ney C. Landrum, *The State Park Movement in America: A Critical Review* (Columbia, MO: University of Missouri Press, 2013), 79.

24 Pearl Chase to Stephen T. Mather, January 17, 1928, 1, Stephen Tyng Mather Papers, BANC MSS C-B 535, The Bancroft Library, University of California, Berkeley, CA.

25 Donald C. Swain, "Harold Ickes, Horace Albright, and the Hundred Days: A Study in Conservation Administration," *Pacific Historical Review* 34, no. 4 (November 1965), 455–465.

26 Pearl Chase, interview by Charles Bridgham Hosmer, Jr., August 8, 1971, in *The New York Preservation Archive Project*, 65–66.

27 Susan R. Schrepfer, *The Fight to Save the Redwoods: A History of the Environmental Reform, 1917–1978* (Madison, WI: University of Wisconsin Press, 1983), 175.

28 Pearl Chase to Duncan McDuffie, June 14, 1928, Ia_214_3_1, CDCC.

29 Pearl Chase to Newton Drury, June 19, 1928, Ia_214_3_1, CDCC.

30 Newton Bishop Drury, "Save The Redwoods League and State Parks," 1972, transcript, oral history, University of California, 183.

31 Consisting of representatives from: municipal park administrators; prominent natural scientists; landscape architects; the Sierra Club, the national municipal league, the American Scenic and Historic Preservation Society, the General Federation of Women's Clubs, the Garden Club of America, the US Bureau of Biological Survey, the Federal

Highway Council, and the National Park to Park Highway Association. Delegates also included a wide range of local and state organizations, birding clubs, historical societies, farm and garden associations, wildflower preservation societies, commercial clubs, civic leagues, and nature study groups. In addition, there were a few publishers of outdoor magazines.

32 Conard, 28–43.

33 *Ibid.*, 35.

34 Landrum, 120. "In 1925, the NCSP joined the Federated Societies on Planning and Parks, consisting of the American Civic Association (ACA), the National Conference on City Planning (NCCP), the American Institute of Park Executives (AIPE), and the American Park Society (APS), to render to communities and individuals more convenient and effective service, and to do so with a minimum expenditure of effort and money. Money was always an issue for the NCSP and during the middle years of the depression without any material means of support it struggled to exist. Its solution was to join with another organization of compatible interest. The choice of partners was the American Planning and Civic Association (APCA), itself formed through a merger of the ACA and the NCCP. The merger proved harmonious. In return for assuming a modest share of expenses, the NCSP got office space, clerical support, and an information outlet through the APCA's quarterly publication, *Planning and Civic Comment.* It also got Harlean James as its executive secretary."

35 Harlean James, *Romance of the National Parks* (New York, NY: Macmillan, 1939), 237.

36 Landrum, 121. "The old ten-member executive committee (which had no term limits) was replaced with a board of fifteen directors to be elected by the conference membership for five-year staggered terms."

37 *Ibid.*

Chapter 14

1 Glenda Riley, "Victorian Ladies Outdoors: Women in the Early Western Conservation Movement, 1870–1920," *Southern California Quarterly* 83, no. 1 (Spring 2001), 71.

2 Alice Van de Water, "The Garden Club of Santa Barbara, 1916–2016: A Centennial History," *Noticias: The Quarterly Magazine of the Santa Barbara Historical Society* 55, no. 1 (2016), 11.

3 *Ibid.*

4 Pearl Chase, interview by Gibbs Smith, ca. 1972–1973, OH 115, transcript, Pearl Chase Oral History, Department of Special Collections, UC Santa Barbara Library, Santa Barbara, CA.

5 The California Garden Club Federation was admitted to membership of the National Council of State Garden Clubs (now National Garden Clubs, Inc.) in December 1932.

6 Claire Claudill et al., *A History of Conservation and National Affairs & Legislation: The Garden Club of America: 1913–2013*, https://www.orindagc.org/uploads/1/2/5/9/125995757/history_of_conservation_2018.pdf. "Soon, Arbor Day and tree-planting became popular garden club activities. During the 1920s, the GCA reorganized itself and its seventeen committees. Wildflower preservation, forestry, native plants, and bird protection committees were merged into the larger National Conservation Committee; the roadside and billboard committees were combined to "urge restriction of all outdoor advertising." At the same time, members agreed to expand conservation education in the GCA. Educational exhibits were added to the International Flower Show in New York City. GCA also gave scholarships to "Nature Camps" to train teachers to educate students about conservation."

7 *Ibid.*

8 *Ibid.*

9 Claudill et al., 8. However, Mrs. William A. Hutcheson rhetorically asked: "Whether in finding billboards to suppress, rubbish to pick up, national parks to protect, Congress to influence, nurserymen to endorse, wild-flowers to save, school children to inspire, and towns to plant, we are not in danger of losing sight of our original object, to set a standard (for) 'the finest gardens America can produce.'"

10 "FDR's Conservation Legacy," National Parks Service, US Department of the Interior, https://www.nps.gov/articles/fdr-s-conservation-legacy.htm.

11 It was also recognized that schoolchildren were critical to making this work a success. They were not only the voters of tomorrow, but also potential leaders in the movement itself. All indications were that the schools could be enlisted to promote conservation-related agendas, and that educators were willing to step up. Government agencies soon began to promote their own mandated management agendas in schools.

12 Under his leadership, FDR's programs introduced new concepts on a national level in planning for the responsible use of our natural and historic resources.

13 Pearl Chase, interview by Gibbs Smith, ca. 1972–1973, OH 115, transcript, Pearl Chase Oral History, Department of Special Collections, UC Santa Barbara Library, Santa Barbara, CA.

14 "Pearl Chase, A Joyous Celebration for a Great Lady" November 2, 1979, Chase Papers, family clippings, Gledhill Library, Santa Barbara Historical Museum, Santa Barbara, California, CA.

15 Pearl used the services of four different printing companies in Santa Barbara who charged very little because they were interested in the work themselves.
16 Pearl Chase to Donald Welch, September 14, 1952, Ia_223_12_1, CDCC.
17 Chase, interview.
18 Pearl Chase, *California's Natural Wealth: A Conservation Guide for Secondary Schools* (Sacramento, CA: State Department of Education, 1940) ix.
19 Chase, interview.
20 This remark was made by John Ward Studebaker, a noted educator, whom Pearl greatly respected.
21 Chase, *California's Natural Wealth*, 14.
22 Pearl Chase to Bertram D. Blyth, February 25, 1940, Ia_65_21_4_5, CDCC.
23 Pearl Chase Undated 1935, V_788_15, CDCC.
24 Pearl Chase to Bernhard Hoffmann, Undated, V_788, 15, CDCC.
25 Chase, *California's Natural Wealth*.
26 Pearl selected the week from April 15 to 21 as the starting point of the campaign.
27 Katherine Glover, "Blue Ribbon Citizen: II. The Stateswoman," *The Survey Graphic: Magazine of Social Interpretation* (March 1940), 181.
28 In the following years, Conservation Week was celebrated over eight days, March 7–14. It was no coincidence that March 7 was both horticulturalist Luther Burbank's birthday and California's Arbor Day.
29 Pearl Chase, "Conservationists Must Educate and Cooperate," March 9, 1941. Although conservation week celebrations existed in other communities, this was the first time in America that representatives of all agencies interested in some phase of conservation or nature study were brought together for planning.
30 Glover, 181.
31 *Ibid.*
32 Chase, interview.
33 Kathleen Weiler, *Democracy and Schooling in California: The Legacy of Helen Heffernan and Corinne Seeds* (New York, NY: Palgrave Macmillan, 2011), 8. Born in the industrial city of Lawrence, Massachusetts, she was the youngest of seven children. Her father, a working-class brickmason, died when she was six, and her family later moved to Goldfield, Nevada. She attended UC Berkeley, independently supporting herself as a teacher, and completed her undergraduate degree by taking five political science courses in the fall semester of 1922.
34 "Education: Supt. Kersey Goes to War," *TIME* 39, no. 15 (April 1942).
35 Weiler, 39.
36 Politically, her conception of education was grounded in the belief in human potential and the possibility of strong state institutions.
37 "An Interview with Helen Heffernan, *Young Children*, 23 (3), January 1968, pp. 146–147, accessible online: http://www.jstor.org/stable/42658431.
38 Chase, interview.
39 Hattie Beresford, "The Way it Was: Rocky Nook Park," *Montecito Journal* 22, no. 9 (March 2016).
40 Included in the studies were birds, plants, stars, geology, and shore life. One of the main aims was to aid in teaching Boy Scout leaders and teachers and members of the 4-H club in instructing children in nature study.
41 "Teachers to go to nature camp in Rocky Nook," *Santa Barbara State College Roadrunner* 12, no. 33 (May 1933), 1.
42 S.G. Kolhstedt, "Nature, Not Books: Scientists and the Origins of the Nature Study Movement in the 1890s," *Isis* 96, no. 3 (September 2005), 324–352. "Nature study had its origins in the nineteenth century. During the early years of the twentieth century, it was the standard approach for introducing elementary and grammar school students to their natural world. Nature study's formulation reflected contemporary interest in the emerging science of ecology, the concerns of preservationists and conservationists, and an agreement throughout society at large that children should be taught about the natural world."
43 By the mid-1930s, a much more closely prescribed course of elementary science was becoming standard in schools with the result that it survived only a generation or so.
44 Pearl Chase, "The California Conservation Council," Undated, 1940, V_788_15, CDCC.
45 Patricia O'Neill Mountfort to Mrs. Weston Walker, February 20, 1967, Ia_228_15_1, CDCC.
46 *Ibid.*
47 A series of standing committees functioned throughout the year: public information including, press, radio, magazines, and publications; speakers and writers; county committees; the Women's Committee; cooperation of governmental agencies; cooperation of schools; and cooperation of statewide organizations. Other special committees were appointed when necessary.
48 Pearl Chase to Hezekiah Chase, July 17, 1940, V_758_15, CDCC.
49 Pearl Chase, "The California Conservation Council", Undated, 1940, V_788_15, CDCC.
50 These included features on wildflowers, birds, soil, trees, forests, parks, and water.
51 Edward McCrea, "The Roots of Environmental Education: How the Past Supports the Future," Environmental Education and Training Partnership (2006), https://files.eric.ed.gov/fulltext/ED491084.

pdf. "In 1935, the National Education Association assumed a leadership role for conservation education in schools. Wisconsin became the first state to enact a statute requiring pre-service teachers to have "adequate preparation in the conservation of natural resources."

52 Written by experts in their fields to assist teachers in the development of suitable instructional materials in conservation and in relating those materials to the school curriculum, it was divided into ten chapters with a bibliography covering a wide range of topics such as planning; prevention of waste, water, soil and agriculture; native flora and forests; wildlife; recreation; and mineral resources.

53 Newton Drury to Pearl Chase, February 8, 1941, 1a_64_20_6, CDCC.

54 Chase, interview. (Pearl Chase arranged a meeting by telephone and drove to Clements's house.)

55 *Ibid.*, p. 5.

56 Glover, 18.

57 Chase, interview.

58 Pearl Chase to Helen Heffernan, September 21, 1966,30_14, Save_The_Redwoods_League_records_BANC MSS 88/15c, The Bancroft Library, University of California, Berkeley, CA.

59 Newton Drury to Dr. Robert Gordon Sproul, May 20, 1946, 4_15_291_Aubrey Neasham papers, MS0004, Center for Sacramento History, Sacramento, CA.

60 Mather became the first director of the National Park Service; Albright was the second.

61 UC Berkeley Institute for Parks, People, and Biodiversity, "The Birth of America's best idea at UC Berkeley," Rausser College of Natural Resources (Berkeley, CA: UC Berkeley), https://parks.berkeley.edu/about/history.

62 Paul Casamajor, *Forestry Education at the University of California: The First Fifty Years* (California Alumni Foresters, 1965) 40.

63 Harvey Helfand, *University of California, Berkeley: An Architectural Tour* (Princeton Architectural Press, 2002), 154.

64 Chase, interview.

Chapter 15

1 Carolyn Merchant, *American Environmental History* (New York, NY: Columbia University Press, 2007), xviii-xix.

2 This involved an attempt to open a naval oil reserve in Wyoming to commercial exploitation.

3 "The passage of the Bursum Bill of 1921 would have given Anglo and Hispanic homesteaders a legal advantage in acquiring Pueblo lands and the adjoining water rights. As a consequence, the bill would have dispossessed Pueblo communities of lands and resources that had been their ancestral heritage for three millennia. When the purpose of the bill became publicly known, groups including the All Pueblo Council (APC), the General Federation of Women's Clubs (GFWC), and the American Indian Defense Association (AIDA) began a legal, diplomatic, and public relations campaign to defeat the bill." See Edwards, Robert Scott, "The Bursum Bill and the Pueblo Lands Board Act: Culture, Law, and politics in the Borderlands of the American Southwest" (University of California, San Diego, 2017).

4 Under the terms of the act, Indian reservation lands had been allotted in 160-acre or smaller plots to individual Indians, and surplus lands opened to homesteading. Several reservations were wiped out, others reduced, and thousands of Native Americans sold or leased their holdings, leaving them landless.' See Edwards, "The Bursum Bill and the Pueblo Lands Board Act."

5 Kenneth R. Philip, "Albert B. Fall and the Protest from the Pueblos, 1921–23," *Arizona and the West* 12, no. 3 (Autumn 1970), 238.

6 "The APC, GFWC, and AIDA then moved to implement an alternative bill that was designed to protect Pueblo interests. They succeeded in their attempt, and in 1924 the Pueblo Lands Board Act (PLBA) was passed in Congress, which made the federal government responsible for protecting Pueblo lands from the encroachment of settlers and corporate interests." See Edwards, "The Bursum Bill and the Pueblo Lands Board Act."

7 Robert Mullins, "Santa Barbara and American Indian Reform," *Soundings: Collections of the University Library, University of California Library at Santa Barbara* 4, no. 2 (December 1972), 21–40.

8 Born in 1884 in Atlanta, Collier came from a privileged background. His father served as mayor of the city (1887–1899).

9 In 1920 he was invited by Mabel Dodge Luhan, a wealthy patroness of the arts, to join her literary colony in Taos along with other intellectuals, including D.H. Lawrence and his wife Freida, the artist Andrew Dasburg, and the painter Dorothy Brett.

10 Kenneth R. Philp, *John Collier's Crusade for Indian Reform, 1920–1954* (Tucson, AZ: University of Arizona Press, 1977), xiii.

11 *Ibid.*, 1.

12 Karin L. Huebner, "An Unexpected Alliance Stella Edward the California Club Women, John Collier, and the Indians of the Southwest, 1917–1934," *Pacific Historical Review* 78, no. 3 (August 2009), 348.

13 Tomas Salinas, "Pearl Chase, John Collier, and Indian Reform Through the New Deal Native

American Affairs in California and the West, 1880–1937" (PhD diss., University of California, Santa Barbara, 1995), 120. Stella Atwood served on its executive committee from its inception along with other directors including Harold Ickes, future Secretary of the Interior. It "initiated a new and more assertive reform movement that would first question and then overturn federal government Indian policy."

14 The conference was held on June 9, 1923.

15 Mullins, 21–40.

16 *Ibid.*

17 Salinas, 125.

18 Tom Storke, the newspaper baron, also attended the conference and made sure that the conference and Pearl's efforts for the Native American received full coverage in his newspapers, a trend he continued in later years.

19 John Collier to Pearl Chase, June 13, 1923, Ia_436_2_1, CDCC.

20 Stella Atwood to Pearl Chase, August 8, 1923, Ia_435_1_7, CDCC.

21 In keeping with Pearl's belief that a man should preside, Franklin Price Knott, a noted photographer and Santa Barbara resident who took some of the first color images to appear in *National Geographic* including Native American Indians, was elected SBIDA president. Pearl was one of three vice presidents, along with Mabel Washburn and S.L. Hoffman, corresponding secretary.

22 Pearl Chase to Dr. Walter Dickie, October 1, 1923, Ia_437_3_10, CDCC.

23 Kenneth R. Philp et al., "John Collier and the American Indian, 1920–1945," *Essays on Radicalism in Contemporary America: The Walter Prescott Webb Memorial Lectures* (Austin, TX: University of Texas Press, 1968), 73–79.

24 Mullins, 24–25.

25 *Ibid.*, 25.

26 Hosmer, Jr., 73 (see chap. 4, n. 9).

27 Mullins, 26. Pearl "organized teas, luncheons, and dinners to raise funds and increase membership. At Christmastime, an annual drive was held to send clothing, food, toys, and other gifts to reservations in California and the southwest. She personally wrote letters of support to help various California-based Indian-owned companies get started and secure contracts. She and her colleagues also purchased Indian-made goods from reservations or displayed them for sale in Santa Barbara."

28 Pearl Chase to Dr. John Gehring, October 11, 1927, V_752_9, CDCC.

29 *Ibid.*

30 Pearl Chase to James Ford, December 7, 1928, Ia_214_3_1, CDCC.

31 Hosmer, Jr., 71.

32 Mullins, 27.

33 The SBIDA sent 80 percent of its funds to the headquarter office in New York, which paid for the firm of Hanna and Wilson's litigation costs in the Pueblo cases, legislative representation in Washington, and Collier's monthly salary.

34 Pearl Chase to Dr. Prynce Hopkins, September 18, 1957, Ia_18_11_1, CDCC.

35 Pearl Chase, "Recollections and Memorabilia re: William Bingham, 2nd, September 23, 1955, V_744_1, CDCC.

36 Pearl Chase to Dr. Milton C. Winternitz, June 24, 1932, 1a_217_6_1, CDCC.

37 Gehring was born in 1857, the son of German immigrants. Slight, trim, and dapper, he was known to smoke cigars and dress formally. Despite appearances, he was a physically active man and encouraged his clients to partake in robust activity. The growing tension reached breaking point during Bingham's journey home to Bethel via the Canadian Pacific in a private car in 1923. Pearl and Hezekiah were invited but left the party at Banff after the strain between Miss Pease and Mrs. Gehring became unbearable. Miss Pease later returned to Santa Barbara without Mr. Bingham, where she lived under the care of Pearl and a companion Bingham employed until she died in December 1934. Dr. Gehring died in 1932 and his wife, Marian, in 1936.

38 His philanthropies were many, chief among them the Bingham Associates Fund, the New England Center Hospital, the Gould Academy in Bethel, and the Betterment Fund. Pearl remained close to Bingham, visiting him on a few occasions in the late 1920s and maintaining correspondence with him until his death in 1955.

39 Salinas, 119.

40 The SBIDA went on to provide valuable leadership in helping to expose and defeat further bills sponsored by the Interior Department that threatened Indian interests.

41 Stella Atwood to Pearl Chase, May 3, 1933, Ia_23_4_2, CDCC.

42 Salinas, 253. In May 1933, Pearl and the other officers of the branch issued a memorandum to the board recommending that the association remain intact.

43 "Haven Emerson," Obituary, *American Journal of Public Health and the Nation's Health* 47, no. 8 (August 1957).

44 Pearl Chase to Haven Emerson, May 18, 1933, Ia _437_3_13, CDCC. She felt she was not "qualified to do all the work that Mr. Collier carried on so long and so effectively."

45 Jessie Kratz, "Indian New Deal," *Pieces of History* (Washington, DC: US National Archives, November 30, 2015). "Among Collier's influences were the following initiatives: anthropologists were hired to document Indian languages and ways of life; photographers were used to capture Native American culture; an Arts and Crafts Board was established to provide some economic development; curricular committees serving Native American education were encouraged to incorporate languages and customs; and the Johnson-O'Malley Act of 1934, which Collier helped steer through Congress, offered states federal dollars to support Native American education, healthcare, and agricultural assistance programs."

46 John Collier, *From Every Zenith: A Memoir, and Some Essays on Life and Thought* (New York, NY: Sage, 1963). Collier referred to it as the "Indian New Deal" stating that it held two purposes. "One was the conservation of the biological Indian and of Indian culture, each with its special purposes. The other purpose was conservation of the Indian's natural resources—the pitiful remnant of what had been their vast land—their vast land conserved by them through ten thousand years.

47 Wilbert T. Ahlstedt, "John Collier and Mexico in the Shaping of U.S. Indian Policy: 1934–1945" (PhD diss., University of Nebraska, Lincoln, 2015), 6.

48 Pearl Chase to Hezekiah Chase, July 12, 1934, V _721_4, CDCC.

49 His 1929 novel *Laughing Boy*, which was about the struggles of the Navajos in the Southwest to reconcile their culture with that of the US, was winner of the Pulitzer Prize.

50 Mullins, 32. In her reply on behalf of the SBIDA written in early August 1934, Pearl, who was organizing it on the same lines as before Collier's departure, albeit with reduced funds, stated that her organization was against a merger.

51 Mullins, Pearl insisted that the organization have the words American Indian in its name and "that Allen G. Harper, former Secretary of the American Civil Liberties Union of Pennsylvania and then-executive secretary of the AIDA, remain in that post because he was trusted by the California branches. She also emphasized that the California branches remain semi-autonomous as they had been with AIDA."

52 Mullins, 36.

53 *Ibid.* "She was favorable to a national leadership that included La Farge, Harper and Emerson and she insisted that the new association always remain national in its outlook regarding solutions to the problems of American Indians."

54 Oliver La Farge to Pearl Chase, January 13, 1936, Ia_437_3_14, CDCC.

55 Mullins, 37.

56 Oliver La Farge to Pearl Chase, September 22, 1936, Ia_437_3_14, CDCC.

57 Dr. Haven Emerson to Pearl Chase, January 3, 1938, Ia_15_8_1, CDCC. Emerson was a bit biased, having helped La Farge to secure a position at Columbia University as instructor in writing in 1936.

58 Pearl Chase to Miss Anne M. Mumford, October 26, 1938, Ia_17_10_1-19, CDCC.

59 Paul C. Rosier, "The Association on American Indian Affairs and the Struggle for Native American Rights, 1948–1955." *The Princeton University Library Chronicle* 67, no. 2 (Winter 2006), 366.

60 Paul Kleinpoppen, "Some Notes of Oliver La Farge," *Studies in American Indian Literatures* 10, no. 2, monograph no. 1, (Spring 1986), 69–120. "In 1937 "La Farge published *Enemy of the Gods*, which says much about his thinking. The story centers on the inability of the Navajo to adapt to white civilization. His portrait of the BIA and Commissioner Trubee, who is based on Collier, is open to charges of idealization in a book that everywhere else, is scrupulously accurate. His brief coverage of the Navajo's response to the Reorganization Act and the federal herd reduction programs that were intended to control soil erosion on the reservation leaves him in the awkward position of appearing to be not a documentary realist but an apologist for his friend Collier."

61 Rosier, 371.

62 Association on American Indian Affairs Archives, 134_18_Oliver La Farge to LaVerne Madigan, January 17, 1961, quoted in Rosier, Paul, p. 371.

63 Salinas, p. 258.

64 La Farge and Emerson remarked that "unless such governmental agencies are continuously watched by a group of well-informed citizens, they inevitably tend to fossilize, if not become corrupt." See Oliver La Farge and Haven Emerson, "Why Have an Indian Association?", 1939, Ia_12_5_7, CDCC.

65 Pearl Chase to John Collier, April 4, 1945, Ia_17_10_1-19, CDCC.

66 Timothy G. Haller, "The Legislative battle over the California-Nevada interstate water compact: A question of might versus Native American right," *Nevada Historical Society Quarterly* 32, no. 3 (Fall 1989), 198–222. "Pyramid Lake, the second largest lake in the US, located in the middle of the Paiute reservation, had fallen over eighty feet since 1910 because Nevada's Truckee-Carson irrigation district was diverting vast amounts of water. Although there was no immediate danger, the lake would dry up; many of the fish, which the Indians relied on, were dying as the water became more concentrated.

The Department of the Interior charged that the compact agreed in draft in 1968 would contribute to the lake's destruction because the allocation agreement called for the construction of new reservoirs up stream on the River Truckee, which would further reduce the volume of water entering the lake. Secretary of the Interior Stewart Udall and his successor, Walter Hickel, were determined to protect the lake, as well as Indian water rights and the health of the Paiute tribal economy. Their stand received strong support from Pearl and others concerned with protecting the environment and with the plight of American Indians. In 1970, the compact was ratified into law in California and the following year in Nevada. However, because of federal opposition from the Departments of Justice and Interior and the Office of Management and Budget, the compact was not acted upon by Congress. Ironically, no one won the battle over the compact. Although the Pyramid Lake Paiutes succeeded in preventing final passage, they failed to secure sufficient water to preserve the lake. The compact proponents won in California and Nevada, but failed with Congress, thus continuing the uncertain status of the area's water availability."

Chapter 16

1 Wikipedia, s.v. "New Deal," last modified April 25, 2022, 23:17, https://en.wikipedia.org/wiki/New_Deal. It "comprised a series of programs, public work projects, financial reforms, and regulations aimed at providing support for farmers, the unemployed, youth and the elderly. Some of the major federal programs and agencies included were the Civil Works Administration, the Farm Security Administration, the National Industrial Recovery Act of 1933, the Social Security Administration and the Civilian Conservation Corps (CCC). The New Deal produced a political realignment making the Democratic Party the majority (as well as the party that held the White House for seven out the nine presidential terms from 1933–1969) with its base in liberal ideas, newly empowered labor unions, and various ethnic groups."

2 Pearl Chase to Mrs Helen Oakleigh Thorne, October 31, 1936, Ia_219_8_1, CDCC.

3 Heinz Eulau, "Neither Ideology nor Utopia: The New Deal in Retrospect," *The Antioch Review* 19, no. 4 (Winter 1959–1960), 523–537.

4 Susan R. Schrepfer, *The Fight to Save the Redwoods: A History of Environmental Reform, 1917–1978* (Madison, WI: University of Wisconsin Press, 1983), 65–66. Unhappy with bureaucracies, they favored administrative expertise balanced by advisory boards or appointive committees.

5 John A. Salmond, *The Civilian Conservation Corps, 1933–1942: A New Deal Case Study* (Durham, NC: Duke University Press, 1967).

6 *Ibid.*

7 Joseph M. Speakman, "Into the Woods: The First Year of the Civilian Conservation Corps," *Prologue Magazine* 38, no. 3 (Fall 2006), https://www.archives.gov/publications/prologue/2006/fall/ccc.html.

8 Salmond.

9 Robert Fetchner, "The Civilian Conservation Corps Program," *The Annals of the American Academy of Political and Social Science* 194 (November 1937), 129–140.

10 John C. Paige, *The Civilian Conservation Corps and the National Park Service, 1933–1942: An Administrative History* (Washington, DC: National Park Service, 1985), https://files.eric.ed.gov/fulltext/ED266012.pdf.

11 The main goal of the California missions was to convert Native Americans into devoted Christians and Spanish citizens. Spain used mission work to influence the natives with cultural and religious instruction. Another motivation for the missions was to ensure that rival countries, such as Russia and Great Britain, did not try to occupy the California region first.

12 Interested in restoring property, they deeded it to the Landmarks Club in 1905. The Club was unable to raise funds to undertake the preservation, and the title reverted to the Union Oil Company.

13 La Purísima Mission State Historic Park, "Guide to the La Purísima Mission State Historic Park Collection," Organizational History (Lompoc, CA: California State Parks, 2003), https://www.parks.ca.gov/pages/1080/files/fa_513_001.pdf.

14 They were headed by Wallace "Wally" Penfield, Santa Barbara County Planning Commission engineer, with a particular interest in harbours and beaches, a representative of the State Park Committee and a member of Pearl's Santa Barbara Roadside Committee.

15 Members suggested by Penfield in February 1935 included Pearl; Frederic Clements, the first director of the Santa Barbara Botanic Garden and Carnegie Institute; Carleton Monroe Winslow, a key proponent of the Spanish Revival architecture, best known for the Santa Barbara public library and Museum of Natural History; Kelley Hardenbrook, a deputy district attorney at Lompoc; Dr. William Ellison, History Department the State College; and L. Deming Tilton. Ex-officio members included Ronald Adam, Santa Barbara County supervisor; Frank Dunne, Santa Barbara County forester; H.W. Whitsett, National Park Service architect; and Fred Hageman, National Park Service architect.

Membership would change over the years as people left the state, were unable to attend meetings, or because of other interests. Other people serving as LPAC members in the pre-WWII years included Edith B. Webb, artist and author; Father Patrick Roddy, OFM, of the Santa Barbara Mission; and Father Maynard Geiger, OFM, historian and archivist of the Santa Barbara Mission.

16 Southworth also owned the Covarrubias Adobe in Santa Barbara, built in 1817.

17 *Online Archive of California*, "Guide to the Joseph Russell Knowland Papers, 1889–1961," Collection Number MS 3154, California Historical Society, San Francisco, CA. In 1899, at the age of twenty-five, Knowland was elected to the California State Assembly and served two terms. In 1902, he was elected to the California State Senate. He went to Washington in 1904 as a United States representative to Congress, where he stayed until 1914.

18 This experience resulted in the 1941 publication of *California: A Landmark History*.

19 Pearl Chase, interview by Charles Bridgham Hosmer, Jr., August 8, 1971, in *The New York Preservation Archive Project*.

20 *Ibid.*, 6.

21 *Ibid.*, 9.

22 Walker A. Tompkins, *Old Mission Canyon, Neigborhood* Series 2 (Santa Barbara, CA: The Santa Barbara Board of Realtors, 1977). "It took until 1948 to complete, but this committee rescued and continued to preserve the ten-acre Mission Historical Park with its ruins of Mission Santa Barbara's old waterworks, tannery vats, grassed areas, and City Rose Garden."

23 Fields related to parks and planning and city beautification.

24 Charles Bridgham Hosmer, Jr., 78–79.

25 Pearl Chase, "Public Participation in Park Work," October 1938, Ia_464_6_15, CDCC.

26 Pearl Chase to Mr. Bourne, March 28, 1935, Ia_218_7_1, CDCC.

27 Hosmer, Jr., 35.

28 In fact, the report became a master plan and influenced management of the unit for over half a century. The committee made an annual report to the state commission.

29 Hosmer, Jr., 39.

30 *Ibid.*, 50.

31 *Ibid.*, 32.

32 Born in Bountiful, Utah, eleven years before Pearl, Webb was educated at Hammond Hall in Salt Lake City.

33 Hosmer, Jr., 56.

34 Islapedia, "Woodward, Arthur," s.v., last modified August 28, 2021, 04:25, https://www.islapedia.com/index.php?title=WOODWARD,_Arthur. "Woodward was born in Des Moines, Iowa in 1898, and his family moved to San Francisco in 1907. After serving in the infantry in World War I, he enrolled at the University of California at Berkeley in 1920, where he studied anthropology, history, and English. He left after two years to take a reporting job with the *New York Evening Journal*, working as a journalist for about three years. Woodward's first job after journalism was museum curator with the Museum of American Indians in New York in 1925. He moved later that year to work at the Los Angeles County Museum, where he was curator until he retired."

35 Holly Rose Larson, "M.R. (Mark Raymond) Harrington Papers MS.214" [finding aid] (Los Angeles, CA: Autry National Center, Braun Research Library). "Harrington spent his childhood roaming the area around Ann Arbor, Michigan, his hometown, learning tribal languages from Indian friends and, when his family moved to Mount Vernon, New York, excavating and collecting local artifacts, thus feeding an early and lifelong interest in Native American culture. In 1930 he bought the Romulo Pico Adobe near the San Fernando Rey Mission, one of the oldest residences in Los Angeles. He rebuilt the property and lived there with his wife for fifteen years."

36 Hosmer, Jr., 39.

37 *Ibid.*, 39–40.

38 *Ibid.*, 40.

39 Christine Savage Palmer, "Mission La Purísima Reconstruction: The Civilian Conservation Corps Story," *Noticias: The Quarterly Magazine of the Santa Barbara Historical Society* 50, no. 2 (Summer 2004), 58.

40 *Ibid.*, 58.

41 Edith Buckland Webb, *Indian life at the Old Missions* (Los Angeles, CA: Warren F. Lewis, 1952), 41. "The little agricultural town of Lompoc generally welcomed the CCC camp members. Young local men did not appreciate competition for the young women of the community, causing occasional scuffles at the tavern on H Street, but most of the enrolees behaved themselves." According to one of the men, "The local boys didn't stand a chance because we outnumbered them." If any parent came to camp to complain, "Please keep your boys away from our girls," the Army commander's stock reply was. "Please keep your girls away from our boys."

42 H.V. Smith, "Mission La Purísima: A Glance Through Its History and The Story of Its Restoration 1938–1939" (Los Angeles, CA: Charles E. Young Research Library, University of

California, Los Angeles), https://oac.cdlib.org/view?docId=hb6n39p3qk&brand=oac4&doc.view=entire_text.

43 Pearl Chase, "Public Participation in Park Work", October 1938, V_771_1, CDCC.

44 *Ibid.*

45 *Ibid.*

46 *Ibid.* and Vernon Aubrey Neasham to Newton B. Drury, August 19, 1938, 4_4.1_6.5_Pearl Chase Papers 1935–1998, California State Parks, La Purísima Mission State Historic Park Collection, La Purísima Mission State Historic Park, Lompoc, CA.

47 Elizabeth Kryder-Reid, *California Mission Landscapes: Race, Memory, and the Politics of Heritage*, (Minneapolis, MN: University of Minnesota Press), 105.

48 *Ibid.*, 109. "Bringing in some outside expertise, the LPAC hired the services of Harry Shepherd, an associate professor of landscape design at UC Berkeley. His garden plan met with some resistance from NPS regional historians who took a purist view of how the garden should look. Knowing that they would not satisfy everyone the LPAC took a diplomatic stance proclaiming that in principle the requirement of historical accuracy was paramount while making a case to proceed with Shepherd's garden plan because it would enhance visitor experience."

49 *Ibid.*, 109.

50 La Purísima Advisory Committee report to National Park Service, quoted in Kryder-Reid, 110. The LPAC's own set of principles "rationalized the historical appropriateness of a mission garden by emphasizing the water features (they called fountains) and insisting on authentic plant material. They were also particularly concerned about the visual effect of the garden on the architecture, insisting that it "must be of generous scale in accord with the building and outlying structures" and that it "should not obscure the building, but rather should provide a setting."

51 Kryder-Reid, 111.

52 Susan Chamberlin, "The CCC 'Mission Garden' at La Purísima and its Forgotten Designers," *Eden: Journal of the California Garden & Landscape History Society* 22, no. 4 (Fall 2019), 14–38. However, "work on the octagonal fountain and lavanderias in the garden was not completed until 1938."

53 Hosmer, Jr., 74. The policy of the church was to keep them in separate housing, so that the Indian men would not run away. However, this did not solve the question of the use of the buildings once they were constructed and their long-term maintenance once the CCC period was over.

54 How to implement it, the question of what animals to have, what use the garden would be and who would live on site. The LPAC tried to think about things that could be made on site and sold to visitors to provide revenue to support employees, "because while housing could be provided, certainly there wasn't any source of money that could be expected for salaries for that type of demonstration." *Ibid.*

55 *Ibid.*, 75.

56 *Ibid.*, 53. She asked Charles A. Storke, the son of Tom Storke, to act as Chairman. She thought that he had reached the point where he ought to be chairman of something.

57 Graduating from Cornell University in 1932, aged twenty-one, Charles Storke had begun working his way up the ladder in the *News-Press* organization owned by his father. Cut from a different cloth to his father, Storke II was much more interested in the history of design. He admitted using his newspaper to promote things that were good for Santa Barbara, and he considered Pearl to be one of them. During the 1950s, when he edited the paper, he provided her with pounds of paper and gallons of ink.

58 Hosmer, Jr., 54.

59 The other members comprised forty-eight leading men and women from within the county. Twenty-one county organizations and groups also cooperated.

60 The Roman Catholic feast day of Saint Barbara was December 4, and her name was bestowed on Mission Santa Barbara founded on December 4, 1786. Mission La Purísima had been founded on the feast of the Immaculate Conception on December 8, 1787. The program included receptions, exhibits, religious ceremonies, illustrated talks, tours, sacred concerts, dinners and fiestas, to be held at the Santa Barbara and La Purísima Missions.

61 Hosmer, Jr., 54–55.

62 *Ibid.*, 55.

63 Buckland Webb, 154–155.

64 *Ibid.*

65 *Ibid.*

66 John A. Salmond, *The Civilian Conservation Corps, 1933–1942: A New Deal Case Study* (Durham, NC: Duke University Press, 1967), https://www.nps.gov/parkhistory/online_books/ccc/salmond/chap13.htm.

67 La Purísima Mission State Historic Park Collection, Series 4.1_5_26_"The Meeting of the Advisory Committee," January 11, 1964.

68 Hosmer, Jr., 79.

Chapter 17

1 Pearl Chase to Friend, April 19, 1935, Ia_218_7_1, CDCC.
2 Mary Louise Days, "Speech at Luncheon in Honor of Pearl Chase Centennial," November 16, 1988.
3 *The Survey Graphic* was a social welfare periodical, with a circulation in the thousands edited by Paul Kellogg.
4 Katharine Glover, co-author of the article.
5 Established in 1941 as an army training base for infantry and armoured forces, in 1958 most of Camp Cooke was renamed Vandenberg AFB.
6 Charles Leo Preisker, a Republican County supervisor, known as "Mr. Politics," was one of the most influential and controversial figures in the political history of twentieth-century Santa Barbara County.
7 Pearl Chase to Frank Taylor, March 21, 1942, V_789_16, CDCC.
8 Pearl Chase to Dr. Aurelia Reinhardt, April 21, 1940, V_758_15, CDCC.
9 On June 10, 1940, Pearl, along with her brother Harold and her friend Alice Bentz, attended the 83rd annual commencement. (Interestingly, both were also present in 1909 when Pearl graduated from UC Berkeley.)
10 Dr. Aurelia Reinhardt, June 10, 1940, 2_25, Reinhardt Papers_1877–1948_Office of the President Mills College, F.W. Olin Library, Special Collections and Archive, Oakland, CA.
11 Alice Bentz to Pearl Chase, April 1940, V_758_15, CDCC.
12 Craig Baker, "Moreton Bay Fig Tree," March 20, 2018, https://www.hmdb.org/m.asp?m=115203. This site is at Chapala and West Montecito streets. Though called a fig tree, it was in fact a Ficus Macrophylla, a cousin of the rubber tree.
13 Further measurements have been taken over the years, and in 1997 the circumference of the tree was 498 inches, or 41.5 feet. The average crown spread was 176 feet and the total height was 80 feet.
14 Mary Louise Days wrote in the 1977 *Santa Barbara Parks History*: "In September 1970 the tree became the city's first officially designated tree of notable historic interest. Which meant it could not be destroyed or cut down. Six years later the southern Pacific transportation company deeded the corner of land containing the tree to the city there were no restrictions in the grant deed."
15 Pearl Chase to John Collier, January 2, 194, Ia_17_10_1-19, CDCC.
16 Pearl Chase, Notes for Speech at AAUW National Convention, Cincinnati, Ohio, May, 1941, Ia_6_2_10, CDCC.

Chapter 18

1 Tompkins, 106 (see chap. 2, n. 5).
2 *Ibid.*, 105.
3 *Ibid.*
4 *Ibid.*, 106.
5 Pearl Chase to Mr. J Wright, January 3, 1943, Ia_221_10, CDCC.
6 Pearl Chase to Santa Barbara Gas Ratio Board, November 1, 1943, V_759_16, CDCC.
7 Pearl Chase to Mrs. Ednah Morse [Rich], July 16, 1943, Ia_42_3_8, CDCC.
8 Pearl Chase, interview by Gibbs Smith, ca. 1972–1973, OH 115, transcript, Pearl Chase Oral History, Department of Special Collections, UC Santa Barbara Library, Santa Barbara, CA.
9 Pearl Chase to Mrs June Cunningham, January 24, 1946, V_759_16, CDCC.
10 *Ibid.*
11 Tom Modugno, "The Marines Invade Goleta: Goleta Marine Base," *Goleta History*, February 23, 2016, https://goletahistory.com/the-marines-invade-goleta/.
12 Globalsecurity.com, "Vandenberg AFB," https://www.globalsecurity.org/space/facility/vafb-over.htm.
13 *Ibid.*
14 Justin Ruhge, "Remembering Camp Cooke for 75th Anniversary of D-Day Landing," *Noozhawk*, June 5, 2019, https://www.noozhawk.com/article/justin_ruhge_remembering_camp_cooke_75th_anniversary_d_day_landing_20190605.
15 Walker A. Tompkins, "The Samarkand," *Neighborhood Series 5* (Santa Barbara County Board of Realtors, 1977).
16 *Ibid.*
17 Hattie Beresford, "World War II, Home Front: A Sentimental Journey," extract from *The Montecito Journal*, in "Historic Posts, Camps, Stations and Airfields: Santa Barbara Army Ground and Services Forces Redistribution Station," http://www.militarymuseum.org/SBAG%26SFRedistStn.html.
18 Graffy, 83 (see chap. 2, n. 1).
19 "Take a Closer Look: America Goes to War," The National World War II Museum, December 13, 2021, https://www.nationalww2museum.org/students-teachers/student-resources/research-starters/america-goes-war-take-closer-look.
20 Graffy, 85 (see chap. 2, n. 1).
21 "Take a Closer Look."
22 Susan Levine, "Home Front's Call to Duty," *Washington Post*, May 23, 2004, https://www.washingtonpost.com/archive/local/2004/05/23/home-fronts-call-to-duty/bd19e8aa-da83-4c4b-84fc-6f67d06c686d/.
23 Pearl Chase to Mayor Norris Montgomery, October 1, 1948, Ia_222_11, CDCC.

24 Chase, interview.
25 Pearl Chase to Jane Manning, September 11, 1945, V_759_16, CDCC.
26 Chase, interview.
27 Initially, the Department of Defense wanted to control every aspect of the soldier's life; however the chairmen of six civilian service organizations, including the YMCA and YWCA, thought that their organizations were better suited for the responsibility. In the end, a compromise was reached: they would be in charge, and the military would provide building supplies, locations, and labor when needed and available.
28 Alma Whitaker, "Barbarenos Go All Out to Aid Servicemen," *Los Angeles Times*, November 26, 1942.
29 Chase, interview.
30 The original building, which was damaged by the 1925 earthquake, was one of twelve in Santa Barbara reconstructed in the Spanish Revival style, with funding from the Bothin Helping Fund of San Francisco.
31 Alma.
32 *Ibid.*
33 The El Paseo complex in downtown Santa Barbara included a restaurant, shops, and offices.
34 Chase, interview.
35 Alma.
36 The AWVS, which established Welcome House next to the Greyhound Bus terminal in May 1943, catered for the families of servicemen the USO could not. A kitchen, office, sitting room, and fully equipped nursery were provided. It was, however, the assistance the AWVS provided in finding places to live and sharing local information that was of most value. As soon as a vacancy was telephoned to the AWVS, they made it available to a service family. By the end of the war, 30,766 people had used its services, with a staff of volunteers having given approximately 15,000 hours.
37 Christopher Michael Head, "The Armor of Democracy: Volunteerism on the Home Front in World War II, California," (master's thesis, California Polytechnic State University, San Luis Obispo: March, 2009), 43. "The American Red Cross (colloquially, 'Red Cross') also played an integral role in providing aid to American soldiers. Founded by famous Civil War nurse Clara Barton in 1881, the Red Cross, by World War II, had become America's most recognizable and influential volunteer organization. It became so influential that it was called the 'big sister' to the Army. It was also one of the most popular organizations with which to volunteer, not least because it was one way of providing aid to the suffering in Europe and Asia."
38 Head, 43. She participated by fabricating clothing and bandages to aid and comfort the troops.
39 Alma Whitaker, "Barbarenos Go All Out to Aid Servicemen," *Los Angeles Times*, November 26, 1942.
40 Melissa A. McEuen, Women, Gender, and World War II," *Oxford Research Encyclopedia of American History* (Oxford, UK: June 2016), 6, https://doi.org/10.1093/acrefore/9780199329175.013.55.
41 Michael Redmon, "The Little Town Club: One of the Oldest Women's Organizations in Santa Barbara." *Santa Barbara Independent*, January 10, 2011, https://www.independent.com/2011/01/10/little-town-club/.
42 Michael Redmon, "Q: 'Who was Anna McCaughey?,'" *Santa Barbara Independent*, March 8, 2007, https://www.independent.com/2007/03/08/q-who-was-anna-mccaughey/. Others included: Ernestine Koefod, wife of the Chase family doctor and devoted to promoting cultural ventures including music, drama, art, education, libraries, and museums; Elma Levy, a former member of the CAA and chair of the Woman's Club; Grace Ruth Southwick, who pioneered adult education and YMCA work in city; and Anna McCaughey, who was a charter member of the Reina del Mar parlor of the Native Daughters of the Golden West, and a ubiquitous presence on the local social work scene.
43 Mrs. Edith Hancock, later a city councilwoman.
44 Nancy Schwarz, Interview with Sue Higman, January 12, 1982, Gledhill Library, Santa Barbara Historical Museum, Santa Barbara, CA.
45 Some of these women included: Lutah Maria Riggs, Santa Barbara-based architect; Dorothy Heaney, wife of Jack Heaney, senior partner of the law firm Heaney, Price, Postel & Parma; Kathleen Burke Hale, a British-American philanthropist and war worker, decorated by seven European nations for her volunteer work during the two world wars, formerly married to Frederick Forest Peabody, who after the Second World War along with her third husband adopted an entire village in France; Lee Ott, former president of the women's board of the Community Arts Music Association; Deborah Pelissero (née Spalding), whose father, Silsby, bought the Tecolote Ranch west of Goleta; Julia Forbes, former president of the Junior League of Santa Barbara and head of the Santa Barbara Historical Society; and Beverley Jackson, a society reporter for the *News-Press* who was revered for her comical accounts about meeting celebrities during the 1970s.
46 Charlotte D. Elmott to Pearl Chase, June 8, 1964, Ia_478_1_14-16, CDCC.
47 McEuen.

Chapter 19

1 Pearl Chase, Letter to the Editor, *Santa Barbara News-Press*, April, 28, 1961, Ia_225, CDCC.

2 As owner of the local newspaper and founder of radio station KTMS, Thomas Storke was the most powerful man in the community. A Democrat, on November 9, 1938, he was appointed to the US Senate to fill the vacancy caused by the resignation of his great friend and Montecito resident, William Gibbs McAdoo, before the post was taken up the following January by Sheridan Downey, McAdoo's elected successor.

3 Pearl Chase to Stanley Barnes, November 4, 1946, Ia_497_1_9, CDCC and Pearl Chase to Dr. Charles L. Jacobs, March 27, 1945, Ia_41_2_7-11, CDCC.

4 Pearl Chase to Robert Gordon Sproul, November 8, 1950, Ib_16_2, CDCC.

5 Pearl Chase, "Women and the University", 1943, V_789_16, CDCC.

6 Pearl Chase to Dr. Clarence Phelps, February 1, 1958, Ia_224_13_1, CDCC.

7 The first building was not completed until 1941 when an industrial and vocational education building opened. Faculties for teacher training in industrial education were judged to be best of any institution in US.

8 Roger L. Geiger, *American Higher Education since World War II: A History* (Princeton, NJ: Princeton University Press, 2021), xviii.

9 Thomas M. Storke. *California Editor* (Santa Barbara, CA: *News-Press* Publishing Company, 1958), 434.

10 *Ibid.*

11 *Ibid.*, 435.

12 Harold Chase had gone to Berkeley with him, and both men were members of the Bohemian Club in San Francisco. He occasionally used Harold's cottage at Hope Ranch on his visits to the city. Harold, who was a life member of the California Alumni Association at Berkeley, was also one of the California Alumni Committee for Earl Warren's gubernatorial election in 1942. Warren ran first and foremost as an advocate of planned growth.

13 Warren would go on to serve as governor of California for ten years and eight months, the longest gubernatorial term in California history at the time. He then assumed an office, chief justice of the US, second only to the presidency in importance, and in that office earned a secure place in the history of the country.

14 Kevin Starr, *Embattled Dreams: California in War and Peace, 1940–1950*, (Oxford, UK: Oxford University Press, 2002), 242. "In his family, he allowed himself a measure of display and ego aggrandisement. Before the Kennedys, he understood the power of family and family values in political life. Californians in turn, worshipped the Warren family, especially the girls and followed their progress through life with unflagging interest." *Ibid.*, 242.

15 Pearl Chase to Ednah Morse [Rich], July 16, 1943, Ia_42_3_8, CDCC.

16 UArch FacP 41_1_11_Florence Clark Meredith Papers, Department of Special Collections, UC Santa Barbara Library_Oral History_Interview conducted by Elle Bellekitchen, December 11-12, 1979, p. 39.

17 Pearl Chase, "Santa Barbara College, The Growth of an Idea, a School, a College." (undated), Ia_41_2_3, CDCC.

18 Storke, *California Editor*, 434.

19 *Ibid.*

20 Pearl Chase, "Santa Barbara College, The Growth of an Idea, a School, a College." (undated), Ia_41_2_3, CDCC.

21 The other satellite locations, which included Los Angeles, the University Farm School at Davis, the Citrus Experiment Station at Riverside, an oceanography laboratory in San Diego, UC Irvine, the Medical Department at San Francisco, and Mount Hamilton (later UC Santa Cruz), were all subordinate to the administrators at the Berkeley campus. It was not until 1958 that the Regents started promoting these to general campuses.

22 Lanny Ebenstein, "The Rise of UCSB," *Noticias: The Quarterly Magazine of the Santa Barbara Historical Society* 54, no. 3 (Fall, 2015), 134.

23 Starr, *Embatteld Dreams*, 312. Born in San Francisco on May 22, 1891, Sproul graduated from UC Berkeley in 1913 with a BS in engineering and the distinction of being a two-year letterman in track and field. "Deciding to find employment at Berkeley he went directly to work in the controller's office and worked his way up the ladder becoming president in 1930."

24 Like Pearl, Sproul was active in conservation circles and served on the National Park Advisory Board. He was also a member of the Bohemian Club where he knew and had a very happy association with Harold and Earl Warren.

25 Newton Bishop Drury, interview by Amelia Roberts Fry and Susan Schrepfer, ca. 1959–1970, transcript, Regional Oral History Office, Bancroft Library, UC Berkeley, Berkeley, CA.

26 George A. Pettitt to Pearl Chase, May 21, 1952, Series 3, President Sproul, University of California (System). Office of the President. Records: Numerical bound folders, CU-5, University Archives, The Bancroft Library, University of California, Berkeley, CA.

27 Storke, *California Editor*, 436.

28 Anson Thacher, the headmaster of the Thacher School in Ojai and son of the school's founder Sherman Day Thacher, was one such individual.
29 Pearl Chase to Stanley Barnes, November 4, 1946, Ia_497_1_9, CDCC.
30 Paul Yost succeeded Pearl's cousin and San Francisco attorney Charles Stetson Wheeler, Jr., who had held the post previously.
31 Paul Yost to Pearl Chase, June 20, 1944, Ia_41_2_7-11, CDCC.
32 Also elected as first vice president of CAA in 1942 was Earl Warren. CAA's second vice president was Stanley "Stan" Nelson Barnes, a noted football player at Berkeley, Republican, and friend of Earl Warren, later appointed US assistant attorney general and US circuit judge of the US court of appeals for the ninth circuit.
33 The following January, Yost was replaced by Jean Witter, Dean's cousin and investment bank cofounder. Pearl's committee was enlarged to include Yost himself.
34 "UC Santa Barbara Alumni History," UC Santa Barbara Alumni, https://www.alumni.ucsb.edu/about/history.
35 Gordon Sproul, interview by Herman Phelger, transcript, Regional Oral History Office, Bancroft Library, UC Berkeley, Berkeley, CA, https://digitalassets.lib.berkeley.edu/roho/ucb/text/sproul_v1.pdf.
36 Pearl Chase to Stanley Barnes, November 4, 1946, Ia_497_1_9, CDCC.
37 The committee included Robertson, Ward, Wallace "Wally" Penfield, and L. Deming Tilton. Consultants included Provost Phelps; James Corley, UC Comptroller; George Geib, business manager; Winsor Soule, supervising architect; R.D. Evans, university architect; Mayor Weyler; the Board of Supervisors; and the UC Alumni Association.
38 Pearl Chase to Dr. Charles L. Jacobs, March 27, 1945, Ia_41_2_7-11, CDCC.
39 Starr, *Embattled Dreams*, 191.
40 *Ibid.*
41 "Servicemen's Readjustment Act (1944)," National Archives and Records Administration, https://www.archives.gov/milestone-documents/servicemens-readjustment-act. "It is estimated that between 1944 and 1951, under the act, approximately 8 million veterans received educational benefits, 2.3 million attended colleges and universities, 3.5 million received school training, and 3.4 million received on-the-job training."
42 Starr, *Embattled Dreams*, 191.
43 "Servicemen's Readjustment Act (1944)," https://www.archives.gov/milestone-documents/servicemens-readjustment-act.
44 Geiger, ix.
45 Thomas M. Storke, "Reminiscences of La Mesa," (presentation, La Mesa Improvement Association meeting, March 26, 1953).
46 Pearl Chase to James Corley, November 4, 1946, Ia_497_1_9, CDCC.
47 Pearl Chase to Robert Gordon Sproul, November 3, 1947, Ia_497_1_9, CDCC.
48 University of California Academic Senate, "J. Harold Williams, Education: Los Angeles and Santa Barbara," in *1985, University of California: In Memoriam* (Berkeley, CA: University of California, 1985), http://content.cdlib.org/view?docId=hb4d5nb20m&doc.view=frames&chunk.id=div00176&toc.depth=1&toc.id. "He often invited groups of faculty members to meet with him at his home in Santa Barbara to discuss current problems and to plan strategy for coping with them. According to members of his staff he was noted for his precise, clipped speech. In faculty meetings he encouraged questioners to formulate precise questions through his preference for yes and no answers. His dour exterior masked a fine sense of humor and a kind heart filled with warm understanding."
49 $64,652 was expended by the city to convert the open barracks to student and family apartments, which were then rented for $31–$36 a month.
50 Pearl Chase to Harold Williams, March 24, 1947, Ia_497_1_10, CDCC.
51 Harold Williams to Pearl Chase, April 14, 1947, 1a_497_1_10, CDCC.
52 Editor "Sproul Welcomes College Students and Vice Versa," *Santa Barbara News-Press*, October 3, 1947.
53 University of California, *Santa Barbara Daily Nexus* and antecedent newspapers, *El Gaucho*, date unknown.
54 Storke, *California Editor*, 435.
55 *Ibid.*
56 University of California History Digital Archives, "Santa Barbara: Historical Overview," March 20, 2021, https://www.lib.berkeley.edu/uchistory/general_history/campuses/ucsb/overview_print.html.
57 *Ibid.*
58 George A. Pettitt to Pearl Chase, May 21, 1952, Series 3, President Sproul, University of California (System). Office of the President. Records: Numerical bound folders, CU-5, University Archives, The Bancroft Library, University of California, Berkeley, CA.
59 Pearl Chase to Mr. E.W. Jacobsen, March 20, 1950, Ia_222, CDCC.
60 Mary Louise Days and Randy Bergstrom, "The Riviera Campus," *La Campana* 41, no. 1 (Winter 2015), 15–26.

61 Selmer O Wake's History of the SB Community College District. SBCC College Histories. The site continued to pass through various hands until, in 1973, philanthropist and developer Michael Towbes of the Towbes Group bought the site. Michael Towbes was a close friend and admirer of Pearl.

62 UC Santa Barbara Art, Design, & Architecture Museum. "UCSB Campus Architecture, Design and Social Change: 1950s and 1960s, Pereira and Luckman, campus planners and executive architects," March 20, 2021, http://www.adc-exhibits.museum.ucsb.edu/exhibits/show/ucsbcampusarchitecture/pereiraandluckman.

63 *Ibid.*

64 Ebenstein, 136.

65 Pearl Chase, "Notes Re: Master Plan", October 5, 1953, Ia_497_1_10, CDCC.

66 Pearl Chase to Mrs. William Earle Chamber, May 20, 1954, Ia_223, CDCC.

67 AD&A Museum, UCSB, "UCSB Campus Architecture, Design and Social Change: 1950s and 1960s, Pereira and Luckman, campus planners and executive architects", available online: http://www.adc-exhibits.museum.ucsb.edu/collections/show/6. The hall featured a sewing room, "house mother," and an 11 p.m. curfew.

68 He was also president of the Episcopal Church National Council for Churchmen.

69 Pearl Chase to Dr. Lynn White, March 30, 1955, V_761_18, CDCC.

70 Pearl also took a keen interest in the access boulevard to the university. It was one of the few contentious and long-discussed issues in the construction of the campus. In 1955, the 2.5-mile-long spur, which ran from US 101 to campus, was named the Clarence Ward Memorial Boulevard in memory of the senator who did so much to develop the university. Funds were made available from the State Highway Fund. Today it is also known as Route 217.

71 Pearl Chase to Tom Storke, September 4, 1958, Ia_225, CDCC.

Chapter 20

1 History.com editors, "V-E Day is celebrated in America and Britain," *History.com*, November 16, 2009, https://www.history.com/this-day-in-history/victory-in-europe.

2 Nancy A. Prieston, *I'll Never Leave You* (Xlibris Corporation, 2012), 264.

3 Sarah Pruitt, "The Post World War Boom: How America got into gear," *History.com*, May 14, 2020, available online: https://www.history.com/news/post-world-war-ii-boom-economy.

4 Pearl Chase to Mayor Norris Montgomery, October 1, 1948, Ia_222_11_1, CDCC.

5 Pearl Chase to Santa Barbara Foundation, December 6, 1958, Ia_225_14_1, CDCC.

6 Fukuo Akimoto, "The birth of Architectural Control in Santa Barbara," (presentation, The 12th International Planning History Conference, New Delhi, India, 2006), 21.

7 *Ibid.*

8 Pearl Chase to Mayor and Members of City Council Santa Barbara, May 17, 1948, Ia_222, CDCC.

9 Hill Blanco, "Style Matters: The Case of Santa Barbara [The Promise of New Urbanism]," *Places* 13, no. 2 (2000), 59.

10 Santa Barbara City Council, "Postwar Development Boom (1945–1970)", *2011 General Plan Appendix C History of the City*, (Santa Barbara, CA: City of Santa Barbara, 2011), https://www.santabarbaraca.gov/civicax/filebank/blobdload.aspx?BlobID=16916.

11 Mr. C. Monsen to Mr. Bell, "Speech at Pearl Chase testimonial dinner, at the Miramar hotel," November 18, 1965, V_771_1, CDCC.

Chapter 21

1 "Conservation Need of U.S.," *Oakland Tribune*, March 13, 1942.

2 "Conservation Week will begin today," *Los Angeles Times*, March 7, 1943.

3 "Special Events will emphasize Conservation," *The Fresno Bee, The Republican*, March 4, 1945.

4 "Ninth California Conservation Week – March 7–14, 1943", (California Conservation Council, 1943). IIJ_35, Reinhardt Papers_1877–1948_Office of the President, Mills College, F.W. Olin Library, Special Collections and Archive, Oakland, CA.

5 Pearl Chase, interview by Gibbs Smith, ca. 1972–1973, OH 115, transcript, Pearl Chase Oral History, Department of Special Collections, UC Santa Barbara Library, Santa Barbara, CA.

6 "Mrs. Mountfort, 79, Committee Aide, Dies," *Santa Barbara News-Press*, April 17, 1967.

7 Pearl Chase to Father Oliger, Santa Clara University, June 13, 1967, V_789_16, CDCC.

8 *Ibid.*

9 Pearl Chase to Ethel Winthrop, February 24, 1940, V_758_15, CDCC.

10 The California Association of School Superintendents, the California Elementary School Principals Association, the California Secondary School Principals Association, and the California School Supervisors Association were all supportive.

11 Pearl Chase to Mrs. Wood May 15, 1943, Ia_221_10_1, CDCC.

12 *Ibid.*

13 California Department of Education and Department of Natural Resources, *Guidebook*

For Conservation Education: A Proposal for a Program of Action in the Schools of California (California Department of Natural Resources, in cooperation with Department of Education, 1950), 1–48. "The function of the subcommittee was to investigate the teaching of conservation in the schools of California, appraise its present extent and effectiveness, determine educational needs regarding conservation education, and make recommendations for improving teaching and for giving better training to both teacher trainees and in-service teachers." The subcommittee included notable educationists from all over the state including Pearl's close colleague Helen Heffernan from the state Department of Education; Heffernan's lover, Corinne Seeds, from the University of California at Los Angeles; and Dr. Leo F. Hadsall of Fresno State College. Serving as chairman was Bernice Baxter, coordinator of instruction for public elementary and junior high schools in Oakland. Pearl also received advice and support from Dr. Ray Wilbur, chancellor of Stanford, and Aurelia Reinhart, who had just retired as president of Mills College in Oakland.

14 *Ibid.*

15 Brigadier General Warren Thomas Hannum was director of Natural Resources, and Roy E. Simpson of the Department of Education.

16 California Department of Education and Department of Natural Resources, *Guidebook For Conservation Education*, foreword.

17 *Ibid.*, 15.

18 Chase, interview.

19 Edward A. Johnson and Michael J. Mappin, *Environmental Education and Advocacy: Changing perspectives of Ecology and Education* (Cambridge, UK: Cambridge University Press, 2005), 141. It promoted "conservation at all levels, encompassing all aspects of the natural and man-made world upon which people relied for the development and maintenance of a desirable social, economic, scientific, cultural and political climate. Both its membership and its leadership consisted of a mixture of professional educators, professional natural resource managers, public information specialists employed by government agencies and resource-associated industries, and representatives of non-governmental organizations (NGOs). Within CEA these groups worked together to promote education about balanced interrelationships between humans and the natural environment."

20 Dr. Aubrey Neasham Memo for files, April 1, 1946, 4_17_312, Aubrey Neasham papers, MS0004_ Center for Sacramento History, Sacramento, CA, Other organizations involved in the project included the Save the Redwoods League, the Sierra Club, California Fish and Game Commission, California Division of Forestry, US Forest Service, US Soil Conservation Service, and the University of California School of Forestry. As the discussion between these representatives developed, the CalCC was asked to act as a coordinating agency for the Institute. Chase was delighted with the opportunity.

21 The committee included Neasham; Helen Heffernan; Edward F. Dolder, supervisor of conservation and education from the state department of beaches and parks; Fred W. Herbert, assistant state conservationist, US Soil Conservation Service; Wallace I. Hutchinson, chief, US Forest Service Division of Information and Education; Charlotte Mauk, Sierra Club; and Dr. Cornelius Siemens, assistant professor of education, UC Extension.

22 Pearl Chase to Dr. Aubrey Neasham, July 20, 1946. 4_17_312, Aubrey Neasham papers, MS0004_ Center for Sacramento History, Sacramento, CA.

23 Fritz Emmanuel to Miss Helen Hammarberg, UC Extension Division Campus, July 3, 1946, 4_17_312, Aubrey Neasham papers, MS0004_ Center for Sacramento History, Sacramento, CA.

24 Pearl Chase, "25th California Conservation Week, March 7–14, 1959", Ia_181_30_9, CDCC.

25 George Van Dusen, "Politics of 'Partnership': The Eisenhower Administration and Conservation, 1952–1960" (PhD diss., Loyola University, 1974), 53–56. "The Mid-Century Conference was funded by the Ford Foundation and organized by Resources for the Future, Inc., an independent organization dedicated to studying and evaluating federal conservation policies. One of Resources for the Future's leading spokesmen was Horace M. Albright. Since he was both a Republican and a businessman, Albright was ably suited to act as a bridge between the White House and the conservationists." "Well aware of the tensions between the conservationists and the new administration, Albright informed the White House that the president's speech to the conference ought to 'strongly' confirm the policies established by Theodore Roosevelt. He warned that "a general impression has spread over the country that this administration is somehow or other going to weaken the conservation policies that have been built up to control our renewable and non-renewable resources since the days of Theodore Roosevelt." "This impression, he said, had been created by the offshore oil issue, the D'Ewart grazing bill, the dismissal of certain civil service employees (e.g., Day and Clawson), and concern over Olympic National Park and Glacier

View Dam. The president's speech, to his mind, was thus an opportunity for the administration to reassure conservationists that it understood and was sympathetic to their problems. The Mid-Century Conference, held between December 2–4, 1953 at the Shoreham Hotel in Washington, DC, was attended by about 1,600 conservationists, business leaders, and labor officials."

26 Pearl Chase speech, in Henry Jarrett, *The Nation Looks at its Resources: Report of the Mid-Century Conference on Resources for the Future, Washington, D.C. December 2,3,4, 1953* (Routledge Revivals, 2016), 340.

27 Pearl Chase, "Conservationists Must Educate and Cooperate", March 9, 1941, V_788_15, CDCC.

28 Katherine Glover, "Blue Ribbon Citizen: II. The Stateswoman," *Survey Graphic: Magazine of Social Interpretation* (March 1940), 181.

29 Newton Bishop Drury, interview by Amelia Roberts Fry and Susan Schrepfer, oral history, transcript, Harry S. Truman Library and Museum. He was devoted to his family and friends and life in the West. Like Pearl, he had a fine appreciation of history, and in 1935 his *California: An Intimate Guide* became the most popular of the state's histories for the next twenty-five years. His primary hobby was books, and he "got a lot of pleasure in browsing old bookstores, and accumulated a terrific tonnage of books as a consequence."

30 Pearl Chase to Robert Gordon Sproul, November 9, 1950., Series 3, President Sproul, University of California (System). Office of the President. Records: Numerical bound folders, CU-5, University Archives, The Bancroft Library, University of California, Berkeley, CA.

31 Pearl Chase to Friend, January 30, 1951, V_760_17, CDCC.

32 "H.G. Chase," *Santa Barbara News-Press*, January 30, 195.

33 Kathleen Jackson to Dr Harold Crowe, President Sierra Club, November 5, 1952, Ia_480_1_1, CDCC.

34 Rudolf F. Grah, Robert A. Cockrell, and John A. Zivnuska, "Woodbridge Metcalf, Forestry; Agricultural Extension: Berkeley," *University of California: In Memoriam, July 1975* (Berkeley, CA: University of California Regents, 2011), http://texts.cdlib.org/view?docId=hb9t1nb5rm;NAAN=13030&doc.view=frames&chunk.id=div00045&toc.depth=1&toc.id=&brand=calisphere. An exact contemporary of Pearl, "Professor Woodbridge "Woody" Metcalf was "born in Grosse Point Farms, Michigan, receiving his BA and MS in forestry from the University of Michigan in 1911. He moved to UC Berkeley in 1914 and served as extension forester from 1926 until 1956. His life was filled with the joy of living and service to his fellow citizens. He had an open friendliness and willingness to accept all who crossed his path as friends and as potential students to whom he could teach conservation." Rather like Pearl, he maintained a special tie to young people, recognizing that the attitudes of people depended on youthful exposure to dynamic ideas. He wrote a great many articles and several books that established him as an authority on trees. During his years as president of the CalCC, he co-authored, with Pearl, a number of pamphlets and leaflets on conservation subjects, including Arbor Day, tree planting, common birds, wildflowers, fires, floods, and soil. "He was an enthusiastic and gregarious man, and one of his special qualities was his talent as an outstanding group song leader. There were few people that ever attended a professional meeting where he was present who could forget his energetic and infectious leadership of songs like "Alouette" and, where appropriate, "Hail to California." He was also a sailor of superior ability; with Glen Waterhouse, he won the international Star Class World Championships in 1933, and in 1936 they represented the US in the Olympic sailing competitions in Kiel, Germany."

Chapter 22

1 A population of 10.5 million as of 1950 reached 15.7 million by the end of the decade.

2 Kevin Starr, *Golden Dreams* (Oxford, UK: Oxford University Press, 2009), xi.

3 Michael McCloskey, "Wilderness Movement at the Crossroads, 1945–1970," *Pacific Historical Review* 41, no. 3 (August 1972), 348.

4 John D. Leshy, "Legal Wilderness: Its past and some speculations on its future," *Environmental Law* 44, no. 2 (Spring 2014), 549–622.

5 Ney C. Landrum, *The State Park Movement in America*, (Columbia, MO: University of Missouri Press, 2004), pp. 178–199.

6 The STRL was founded in 1918 to protect and restore redwood forests for future generations by John Campbell Merriam, a palaeontologist and, later, president of the Carnegie Institute; Madison Grant, a lawyer, writer, and zoologist known for his work as a eugenicist; and Henry Fairfield Osborn, a palaeontologist, geologist, and eugenics advocate. Other prominent individuals involved in its early formation included Stephen T. Mather, first director of the NPS; Congressman William Kent, author of the bill creating the National Park Service; and Newton Drury.

7 The Council was the League's voting membership.

8 Elizabeth Kenneday, "Art, Ecology and the Giant Sequoia Project," in Rachel Mason and Teresa Eca, eds., *International Dialogues about Visual Culture, Education and Art* (Bristol, UK: Intellect Books, 2008), 182.

9 David Vogel, *California Greenin': How the Golden State became an Environmental Leader* (Princeton, NJ: Princeton University Press), 71–72.

10 Pearl Chase to Hezekiah Chase, undated 1908, V_719_2, CDCC.

11 Pearl Chase, "A Gift to California," 1934.

12 *Ibid.* She admired that some Sequoia Sempervirens were 20 feet in diameter, 360 feet high, and estimated to to be about 3,000 years old, their rings recording the cycles of dry years and those of heavy rainfall since the time of Christ and before.

13 Edwin Markham, quoted in Pearl Chase, "A Gift to California."

14 Save the Redwoods League, "The Garden Club of America Grove" (2022), https://www.savetheredwoods.org/what-we-do/our-work/partner/conservation-organizations/the-garden-club-of-america-grove/.

15 Later renamed *Arts and Architecture.*

16 Chase, "A Gift to California."

17 Over the following decades the STRL, GCA, and CSP partnered to protect more priority lands surrounding the initial acreage of 2,552. GCA members and clubs were encouraged to contribute to the League to cover one-half of land purchase prices, as they had done during the initial acquisition. Such has been their success that the GCA Grove now contains more than 5,100 acres, the third-largest dedicated grove in the entire state parks system.

18 Pearl Chase to Newton Drury, May 25, 1966, Ia_228, CDCC.

19 Deborah Zierten, "Happy Anniversary to our State Tree," Save the Redwoods League, August 27, 2014, https://www.savetheredwoods.org/blog/happy-anniversary-to-our-state-tree/. "Interestingly enough, the senate bill did not name a particular species but simply stated 'the California redwood.' The use of that general term left room for people to wonder which redwood, exactly, was the state tree? There were actually two species that would qualify, the coast redwood, Sequoia sempervirens, and the giant sequoia, Sequoia gigantea (now called Sequoiadendron giganteum). To answer this question, California's attorney general stated that both species of redwood would be the state tree. So, in 1953, the original law was amended to officially recognize both the coast redwood and the giant sequoia as the state trees. It seems only fitting that the tallest and largest trees in the world both equally represent the spectacular and varied natural landscape of California."

20 In June, 1945, Pearl was involved with the California Garden Clubs, Inc. that endorsed the STRL's "National Tribute Grove" to honor the men and women of the US WWII Armed Forces. The grove is in primeval forest lands in the Mill Creek-Smith River region on the Redwood Highway, five miles northeast of Crescent City. In the fall of 1947, she promoted the purchase of a forty-acre redwood grove in the name of Garden Clubs. The sum of $5,130 was raised, and that amount was matched by the state. Pearl received a personal note of congratulations from Aubrey Drury for Santa Barbara's "fine showing." Aubrey Drury to Pearl Chase, February 6, 1948, 30_13, Save_The_Redwoods_League_records_BANC MSS 88/15c, The Bancroft Library, University of California, Berkeley, CA.

21 In 1949, "due to the state president's enthusiasm for the project, the National Council of State Garden Clubs, Inc. adopted a project to buy an adjoining 40-acre grove to further its efforts to preserve some of the country's national heritage, and to mark the 20th anniversary of the founding of National Council." See http://californiagardenclubs.com/sites/default/files/Publications/TheDiamondYearsOnline.pdf.

22 Pearl Chase to Mrs. John Glascock Baldwin, Redwood Grove Ctte, GCA, June 25, 1968, 30_13, Save_The_Redwoods_League_records_BANC MSS 88/15c, The Bancroft Library, University of California, Berkeley, CA.

23 *Ibid.*

24 The Editors of Encyclopedia Britannica. "Sierra Club," *Encyclopedia Britannica*, January 28, 2019, https://www.britannica.com/topic/Sierra-Club.

25 *Ibid.* "Among its first successes was the defeat of efforts to constrict the size of Yosemite National Park, which in 1905 was transferred from state to federal control."

26 The meeting was organized by LeMoille Pugh, a former teacher from Huntington Park High School in Los Angeles.

27 Pearl Chase to Friends, June 13, 1972, V_765_22, CDCC.

28 Kathleen Goddard Jones, interview by Anne Van Tyne, 1984, transcript, Oral History Program of the Sierra Club, *Sierra Club Nationwide II*, Sierra Club History Committee, https://digitalassets.lib.berkeley.edu/roho/ucb/text/sierra_club_nationwide2.pdf.

29 "'New Sierra Club Can Help Conservation,' says Miss Chase," *Santa Barbara News-Press*, February 7, 1951.

30 *Ibid.*

31 In 1952, the group achieved the formation of the Los Padres Chapter which served Santa Barbara and Ventura counties.

32 Lena Eyen, "David Brower, Building Bridges and Stopping Dams," Markkula Center for Applied Ethics, Santa Clara University, https://www.scu.edu/environmental-ethics/environmental-activists-heroes-and-martyrs/david-brower.html. Born in Berkeley on July 1, 1912, "Brower graduated from Berkeley High School in 1929. He attended UC Berkeley for two years as an entomology major, but, rather than graduating four years later, he joined the Sierra Club through sponsorship from artist and environmentalist Ansel Adams. During this time, he worked towards becoming a world-class mountain climber, making over seventy first ascents. He eventually settled into the position of editor for the *Sierra Club Bulletin*, and later became editor at the University of California Press, where he met his wife, Anne Hus. He served as a lieutenant in the Tenth Mountain Division during World War II. After the war, he returned to his job at the UCP and began editing the *Bulletin* in 1946."

33 "Who Was David Brower?," David Brower Center, February 1, 2017.

34 Pearl Chase to Harlean James, April 7, 1956, 1a_224_13_1, CDCC.

35 David Brower, "The Need for a Scenic Resources Review," address to Channel City Club, April 4, 1956.

36 *Ibid.*

37 Michigan in the World and the Environmental Justice HistoryLab, "National Parks and the 1964 Wilderness Act, Give Earth a Chance: Environmental Activism in Michigan," University of Michigan History (LSA), https://michiganintheworld.history.lsa.umich.edu/environmentalism/exhibits/show/main_exhibit/origins/wilderness-act. "The act would provide 'outdoor recreation' for Americans and protect beautiful and fragile lands from development by logging, mining, and oil companies."

38 Walker A. Tompkins, "Civic Activities Over Years Varied", *Santa Barbara News-Press*, September 13, 1959.

39 Editor, "11 Southlanders Capture 1950 Honors as Achievement Leaders," *Los Angeles Times*, December 31, 1950.

40 Editor, "Miss Pearl Chase to be presented Medallion Award," *Santa Barbara News-Press*, April 11, 1971.

41 *Ibid.*

42 *Ibid.*

43 Editor, "Architects Honor Pearl Chase, Hear History of City's Building," *Santa Barbara News-Press*, January 12, 1955.

44 SBHC_Mss_1_5_771_1 "Woman of the Year of Santa Barbara for 1956."

45 Editor, "Architects Honor Pearl Chase, Hear History of City's Building." *Santa Barbara News-Press*, January 12, 1955.

46 Pearl Chase, "Recognition Awards," V_771, CDCC.

47 Editor, "Architects Honor Pearl Chase, Hear History of City's Building." *Santa Barbara News-Press*, January 12, 1955.

48 *Ibid.*

49 Kevin Starr, *Golden Dreams: California in an Age of Abundance, 1950–1963*, (Oxford, UK: Oxford University Press, 2008), 33. Born on May 17, 1911, in Stony Creek, Pennsylvania, Clark Kerr earned his MA at Stanford and his PhD in economics at Berkeley in 1939. He became a convert to the university, becoming the first chancellor of Berkeley in 1952. Joking that his job was to provide "parking for faculty, sex for the students, and athletics for the alumni," he showed himself to be a brilliant administrator and leader.

Chapter 23

1 John F. Kennedy Presidential Library and Museum, TNC:191-E5 (excerpt) *Historic Speeches*, "Acceptance of Democratic nomination for President," July 15, 1960.

2 Pamela Dwight, *Landmark Yellow Pages* (Washington, DC: Preservation Press, 1993), 118–121. "Chronology: Historic Preservation Movement in the United States," https://files4.1.revize.com/pontiac/departments/community_development/hdc/docs/HistoricPreservationChronology2018.pdf.

3 Editor, "Citizen Role in Planning Job Stressed," *Santa Barbara News-Press*, January 12, 1954.

4 Cordell Hicks, Steps Taken by Santa Barbara to Preserve Landmarks Hailed," *Los Angeles Times*, April 25, 1956.

5 Nadine Ishitani Hata, *The Historic Preservation Movement in California: 1940–1976* (Sacramento, CA: California Department of Parks and Recreation, Office of Historic Preservation, 1992), 91.

6 Editor, "Citizen Role in Planning Job Stressed," *Santa Barbara News-Press*, January 12, 1954.

7 Eleanor Boba and Carol Snook Weare, "Studies of a Growing Community: Santa Barbara, 1930–1980," *Public Historical Studies* 5, no. 4 (1982), 50.

8 Pearl Chase to Friend, September 12, 1958, Ia_225_14_1, CDCC.

9 The Santa Barbara Historical Society was established in 1932.

10 *Ibid.*

11 Ishitani Hata, 92.

12 Ishitani Hata, 92. Resolution no. 4125 of city of Santa Barbara creating the Santa Barbara Advisory

Landmark Committee, May 10, 1960.

13 Mary Louise Days, et al., *Santa Barbara: a Guide to El Pueblo Viejo* (Santa Barbara, CA: The Santa Barbara Conservancy, 2016), 120. "Founded on April 21, 1782, the Spanish empire had almost three centuries of frontier experience which they fully used in the plan and construction of the Presidio. The structure's plan was based on similar forts built elsewhere in the Spanish empire. The resulting design a square four hundred feet to the side enclosed in the nine-foot-high defense wall with two diamond-shaped bastions located on the diagonal, theoretically would enable soldiers to protect the four sides of the fort with enfilading fire. Other standard features included a two-story high chapel opposite the main gate, and parallel rooms to the east and west with adjoining vegetable gardens for soldiers and their families. The Commandante, priest and officers enjoyed somewhat larger quarters adjacent to the chapel. The whole was an entirely planned structure, one the Spanish had perfected over several centuries of frontier military experience. In all likelihood, the structure was more a garrisoned outpost than it was a military fort."

14 California Department of Parks and Recreation, "El Presidio de Santa Barbara State Historic Park" (State of California, 2022), https://www.parks.ca.gov/?page_id=608. "By contrast with Monterey, which was the political capital of California during most of the Spanish and all the Mexican periods, the majority of the ruling class preferred the climate and beautiful surroundings of Santa Barbara. Local Chumash Indians working under the supervision of Spanish soldiers erected the presidio's buildings and walls using sun-dried adobe bricks laid upon foundations of sandstone boulders. Timbers from the nearby forests supported roofs of red clay tile and the finished walls were covered with whitewash."

15 Santa Barbara Trust for Historic Preservation, "El Presidio de Santa Bárbara State Historic Park, History" (Santa Barbara, CA: Santa Barbara Trust for Historic Preservation, 2022), https://www.sbthp.org/history. "In 1821, Mexico achieved independence from Spain. Those Spanish soldiers and settlers who would not pledge loyalty to the Mexican government were then expelled from the Presidio, so the Presidio fell into disrepair. By the 1840s, the compound stood in partial ruins. The Presidio's military role ended in 1846 when Colonel John C. Frémont's troops claimed the city for the United States. It should be noted that the Presidio of Santa Barbara remained in use long after California's other presidios had been abandoned. Santa Barbara's streets were surveyed in the 1850s and laid directly through the Presidio site in the 1870s. Although several portions of the Presidio quadrangle survived into the 20th century, most original structures were lost to the forces of nature and to Santa Barbara's growth as a city."

16 Raymond Chong, "Faded memories of a Lost Chinatown in Santa Barbara on the California coast," *AsAm News*, August 1, 2020, https://asamnews.com/2020/08/01/how-one-of-californias-chinatown-disappeared-into-distant-memory/.

17 Pearl Chase to Thomas M. Storke, April 3, 1957, Thomas M. Storke Papers, The Bancroft Library, University of California, Berkeley, CA.

18 Ishitani Hata, 54.

19 *Ibid.*, 49–50.

20 Pearl Chase to Olaf Jenkins, Chief, Division of Mines, July 3, 1956, Ia_224_13_1, CDCC.

21 At that time, California had not yet passed enabling legislation that would give municipalities the authority to enact and enforce their own historic district ordinances.

22 Cathy Randolph, "Santa Barbara Trust for Historic Preservation: A Brief History" (Santa Barbara, CA: Santa Barbara Trust for Historic Preservation, 1986), 1. Pearl pressed the Santa Barbara Foundation for help, of which her brother, Harold Chase, was a trustee.

23 *Ibid.* 1.

24 There were numerous success stories she could point to, including: Ann Pamela Cunningham and the Mount Vernon Ladies' Association; Susan Pringle Frost of Charleston, South Carolina; Elizabeth Thomas Werlein of New Orleans, Louisiana; and Ida Krus McFarlane, who led the efforts to restore Colorado's Central City.

25 Barbara J. Howe, "Women in Historic Preservation: The legacy of Ann Pamela Cunningham," *The Public Historian* 12, no. 1 (Winter 1990), 31–61.

26 Wes Chapin and Dr. Anne Petersen, "Interpretation Master Plan: El Presidio de Santa Barbara State Historic Park," (California State Parks, 2012), 48–49, https://www.parks.ca.gov/?page_id=27862.

27 "Royal Presidio State Landmark No. 636," *Noticias: Magazine of the Santa Barbara Historical Society* 46, no. 3 (Summer, 1958): 12-13.

28 In 1961, the division of beaches and parks merged with the division of recreation and the division of small craft harbours within the department of parks and recreation.

29 Pearl Chase to Thomas M. Storke, October 30, 1959, Thomas M. Storke Papers, Mss_73/72c, The Bancroft Library, University of California, Berkeley, CA.

30 Ishitani Hata, 49–54.

31 Editor, "Presidio Reconstruction," *Santa Barbara News-Press*, December 8, 1961.

32 Santa Barbara Trust for Historic Preservation, 2. John Rickard, former mayor and attorney, presided over the board.
33 Francis Price, attorney with Price, Postel & Parma, was elected second vice president and trustee for two years. Of the twelve members of the board, four were women. Among the other incorporators present at the first meeting held in the conference room of the *News-Press* included Fr. Maynard Geiger, Harold Chase, and Edwin Gledhill. Those absent included, among others, Tom Storke and Dwight Murphy. Ex officio members included the state senator and assemblyman, the supervisor of Santa Barbara County, and the mayor.
34 Editor, "Historical Preservation Trust Names Rickard as President," *Santa Barbara News-Press*, February, 19, 1963.
35 *Ibid.*
36 *Ibid.*
37 The other adobe was the Canedo Adobe, built around 1788 to serve as officers' quarters.
38 Chapin et al., 48–49. "El Cuartel was previously part of a row of thirteen buildings that formed the West Wing soldiers' quarters of the quadrangle. In 1846, the structure was deeded to Jose Jesus Valenzuela and appears to have remained in his family until 1925. In 1941, a group of citizens purchased the adobe for $6,500 for the Mission Council of the Boy Scouts of America to use as their headquarters. As one of the few adobes in the city and state which had not been reconstructed with modern materials, the property was deemed to be one of the most historically significant structures in California."
39 Ed Ainsworth, "Santa Barbara's Delightful Blend," *Los Angeles Times*, April 3, 1964.
40 Chapin et al., 48–49.
41 Roger Boleyn, *Liberal or Capitalist?: A Historical Documentary of America's Two-Party Political System* (Morrissville, NC: Lulu Publishing Services, 2019).
42 *Ibid.*
43 National Park Service, "National Historic Preservation Act," December 2, 2018, https://www.nps.gov/subjects/historicpreservation/national-historic-preservation-act.htm.
44 Ishitani Hata, 111.
45 National Park Service, "National Historic Preservation Act."
46 Ishitani Hata, 111.
47 Ishitani Hata, 227–249. "Although federal and state programs dominated the preservation scene in the years following the passage of the landmark 1966 federal legislation, local preservation organizations such as the SBTHP did much to strengthen and change the practice and direction of preservation in California. Despite the emergence of these local organizations, there was no single state-wide preservation organization or official state historical society to lobby for preservation concerns, an activity the National Trust for Historic Preservation was prohibited from doing. Not until March 1984 when the Californians for Preservation Action (CPA) and the California Preservation Foundation (CPF) merged into the CPF did this become a reality."
48 The cost was $145,000.
49 Chapin et al., 48–49.
50 *Ibid.*
51 Pearl Chase to Dwight Murphy, January 31, 1968, Ia_228_17_1, CDCC.
52 Pearl Chase to Edwin Gledhill, June 28, 1966, Ia_228_17_1, CDCC.
53 Pearl Chase to Mrs. and Mr. Robert Phelan, May 5, 1966, Ia_228_17_1, CDCC.
54 Bill Luton, Jr., in discussion with the author, February 26, 2019.
55 *Ibid.*
56 Chapin et al., 48–49.
57 Marco Farley, "The Legacy of Pearl Chase," (Santa Barbara, CA: Santa Barbara Trust for Historic Preservation, 1988), 24.
58 Pearl Chase to Mr. Raleigh A. Taylor, State Division of Forestry, January 3, 1964, Ia_226_15_1, CDCC.

Chapter 24

1 Carolyn Merchant, *American Environmental History* (New York, NY: Columbia University Press, 2007), 193.
2 *Ibid.*, 193–194.
3 Lewis L. Gould, Lewis, *Lady Bird Johnson and the Environment* (Lawrence, KS: University Press of Kansas, 1988), 6.
4 US Department of Labor, "Eras of the New Frontier and the Great Society 1961–1969," https://www.dol.gov/general/aboutdol/history/dolchp06.
5 Merchant, 196.
6 Gould, 43. Born to Mormon parents on 31 January 30, 1920, in St. Johns, Arizona, Udall attended the University of Arizona, later serving as an air gunner in Europe during the Second World War. After the war, he finished college and obtained a law degree. In 1954, he ran for Congress and served three terms.
7 *Ibid.*
8 Pearl Chase to Miss Hellene Smith, March 9, 1964, Ia_226_15_1, CDCC.
9 Lyndon B. Johnson, "Remarks Upon Signing the Wilderness Bill and the Land and Water Conservation Fund Bill," The American Presidency Project, UC Santa Barbara, https://www.presidency.ucsb.edu/documents/remarks-upon-signing-the-

wilderness-bill-and-the-land-and-water-conservation-fund-bill.

10 John de Graff, "A National Beautification Campaign Revitalized Communities in the '60s and Could Again Today," *Truthout*, January 1, 2018, https://truthout.org/articles/a-national-beautification-campaign-revitalized-communities-in-the-60-and-could-again-today/.

11 Rita G. Koman, "…To Leave This Splendour for Our Grandchildren: Lady Bird Johnson, Environmentalist Extraordinaire," *OAH Magazine of History* 15, no. 3 (Spring 2001), 31.

12 Kim Kennedy White and Leslie A. Duram, *America Goes Green: An Encyclopedia of Eco-Friendly Culture in the United States*, (ABC-CLIO, 2012), 598.

13 Lauren A. Stealey, "Lady Bird Johnson, Betty Ford, and Second Wave Feminism" (master's thesis, University of Southern Mississippi, 2014), 28, https://aquila.usm.edu/cgi/viewcontent.cgi?article=1249&context=honors_theses.

14 Koman, 31.

15 *Ibid.*

16 Lyndon B. Johnson, "Special Message to the Congress on Conservation and Restoration of Natural Beauty," American Presidency Project, UC Santa Barbara, https://www.presidency.ucsb.edu/documents/special-message-the-congress-conservation-and-restoration-natural-beauty.

17 *Ibid.*

18 Michigan in the World and the Environmental Justice HistoryLab, "Environmentalism and the Great Society," University of Michigan History (LSA), http://michiganintheworld.history.lsa.umich.edu/environmentalism/exhibits/show/main_exhibit/origins/environmentalism-and-the-great.

19 Editor, "Conference 'Well-Organized,' Pearl Chase Enthusiastic Over White House Operation Lady Bird," *Santa Barbara News-Press*, June 20, 1965.

20 *Ibid.*

21 Lyndon Baines Johnson, *Public Papers of the Presidents of the United States: Lyndon B. Johnson, 1965*, book one, 165.

22 Gould, 74.

23 Catherine Guidis, *Buyways: Billboards, Automobiles, and the American Landscape* (New York, NY: Routledge, 2004), 216. "The reformers did acquire some powerful allies of their own, including the Automobile Association of America (AAA), which entered the fray in 1940 in support of comprehensive state-wide zoning plans. AAA drafted a model roadside zoning bill that borrowed greatly from the 1931 proposals of the National Roadside Council."

24 The National Association of Real Estate Boards (NAREB) and the American Society of Planning Officials supported the bill, which was frequently defeated by the billboard lobby but for the states of California, Oklahoma, and Oregon.

25 Guidis, 216.

26 *Ibid.*, 219.

27 *Ibid.*, 220–221. Ironically, shortly after the war, "the NRC dissolved in an untimely way just as the outdoor advertising industry was becoming a devastatingly effective lobbying machine." As one reformer sympathizer explained, "This lobby shrewdly puts many legislators in its debt by giving them free sign space during election time, and it is savage against the legislator who dares oppose it. It subsidizes his opposition and foments political trouble in his home district."

28 *Ibid.*, 219.

29 In 1958, "Congress adopted the 'Bonus Act' that left billboard control in state hands. States that regulated billboards within established federal standards would receive a 'bonus' of 0.5 percent more than the 90 percent federal subsidy of the interstate system."

30 Pearl Chase to Senator John F. McCarthy, December 1, 1958, Ia_225_14_1, CDCC.

31 Guidis, 221. "Despite their efforts, by the time the extended 'Bonus' act expired on June 30, 1965, only twenty-three states were signed up, relatively few miles of interstate had been affected, and only seven states had fulfilled the requirements and received bonuses."

32 *Ibid.*, 223.

33 Knowing that Mrs. Johnson was attending a conference on California's beauty in Los Angeles, Pearl sent her an invitation to visit and speak in Santa Barbara during her trip west. Pearl thought Lady Bird's "willingness to participate in activities which stimulate widespread interest has been both unique and highly encouraging especially to those of us who have been working with public agencies and private organizations at the State and County level." Pearl Chase to Mrs. Lyndon B. Johnson, November 17, 1965, Ia_227_16_1, CDCC. Unfortunately, due to another commitment, Mrs. Johnson was unable to accept the invitation.

34 Guidis, 223–224.

35 *Ibid.*, 224.

36 "The president admitted that the act was a compromise. Firstly, the federal government allocated only a tiny fraction of the funds that it promised for billboard removals, so few removals ever occurred; secondly, the act prevented the states from controlling the billboards on their own through a mechanism called amortization, which offered a phase-out period in lieu of cash; thirdly, the outdoor advertising industry simply found other

billboard locations—the industry recognized that its investment could not be lost, as governments were required to pay full cash compensation for removals; fourthly, the act led to billboards bigger than any previously seen and placed strategically outside the corridor regulated by the act." *Ibid.*, 224–225.

37 Guidis, 225.

38 Helen Reynolds, Letter to the Editor of the *Atlantic Monthly*, December 15, 1965, Beautification files, White House Conference on Natural Beauty, White House Social Files, Box 14, LBJ Library, quoted in Guidis, 225.

39 Guidis, 225.

40 Pearl Chase, interview by Gibbs Smith, ca. 1972–1973, OH 115, transcript, Pearl Chase Oral History, Department of Special Collections, UC Santa Barbara Library, Santa Barbara, CA.

41 In 1965, Reynolds and some conservationists in Marin County formed the Planning and Conservation League (PCL) to remedy California's fast-paced development. To continue supporting and promoting legislation, the PCL acted as a conduit for the CRC. Reynolds maintained CRC's "The Bulletin" until 1973, and by 1976 the organization had merged with the PCL.

42 Rozella Jewett, "Santa Barbara Beautiful: The Early Years," *History of Santa Barbara Beautiful*, (1979), https://sbbeautiful.org/about-us/history/.

43 *Ibid.*

44 Kevin Starr, *Golden Dreams: California in an Age of Abundance, 1950–1963* (Oxford, UK: Oxford University Press, 2009), ix.

45 Joseph A. Califano, Jr., "What Was Really Great About the Great Society," *Washington Monthly*, October 1, 1999, https://washingtonmonthly.com/1999/10/01/what-was-really-great-about-the-great-society/.

46 Professor W. Elliot Brownlee, in discussion with the author, conducted on May 15, 2018.

47 Pearl Chase to Harold Chase, June 9, 1965, V_725_8, CDCC.

Chapter 25

1 David Gebhard and Robert Winter, *A Guide to Architecture in Los Angeles & Southern California*, (Santa Barbara, CA: Peregrine Smith Inc., 1977), 28.

2 Frances Woo, "Vietnam War Protests," *Living History Project*, Associated Students of UC Santa Barbara (Santa Barbara, CA: UC Santa Barbara, 2019).

3 Two services were held for Mountfort in the Old Mission, and she was buried in Goleta Catholic Cemetery near Santa Barbara. Gifts in her memory amounted to $600, which Pearl allocated for activities in which Mountfort had an interest, including tree planting in school grounds, the sowing of wildflower seeds on barren hillsides, and for junior conservation scholarships.

4 While undergoing tests at the Cottage Hospital in mid-May, Harold suffered a stroke which paralyzed the left side of his body. His mind remained clear, and he was able to speak. Between treatments, exercise, and massage, he enjoyed listening to the baseball on the radio and other very limited forms of recreation.

5 Editor, "Harold Chase: A Great Citizen," *Santa Barbara News-Press*, April 28, 1970.

6 Pearl Chase to Harold and Gertrude Chase, July 6, 1954, Ia_245_3_1–6, CDCC.

7 Ronald L. Nye, "The Influence of the Chase Family on Santa Barbara History" (presentation, West Coast Symposium on Family History, UC Santa Barbara, May 1, 1976).

8 ForestWatch, "San Rafael Wilderness: 50 Years of Preserving Santa Barbara's Backcountry", *Los Padres ForestWatch*, October 23, 2014, https://lpfw.org/san-rafael-wilderness-50-years-of-preserving-santa-barbaras-backcountry/.

9 Department of Agriculture, Forest Service, California Region, San Francisco, "Report on the proposed San Rafael Wilderness, Los Padres National Park, California," H.R. Rep. 90, at 10–91 (1967).

10 ForestWatch, "San Rafael Wilderness." Robert "Bob" Easton, a local author, journalist, and faculty member at Santa Barbara City College whose wife Jane Faust, was one of Chase's sorority sisters at Berkeley, became chair of the Citizens Committee and met frequently with Congressman Charles Teague, the area's representative. Easton's group enlisted the support of the city council, along with the county planning commission and board of supervisors, and the group's leaders mobilized the community to speak out in support of the larger citizens' wilderness proposal.

11 *Ibid.*

12 Pearl Chase to Mr. Charles A. Connaughton, February 22, 1964, Ia_226_15_1, CDCC.

13 John Alexander, "Teague Offers Aid on Wilderness Act", *Santa Barbara News-Press*, November 9, 1965.

14 Speakers at the wilderness hearing included Congressman Charles M. Teague, the ranking republican member of the House subcommittee on forests; Carl Buckheister, president of the National Audubon Society from New York; Michael McCloskey, northwest field representative of the Sierra Club and, in 1969, the club's second executive director; Lamarr Johnston of the California Cattlemen's association; and Fred Eissler, mountaineer, teacher at the Santa Barbara San Marcos High School, Sierra Club director, and close friend of David Brower.

15 ForestWatch, "San Rafael Wilderness."
16 Anne Eisner, in discussion with the author, February 27, 2019.
17 Robert Olney Easton and David E. Russell, "Writing: The Early Years," (Santa Barbara, CA: UC Santa Barbara Oral History Program, 1988), 241.
18 John Alexander, "Teague Offers Aid on Wilderness Act," *Santa Barbara News-Press*, November 9, 1965.
19 Easton and Russell, 241.
20 Lyndon B. Johnson, "Remarks Upon Signing the Bill to Designate the San Rafael Wilderness, California," The American Presidency Project, UC Santa Barbara, https://www.presidency.ucsb.edu/documents/remarks-upon-signing-bill-designate-the-san-rafael-wilderness-california.
21 Pearl Chase to Lawrence Stuart, December 30, 1968, Ia_228_17_1, CDCC.
22 Pearl Chase to Horace Albright, July 8, 1974, V_767_24, CDCC.
23 Helen Baker Reynolds, interview by Carla Ehat and Anne T. Kent, February 28, 1979, transcript, Marin County Free Library.
24 Michigan in the World and the Environmental Justice HistoryLab, "Environmental Crisis in the Late 1960s," University of Michigan History (LSA), https://michiganintheworld.history.lsa.umich.edu/environmentalism/exhibits/show/main_exhibit/origins/-environmental-crisis--in-the-#content
25 Women have provided the inspiration and grassroots activism for many areas of the environmental movement, animal rights movement, vegetarianism, and veganism.
26 National Park Service, "Lyndon B. Johnson and the Environment," US Department of the Interior, https://www.nps.gov/lyjo/planyourvisit/upload/environmentcs2.pdf.
27 John A. Farrell, "The Inside Story of Richard Nixon's Ugly, 30-Year Feud with Earl Warren," *Smithsonian* magazine (March 2017), https://www.smithsonianmag.com/history/inside-story-richard-nixons-ugly-30-year-feud-earl-warren-180962614/.

Chapter 26

1 "Anguish, Anger and Activism: Legacies of the 1969 Santa Barbara Oil Spill," UC Santa Barbara Library, https://spotlight.library.ucsb.edu/starlight/oil-spill.
2 Keith C. Clarke and Jeffrey J. Hemphill, "The Santa Barbara Oil Spill: A Retrospective," *Yearbook of the Association of Pacific Coast Geographers, 2002*, 64 (2002), 160.
3 It was reported that approximately fifteen hundred birds died in the centers by the end of February.
4 Teresa Sabol Spezio, *Slick Policy* (Pittsburgh, Pennsylvania: University of Pittsburgh Press, 2018), 139.
5 Get Oil Out, "1969 Oil Spill" (2018), https://getoilout.org/?p=113.
6 "Santa Barbara Oil Spill," *Environmental Encyclopedia*, Encyclopedia.com, https://www.encyclopedia.com/environment/encyclopedias-almanacs-transcripts-and-maps/santa-barbara-oil-spill.
7 UCSB, "Anguish, Anger and Activism."
8 Nick Welsh, "Get Oil Out Founder and Dolphin Sculptor Bud Bottoms Dies," *Santa Barbara Independent*, September 24, 2018, https://www.independent.com/2018/09/24/get-oil-out-founder-and-dolphin-sculptor-bud-bottoms-dies/. Bottoms was a twinkly-eyed forty-year-old who embodied to an uncommon degree the ideal of man-about-town and engaged public citizen.
9 *Ibid.*
10 Jonathan Bastian, "How the 1969 Santa Barbara Oil Spill Sparked Earth Day," *News Stories*, KCRW, April 21, 2017, https://www.kcrw.com/news/articles/how-the-1969-santa-barbara-oil-spill-sparked-earth-day.
11 They were Marvin Stuart and Alvin Weingand, a former Democratic senator in the state legislature.
12 Tim Hazeltine, in discussion with the author, February 25, 2018.
13 James "Bud" Bottoms, "In Their Own Voice, The Legacy of Seventeen Past Presidents, Santa Barbara Beautiful," *Santa Barbara Beautiful: An Oral History, Volume 1, 1965–2008* (1967), 4.
14 At the end of the nineteenth century, an economic boom accompanied the development of the Summerland oil field, six miles from Santa Barbara, which transformed the spiritualist community of Summerland into an oil town. By 1903, as Santa Barbara was beginning to establish itself as a health resort and tourist destination with dramatic natural scenery, unspoiled beaches, and a perfect climate and H.G. Chase Real Estate opened for business, California became the leading oil-producing state in the US.
15 Unregulated drilling.
16 Editor, "Letter from an Eastern Visitor", *Morning Press*, February 21, 1929.
17 The local newspapers, the Chamber of Commerce, women's club, Business and Professional Women's Club, AAUW, Parent-Teacher Federation, the building trades, automobile dealers, a considerable number of real estate dealers, including H.G. Chase, the insurance men, the better class of shop owners, homeowners in the city and in Montecito.
18 Pearl Chase to the Mayor and City Council, Santa Barbara, February 7, 1929, Ia_215_4_1, CDCC.
19 Wikipedia, s.v. "Mesa Oil Field," last modified October 11, 2021, 02:43, https://en.wikipedia.org/wiki/Mesa_Oil_Field.

20 S.G. Dolman, "Mesa Oil Field," *California Division of Oil and Gas, Summary of Operations* 24, no. 2 (1938), 5–14. According to S.G. Dolman, writing in 1940, "It is doubtful if the field has returned in dividends the money invested. Like most town-lot fields, there are 10 wells where one would have sufficed."
21 F.B. Kellam to Camillo Fenzi, April 28, 1933, Ia_218_7_1, CDCC.
22 However, a protracted dispute between the federal government and the state over the ownership of this offshore oil restricted offshore platform construction and drilling.
23 Bureau of Ocean Energy Management, "Submerged Lands Act (SLA), 1953," https://www.boem.gov/sites/default/files/uploadedFiles/BOEM/Oil_and_Gas_Energy_Program/Leasing/Outer_Continental_Shelf/Lands_Act_History/submerged.pdf.
24 A tug of war on oil revenues ensued. She remained strongly opposed when Mayor Edward L. Abbott announced a revenue study. She felt his position was "the most serious situation ever to threaten Santa Barbara's future and its present reputation."
25 Editor, "Tug of War Set on Oil Revenues," *Los Angeles Times*, April 23, 1962.
26 Kate Wheeling and Max Ufberg, "'The Ocean Is Boiling': The Complete Oral History of the 1969 Santa Barbara Oil Spill," *Pacific Standard* (April 2017), https://psmag.com/news/the-ocean-is-boiling-the-complete-oral-history-of-the-1969-santa-barbara-oil-spill. According to one local, "I remember when they built the oil platforms. Until then, it was beautiful. It was just the moonlight on the water. I remember the oil companies saying when they built the oil platforms, they were going to obscure them with clouds, so that you would never see them. They were telling us whatever we wanted to hear to get it approved."
27 Wheeling and Ufberg.
28 Pearl Chase to Mrs. Tutenberg, January 21, 1960, Ia_225_14_1, CDCC.
29 UCSB, "Anguish, Anger and Activism."
30 Meir Rinde, "Richard Nixon and the Rise of American Environmentalism," *Distillations, Science History Institute* (June 2017), https://www.sciencehistory.org/distillations/richard-nixon-and-the-rise-of-american-environmentalism.
31 *Ibid.* "He ran on a platform of law and order and ending the Vietnam War, and vowed to cut back Lyndon Johnson's social programs. But he also recognized the huge political power of environmentalism, which blossomed into a popular movement just around the time of his election. He had picked as his top domestic adviser John Ehrlichman, who believed in safeguarding natural resources." See: Rinde, Meir, "Richard Nixon and the Rise of American Environmentalism."
32 Indy Staff, "Naomi Klein Discusses our Environmental Future: Author Delivers May 17 Granada Theatre Speech on Climate Crisis," *Santa Barbara Independent*, May 25, 2017, https://www.independent.com/2017/05/25/naomi-klein-discusses-our-environmental-future/.
33 Get Oil Out. "Union Oil suffered millions in losses from the clean-up efforts, payments to fishermen and local businesses, and lawsuit settlements."
34 Federal and state regulations governing oil drilling were also strengthened.
35 Elizabeth Goldstein, "California State Parks Foundation," *San Francisco Business Times*, August 6, 2006, https://www.bizjournals.com/sanfrancisco/stories/2006/08/07/story18.html. "Since 1969, CSPF has raised more than $120 million to benefit state parks. CSPF is committed to improving the quality of life for all Californians by expanding access to the natural beauty, rich culture and history, and recreational and educational opportunities offered by California's 279 state parks. The largest state park system in the United States. In 1972 the California Coastal Commission was created from a state-wide initiative. This commission today has broad control over human activities that affect California's coastal areas."
36 Wheeling and Ufberg.
37 EarthDay.org, "About Us: The History of Earth Day," https://www.earthday.org/history/.
38 *Ibid.*

Chapter 27

1 Pearl Chase, "Planning for Growth in Santa Barbara County", April 5, 1962.
2 Mary Louise Days, "History of Santa Barbara's Building Heights," *Santa Barbara Independent*, October 7, 2009, https://www.independent.com/2009/10/07/history-santa-barbaras-building-heights/. "It lowered the maximum allowable heights to four stories and sixty feet in the general commercial and manufacturing/industrial zones; to three stories and forty-five feet in multiple-family zones; and to two stories and thirty feet in single-family and two-family zones."
3 Hattie Beresford, "El Mirasol: From Graceful Swan to Ominous Albatross," *Noticias: The Quarterly Magazine of the Santa Barbara Historical Society* 47, no. 1 (Spring 2001), 21.
4 *Ibid.*
5 Pearl Chase to Herbert J. Stevens, November 30, 1967, V_763_20, CDCC.
6 Hattie Beresford, "El Mirasol: From Graceful Swan to Ominous Albatross," *Noticias: The Quarterly*

Magazine of the Santa Barbara Historical Society 47, no. 1 (Spring 2001), 21.

7 *Ibid.*

8 *Ibid.*

9 Pearl Chase to the Mayor of Santa Barbara, November 20, 1967, Ia_228_17_1, CDCC.

10 Pearl Chase to Horace Albright, October 21, 1968, V_763_20, CDCC.

11 Both of these zones had a height maximum of forty-five feet and/or three stories.

12 Beresford, "El Mirasol," 21.

13 Mary Louise Days, "The Public Shapes Public Policy: Regulation of High-Rise Construction in Santa Barbara," (Prepared for the Santa Barbara City College Political Science Class, December 1982), 2.

14 Pearl Chase to Mrs. McCormick, November 22, 1967, Ia_228_17_1, CDCC.

15 Beresford, "El Mirasol," 21.

16 David Van Horne in discussion with the author, February 28, 2019.

17 "William Alexander Obituary", *Santa Barbara News-Press*, July 17, 2016. "Bill Alexander was born on October 20, 1920, in Mooresville, North Carolina. He graduated from Mooresville High School in 1937, and the University of North Carolina at Chapel Hill with a degree in business in 1942. After graduation, he spent three years in the US Coast Guard as a training school instructor, and subsequently served aboard a troop transport in both the Atlantic and Pacific theatres during World War II. Following the war, he married Betty Stearns in Berkeley, California, ultimately settling in the Los Angeles area. He worked briefly for the Signal Oil Corporation, but it was his fortuitous meeting with developer Lionel Mayell that set the course for his professional business life. After Bill joined the firm of Lionel Mayell Enterprises, one pioneering the concept of cooperatively owned apartments, the Alexanders moved with their children Jeffrey, Dana, and Nancy, to Santa Barbara, where Bill built his first condominium project in 1953. His work for Mayell was so successful that he soon went into business for himself as president of William Alexander and Associates."

18 Nick Welsh, "So long to Jerry Beaver: Poodle gets misty over a cordial developer," *Santa Barbara Independent*, December 6, 2018, https://www.independent.com/2018/12/06/so-long-jerry-beaver/. "Jerry Beaver was born on July 30, 1932, in Springfield, Illinois. He went west to Arizona State University and then the University of Colorado at Boulder, where he studied architecture. He served in the U.S. Army as an officer in the Corps of Engineers during the Korean War. He married Helene Giljum, who had come to the United States as a refugee after World War II. The couple moved to Santa Barbara in 1960 where Beaver started out as an appraiser and then as a broker and developer. According to a friend, "Back in the day, when the psycho-politics of Santa Barbara needed someone to play the Big, Bad Developer, Jerry Beaver was it. And he didn't merely play at it; as they say in Hollywood, he inhabited the role. He owned it. He embraced it."

19 "William Alexander Obituary", *Santa Barbara News-Press*. Alexander had a reputation for honesty, generosity, creativity, and amazing energy.

20 Pearl Chase to Mr. W.H. Ferry, October 16, 1968, Ia_228_17_1, CDCC.

21 Days, 3.

22 Beresford, "El Mirasol," 25.

23 Editor, "Our life with Pearl Chase: Memories shared by Penny and Terry Davies," *Santa Barbara News-Press*, November 17, 2011.

24 Pearl Chase to Mr. Irving Stone, October 17, 1968, Ib_16_2, CDCC.

25 Editor, "Our life with Pearl Chase."

26 Days, 4.

27 *Ibid.*

28 Editor, "Our life with Pearl Chase."

29 John Sink was born in Atlanta, Georgia in 1928. He graduated from Harvard University, Harvard Law School, and served in the US Marine Corps during the Second World War. He practiced in Los Angeles before moving to Santa Barbara in 1960.

30 Days, 5.

31 *Ibid.*

32 Beresford, "El Mirasol," 27.

33 Editor, "Our life with Pearl Chase."

34 Mary Louise Days, "History of Santa Barbara's Building Heights," *Santa Barbara Independent*, October 7, 2009, https://www.independent.com/2009/10/07/history-santa-barbaras-building-heights/. "Organized by the Citizens' Planning Association and the Santa Barbara City College Adult Education Division, and with Chase's assistance, a three-meeting forum called "Should Santa Barbara Go High-Rise?" was held in the spring of 1970. There were fourteen cooperating organizations and a large attendance. At the same time, a city General Plan Goals Committee recommended that the current building height limits be incorporated into the city charter.
In March 1972, the city council adopted an amendment which recommended that the present building height maximums be maintained or reduced in certain areas, such as El Pueblo Viejo. Later that year, city council voted 6–1 to place a measure on the November general election ballot. On November 7, it carried on a vote of 26,499

to 8,048. Its opening lines read, "It is hereby declared the policy of the City that high buildings are inimical to the basic residential and historical character of the City."

35 James "Bud" Bottoms, "In Their Own Voice, The Legacy of Seventeen Past Presidents, Santa Barbara Beautiful," *Santa Barbara Beautiful: An Oral History, Volume 1, 1965–2008* (1967), 4.

36 Edward A. Hartfeld, *California's Knight on a Golden Horse: Dwight Murphy, Santa Barbara's Renaissance Man* (Santa Barbara, CA: The Dwight Murphy Memorial Project, 2007), 109.

37 Mary Louise Days, in discussion with the author, May 30, 2018.

38 Beresford, 28.

39 Michael Redmon, "Nine-Story Towers Were Proposed for Alice Keck Park Gardens," *Santa Barbara Independent*, October 13, 2015, https://www.independent.com/2015/10/13/nine-story-towers-were-proposed-alice-keck-park-gardens/.

Chapter 28

1 Pearl Chase, interview by Charles Bridgham Hosmer, Jr., transcript, August 8, 1971, transcript, The New York Preservation Archive Project.

2 "Anguish, Anger and Activism: Legacies of the 1969 Santa Barbara Oil Spill," UC Santa Barbara Library, https://spotlight.library.ucsb.edu/starlight/oil-spill.

3 Committee to Save East Beach, "Summary of a plan for East Beach", July 22, 1972, Ia_263_1_4, CDCC.

4 The battle waged for a further ten years during which time the Hyatt and Southern Pacific bowed out and sold a small portion of their land to Fess Parker, who leveraged that into a controlling interest. Pearl never lived to see Fess Parker's Red Lion Inn, built in 1985.

5 Sheila Lodge, *Santa Barbara: An Uncommonplace American Town* (Santa Barbara, CA: Olympus Press, 2020), 77.

6 UCSB College of Creative Studies, "Chancellor Vernon Cheadle," https://ccs.ucsb.edu/ccs-profiles/chancellor-vernon-cheadle-3750. "Born on February 6, 1910, in Salem, South Dakota, Vernon Cheadle earned a BA with honors in Botany, magna cum laude, from Miami University in 1932. After receiving an MA and PhD from Harvard University in 1934 and 1936, respectively, he joined the University of Rhode Island faculty, where he quickly earned international recognition as a botanist and rose to the rank of full professor in just five years. It was at URI that Chancellor Cheadle met his wife Mary, and they were married in 1939. After sixteen years at URI, he began a twenty-five-year run at the University of California, when he accepted the chair of botany at UC Davis in 1952. Ten years later, he was appointed chancellor at UCSB, where he led the campus for fifteen years until he reached the then-mandatory retirement age of sixty-seven."

7 Eileen Kadesh, "Dedication of 'Pearl Chase Garden,'" April 23, 1972.

8 Pearl Chase, "Dedication of 'Pearl Chase Garden,'" April 23, 1972.

9 Pearl Chase to Newton Drury, June 16, 1970, 30_15_Save the Redwoods League Records, Mss 88/15c, University Archives, The Bancroft Library, University of California, Berkeley, CA.

10 *Ibid.*

11 Nancy Schwarz, "Pearl Chase: Citizen Leader," *UCSB Environmental Studies* 192 (June 1982), 2.

12 *Ibid.*

13 Daniel Alef, "Pearl Chase: 'Joan of Arc with a trowel,'" *Santa Barbara News-Press*, January 29, 2005.

14 Pearl Chase to June Wilson, December 31, 1968, V_763_20, CDCC.

15 Pearl Chase to Newton Drury, August 24, 1970, 30_15_ Save the Redwoods League Records, Mss 88/15c, University Archives, The Bancroft Library, University of California, Berkeley, CA.

16 UCSB College of Creative Studies, "Chancellor Vernon Cheadle."

17 Vernon Cheadle, "Chancellor's Dedication of Pearl Chase Garden," April 23, 1972.

18 Vernon Cheadle to Pearl Chase, June 29, 1976, V_767_24, CDCC.

19 Vernon Cheadle to Pearl Chase, April 5, 1971, Ib_16_8, CDCC.

20 Pearl Chase to William Penn Mott, May 4, 1972, V_765_22, CDCC.

21 Pearl Chase to Lady Georgina Hamilton, June 15, 1971, V_748_5, CDCC.

22 Pearl Chase to Winifred Pomeroy, November 8, 1973, V_766_23, CDCC.

23 Michael Heskett to Pearl Chase, May 30, 1972, Ib_16_8, CDCC.

24 *Ibid.*

25 Roseanne M. Barker, "Small Town Progressivism: Pearl Chase and Female Activism in Santa Barbara, 1909–1929" (PhD diss., UC Santa Barbara, 1994), 15.

26 The Watergate scandal had stemmed from his administration's attempts to cover up its involvement in the June 17, 1972, break-in of the Democratic National Committee headquarters at the Watergate Office Building.

27 Richard Nixon, "Annual Message to the Congress on the State of the Union: January 22, 1970," *The American Presidency Project* (Santa Barbara, CA: UC Santa Barbara), https://www.presidency.ucsb.edu/documents/annual-message-the-congress-the-state-the-union-2.

28 Kathleen Wilson Balsdon to Pearl Chase, May 21, 1973, V_766_23, CDCC.
29 Sarah Booth Conroy, "Her Solution to Pollution," *Washington Post*, May 9, 1973.
30 *Santa Barbara News-Press*, July 8, 1973, and *The Independent*, May 9, 1973.
31 Vivian "Vie" Obern, "Remembering Pearl Chase," *La Campana* (Santa Barbara Trust for Historic Preservation, Fall 1988), 12.
32 Pearl Chase to Cousins, July 26, 1973, V_766_23, CDCC.
33 Pearl Chase to William 'Bill' F. Luton, Snr., August 2, 1973, V_766_23, CDCC.
34 They were Robert "Bob" Easton, Sue Higman, and Vivian "Vie" Obern.
35 Vivian Obern, Robert Easton, Sue Higman to Friend of Pearl and Harold S. Chase, September 19, 1982, V_773_2, CDCC.
36 Pearl Chase, "East Cabrillo Boulevard – How It Happened, 1924–1927," reprinted from *Noticias: The Magazine of the Santa Barbara Historical Society* (Summer, 1959), 12.
37 Nancy Schwarz, "Pearl Chase: Citizen Leader," *UCSB Environmental Studies* 192 (June 1982), 6–8.

Chapter 29

1 "The Legacy of Pearl Chase," *Santa Barbara News-Press*, October 25, 1979.
2 "Woman Who Shaped Image of a City Dies," *Los Angeles Times*, October 29, 1979.
3 *Ibid.*
4 "DAR honors Dr. Chase," *Santa Barbara News-Press*, October 30, 1979. Among others to recognize Pearl Chase were The Daughters of the American Revolution.
5 "Dr. Pearl Chase dies at age 90," *Santa Barbara News-Press*, October 28, 1979.
6 Vernon Cheadle, "Miss Chase unequalled," *Santa Barbara News-Press*, October 30, 1979.
7 Acting temporarily for Mayor David Shiffman while he visited China.
8 Hal Conklin, "Pearl Chase Set Style," *Santa Barbara News-Press*, October 26, 1979.
9 "Pearl Chase Succumbs," *UCSB Alumni Magazine*, November 1979.
10 Those present were Lady Georgina Hamilton, Pearl's great-niece; Sue Higman; and Mary Louise Days.
11 Lady Georgina Hamilton, in discussion with the author, August 1, 2019.
12 "Pearl Chase left $67,800 to groups," *Santa Barbara News-Press*, November 9, 1979.
13 Sue Higman, "Honor name of Chase," *Santa Barbara News-Press*, November 13, 1979.

Chapter 30

1 The name was coined three years after her death at the bicentenary of the Presidio, by Richard "Feltie" Felton, a regional director of the State Parks and Recreation department.
2 Nancy Schwarz interviews conducted April 1982, Gledhill Library, Santa Barbara Historical Museum, Santa Barbara, CA.
3 Beverley Jackson, "Pearl Chase 100th birthday fete attracts many fans, admirers." *Santa Barbara News-Press*, November 20, 1988.
4 Editor, "Plaque in the Park." *Santa Barbara News-Press*, November 17, 1982.
5 Jackson.
6 Mary Louise Days, "Speech at Luncheon in Honor of Pearl Chase Centennial, November 16, 1988," Mary Louise Days Collection, Santa Barbara, CA.
7 *The Pearl Chase Society*, "About Us." Available online: https://www.pearlchasesociety.org/about-us.
8 Sheila Lodge, *Santa Barbara: An Uncommonplace American Town: How Thoughtful Planning Shaped a City* (Olympus Press, Santa Barbara, 2020), p. 100.
9 Newton Drury to Miss Helen E. Murphy, October 27, 1965, 30_15, Save the Redwoods League Records, Mss 88/15c, University Archives, The Bancroft Library, University of California, Berkeley, CA.
10 Pearl Chase, interview by Gibbs Smith, ca. 1972–1973, OH 115, transcript, Pearl Chase Oral History, Department of Special Collections, UC Santa Barbara Library, Santa Barbara, CA.

BIBLIOGRAPHY • ARCHIVAL SOURCES

Art and Design Collection, Art, Design & Architecture Museum, University of California, Santa Barbara, CA
Riggs (Lutah Maria) Papers
Santa Barbara Community Arts Association Records
Soule, Murphy & Hastings Drawings
Stevens (Ralph T.) Landscape plan for Harold S. Chase estate

Bancroft Library, University of California, Berkeley, CA
Grinnell (Joseph) Papers
Knowland (Joseph R.) Papers
Marshall (George) Papers
Mather (Stephen T.) Papers
Merriam (C. Hart) Papers
Metcalf (Woodbridge) Papers
Save the Redwoods League Records
Sierra Club Records
Sproul (Robert Gordon) Papers
Storke (Charles A.) Papers
Storke (Thomas M.) Papers
Photographs of Earl Warren (graphic) 1925–1973

Bentley History Library, University of Michigan, Ann Arbor, MI
Backus (Standish) Papers

Boston Public Library, Boston, MA
Newspaper Archive

Boston Tax Department, Boston, MA
Boston Tax Records 1822–1912

Bowood Collection, Bowood House, Calne, UK
Chase (Harold S.) Papers
Chase (Pearl) Papers
Lansdowne (Barbara) Papers

The Carl A. Kroch Library, Rare and Manuscript Collections, Cornell University, NY
Ewald (William R.) Papers

Center for Sacramento History, Sacramento, CA
Neasham (Vernon Aubrey) Papers

Charles Babbage Institute Archives, Elmer L. Andersen Library, University of Minneapolis, MN
Burroughs Corporation Records

City Hall, Santa Barbara, CA
Map of Santa Barbara, 1912

Colorado School of Mines, Golden, CO
Colorado Historic Newspapers Collection

County of Santa Clara Office of the County Clerk-Recorder, San Jose, CA
Government Listings

Denver Public Library, Colorado, CO
Census Records

Gilroy Public Library, Gilroy, CA
City Directories

Gledhill Library, Santa Barbara Historical Museum, Santa Barbara, CA
Chase (Pearl), Berkeley Scrapbook and various other papers under same subject name
Chase (Pearl), Scrapbook of Pearl Chase, Omega Chapter, UC Berkeley 1905-1909, Digital Facsimile (Property of Kappa Alpha Theta Fraternity, Indianapolis, IN)
Jackson (Beverley) Newspaper Columns
Jackson (Beverley) Photograph Collection
Newspaper Archive

Oral History Program, Santa Barbara Historical Society

Haverhill Public Library, Haverhill, MA
Newspaper Archive

Huntington Library, San Marino, CA
Johnson (Reginald D.) Collection
Los Angeles Times Records

Josiah Hamilton Collection, Montecito, CA
Chase Family Photographs

Judy and Harold Whiting Collection, Santa Barbara, CA
Chase (Harold) Papers
Hope Ranch Papers

Kathi Brewster Collection, Santa Barbara, CA
Newspaper Clippings

Kappa Alpha Theta, Indianopolis, IN
Chase (Pearl), Scrapbook of Pearl Chase, Omega Chapter, UC Berkeley 1905-1909

La Purísima Mission State Historical Park Archive, Lompoc, CA
Chase (Pearl) Papers

Marin County Free Library, San Rafael, CA
Oral History Project: Interview with Helen Baker Reynolds

Mary Louise Days Collection, Santa Barbara, CA
Newspaper Clippings
Santa Barbara Photographs

Newton Free Library, Newton, MA
Newspaper Archive

Price, Postel & Parma LLP Archives, Santa Barbara, CA
Chase (Harold) Papers

Robert Mercer-Nairne Collection, Perth, Scotland
Chase (Harold S.) Papers
Chase (Pearl) Papers
Lansdowne (Barbara) Papers

Santa Barbara Club Archive, Santa Barbara, CA
Visitors Register

Santa Barbara County's Clerk-Recorder Office, Santa Barbara, CA
Index to Deeds

Santa Barbara County Courthouse, Santa Barbara, CA
Chase (Gertrude Boyer) Estate of – Will & Codicil
Chase (Pearl), Estate of – Will & Codicil

Santa Barbara Junior League, Santa Barbara, CA
Annual Reports
Newspaper Archive
The Sunshiner Magazine

Santa Barbara Little Town Club, Santa Barbara, CA
Annual Meeting Minutes of Board of Directors and Members
Members By-Laws and House Rules

Santa Barbara Trust for Historic Preservation, Presidio Research Center, Santa Barbara, CA
Chase (Pearl) Papers
Native Daughters of the Golden West Scrapbook
Santa Barbara Directories

Shelley Marks Collection, San Francisco, CA
Backus Family Papers

Special Collections, F.W. Olin Library, Mills College, Oakland, CA
Keep (Rosalind) Papers
Reinhardt (Aurelia H.) Papers

University of California, Santa Barbara, Special Research Collections, UCSB Library, Santa Barbara, CA

ACCESS Collection
Chase (Harold S.) Oral History
Chase (Pearl) Oral History
Chase (Pearl) Correspondence
Community Development and Conservation Collection also known as the Pearl Chase Collection
Community Environmental Council Records
Easton (Robert O.) Collection
Friends of the UCSB Library Records
Hoover (Herbert) Letters
Johnson, (Dr. Marian Ashby) Santa Barbara Oral History
Menzies (Jean Storke) Collection
Meredith (Florence Clark) Papers
Rowny (J.F.) Press Records
Tompkins (Walker A.) Collection
University of California, Santa Barbara, History and Antecedents Collection
University of California, Santa Barbara, Office of the Chancellor, Chancellor's Records
University of California, Santa Barbara, Public Historical Studies Program Records
Veblen (Paul) Papers

Virginia Vanocur Collection, Montecito, CA

Backus Family Papers

Online Primary Sources

Adam Matthew Explorer
Alexandria Digital Research Library, University of California, Santa Barbara
California Digital Newspaper Collection
Calisphere, University of California
Digital Public Library of America
Gale Primary Sources
Google Books
Google Scholar
HathiTrust Digital Library
History Vault
Newspapers.com
Online Archive of California
ProQuest History Vault
Smithsonian Institution
The U.S. Library of Congress
The U.S. National Archives and Records Administration
WorldCat

Secondary Sources

Details of secondary sources are given in the relevant endnotes.

ILLUSTRATION CREDITS

Frontispiece. CDCC_Mss1_v_790_17, SRC

1. Orange Smile.com, Santa Barbara and Environs, 2022
2. GIS Geography.com Map of California, 2022
3. Courtesy of Santa Barbara Beautiful
4. Meikleour House Collection, reproduced with permission
5. CDCC_Mss1_vi_805_11-14, SRC
6. Meikleour House Collection, reproduced with permission
7. Library of Congress
8. Library of Congress
9. SBHC_Mss1_0800, SRC
10. Edson Smith Photo Collection, 18_66, Santa Barbara Public Library, Santa Barbara, CA
11. California State Library,2009-0279, (C)001 423653CSL01-Aleph, Sacramento, CA
12. SBHC_Mss1_g00165, SRC
13. CHS-6752
14. Courtesy of Calisphere
15. CDCC_Mss1_v_790_17, SRC
16. Meikleour House Collection, reproduced with permission
17. CHS-2580
18. WC, Brück & Sohn Kunstverlag Meißen, 1903
19. Courtesy Angela Meloney, photography Tom Ploch
20. CDCC_Mss1_vi,_802, SRC
21. CDCC_Mss1_vi,_802, 11, SRC
22. 1965.232.153, Gledhill Library, Santa Barbara Historical Museum
23. Courtesy of Josiah Hamilton
24. CHS-14386
25. California State Library, 2015-1871, (C)001 545266CSL01-Aleph, Sacramento, CA
26. Meikleour House Collection, reproduced with permission
27. Kappa Alpha Theta Archives, Pearl Chase Scrapbook
28. Kappa Alpha Theta Archives, Pearl Chase Scrapbook
29. Kappa Alpha Theta Archives, Pearl Chase Scrapbook
30. Julia Morgan Records, Environmental Design Archives, University of California, Berkeley, CA
31. Kappa Alpha Theta Archives, Pearl Chase Scrapbook
32. WC, 1902 Cornell University yearbook
33. Kappa Alpha Theta Archives, Pearl Chase Scrapbook
34. George Williford Boyce Haley, (Nation Archives and Record Administration, NARA record: 4472976
35. Kappa Alpha Theta Archives, Pearl Chase Scrapbook
36. Kappa Alpha Theta Archives, Pearl Chase Scrapbook
37. CDCC_Mss_1_vi_803_12, SRC
38. Kappa Alpha Theta Archives, Pearl Chase Scrapbook
39. Kappa Alpha Theta Archives, Pearl Chase Scrapbook
40. Courtesy of Geneastar
41. Kappa Alpha Theta Archives, Pearl Chase Scrapbook
42. Kappa Alpha Theta Archives, Pearl Chase Scrapbook
43. Kappa Alpha Theta Archives, Pearl Chase Scrapbook
44. UArch_112-g01612, SRC
45. WC, Nickolas Muray, Shadowland, 1922
46. Bowood House Collection, reproduced with permission
47. 2002-028, Gledhill Library, Santa Barbara Historical Museum
48. CDCC_Mss1_v_773_2, SRC
49. Meikleour House Collection, reproduced with permission
50. Library of Congress, 2016820018

51. Kappa Alpha Theta Archives, Pearl Chase Scrapbook
52. WC, Architect and Engineer, San Francisco Public Library
53. Guild Hall, East Hampton, Arnold Genthe, Gift of Mr Robert Schey, Accession No, x5.7 – Gary Mamay Photography
54. Library of Congress, George Grantham Bain Collection, Reproduction Number: LC-DIG-ggbain-20918
55. CDCC_Mss1_vi_804_11-14, SRC
56. Library of Congress, Bain News Service
57. Alamy
58. Aurelia Henry Reinhardt Papers, Record Group II - Office of the President Files, (1916-1943), 34. Special Collections, F. W. Olin Library, Mills College at Northeastern University, Oakland, CA
59. MS-01 Pearl Chase Collection, Lantern Slide Images: pc_0640, courtesy of the Santa Barbara Trust for Historic Preservation
60. WC, Konrad Summers
61. WC
62. MS-01 Pearl Chase Collection, Lantern Slide Images: pc_0641, courtesy of the Santa Barbara Trust for Historic Preservation
63. Library of Congress, 6950361704
64. WC, US Government, SSA
65. CDCC_Mss1_vi_835_41b, SRC
66. WC
67. Library of Congress, 2016861362
68. SBHC_Mss1_g00164, SRC
69. American Civic Annual, ed. Harlean James, (Washington D.C. 1929). p.140
70. CDCC_Mss1_vi_SRC
71. 340.0, Gledhill Library, Santa Barbara Historical Museum
72. WC
73. Bowood House Collection, reproduced with permission
74. Library of Congress, Bain Collection
75. WC
76. National Park Service Historic Photo Collection, George Grant, HFCA 1607
77. WC, Official Portrait Dept of Interior
78. National Archives and Records Administration, NARA 533461
79. Joseph and Hilda W. Grinell Papers_Banc_Mss_73_25c_10_18 @ The Regents of the University of California, The Bancroft Library, University of California, Berkeley, CA
80. Woodbridge Metcalf Papers_C-B_1018_20, @ The Regents of the University of California, The Bancroft Library, University of California, Berkeley, CA
81. Joseph and Hilda W. Grinell Papers_Banc_Mss_73_25c_10_18 @ The Regents of the University of California, The Bancroft Library, University of California, Berkeley, CA
82. Woodbridge Metcalf Papers_C-B_1018_22, @ The Regents of the University of California, The Bancroft Library, University of California, Berkeley, CA
83. CDCC_Mss1_vi_803_12, SRC
84. CHS-1337
85. CDCC_Mss1_vi_803_12, SRC
86. Bowood House Collection, reproduced with permission
87. Bowood House Collection, reproduced with permission
88. WC, Calbraith Bourn Perry
89. CDCC_Mss1_vi_830_36_3, SRC
90. CHS-2260
91. Courtesy of the California State Parks, La Purísima Mission State Historic Park Collection, La Purísima Mission State Historic Park, Lompoc, CA. 090-32172
92. CDCC_Mss1_v_765_22, SRC
93. CDCC_Mss1_vi_830_36_5, SRC
94. Courtesy of the California State Parks, La Purísima Mission State Historic Park Collection, La Purísima Mission State Historic Park, Lompoc, CA. 090-29348
95. CDCC_Mss1_vi_839_45, SRC
96. UArch_112_g04426_SRC
97. National Archives and Records Administration, NARA 1985.0851.05
98. SBHC-Mss1_g00543, SRC
99. WC
100. WC

101. WC
102. Library of Congress, n80142711
103. WC
104. Library of Congress, 2004672767
105. UArch_112_g02068, SRC
106. WC
107. Uarch_112-g04426, SRC
108. Uarch_112-g01890, SRC
109. CDCC_Mss1_vi_808_16, SRC
110. Woodbridge Metcalf Papers_C-B_1018_20, @ The Regents of the University of California, The Bancroft Library, University of California, Berkeley, CA
111. Woodbridge Metcalf Papers_C-B_1018_20, @ The Regents of the University of California, The Bancroft Library, University of California, Berkeley, CA
112. Meikleour House Collection, reproduced with permission
113. Bowood House Collection, reproduced with permission
114. Woodbridge Metcalf Papers_C-B_1018_20, @ The Regents of the University of California, The Bancroft Library, University of California, Berkeley, CA
115. Bowood House Collection, reproduced with permission
116. CDCC_Mss1_vi_800_8, SRC
117. CDCC_Mss1_vi_835_41a, SRC
118. CHS-m7559
119. WC, Eugene Zelenko, 2007
120. Lyndon Baines Johnson Presidential Library and Museum, Arnold Newman
121. Lyndon Baines Johnson Presidential Library and Museum, Serial Number: B7409-10A
122. Bowood House Collection, reproduced with permission
123. WC, Mary C. Rabbitt, 1989, "The United States Geological Survey: 1879-1989," US Geological Survey, Circular 1050, Figure 43, p.43
124. Alamy
125. CDCC_Mss1_v_790, SRC
126. WC, G.H. Eldridge
127. National Archives Catalogue, Richard Nixon Library, Oliver F. Atkins, Record group: Collection RN-WHPO: (National Archives Identifier: 1179)
128. WC
129. Sourisseau Academy for State and Local History, Waterhouse (Clark B.) Photograph Collection
130. WC
131. WC
132. UArch_112_g00384, SRC
133. UArch_112_g00383, SRC
134. UArch_112_g01075, SRC
135. UArch_11_49_74, SRC
136. WC
137. WC
138. Author photo

Plate 1. Library of Congress, Geography and Map Division Washington, D.C. 75693112

Plate 2. Alamy

Plate 3. CDCC_Mss1_v_790_17, SRC

Plate 4. Kappa Alpha Theta Archives, Pearl Chase Scrapbook

Plate 5. Kappa Alpha Theta Archives, Pearl Chase Scrapbook

Plate 6. Bowood House Collection, reproduced with permission

Plate 7. Architecture and Design Collection. Art, Design & Architecture Museum, University of California, Santa Barbara, Community Arts Association records 0000172, Box 3, Folder 58

Plate 8. MS-01 Pearl Chase Collection, Lantern Slide Images: pc_0403, courtesy of the Santa Barbara Trust for Historic Preservation

Plate 9. Courtesy of the California State Parks, La Purísima Mission State Historic Park Collection, La Purísima Mission State Historic Park, Lompoc, CA. 090-29313

Plate 10. CDCC_Mss1_vi_800_8, SRC

Plate 11. Meikleour House Collection, reproduced with permission

Plate 12. Alamy

Plate 13. Alamy
Plate 14. Courtesy of Santa Barbara Beautiful
Plate 15. Alamy
Plate 16. WC
Plate 17. Alamy
Plate 18. UArch_112_g00381, SRC
Plate 19. Meikleour House Collection, reproduced with permission

ACKNOWLEDGMENTS

There were many people that were of great help to me during the five years of study and writing of this biography. As a relative of Pearl Chase, I was fortunate to have had exceptional opportunities of research extended to me which enabled me to access materials previously unseen.

At the Special Collections Research Department of the University of California, Santa Barbara Library, I was helped by the former director Danelle Moon, Ed Fields, Assistant Head, Daisy C. Muralles, former Information and Reference Specialist, Zachary Liebhaber, Archival Processor, Raul Pizano, Archivist, and the student support staff. I owe a huge debt to Daisy for her support. At UCSB Library I would also like to thank the librarians.

Julia Larson, former Reference Archivist and Felicity Frisch, Assistant Archivist, Architecture and Design Collection, Art, Design & Architecture Museum, University of California, Santa Barbara, were extremely helpful.

At the Santa Barbara Trust for Historic Preservation, Dr. Anne Petersen, Executive Director and Laurie Hannah, former librarian and archivist, came to my aid. Dez Alaniz, Director of the Presidio Research Center produced striking images. Michael Redmon, Former Director of Research and Chris Ervin, Archivist, Gledhill Library, Santa Barbara Historical Museum, alerted me to first-rate material. In Santa Barbara I also wish to thank, Dianne Elliott, Media Administration Assistant at *The Santa Barbara News-Press*, Terri Sheridan, Museum Librarian, Santa Barbara Museum of Natural History, Brittany Bratcher, Associate Archivist and Program Coordinator, Santa Barbara Mission Archive-Library, Joan Muhr, Office Secretary, Junior League Santa Barbara, Grace Thomas and Beth Williamson, Veronica Springs Baptist Church, Dacia Harwood, Executive Director, Santa Barbara Historical Museum, Dory Turk, Office Manager, The Little Town Club, Lani Wollschlager, Administrator, Santa Barbara Foundation, Linda Hill, Administrator, Santa Barbara Association of Realtors, the Administrators at the Clerk Recorders Office, the Administrators at the Community Development Department, Building and Safety and staff at the Book Den, and the Tecolote Book Shop in Montecito.

Further afield, Shyra Liguori, California State Parks, La Purísima Mission SHP, Lompoc shared her expertise on the State Parks. I would like to thank Dr. Steve Hindle, then Interim President and W.M. Keck Foundation Director of Research at the Huntingdon Library in San Marino, and his support staff. In Northern California, at the Bancroft Library of the University of California,

Berkeley, I would like to thank Susan Snyder, Head of Access Services, Lorna Kirwan, Collections Manager, and the librarians. I would like to thank Carla von Merz, at Save the Redwoods League, San Francisco. Kim Hayden, archivist, at the Center for Sacramento History, Sacramento, was particularly supportive. As was Janice Braun, Library Director and Special Collections Curator, F.W. Olin Library, Mills College, Oakland. Staff at the Clerk-Recorder's Office, San Jose, came to my aid. I would like to thank Henry Bankhead, Assistant Librarian and Recreation Director, City of San Rafael, Eva Patterson, Librarian Marin County Free Library and Carol Acquaviva, Librarian, Anne T. Kent California Room, Marin Free County Library for their assistance.

Outside California, the librarians at the Oregon Historical Society, and the Public Library in Portland were extremely helpful. I am indebted to Professor David Spadafora, President at the Newberry Library in Chicago, and Professor D. Bradford Hunt, Vice President for Research and Academic Programs. Also in Chicago, I would like to thank Sarah Rogers, Archives Specialist, National Archives of Chicago, Lesley Martin, Reference Librarian, Chicago History Museum Research Center and staff at the Cook County Recorder of Deeds.

In Denver, Rick Martinez, Archives Specialist at the National Archives proved helpful, as did Sarah Ganderup, Reference Librarian, Western History/Genealogy Dept., Denver Public Library. In Colorado I was assisted by Alexis Ehrgott at Clear Creek County Archives. Georgetown and Lisa G. Dunn, Research Librarian and Special Collections Manager at Arthur Lakes Library, Colorado School of Mines, at Golden. I would particularly like to thank Lisa for invaluable support.

In Boston, I was assisted by Daniel Fleming, Archives Technician, National Archives, Shelby Wolfe, Librarian, Massachusetts Historical Society, Librarians at the Kirstein Business Library and Innovation Center, and the Research Services Department at the Boston Public Library, Kayla Skillin, Assistant Archivist, City of Boston Archives, Kathleen Kaldis, Genealogist, New England Historic Genealogical Society.

In Newton, I would like to thank Ginny Audet, Reference and Genealogy Librarian and Georgina J. Flannery, Reference Librarian at the Newton Free Library, Lisa S. Dady, Executive Director, at Historic Newton and Katy Hax-Holmes, Chief Preservation Planner. In Haverhill I would like to thank the staff in the Special Collections, at the Public Library.

In Ann Arbor, I would like to thank Diana Bachman, Archivist for Researcher Services and Librarians and Reference Staff, Bentley Historical Library, University of Michigan. In Minneapolis, I was assisted by Amanda Wick, Elmer L. Andersen Library, University of Minnesota Libraries and Hannah O'Neill, Researcher. At Cornell University at Ithaca, New York, I would like to thank Eisha Neely, Reference Services Librarian, Division of Rare and Manuscript Collections, Carl

A. Kroch Library, Peter Corina, Reference Specialist and Reproductions Coordinator and Ronda Roaring, Researcher. In Indianapolis, Indiana, I am grateful to Noraleen C. Young, Archivist, Kappa Alpha Theta Fraternity.

In the UK I am indebted to the staff at the British Library in London for all the assistance I received.

Of the many people I interviewed and corresponded with about Pearl Chase I am especially appreciative to Marc Appleton, the late Jerry Beaver, the late Keith C. Berry, Jerry and Geri Bidwell, Kathi Brewster, the Late John A. Bross, Professor Eliot Brownlee, Doug Campbell, the late Mrs. Helen Cornell, Caroline Dawnay, Mary Louise Days, John Doordan, Anne Eissler, the late Georgina Fitzmaurice, the late Kellam de Forest, John Free, Eric Gaensler, Nicholas Gaensler, Guy and Cynthia Hamilton, Josiah, Justine, Dash, and Milly Hamilton, the late Ed Hartfield, Tim Hazeltine, Bea Hemming, David van Horne, Amanda Karby, Sir Henry Keswick, Michael Johnson, Charlie Lansdowne, Bill Luton, Jr., Emma, Dave and Stella Malina, Shelley Marks, Tim Marks, Angela Meloney, Timothy E. Metzinger, Ronald L. Nye, Debbie Owen, Pam Post, Professor Jane Ridley, Geoffrey Claflin Rusack, Sir Matthew Rycroft, Anita Sciutto, Lee A. Simpson, Monica Tucker, Suzanne Tucker, Ginny Vanocur, Harold Whiting, Judith Whiting, Suzanne Williams, and Alison Elizabeth Wrigley.

Judy C. Bross and Robert Mercer-Nairne read an early draft of the book. With their unfailing and generous assistance this book has had valuable corrections.

Ian Strathcarron, Chairman and Commissioning Editor of Unicorn Publishing Group, was enthusiastic for the subject and discerning as to how the book should be produced. Ryan Gearing, Simon Perks and Felicity Price-Smith at Unicorn showed both common sense and humour.

Most of all I would like to thank my wife Nadine and son George, to whom this book is dedicated, who have had to put up with even more than usual.

INDEX

Locators in *italics* refer to illustrations. Additional information may be found under named entries. 'PC' in entries and subheadings refers to Pearl Chase.

T